Oracle Tuning Power Scripts
With 100+ High Performance SQL Scripts
Second Edition

Oracle In-Focus Series

Harry Conway
Mike Ault
Donald Burleson

I dedicate this book to my father, Albert Edward Conway, who passed away in October 2004. My dad was a good man, with a big heart and that makes him one of the most successful people I will ever know. I will miss him, but he is not gone for in me, he lives on.

~Harry Conway

Oracle Tuning Power Script
With 100+ High Performance SQL Scripts
Second Edition

By Harry Conway, Mike Ault, and Donald Burleson

Copyright © 2014 by Rampant TechPress. All rights reserved.

Printed in the United States of America.

Published in Kittrell, North Carolina, USA.

Oracle In-Focus Series: Book #10

Series Editor: Don Burleson

Editors: Janet Burleson, John Lavender, and Robin Haden

Production Editor: Teri Wade

Cover Design: Bryan Hoff

Printing History: July 2005 for First Edition, March 2014 for Second Edition

Oracle, Oracle7, Oracle8, Oracle8i, Oracle9i, Oracle10g, and Oracle 11g are trademarks of Oracle Corporation.

Many of the designations used by computer vendors to distinguish their products are claimed as Trademarks. All names known by Rampant TechPress to be trademark names appear in this text as initial caps.

Flame Warriors illustrations are copyright © by Mike Reed Illustrations Inc.

ISBN: 978-0-9916386-4-2

Library of Congress Control Number: 2014935541

Table of Contents

Using the Online Code Depot

The purchase of this book provides complete access to the online code depot that contains the sample code scripts. All of the code depot scripts in this book are located at the following URL:

rampant.cc/power_script.htm

All of the code scripts in this book are available for download in zip format, ready to load and use. If technical assistance is needed with downloading or accessing the scripts, please contact Rampant TechPress at info@rampant.cc.

Got Scripts?

This is the complete Oracle script collection from Mike Ault and Donald Burleson, the world's best Oracle DBA's.

Packed with over 600 ready-to-use Oracle scripts, this is the definitive collection for every Oracle professional DBA. It would take many years to develop these scripts from scratch, making this download the best value in the Oracle industry.

It's only $79.95.

For purchase and download go to: www.oracle-script.com or call 252-431-0050.

Conventions Used in this Book

It is critical for any technical publication to follow rigorous standards and employ consistent punctuation conventions to make the text easy to read.

However, this is not an easy task. Within Oracle there are many types of notation that can confuse a reader. Some Oracle utilities such as STATSPACK and TKPROF are always spelled with CAPITAL letters, while Oracle parameters and procedures have varying naming conventions in the Oracle documentation.

It is also important to remember that many Oracle commands are case sensitive, and are always left in their original executable form; never altered with italics or capitalization.

Hence, all Rampant TechPress books follow these conventions:

Parameters - All Oracle parameters will be lowercase italics. Exceptions to this rule are parameter arguments that are commonly capitalized (KEEP pool, TKPROF), these will be left in ALL CAPS.

Variables - All PL/SQL program variables and arguments will also remain in lowercase italics (*dbms_job*, *dbms_utility*).

Tables & Dictionary Objects - All data dictionary objects are referenced in lowercase italics (*dba_indexes*, *v$sql*). This includes all *v$* and *x$* views (*x$kcbcbh*, *v$parameter*) and dictionary views (*dba_tables*, *user_indexes*).

SQL - All SQL is formatted for easy use in the code depot, and all SQL is displayed in lowercase. The main SQL terms (select, from, where, group by, order by, having) will always appear on a separate line.

Programs & Products - All programs and products that are known to the author are capitalized according to the vendor specifications (IBM, DBXray, etc). All names known by Rampant TechPress to be trademark names appear in this text as initial caps. References to UNIX are always made in uppercase.

Acknowledgements

Composing this type of reference book requires the dedicated efforts of many people. Even though we are the authors, our work ends when we deliver the content. After each chapter is delivered, several Oracle DBAs carefully review and correct the technical content. After the technical review, experienced copy editors polish the grammar and syntax. The finished work is then reviewed as page proofs and turned over to the production manager, who arranges the creation of the online code depot and manages the cover art, printing distribution, and warehousing.

In short, the authors play a small role in the development of this book, and we need to thank and acknowledge everyone who helped bring this book to fruition:

- **John Lavender**, for the production management, including the coordination of the cover art, page proofing, printing, and distribution.

- **Teri Wade**, for her help in the production of the page proofs.

- **Bryan Hoff**, for his exceptional cover design and graphics.

- **Janet Burleson**, for her assistance with the web site, and for creating the code depot and the online shopping cart for this book.

- **Mike Ault**, for his expert technical review of the content.

- **Donald K. Burleson**, for his invaluable advice and help while writing this book.

With our sincerest thanks,

Harry Conway
Don Burleson

Ion for Oracle

ION for Oracle is the premier Oracle tuning tool. ION provides unparalleled capability for time-series Oracle tuning, unavailable anywhere else.

 ION can quickly find and plot performance signatures allowing you to see hidden trends, fast. ION interfaces with STATSPACK or AWR to provide unprecedented proactive tuning insights.

Get Ion for Oracle now!

www.ion-dba.com

Preface

This book has been designed and laid out as a reference guide with the "hands on" Oracle DBA in mind. The chapters are organized by topical area for easy reference to information on tuning the various areas of the database.

The focus of this book is on Oracle9i and 10g. In fact, each chapter has a specific section dedicated to 10g. Although, some of the scripts are from 8i, they still work quite well in 9i or even 10g. A substantial amount of material is devoted to the new features in 10g, from which an Oracle DBA seasoned in 8i or 9i will still gain even more knowledge.

The text and scripts in this book are targeted for senior Oracle professionals. It is assumed that the reader already has substantial knowledge of SQL and the architecture of an Oracle database.

Wherever possible, a narrative is provided for identifying when and why to use a specific script. An example output for each script is provided with an explanation of the results. In addition, the results include an analysis of how the results can be interpreted. Since, it is important that the DBA understand the when and why of using a specific script in the tuning and monitoring of databases, our goal is to provide an arsenal of scripts for a number of specific tuning needs.

The content in this book is collected from various DBAs with decades of Oracle experience. As with the different versions of Oracle, a DBA is constantly changing and learning. Our hope is that the material in this book aids in furtherance of the DBA's knowledge and skills, which in turn facilitates the advancement of their careers.

CPU, Enqueue, and Wait Event Monitoring

This book is designed to provide DBAs with the scripts required to tune and monitor Oracle databases. In this first chapter, Oracle CPU, Enqueue and Event Monitoring scripts will be detailed. For each of these, a listing and an example output with commentary from running the script will be provided.

CPU Usage Statistics

CPU usage statistics form a critical component of response time analysis. Response time is defined as service time plus wait time. The service time component is CPU usage and can be broken down into CPU parse time, CPU recursive time and CPU other.

If CPU usage constitutes a large part of the response time, the database should be tuned based on the type of CPU usage shown. Tune SQL for the proper access path, less sorting and hashing for CPU other. Furthermore, look at bind variable usage and cursor sharing/caching for CPU parse; and look at excessive data dictionary lookups, excessive dynamic sizing and other recursive operations for CPU recursive time.

The following script will report the CPU time utilized by the database since the last startup of the database.

🖫 CPU_TIME.sql

```
-- ****************************************************
-- Copyright © 2005 by Rampant TechPress
-- This script is free for non-commercial purposes
-- with no warranties.  Use at your own risk.
--
-- To license this script for a commercial purpose,
-- contact info@rampant.cc
-- ****************************************************


rem
rem    CPU_TIME.SQL
rem    Mike Ault
rem

col name     heading  'Statistic'
col value    heading  'Value'

ttitle 'CPU Related Statistics'
spool cpu_stats

select name,value from v$sysstat where upper(name) like '%CPU%'
;
spool off
clear columns
ttitle off
```

The following sample report displays CPU statistics from v$sysstat from an Oracle 9iR2 instance:

```
Wed Sep 22                                            page     1
                         CPU Related Statistics

Statistic                                               Value
-------------------------------------------------- ----------
recursive cpu usage                                     35094
CPU used when call started                             402131
CPU used by this session                               402218
parse time cpu                                          12110
OS User level CPU time                                      0
OS System call CPU time                                     0
OS Other system trap CPU time                               0
OS Wait-cpu (latency) time                                  0
```

8 rows selected.

The service time metric is important and is used in the calculation of the response time metric which determines the breakdown between wait time and CPU time (service time) for a specific system. All of the components for the service time calculation are shown above. Essentially the formula would look something like this: Service Time = CPU Other + CPU Parse + CPU Recursion. CPU Other is calculated by subtracting the sum of Recursive CPU Usage and Parse Time CPU from CPU Used by this session.

SQL by CPU Usage

In order to determine the SQL that may be contributing to the CPU usage, query the *v$sqlarea* view. This view contains statistics about SQL in the shared pool and its usage statistics.

By querying *v$sqlarea* view, the following simple 9i script shows SQL statements by their CPU Usage:

🖫 CPU.SQL

```
-- *************************************************
-- Copyright © 2005 by Rampant TechPress
-- This script is free for non-commercial purposes
-- with no warranties.  Use at your own risk.
--
-- To license this script for a commercial purpose,
-- contact info@rampant.cc
-- *************************************************

rem
rem    CPU.SQL
rem    Mike Ault
rem
rem    SQL by CPU Usage (v$sqlarea)
rem
column sql_text format a40 word_wrapped heading 'SQL|Text'
column cpu_time       heading 'CPU|Time'
column elapsed_time   heading 'Elapsed|Time'
column disk_reads     heading 'Disk|Reads'
column buffer_gets    heading 'Buffer|Gets'
column rows_processed heading 'Rows|Processed'
set pages 55 lines 132
ttitle 'SQL By CPU Usage'
spool cpu
```

```
select * from
        (select sql_text,
                cpu_time/1000000 cpu_time,
                elapsed_time/1000000 elapsed_time,
                disk_reads,
                buffer_gets,
                rows_processed
        from v$sqlarea
        order by cpu_time desc, disk_reads desc
        )
where rownum < 21
/
spool off
set pages 22 lines 80
ttitle off
```

The following example report of SQL statements ordered by *cpu_time*
and *disk_reads* was edited for brevity. Once the problem SQL is isolated,
tune the offending SQL to reduce Logical IO and CPU usage will
usually be reduced as well:

```
Wed Sep 22 page    1
                                                        SQL By CPU Usage

SQL                                         CPU     Elapsed     Disk     Buffer      Rows
Text                                        Time       Time     Reads       Gets Processed
------------------------------------- ---------- ---------- ---------- ---------- ----------
select  OWNER,        SEGMENT_NAME,    .16501 .172953798      140770    5871602          0
SEGMENT_TYPE,         TABLESPACE_NAME,
NEXT_EXTENT from (        select
seg.OWNER,
seg.SEGMENT_NAME,
seg.SEGMENT_TYPE,
seg.TABLESPACE_NAME,
t.NEXT_EXTENT          from
dba_segments seg,
dba_tables t         where
(seg.SEGMENT_TYPE = 'TABLE'        and
seg.SEGMENT_NAME = t.TABLE_NAME
and      seg.owner = t.OWNER        and
NOT EXISTS (
select   TABLESPACE_NAME
from    dba_free_space free
where   free.TABLESPACE_NAME =
t.TABLESPACE_NAME
and     BYTES >= t.NEXT_EXTENT))
union         select   seg.OWNER,
seg.SEGMENT_NAME,
seg.SEGMENT_TYPE,
seg.TABLESPACE_NAME,
c.NEXT_EXTENT         from
dba_segments seg,

SELECT                                      .10371 .118568367     97872     100559        136
EMP.DIVISION,CMD.COLL,EMP.NAME,SUM(CMD.S
ACC_COMM),SUM(DECODE(DLT_TYPE,'P',CMD.AM
T,-1*CMD.AMT)),COUNT(CLM)FROM CMD,EMP
WHERE CMD.DT_TRANS BETWEEN:b1 AND
TO_DATE(:b2)+1 AND
TO_CHAR(DT_TRANS,'HH24MISS')BETWEEN:b3
AND:b4 AND DLT_TYPE||ADJ_TYPE
IN('J1','J5','J7','P ')AND
EMP.NO=CMD.COLL GROUP BY
EMP.DIVISION,EMP.NAME,CMD.COLL ORDER BY
EMP.DIVISION,CMD.COLL
```

Enqueues

Enqueues are shared memory structures that serialize access to database resources and are associated with a session or transaction. In Real Application Clusters (RAC), enqueues can be global to a database. If Real Application Clusters are not enabled, enqueues are then local to one instance.

An enqueue is a lock that protects a shared resource, such as data, in order to prevent processes from updating the same data simultaneously. An enqueue includes a First In First Out (FIFO) queuing mechanism.

Enqueue waits usually point to TX enqueues, TM enqueues, ST enqueues and HW enqueues, explained as follows:

TX Enqueue - This type of enqueue is the most common enqueue wait. For example, one issue could be multiple updates to the same bitmap index fragment. A single bitmap fragment may contain multiple rowids. When multiple users are trying to update the same fragment, a commit or rollback needs to be issued to free the enqueue. The situation is most likely to surface when multiple users are updating the same block. If there are no free ITL slots, a block-level lock could occur. This scenario can be avoided by increasing the *initrans* and/or *maxtrans* to allow multiple ITL slots, and/or by increasing the *pctfree* on the table.

TM Enqueue - This type of enqueue occurs during DML to prevent DDL to the affected object. Indexes on foreign keys should be used to avoid this general locking issue.

ST Enqueue - This type of enqueue is used for space management and allocation for dictionary-managed tablespaces. Use LMTs, or try to preallocate extents or at least make the next extent larger for problematic dictionary-managed tablespaces.

HW Enqueue – This type of enqueue is used with the high-water mark of a segment; manually allocating the extents can circumvent this wait.

The following 9i script will display three simple reports for analyzing the enqueues of the database

🖫 ENQUEUES9i.sql

```
-- **************************************************
-- Copyright © 2005 by Rampant TechPress
-- This script is free for non-commercial purposes
-- with no warranties.  Use at your own risk.
--
-- To license this script for a commercial purpose,
-- contact info@rampant.cc
-- **************************************************

rem
rem    ENQUEUES9i.SQL
rem    Mike Ault
rem
ttitle 'Enqueues Report'
spool enqueues
prompt Enqueues
col name format a25
col lock format a4 heading 'Lock'
col gets format 9,999,999 heading 'Gets'
col waits format 9,999,999 heading 'Waits'
col Mode format a4

SELECT *
FROM v$sysstat
WHERE class=4
;

SELECT chr(bitand(p1,-16777216)/16777215)||
        chr(bitand(p1, 16711680)/65535)  "Lock",
        to_char( bitand(p1, 65535) )     "Mode"
FROM v$session_wait
WHERE event = 'enqueue'
/

Prompt Enqueue Stats

select * from v$enqueue_stat where cum_wait_time>0
order by cum_wait_time desc
/
spool off
ttitle off
```

Code Depot Username = reader, Password = arsenal

```
Enqueues

Wed Sep 22                                         page    1
                          Enqueues Report

INST_ID STATISTIC# NAME                    CLASS       VALUE
```

```
-------  ----------  -------------------------  ----------  ----------
      4          22 enqueue timeouts                     4          65
      4          23 enqueue waits                        4    54133624
      4          24 enqueue deadlocks                    4           0
      4          25 enqueue requests                     4   252483462
      4          26 enqueue conversions                  4      425394
      4          27 enqueue releases                     4   252482896

6 rows selected.

Lock Stats

Wed Sep 22                                                    page     1
                            Enqueues Report

INST_ID Lock Mode
------- ---- ----
      4 US   6
      4 US   6
      4 US   6
      4 TX   6
      4 TX   6

5 rows selected.

Enqueue Stats

Wed Sep 22                                                    page     1
                            Enqueues Report

INST_ID EQ TOTAL_REQ# TOTAL_WAIT#   SUCC_REQ# FAILED_REQ# CUM_WAIT_TIME
------- -- ----------  -----------  ---------- ----------- -------------
      4 US   54876879    53410542    54876822           0    1533644257
      4 TX   63851995      461325    63867209           0      11031417
      4 SQ     585304      243592      585304           0       5375456
      4 CF     234529        1617      234470          59         24744
      4 FB      12902        9571       12902           0         26668
      4 HW      10517        4581       10517           0         16212
      4 TA       2609        1568        2609           0          5491
      4 CU    1594631          35     1594625           0          1426

8 rows selected.
```

The enqueues of concern will show the greatest amount of cumulative wait time (*cum_wait_time*) and will be shown first in the listing. The report also shows the enqueue related wait events and the current lock status for enqueue related activity. Since the report uses the GV version of the dynamic performance tables, it will list results for all instances in a RAC cluster. In the report shown above, instance 4 was the only active instance when the report was run.

Now moving on from Enqueues to Events one of the most important areas to monitor in an Oracle database will be reviewed.

Monitoring Events

Oracle is an event-driven system. This means that sessions wait for calls, locks and latches spin, and processes slumber and wake at the behest of events. The *v$session_event* view tracks all current events by session.

The following script, *events.sql*, will generate a report on current Oracle events. The script, *sys_events_pct.sql*, which then follows, provides a more detailed view of the event profile by adding the CPU contribution and calculating the overall percentages each wait is contributing.

⊟ events.sql

```
-- ****************************************************
-- Copyright © 2005 by Rampant TechPress
-- This script is free for non-commercial purposes
-- with no warranties.  Use at your own risk.
--
-- To license this script for a commercial purpose,
-- contact info@rampant.cc
-- ****************************************************

COLUMN sid                HEADING Sid
COLUMN event              HEADING Event             FORMAT a40
COLUMN total_waits        HEADING Total|Waits
COLUMN total_timeouts     HEADING Total|Timeouts
COLUMN time_waited        HEADING Time|Waited
COLUMN average_wait       HEADING Average|Wait
COLUMN username           HEADING User

BREAK ON username
ttitle "Session Events By User"
SPOOL events
SET LINES 132 PAGES 59 VERIFY OFF FEEDBACK OFF

SELECT
   username,
   event,
   total_waits,total_timeouts,
   time_waited,average_wait
FROM
   sys.v_$session_event a,
   sys.v_$session b
WHERE
   a.sid= b.sid
ORDER BY 1;

SPOOL OFF
PAUSE Press Enter to continue
CLEAR COLUMNS
CLEAR BREAKS
SET LINES 80 PAGES 22 VERIFY ON FEEDBACK ON
```

The following is an example of an event report:

User	Event	Total Waits	Total Timeouts	Time Waited	Average Wait
SYSTEM	enqueue	149	149	44425	298
	control file sequential read	214	0	14	0
	log file sync	61	0	65	1
	SQL*Net message to client	462	0	1	0
	single-task message	2	0	5	2
	SQL*Net break/reset to client	4	0	0	0
	SQL*Net message from client	800	0	735778	920
	SQL*Net message to client	19	0	0	0
	db file sequential read	24987	0	10986	0
	db file sequential read	16	0	10	1
	pmon timer	167133	167130	49031711	293
	rdbms ipc message	163764	163681	49050112	300
	control file sequential read	20	0	2	0
	control file parallel write	163663	0	75411	0
	direct path read	14	0	0	0
	db file parallel write	3300	3300	8	0
	db file scattered read	596	0	750	1
	db file sequential read	248	0	232	1
	log file parallel write	3760	0	1168	0
	log file single write	4	0	0	0
	log file sequential read	4	0	2	1
	library cache load lock	1	1	299	299
	smon timer	1640	1634	47313312	28850
	direct path write	12	0	0	0
	direct path read	14	0	0	0
	control file parallel write	8	0	4	0
	control file sequential read	49110	0	1069	0
	async disk IO	1	0	0	0
	rdbms ipc message	166085	163858	49051891	295

Notice that the report is by username. This can help isolate which database users are generating the most wait events. However, it can be more useful to capture the events as a percentage of all wait time, including that for the CPU usage time. Note that on multi-CPU systems the CPU usage may be skewed high and the need may exist to divide by the number of CPUs to get a useful number for the current CPU used by a session. Next, a different cut of this report that uses a percentage calculation to show the relative weight of each event by percent will be reviewed.

System Events by Percent

The System Events by Percent report shows the major events in the database and their contribution to overall response time.

Comparison of CPU usage to event wait time will help to confirm that wait events are actually the problem. If CPU time is the major component to the response time profile, tuning events will make little difference to the overall performance:

🖫 SYS_EVENTS_PCT.sql

```
-- *****************************************************
-- Copyright © 2005 by Rampant TechPress
-- This script is free for non-commercial purposes
-- with no warranties.  Use at your own risk.
--
-- To license this script for a commercial purpose,
-- contact info@rampant.cc
-- *****************************************************

rem
rem     SYS_EVENTS_PCT.SQL
rem     Mike Ault
rem
rem     This report shows the major events in the database and
rem     their contribution to overall response time.
rem
rem
col event format a30                   heading 'Event Name'
col waits format 999,999,999           heading 'Total|Waits'
col average_wait format 999,999,999 heading 'Average|Waits'
col time_waited format 999,999,999  heading 'Time Waited'
col total_time new_value divide_by  noprint
col value new_value        val       noprint
col percent format 999.990             heading 'Percent|Of|Non-Idle Waits'
col duration new_value millisec       noprint
col p_of_total    heading  'Percent|of Total|Uptime' format 999.9999

set lines 132 feedback off verify off pages 50

select to_number(sysdate-startup_time)*86400*1000 duration
from v$instance
;
select
sum(time_waited) total_time
from v$system_event
where total_waits-total_timeouts>0
    and event not like 'SQL*Net%'
    and event not like 'smon%'
    and event not like 'pmon%'
    and event not like 'rdbms%'
        and event not like 'PX%'
        and event not like 'sbt%'
        and event not in ('gcs remote message','ges remote message',
                          'virtual circuit status','dispatcher timer')
;
select value
from v$sysstat
```

```
where name ='CPU used when call started'
;
ttitle 'System Events Percent'
break on report
compute sum of time_waited on report
spool sys_events

select name event,
       0 waits,
       0 average_wait,
       value time_waited,
      value/(&&divide_by+&&val)*100 Percent,
       value/&&millisec*100 p_of_total
from v$sysstat
where name ='CPU used when call started'
union
select event,
       total_waits-total_timeouts waits,
       time_waited/(total_waits-total_timeouts) average_wait,
       time_waited,
       time_waited/(&&divide_by+&&val)*100 Percent,
       time_waited/&&millisec*100 P_of_total
from v$system_event
where total_waits-total_timeouts > 0
and event not like 'SQL*Net%'
and event not like 'smon%'
and event not like 'pmon%'
and event not like 'rdbms%'
and event not like 'PX%'
and event not like 'sbt%'
and event not in ('gcs remote message','ges remote message',
                  'virtual circuit status','dispatcher timer')
and time_waited > 0
order by percent desc
;

spool off
clear columns
ttitle off
clear computes
clear breaks
```

A sample of the report resulting from this script is presented in the following section.

System Events by Percent - Sample Report

This sample report shows the major events in the database and their contribution to overall response time. From the report, enqueues account for the major part of the response time. This shows that application tuning is critical for the database as most enqueues are generated by incorrect transaction logic.

```
                                System Events Percent

                                                   Percent    Percent
                           Total Average          Non-Idle    of Total
Event Name                 Waits  Waits Time Waited   Waits     Uptime
-------------------------- ------ ------ ----------- --------- ---------
enqueue                        58 15,348     890,203    41.649    3.9893
CPU used when call started      0      0     628,228    29.392    2.8153
db file scattered read    699,633      0     300,691    14.068    1.3475
db file sequential read 1,104,472      0     209,797     9.816     .9402
buffer busy waits         481,491      0      51,478     2.408     .2307
log file sync             796,795      0      36,167     1.692     .1621
latch free                    964     12      11,660      .546     .0523
log file parallel write   727,589      0       8,587      .402     .0385
direct path read (lob)      4,186      0       1,390      .065     .0062
db file parallel write      3,223      0         845      .040     .0038
control file parallel write 7,270      0         210      .010     .0009
direct path write           1,264      0         207      .010     .0009
file open                   1,158      0         182      .009     .0008
library cache lock             11     14         155      .007     .0007
direct path write (lob)       181      0          46      .002     .0002
control file sequential read  401      0          12      .001     .0001
direct path read              277      0           9      .000     .0000
local write wait               69      0           6      .000     .0000
refresh controlfile command    43      0           6      .000     .0000
                                            -----------
sum                                           2,139,879
```

Also note that this report indicates that I/O tuning will gain a maximum of 27 percent, and the big gains will come from code and application changes.

SYS_EVENTS

If the users are complaining the database is slow, the report generated by the following script will probably shed a lot of light on where the poor performance is coming from. This SQL script queries *v$system_event* view and displays the system events in the order of how much system time was spent waiting for a particular wait state.

🖫 SYS_EVENTS.sql

```
-- *****************************************************
-- Copyright © 2005 by Rampant TechPress
-- This script is free for non-commercial purposes
-- with no warranties.  Use at your own risk.
--
-- To license this script for a commercial purpose,
-- contact info@rampant.cc
-- *****************************************************

rem
```

```
rem    SYS_EVENTS.SQL
rem    Mike Ault
rem
set pagesize 100
col event format a30              heading 'Event Name'
col waits format 999,999,999      heading 'Total|Waits'
col average_wait format 999,999,999 heading 'Average|Waits'
col time_waited format 999,999,999  heading 'Time Waited'
ttitle 'System Events'
break on report
compute sum of time_waited on report

spool sys_events

select event,
total_waits-total_timeouts waits,
time_waited/(total_waits-total_timeouts) average_wait,
time_waited
from v$system_event
where total_waits-total_timeouts>0
    and event not like 'SQL*Net%'
    and event not like 'smon%'
    and event not like 'pmon%'
    and event not like 'rdbms%'
    and event not like '%control%'
    and event not like 'LGWR%'
        and event not like 'PX%'
order by time_waited desc
/
spool off
clear columns
ttitle off
```

The following sample report indicates that the *db file waits* are the major contributors to system wait time:

```
Wed Sep 22                                            page    1
                        System Events

                             Total     Average
Event Name                   Waits       Waits  Time Waited
-------------------------- ----------- ----------- -----------
db file scattered read     67,706,470           0   1,556,290
db file sequential read    36,352,060           0   1,334,478
log file sync               3,435,741           0     473,096
latch free                    196,641           1     284,656
log file parallel write     4,021,943           0     258,424
enqueue                        26,542           8     211,480
db file parallel read          40,669           1      26,089
file open                     761,474           0       6,706
log file sequential read      148,109           0       4,833
log file switch completion      2,054           2       4,279
direct path read              906,007           0       1,281
buffer busy waits              12,307           0       1,225
log file single write           3,676           0         564
file identify                   9,302           0         253
```

```
process startup                47           3        160
db file single write        3,349           0        155
direct path write         104,293           0        146
row cache lock                  7          17        120
db file parallel write    107,341           0         73
switch logfile command         17           4         62
library cache pin             120           0         48
log buffer space               67           1         35
single-task message             5           1          6
library cache load lock         1           1          1
reliable message                1           0          0
instance state change           2           0          0
                                               -----------
sum                                          4,164,460

26 rows selected.
```

Leaving off the CPU contribution illustrates that the events at the SYSTEM level are contributing to non-CPU wait time. Another important event is the 4031, or shared pool fragmentation event which will be covered next.

Events Related to ORA-4031 Error

If the system is having recurrent ORA-4031 errors, shared pool excessive fragmentation is usually the cause. The following script must be run from the SYS user. It will show the errors that have occurred and this information will help the DBA isolate the issue:

🖫 SEE_4031.sql

```
--  ***************************************************
--  Copyright © 2005 by Rampant TechPress
--  This script is free for non-commercial purposes
--  with no warranties.  Use at your own risk.
--
--  To license this script for a commercial purpose,
--  contact info@rampant.cc
--  ***************************************************

rem
rem    SEE_4031.SQL
rem    Mike Ault
rem

column kghlurcr heading "RECURRENT|CHUNKS"
column kghlutrn heading "TRANSIENT|CHUNKS"
column kghlufsh heading "FLUSHED|CHUNKS"
column kghluops heading "PINS AND|RELEASES"
column kghlunfu heading "ORA-4031|ERRORS"
column kghlunfs heading "LAST ERROR|SIZE"
```

```
ttitle 'Report on 4031 events (SYS user only)'
spool cpu_stats

select
kghlurcr,
kghlutrn,
kghlufsh,
kghluops,
kghlunfu,
kghlunfs
from
sys.x$kghlu
where
inst_id = userenv('Instance')
;

spool off
clear columns
ttitle off
```

The following report displays data about the current state of the shared pool, showing fragmentation issues.

```
Wed Sep 22                                                              page
1
                       Report on 4031 events (SYS user only)

RECURRENT   TRANSIENT      FLUSHED    PINS AND    ORA-4031 LAST ERROR
   CHUNKS      CHUNKS       CHUNKS    RELEASES      ERRORS        SIZE
---------- ----------   ---------- ----------   ---------- ----------
    10608       17797         9191    1410063            0           0
```

Generally speaking, if there are no 4031 errors, the DBA should simply look at the distribution of chunks and compare it to the number of SQL areas used. This ratio will reveal how many chunks per SQL statements are being utilized and will present a gage as to how much the pool is fragmenting. If an error has occurred, the report will show the size of the area requested which will to allow the DBA to plan space usage more efficiently.

Snap_delta_sys_events_pct90

snap_delta_sys_events_pct90 calculates the delta values between STATSPACK reports for events. It then shows their contribution to the overall wait picture. For analysis of either SQL statements or sections of applications, this report provides detailed wait event reporting for the delta values between two STATSPACK reports. This report also requires that STATSPACK be installed and at least two snapshots covering the time period for the report have been generated.

🖫 Snap_delta_sys_events_pct90.sql

```
-- **************************************************
-- Copyright © 2005 by Rampant TechPress
-- This script is free for non-commercial purposes
-- with no warranties.  Use at your own risk.
--
-- To license this script for a commercial purpose,
-- contact info@rampant.cc
-- **************************************************


rem
rem Mike Ault
rem
rem snap_delta_sys_events_pct90.sql
rem
rem Function: Calculates the delta values between statspacks for events
rem           then shows what they contribute to the overall wait picture
rem
rem total response time=wait time+cpu time (divide_by+val)
rem
ttitle off
col event         format a30          heading 'Event Name'
col waits         format 999,999,999 heading 'Total|Waits'
col average_wait format 999,999,999 heading 'Average|Waits'
col time_waited   format 999,999,999 heading 'Time Waited'
col percent       format 999.990     heading 'Percent|Of|Non-Idle Waits'
col p_of_total    format 999.9999    heading 'Percent|of Total|Uptime'
rem
rem
col total_time new_value divide_by noprint
col value       new_value val        noprint
col duration    new_value sec        noprint
rem
set lines 132 feedback off verify off pages 50
rem
rem Number of seconds since startup (duration->sec)
rem 86400 is number of seconds in a day, total available time is
elapsed*number of cpus
rem
select to_number(sysdate-a.startup_time)*86400*to_number(b.value) duration
from v$instance a,
v$parameter b
where b.name='cpu_count';
rem
rem Total seconds of waiting (total_time->divide_by)
rem in 9.0 this was in microseconds, so we divide by 1000000 to get to
rem seconds
rem
select
sum(b.time_waited_micro-a.time_waited_micro)/1000000 total_time
from stats$system_event a, stats$system_event b
```

```
where (b.total_waits-b.total_timeouts)-(a.total_waits-a.total_timeouts)>0
    and a.event not like 'SQL*Net%'
    and a.event not like 'smon%'
    and a.event not like 'pmon%'
    and a.event not like 'rdbms%'
        and a.event not like 'PX%'
        and a.event not like 'sbt%'
        and a.event not in ('gcs remote message','ges remote message',
                            'virtual circuit status','dispatcher timer')
and a.snap_id=&&first_snap_id
and b.snap_id=&&sec_snap_id
and a.event=b.event
;
rem
rem CPU seconds between snap 1 and snap 2 (value->val)
rem as placed in table the view they are milliseconds
rem divide by 1000 to correct to seconds
rem
select b.value-a.value/1000 value from stats$sysstat a, stats$sysstat b
where a.name ='CPU used when call started'
and b.name ='CPU used when call started'
and a.snap_id=&&first_snap_id
and b.snap_id=&&sec_snap_id;
rem
ttitle 'Snap &&first_snap_id to &&sec_snap_id System Events Percent'
break on report
compute sum of time_waited on report
spool snap&&first_snap_id'_to_'&&sec_snap_id'_sys_events'
rem
rem Now for the report, first we get CPU contribution, then the waits
rem
select 'CPU used when call started' event,
          0 waits,
  0 average_wait,
  &&val time_waited,
  (&&val/(&&divide_by+&&val))*100 Percent,
  (&&val/1000/(&&sec))*100 p_of_total
from dual
union
select a.event,
      (b.total_waits-b.total_timeouts)-(a.total_waits-a.total_timeouts)
waits,       ((b.time_waited_micro-
a.time_waited_micro)/1000000)/((b.total_waits-b.total_timeouts)-
(a.total_waits-a.total_timeouts)) average_wait,
      (b.time_waited_micro-a.time_waited_micro)/1000000 time_waited,
      ((b.time_waited_micro-
a.time_waited_micro)/1000000/(&&divide_by+&&val))*100 Percent,
      (((b.time_waited_micro-a.time_waited_micro)/1000000)/&&sec)*100
P_of_total
from stats$system_event a, stats$system_event b
where (b.total_waits-b.total_timeouts)-(a.total_waits-a.total_timeouts)>0
    and a.event not like 'SQL*Net%'
    and a.event not like 'smon%'
    and a.event not like 'pmon%'
    and a.event not like 'rdbms%'
        and a.event not like 'PX%'
        and a.event not like 'sbt%'
        and a.event not in ('gcs remote message','ges remote message',
                            'virtual circuit status','dispatcher timer')
```

```
        and b.time_waited_micro-a.time_waited_micro>0
        and a.snap_id=&&first_snap_id
        and b.snap_id=&&sec_snap_id
        and a.event=b.event
order by percent desc
/
spool off
clear columns
ttitle off
clear computes
clear breaks
undef first_snap_id
undef sec_snap_id
```

The following report shows the detailed wait event breakdown by percent, including the contribution from CPU usage for the time interval between two STATSPACK runs:

```
Enter value for first_snap_id: 14300
Enter value for sec_snap_id: 14310

Enter value for db: TEST

Wed Sep 22                                             page    1
                      Snap 14300 to 14310 System Events Percent

                                                 Percent   Percent
                          Total    Average       Non-Idle  of Total
Event Name                Waits  Waits Time Waited  Waits    Uptime
------------------------- ------ ----- ----------- -------- --------
CPU used when call started      0     0     257,657   98.985   .0235
jobq slave wait                24    80       1,927     .740   .1758
db file sequential read   584,037    0         460     .177   .0420
control file parallel write 11,730    0         148     .057   .0135
db file scattered read     16,466    0          56     .021   .0051
log file sync               5,562    0          23     .009   .0021
db file parallel write      2,372    0          15     .006   .0013
log file parallel write        55    0           7     .003   .0007
process startup                34    0           2     .001   .0002
async disk IO                  65    0           1     .000   .0001
control file sequential read 8,489    0          1     .000   .0001
enqueue                         3    0           1     .000   .0001
log file sequential read       80    0           1     .000   .0001
log file switch completion     10    0           0     .000   .0000
direct path write             144    0           0     .000   .0000
latch free                     11    0           0     .000   .0000
LGWR wait for redo copy       165    0           0     .000   .0000
direct path read               97    0           0     .000   .0000
log file single write          20    0           0     .000   .0000
wait for stopper event to be i  1    0           0     .000   .0000
ncreased
buffer busy waits               3    0           0     .000   .0000
                                         -----------
sum                                          260,299
```

Oracle10g Wait Events

With the release of Oracle10g came a standard Automatic Workload Repository (AWR) report which contains a *Wait* Events section that

---

displays top wait events. The following query can also be used to allow retrieval of top wait events for a particular AWR snapshot interval:

🖫 wt_events_int_10g.sql

```
-- ****************************************************
-- Copyright © 2005 by Rampant TechPress
-- This script is free for non-commercial purposes
-- with no warranties.  Use at your own risk.
--
-- To license this script for a commercial purpose,
-- contact info@rampant.cc
-- ****************************************************

select event
    , waits "Waits"
    , time "Wait Time (s)"
    , pct*100 "Percent of Total"
    , waitclass "Wait Class"
from (select e.event_name event
                , e.total_waits - nvl(b.total_waits,0)  waits
                , (e.time_waited_micro -
nvl(b.time_waited_micro,0))/1000000  time
                , (e.time_waited_micro - nvl(b.time_waited_micro,0))/
                  (select sum(e1.time_waited_micro -
nvl(b1.time_waited_micro,0)) from dba_hist_system_event b1 ,
dba_hist_system_event e1
                    where b1.snap_id(+)          = b.snap_id
                      and e1.snap_id             = e.snap_id
                      and b1.dbid(+)             = b.dbid
                      and e1.dbid                = e.dbid
                      and b1.instance_number(+)  = b.instance_number
                      and e1.instance_number     = e.instance_number
                      and b1.event_id(+)         = e1.event_id
                      and e1.total_waits         > nvl(b1.total_waits,0)
                      and e1.wait_class          <> 'Idle'
  )  pct
                , e.wait_class waitclass
            from
              dba_hist_system_event b ,
              dba_hist_system_event e
          where b.snap_id(+)          = &pBgnSnap
            and e.snap_id             = &pEndSnap
            and b.dbid(+)             = &pDbId
            and e.dbid                = &pDbId
            and b.instance_number(+)  = &pInstNum
            and e.instance_number     = &pInstNum
            and b.event_id(+)         = e.event_id
            and e.total_waits         > nvl(b.total_waits,0)
            and e.wait_class          <> 'Idle'
        order by time desc, waits desc
  )
```

The sample output of this query looks like the following:

```
SQL> @ wt_events_int_10g.sql

EVENT                     Waits Wait Time (s) Percent of Total Wait Class
------------------------- ----- ------------- ---------------- --------------
control file parallel write 11719     119.13     34,1611762 System I/O
class slave wait             20       102.46     29,3801623 Other
Queue Monitor Task Wait      74        66.74     19,1371008 Other
log file sync               733        20.60      5,90795938 Commit
db file sequential read    1403        14.27      4,09060416 User I/O
log buffer space            178        10.17      2,91745801 Configuration
process startup             114         7.65      2,19243344 Other
db file scattered read      311         2.14       ,612767501 User I/O
control file sequential read 7906       1.33       ,380047642 System I/O
latch free                  254         1.13       ,324271668 Other
log file switch completion   20         1.11       ,319292495 Configuration
```

As shown above, the output of the *wt_events_int_10g.sql* script displays the wait events ordered by wait times in seconds.

Oracle10g Enqueues

Enqueues provide a lock mechanism to coordinate concurrent access to numerous database resources. The name of the enqueue is included as part of the wait event name and takes the form of: enq: *enqueue_type - related_details*. There are several types of enqueues available. Some examples are:

- ST enqueues control dynamic space allocation.

- HW enqueues are used to serialize the allocation of space beyond the high water mark (HWM).

- Waits for TM locks are usually caused by missing indexes on foreign key constraints.

- TX locks are placed in various modes on data blocks when a transaction modifies data within this block. There are several types of TX locks: enq: TX - allocate ITL entry; enq: TX – contention; enq: TX - index contention; enq: TX - row lock contention.

dba_hist_enqueue_stat

The dba_hist_enqueue_stat view displays statistical information about requests for various types of enqueues or locks. This view stores snapshots of the *v$enqueue_statistics* dynamic performance view.

Below is what the *dba_hist_enqueue_stat* view contains

```
SQL> desc DBA_HIST_ENQUEUE_STAT
 Name                                     Null?    Type
 ---------------------------------------- -------- ------------
 SNAP_ID                                  NOT NULL NUMBER
 DBID                                     NOT NULL NUMBER
 INSTANCE_NUMBER                          NOT NULL NUMBER
 EQ_TYPE                                  NOT NULL VARCHAR2(2)
 REQ_REASON                               NOT NULL VARCHAR2(64)
 TOTAL_REQ#                                        NUMBER
 TOTAL_WAIT#                                       NUMBER
 SUCC_REQ#                                         NUMBER
 FAILED_REQ#                                       NUMBER
 CUM_WAIT_TIME                                     NUMBER
 EVENT#                                            NUMBER
```

If wait events with *enqueue* in their name, such as the *enqueue waits* wait event, have significant wait time, the *dba_hist_enqueue_stat* view can be used to drill down to the details about which particular enqueue has a long wait time. The *enq_stat_int_10g* script can be used to query this view:

🖫 enq_stat_int_10g.sql

```
-- ***************************************************
-- Copyright © 2005 by Rampant TechPress
-- This script is free for non-commercial purposes
-- with no warranties.  Use at your own risk.
--
-- To license this script for a commercial purpose,
-- contact info@rampant.cc
-- ***************************************************

select
  ety "Enqueue",
  reqs "Requests",
  sreq "Successful Gets",
  freq "Failed Gets",
  waits "Waits",
  wttm "Wait Time (s)",
  awttm "Average Wait Time(ms)"
from (
select /*+ ordered */
        e.eq_type || '-' || to_char(nvl(l.name,' '))
     || decode( upper(e.req_reason)
              , 'CONTENTION', null
              , '-',          null
              , ' ('||e.req_reason||')')         ety
    , e.total_req#    - nvl(b.total_req#,0)      reqs
    , e.succ_req#     - nvl(b.succ_req#,0)       sreq
    , e.failed_req#   - nvl(b.failed_req#,0)     freq
    , e.total_wait#   - nvl(b.total_wait#,0)     waits
```

```
        , (e.cum_wait_time - nvl(b.cum_wait_time,0))/1000   wttm
        , decode(   (e.total_wait#   - nvl(b.total_wait#,0))
                , 0, to_number(NULL)
                , (   (e.cum_wait_time - nvl(b.cum_wait_time,0))
                / (e.total_wait#    - nvl(b.total_wait#,0))
                )
            )                                               awttm
    from dba_hist_enqueue_stat e
    , dba_hist_enqueue_stat b
    , v$lock_type               l
where b.snap_id(+)               = &pBgnSnap
    and e.snap_id               = &pEndSnap
    and b.dbid(+)               = &pDbId
    and e.dbid                  = &pDbId
    and b.dbid(+)               = e.dbid
    and b.instance_number(+)    = &pInstNum
    and e.instance_number       = &pInstNum
    and b.instance_number(+)    = e.instance_number
    and b.eq_type(+)            = e.eq_type
    and b.req_reason(+)         = e.req_reason
    and e.total_wait# - nvl(b.total_wait#,0) > 0
    and l.type(+)               = e.eq_type
order by wttm desc, waits desc)
```

The following is a sample output from the above script:

```
SQL> @Enq_stat_int_10g.sql

Enqueue                   Requests  Successful Gets Failed Gets  Waits Wait Time (s) Average
Wait Time(ms)
----------------------    --------- --------------- ----------- ------ -------------
RO-Multiple Object          1806           1806           0     153         4,554
29,7647059

TC-Tablespace Checkpoint      81             81           0      27         4,016
148,740741

TQ-Queue table enqueue     19878          19878           0      16         3,596
224,75

CF-Controlfile Transaction 308733        308732           1       2          ,692
346
```

The script output shows activity statistics for particular types of enqueues that allows users to find the ones which cause the most waits and wait times.

The WISE tool has a special report named *Enqueue Activity* that is used to retrieve and chart AWR data from the *dba_hist_enqueue_stat* view as shown in Figure 1.1.

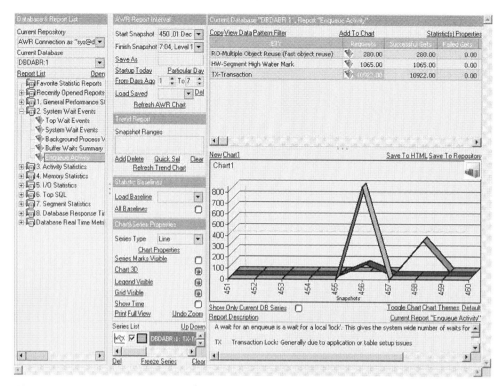

Figure 1.1: *AWR Enqueue Activity chart in WISE.*

Just by looking at the above chart, one can easily find the specific time periods that certain enqueues spike in wait time and are potential bottlenecks on performance

10g Time Model Statistics *dba_hist* Views

Time model statistics show the amount of CPU time that has been required to complete each type of database processing work. Examples include *sql execute elapsed time*, *parse time elapsed* and *PL/SQL execution elapsed time* statistics.

The most important time model statistic is *DB time*, which represents the total time spent by Oracle to process all database calls. In fact, it describes the total database workload. *DB time* is calculated by aggregating the CPU and all non-idle wait times for all sessions in the database after the last startup. Since it is an aggregate value, it is actually possible that the *DB time* statistic could be larger than the total instance runtime.

One common objective in Oracle performance tuning is the reduction of database workload or *DB time*. This reduction can be achieved by minimizing specific components such as the session's SQL parse and processing times, session's wait times, etc.

The time model statistics allow the identification of where the Oracle database spends the most CPU time for processing. The next section looks at the view Oracle provides for this purpose

dba_hist_sys_time_model

The dba_hist_sys_time_model view displays snapshots for the *v$sys_time_model* dynamic view and stores history for system time model statistics.

```
SQL> desc DBA_HIST_SYS_TIME_MODEL

Name                                     Null?    Type
-------------------------------------- -------- ----------
SNAP_ID                                          NUMBER
DBID                                             NUMBER
INSTANCE_NUMBER                                  NUMBER
STAT_ID                                          NUMBER
STAT_NAME                                        VARCHAR2(64)
VALUE                                            NUMBER
```

The statistic names are also available in the *dba_hist_stat_name* view that displays all the statistic names gathered by the AWR and stores snapshots for the *v$statname* dynamic view. This *dba_hist_stat_name* view is also used with the *dba_hist_sysstat* view described below.

This simple script provides valuable information about what percentage of total database processing time and actual time in seconds each metric takes. With this query, users can quickly identify the areas where the database consumes processing time, not wait time, and thus isolate the most resource intensive tasks.

This query can be used to retrieve information from the *dba_hist_sys_time_model* view for a particular AWR snapshot interval:

🖫 sys_time_model_int_10g.sql

```
-- *************************************************
-- Copyright © 2005 by Rampant TechPress
-- This script is free for non-commercial purposes
-- with no warranties.  Use at your own risk.
--
-- To license this script for a commercial purpose,
-- contact info@rampant.cc
-- *************************************************

column "Statistic Name" format A40
column "Time (s)" format 999,999
column "Percent of Total DB Time" format 999,999

select e.stat_name "Statistic Name"
     , (e.value - b.value)/1000000          "Time (s)"
     , decode( e.stat_name,'DB time'
             , to_number(null)
             , 100*(e.value - b.value)
             )/
     ( select nvl((e1.value - b1.value),-1)
     from dba_hist_sys_time_model  e1
        , dba_hist_sys_time_model  b1
     where b1.snap_id              = b.snap_id
     and e1.snap_id                = e.snap_id
     and b1.dbid                   = b.dbid
     and e1.dbid                   = e.dbid
     and b1.instance_number        = b.instance_number
     and e1.instance_number        = e.instance_number
     and b1.stat_name              = 'DB time'
     and b1.stat_id                = e1.stat_id
)
     "Percent of Total DB Time"

  from dba_hist_sys_time_model e
     , dba_hist_sys_time_model b

 where b.snap_id                   = &pBgnSnap
   and e.snap_id                   = &pEndSnap
   and b.dbid                      = &pDbId
   and e.dbid                      = &pDbId
   and b.instance_number           = &pInst_Num
   and e.instance_number           = &pInst_Num
   and b.stat_id                   = e.stat_id
   and e.value - b.value > 0
 order by 2 desc;
```

The output of this query looks like the following:

```
SQL> @Sys_time_model_int_10g.sql

Statistic Name                              Time (s) Percent of Total DB Time
----------------------------------------    -------- ------------------------
DB time                                          169
sql execute elapsed time                         156                       93
DB CPU                                           153                       90
PL/SQL execution elapsed time                     77                       46
background cpu time                                53                       31
parse time elapsed                                 6                        4
hard parse elapsed time                            4                        3
connection management call elapsed time            0                        0
Java execution elapsed time                        0                        0
PL/SQL compilation elapsed time                    0                        0
sequence load elapsed time                         0                        0
hard parse (sharing criteria) elapsed ti           0                        0
hard parse (bind mismatch) elapsed time            0                        0
```

The WISE tool has a report for *dba_hist_sys_time_model* called DB Time
Model Statistics. This report allows users to quickly build time-series
charts for time model statistics. The time-series charts for *DB time* model
statistics allow easy identification of the hot time periods of the database
workload as shown in Figure 1.2.

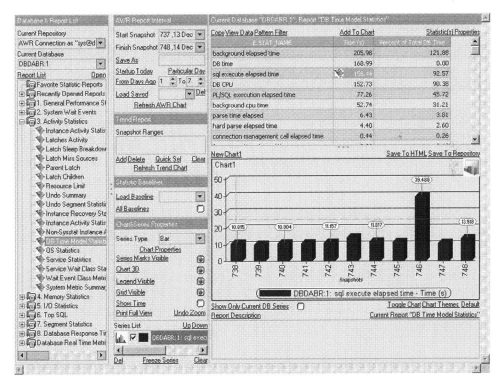

Figure 1.2: *Time Model Statistics chart in WISE.*

In the above figure it can quickly be seen that there is a particular snapshot time period that needs further analysis as it is out of the norm, based on the other snapshot time periods.

Active Session History (ASH) information on enqueues is also maintained. This allows a query such as *ash_enqueues.sql* to produce a report on enqueue waits:

🖫 ash_enqueues.sql

```
-- ****************************************************
-- Copyright © 2005 by Rampant TechPress
-- This script is free for non-commercial purposes
-- with no warranties.  Use at your own risk.
--
-- To license this script for a commercial purpose,
-- contact info@rampant.cc
-- ****************************************************

column begin_interval_time format a10
column req_reason          format a25
column cum_wait_time       head CUM|WAIT|TIME
column total_req#          head TOTAL|REQ#
column total_wait#         head TOTAL|WAIT#
column failed_req#         head FAILED|REQ#

select
   begin_interval_time,
   eq_type,
   req_reason,
   total_req#,
   total_wait#,
   succ_req#,
   failed_req#,
   cum_wait_time
from
   dba_hist_enqueue_stat
 natural join
   dba_hist_snapshot
where
   cum_wait_time > 0
order by
   begin_interval_time,
   cum_wait_time;
```

The following output lists the results with the top waits by time period:

TIME	EQ	REQ REASON	TOT REQUEST	TOT WT NUM	SUCCESS REQ NUM	FAILED REQ NUM	CUM WAIT TIME
1 PM	JS	slave enq get lock1	11	2	11	0	2,990
1 PM	RO	fast object reuse	1,960	31	1,960	0	1,940
1 PM	SQ	contention	244	4	244	0	550
1 PM	TM	contention	121,391	1	121,370	21	100
1 PM	TX	contention	66,793	1	66,793	0	60
1 PM	TX	index contention	1	1	1	0	50
2 PM	JS	slave enq get lock1	22	4	233	0	4,332
2 PM	RO	fast object reuse	1,960	31	1,960	0	5,730
2 PM	SQ	contention	244	4	244	0	950
2 PM	TX	row lock contention	1	1	1	0	870
2 PM	JS	queue lock	1151,724	1	1151,724	0	790
2 PM	SQ	contention	247	4	247	0	550
2 PM	TM	contention	122,513	1	122,492	21	450
2 PM	TX	contention	67,459	1	67,459	0	360
2 PM	TX	index contention	1	1	1	0	250
2 PM	TX	row lock contention	1	1	1	0	170

In the above samples, it is clear that AWR and ASH can be used together to obtain more precise time-series trend pictures of database performance. The top enqueue waits are the areas of concern during the specific time periods. The above type of report will allow the DBA to determine if the same enqueues are a recurring problem or if an enqueue is only a bottleneck at different times.

Conclusion

Monitoring of system wait events and enqueues, combined with CPU usage monitoring provides a complete picture of the response time for the system. By analyzing response time, the key problem areas where the DBA should concentrate their tuning efforts are located.

In this chapter, scripts that allow the DBA the ability to examine the response time components have been presented. Additionally, the following important points were presented:

- CPU usage statistics form a critical component of response time analysis.

- Enqueues are shared memory structures that serialize access to database resources and are associated with a session or transaction.

The enqueues of concern will show the greatest amount of cumulative wait time.

- Oracle is an event-driven system. This means that sessions wait for calls, locks and latches spin, and processes slumber and wake at the behest of events. Be sure to compare CPU usage to event wait time to ensure that wait events are actually the problem. If CPU time is the major component to the response time profile, then tuning events will make little difference to overall performance.

File I/O Monitoring

Monitoring I/O

When complaints begin to surface regarding database performance, the root cause can often be traced to one or more issues with I/O. The one thing to keep in mind when beginning to monitor the I/O of a database is that what is really being reviewed is the success of the physical design model.

All the physical storage characteristics and placements, the table and index designs, and the speed with which it all works are on display when I/O is monitored. A database's main index of performance is measured by how fast I/O needs are satisfied; therefore, it is the responsibility of the DBA to quickly interrogate Oracle to determine if a reported database slowdown is I/O related.

How can a DBA quickly accomplish such a task? While it is true that every situation is different in some regard, one roadmap that can regularly be used is outlined as follows:

- Obtain global measures regarding the I/O of the database and note any standout values.

- Examine global statistics regarding how database objects are being accessed.

- Drill deeper by examining the I/O of the storage structures and noting where the hotspots appear to be on the disk.

- From storage, uncover the objects that appear to be the most in demand.

- If the reported slowdown is currently active, obtain metrics regarding the leading sessions with respect to I/O.

- Once it is known what objects and users are responsible for the most I/O issues, drill further into the situation by locating the SQL being issued. This area will be examined more deeply in a subsequent chapter.

The following section is a detailed analysis of each step showing how using the above steps can quickly pinpoint the I/O hotspots and bottlenecks in databases.

Global Basic Queries

The first step in unraveling any I/O puzzles in databases is to make a quick check of some of the global database I/O metrics.

A query such as the following *globiostats.sql* script can be used to get a bird's eye view of a database's I/O:

globiostats.sql

```
-- ***************************************************
-- Copyright © 2005 by Rampant TechPress
-- This script is free for non-commercial purposes
-- with no warranties.  Use at your own risk.
--
-- To license this script for a commercial purpose,
-- contact info@rampant.cc
-- ***************************************************

select
   name,
   value
from
   sys.v_$sysstat
where
   name in
     ('consistent changes',
      'consistent gets',
      'db block changes',
      'db block gets',
      'physical reads',
      'physical writes',
      'sorts (disk)',
      'user commits',
      'user rollbacks'
     )
 order by
 1;
```

The output from the above query might look like the following:

```
NAME                    VALUE
------------------------ -----
consistent changes          1
consistent gets         70983
db block changes          243
db block gets             612
physical reads          11591
physical writes            52
sorts (disk)                0
user commits               26
user rollbacks              1
```

Some database experts do not believe the buffer cache hit ratio is of much value anymore. There are some valid reasons for assuming such a stance; however, a cursory check should still be performed to get an idea of overall disk I/O activity by using the *buffratio.sql* script:

buffratio.sql

```
-- ****************************************************
-- Copyright © 2005 by Rampant TechPress
-- This script is free for non-commercial purposes
-- with no warranties.  Use at your own risk.
--
-- To license this script for a commercial purpose,
-- contact info@rampant.cc
-- ****************************************************

select
   100 -
   100 *
      (round ((sum (decode (name, 'physical reads',
       value, 0))
         -
       sum (decode (name, 'physical reads direct',
       value, 0)) -
          sum (decode (name,
       'physical reads direct (lob)',
          value, 0))) /
          (sum (decode (name, 'session logical reads',
          value, 1))
           ),3)) hit_ratio
 from
    sys.v_$sysstat
where
   name in
   ('session logical reads',
    'physical reads direct (lob)',
    'physical reads',
    'physical reads direct');
```

The following is a list of quick things to look for in the above statistics:

- Increasing numbers of physical reads and a low hit ratio may indicate insufficient settings for *db_block_buffers* or *db_cache_size* in database versions Oracle9i and above. The hit ratio reading in particular should be observed to see if the ratio is representative of the database's *personality*. The time period that his ratio is monitored depends on the particular characteristics of the database being monitored. Keep in mind that readings below the normal rule of thumb of 90% can be OK.

- High volumes of disk sorts could be indicative of either; a setting for *sort_area_size* in database versions Oracle8i and below; or a setting for *pga_aggregate_target* for Oracle9i and above that is too low or unnecessary sort activities. Seeing large numbers of physical writes in a read-only database may also be indicative of excessive sorting.

- Large numbers of user rollbacks can be undesirable since it indicates that user transactions are not completing for one reason or another.

In addition, do cursory, global checks of the system-level wait events to get an idea of the I/O bottlenecks that may be occurring in the system.

The following script such as the *syswaits.sql* script can be used to perform such a check:

💾 syswaits.sql

```
-- *****************************************************
-- Copyright © 2005 by Rampant TechPress
-- This script is free for non-commercial purposes
-- with no warranties.  Use at your own risk.
--
-- To license this script for a commercial purpose,
-- contact info@rampant.cc
-- *****************************************************

select
   event,
   total_waits,
   round(100 * (total_waits / sum_waits),2) pct_waits,
   time_wait_sec,
   round(100 * (time_wait_sec / greatest(sum_time_waited,1)),2)
   pct_time_waited,
   total_timeouts,
   round(100 * (total_timeouts / greatest(sum_timeouts,1)),2)
   pct_timeouts,
   average_wait_sec
from
(select
      event,
      total_waits,
      round((time_waited / 100),2) time_wait_sec,
      total_timeouts,
      round((average_wait / 100),2) average_wait_sec
from
      sys.v_$system_event
where
      event not in
('lock element cleanup',
 'pmon timer',
 'rdbms ipc message',
 'rdbms ipc reply',
 'smon timer',
 'SQL*Net message from client',
 'SQL*Net break/reset to client',
 'SQL*Net message to client',
 'SQL*Net more data from client',
 'dispatcher timer',
 'Null event',
 'parallel query dequeue wait',
```

```
    'parallel query idle wait - Slaves',
    'pipe get',
    'PL/SQL lock timer',
    'slave wait',
    'virtual circuit status',
    'WMON goes to sleep') and
    event not like 'DFS%' and
    event not like 'KXFX%'),
(select
        sum(total_waits) sum_waits,
        sum(total_timeouts) sum_timeouts,
        sum(round((time_waited / 100),2)) sum_time_waited
from
        sys.v_$system_event
where
        event not in
    ('lock element cleanup',
    'pmon timer',
    'rdbms ipc message',
    'rdbms ipc reply',
    'smon timer',
    'SQL*Net message from client',
    'SQL*Net break/reset to client',
    'SQL*Net message to client',
    'SQL*Net more data from client',
    'dispatcher timer',
    'Null event',
    'parallel query dequeue wait',
    'parallel query idle wait - Slaves',
    'pipe get',
    'PL/SQL lock timer',
    'slave wait',
    'virtual circuit status',
    'WMON goes to sleep') and
    event not like 'DFS%' and
    event not like 'KXFX%')
order by
    2 desc, 1 asc;
```

The output from this query could resemble Figure 2.1 below:

	EVENT	TOTAL_WAITS	PCT_WAITS	TIME_WAIT_SEC	PCT_TIME_WAITED	TOTAL_TIMEOUTS	PCT_TIMEOUTS	AVERAGE_WAIT_SEC
1	control file parallel write	13763	66.1	11.8	43.77	0	0	0
2	direct path write	2216	10.64	4.18	15.5	0	0	0
3	db file sequential read	1874	9	1.76	6.53	0	0	0
4	control file sequential read	1805	8.67	3.86	14.32	0	0	0
5	direct path read	319	1.53	1.11	4.12	0	0	0
6	refresh controlfile command	231	1.11	1.7	6.31	0	0	.01
7	log file parallel write	165	.79	.1	.37	0	0	0
8	db file scattered read	130	.62	.11	.41	0	0	0
9	file open	130	.62	.75	2.78	0	0	.01
10	log file sync	51	.24	.5	1.85	0	0	.01
11	db file parallel write	46	.22	.39	1.45	0	0	.01
12	file identify	35	.17	.06	.22	0	0	0
13	latch free	22	.11	.52	1.93	21	100	.02
14	library cache pin	12	.06	0	0	0	0	0
15	buffer busy waits	10	.05	.12	.45	0	0	.01
16	log file sequential read	5	.02	0	0	0	0	0
17	log file single write	5	.02	0	0	0	0	0
18	instance state change	1	0	0	0	0	0	0
19	library cache load lock	1	0	0	0	0	0	0
20	reliable message	1	0	0	0	0	0	0

Figure 2.1 – *System event waits output*

The following is a list of things to note about the output from the waits SQL script:

- Numerous waits for the *db file scattered read* event may indicate a problem with table scans.

- Many waits for the *latch free* event could indicate excessive amounts of logical I/O activity.

- High wait times for the *enqueue* event pinpoints a problem with lock contention.

DATAFILE I/O

This is the physical part of the database and where the true disk activity occurs. If the datafile I/O balance is not distributed properly, then it is the responsibility of the DBA to reconfigure the system to ensure proper balancing.

Use this simple sql script to identify any "hot spots" and possible I/O contention

🖫 fileio.sql

```
-- ****************************************************
-- Copyright © 2005 by Rampant TechPress
-- This script is free for non-commercial purposes
-- with no warranties.  Use at your own risk.
--
-- To license this script for a commercial purpose,
-- contact info@rampant.cc
-- ****************************************************

rem
rem NAME: fileio.sql
rem
rem FUNCTION: Reports on the file io status of all of the
rem           datafiles in the database.
rem
rem Mike Ault
rem

column sum_io1 new_value st1 noprint
column sum_io2 new_value st2 noprint
column sum_io new_value divide_by noprint
column Percent format 999.999 heading 'Percent|Of IO'
column brratio format 999.99 heading 'Block|Read|Ratio'
column bwratio format 999.99 heading 'Block|Write|Ratio'
column phyrds heading 'Physical | Reads'
column phywrts heading 'Physical | Writes'
column phyblkrd heading 'Physical|Block|Reads'
column phyblkwrt heading 'Physical|Block|Writes'
column name format a30 heading 'File|Name'
column file# format 9999 heading 'File'
column dt new_value today noprint
TTITLE 'FILE I/O Status'
select to_char(sysdate,'ddmonyyyyhh24miss') dt from dual;
set feedback off verify off lines 132 pages 60 sqlbl on trims on
rem
select
     nvl(sum(a.phyrds+a.phywrts),0) sum_io1
from
     sys.v_$filestat a;
select nvl(sum(b.phyrds+b.phywrts),0) sum_io2
from
       sys.v_$tempstat b;
select &st1+&st2 sum_io from dual;
rem
title 'File IO Statistics Report'
spool fileio&&today
select
     a.file#,b.name, a.phyrds, a.phywrts,
     (100*(a.phyrds+a.phywrts)/&divide_by) Percent,
     a.phyblkrd, a.phyblkwrt, (a.phyblkrd/greatest(a.phyrds,1)) brratio,
      (a.phyblkwrt/greatest(a.phywrts,1)) bwratio
from
     sys.v_$filestat a, sys.v_$dbfile b
where
     a.file#=b.file#
union
select
```

```
    c.file#,d.name, c.phyrds, c.phywrts,
    (100*(c.phyrds+c.phywrts)/&divide_by) Percent,
    c.phyblkrd, c.phyblkwrt,(c.phyblkrd/greatest(c.phyrds,1)) brratio,
     (c.phyblkwrt/greatest(c.phywrts,1)) bwratio
from
    sys.v_$tempstat c, sys.v_$tempfile d
where
    c.file#=d.file#
order by
    1
/
spool off
set feedback on verify on lines 80 pages 22
clear columns
ttitle off
```

This script reports all the datafiles in the database ordered by the file number. By changing the "order by" clause, one can view the datafiles in different ways. For instance, ordering by filename could display the files by the mount point in order to analyze load balancing on different mount points.

This report can be utilized to not only see which files are incurring the most I/O, but also to make logical assumptions regarding the type of I/O being performed by examining the block read ratios. By knowing the values for *db_file_multi_block_read_count*, *direct_io_count* and *sort_io_count* for the database (8-32 for the first, 64 for the second and two for the third), the DBA can generate an idea of the type of access a file is seeing.

If the ratio is close to one, mostly single block data or index reads are occurring. If the value is close to *db_file_multi_block_read_count*, the majority of I/O is probably full table scans. If the value is greater than *db_file_multi_block_read_count*, direct I/O is occurring in the file.

This information allows the DBA to not only determine what files are being hit the hardest, but to also determine if the type of access is correct.

For example, excessive direct I/O to the SYSTEM tablespace could indicate bad temporary tablespace assignments in systems using global temporary tables. Excessive I/O to the SYSTEM tablespace in general probably indicates bad default or temporary tablespace assignments. In the example report, a majority of I/O involves the system tablespace. This should be immediately investigated and corrected.

```
Tue Dec 14                                                                    page    1
                                              FILE I/O Status

                                                  Physical Physical Block Block
          File               Physical Physical Percent   Block    Block Read Write
File Name                       Reads    Writes  Of IO    Reads   Writes Ratio Ratio
---- ------------------------ --------- -------- ------- --------- -------- ----- -----
   1 /u03/oradata/PROD/system01.dbf 16009811   69771   3.942  87630332    69771  5.47  1.00
   2 /u03/oradata/PROD/tools01.dbf      2594    2592    .001      2594     2592  1.00  1.00
   3 /u03/oradata/PROD/rbs01.dbf       14521  754697    .189     14521   754697  1.00  1.00
   4 /u03/oradata/PROD/temp01.dbf    2525989  909561    .842   6506288  6729627  2.58  7.40
   5 /u03/oradata/PROD/users01.dbf      2594    2914    .001      2594     2914  1.00  1.00
   6 /u03/oradata/PROD/indx01.dbf     530578  149682    .167    622320   149682  1.17  1.00
   7 /u03/oradata/PROD/PROD01.dbf   35324632  165817   8.702 194423552   165948  5.50  1.00
   8 /u03/oradata/PROD/PROD02.dbf     937126   28027    .237   4443975    28165  4.74  1.00
   9 /u03/oradata/PROD/PROD03.dbf     491937   16034    .125   2484248    16034  5.05  1.00
  10 /u03/oradata/PROD/PROD04.dbf     393073    9081    .099   2069376     9081  5.26  1.00
  11 /u03/oradata/PROD/PROD05.dbf     313332    8533    .079   1652185     8533  5.27  1.00
  12 /u03/oradata/PROD/PROD06.dbf     312113    7358    .078   1681192     7358  5.39  1.00
  13 /u03/oradata/PROD/PROD07.dbf     691411   25523    .176   3299955    25668  4.77  1.01
  14 /u03/oradata/PROD/PROD08.dbf     782111   17235    .196   3599924    17362  4.60  1.01
  15 /u03/oradata/PROD/PROD09.dbf    1010212   13159    .251   4520903    13294  4.48  1.01
  16 /u03/oradata/PROD/PROD10.dbf     690730   25095    .176   3318040    25240  4.80  1.01
  17 /u03/oradata/PROD/PROD11.dbf     819918   18959    .206   3748198    19096  4.57  1.01
  18 /u03/oradata/PROD/PROD12.dbf     606694   23945    .155   2911930    24081  4.80  1.01
  19 /u03/oradata/PROD/PROD13.dbf     785076   28654    .200   3741405    28788  4.77  1.00
  20 /u03/oradata/PROD/PROD14.dbf     771884   18426    .194   3525416    18562  4.57  1.01
  21 /u03/oradata/PROD/PROD15.dbf     717686   17843    .180   3325660    17973  4.63  1.01
  22 /u03/oradata/PROD/PROD16.dbf     860536   26111    .217   4157076    26233  4.83  1.00
  23 /u03/oradata/PROD/PROD17.dbf     826276   26888    .209   3948690    27008  4.78  1.00
  24 /u03/oradata/PROD/system02.dbf  1046800   13323    .260   4673279    13456  4.46  1.01
  25 /u03/oradata/PROD/system03.dbf 54208739   82473  13.311 345876890    82473  6.38  1.00
  26 /u03/oradata/PROD/PROD18.dbf     736361    6036    .182   3696429     6038  5.02  1.00
  27 /u03/oradata/PROD/PROD19.dbf     741042   15088    .185   3700420    15088  4.99  1.00
  28 /u03/oradata/PROD/PROD20.dbf     704588   13635    .176   3482388    13635  4.94  1.00
  29 /u03/oradata/PROD/PROD21.dbf     696834   16406    .175   3496504    16406  5.02  1.00
  30 /u03/oradata/PROD/PROD22.dbf     659906   23790    .168   3275079    23801  4.96  1.00
```

PL/SQL to Calculate I/O per Second Data

Knowing the value for total I/O per second for the database allows the DBA to do resource planning for the number of disks utilized. Generally speaking, a modern disk drive can only support around 100 I/O's per second of non-linear activity. If the value for average I/O's per second exceeds 100 times the number of disks in use, chances are the disks are being over-taxed and more disks should be added.

This report calculates an average since the database was started; therefore, the actual value for peak I/O's per second could be double or more this average value.

io_sec.sql

```
-- ****************************************************
-- Copyright © 2005 by Rampant TechPress
-- This script is free for non-commercial purposes
-- with no warranties.  Use at your own risk.
--
-- To license this script for a commercial purpose,
-- contact info@rampant.cc
-- ****************************************************

rem
rem NAME: io_sec.sql
rem
rem FUNCTION:  PL/SQL to calculate IO/sec data
rem Mike Ault
rem

set serveroutput on
declare
cursor get_io is select
        nvl(sum(a.phyrds+a.phywrts),0) sum_io1,to_number(null) sum_io2
from sys.gv_$filestat a
union
select
        to_number(null) sum_io1, nvl(sum(b.phyrds+b.phywrts),0) sum_io2
from
        sys.gv_$tempstat b;
now date;
elapsed_seconds number;
sum_io1 number;
sum_io2 number;
sum_io12 number;
sum_io22 number;
tot_io number;
tot_io_per_sec number;
fixed_io_per_sec number;
temp_io_per_sec number;
begin
open get_io;
for i in 1..2 loop
fetch get_io into sum_io1, sum_io2;
if i = 1 then sum_io12:=sum_io1;
else
sum_io22:=sum_io2;
end if;
end loop;
select sum_io12+sum_io22 into tot_io from dual;
select sysdate into now from dual;
select ceil((now-max(startup_time))*(60*60*24)) into elapsed_seconds from
gv$instance;
fixed_io_per_sec:=sum_io12/elapsed_seconds;
temp_io_per_sec:=sum_io22/elapsed_seconds;
tot_io_per_sec:=tot_io/elapsed_seconds;
dbms_output.put_line('Elapsed Sec :'||to_char(elapsed_seconds,
'9,999,999.99'));
dbms_output.put_line('Fixed
IO/SEC:'||to_char(fixed_io_per_sec,'9,999,999.99'));
```

```
dbms_output.put_line('Temp IO/SEC :'||to_char(temp_io_per_sec,
'9,999,999.99'));
dbms_output.put_line('Total IO/SEC:'||to_char(tot_io_Per_Sec,
'9,999,999.99'));
end;
/
```

The following sample output from *io_sec.sql* displays the total elapsed seconds since the database was started, the I/O per second for both temporary I/O and fixed I/O as well as the total I/O per second. The report should be run periodically to determine if I/O rates are fluctuating. A version of this report that uses STATSPACK data is also available so that interval I/O rates can be determined.

```
Elapsed Sec : 2,183,399.00
Fixed IO/SEC:       190.96
Temp IO/SEC :          .00
Total IO/SEC:       190.96

PL/SQL procedure successfully completed.
```

I/O Timing Analysis

Calculate I/O Timing Values for Datafiles

The other component of I/O profiling is the amount of time required to complete the I/O to each datafile. Datafiles under stress will exhibit higher I/O times than non-stressed datafiles. The exception would be those datafiles that undergo very little I/O. Generally speaking, if several thousand I/O's for the period monitored are not being seen, then the values may not be accurate.

Here is a script to investigate I/O timing.

⊞ IO_TIMING.sql

```
-- ***************************************************
-- Copyright © 2005 by Rampant TechPress
-- This script is free for non-commercial purposes
-- with no warranties.  Use at your own risk.
--
-- To license this script for a commercial purpose,
-- contact info@rampant.cc
-- ***************************************************
```

```
rem   IO_TIMING.SQL
rem
rem   Purpose: Calculate IO timing values for datafiles
rem
rem   MIKE AULT
rem
col name format a30
set lines 132 pages 45
ttitle 'IO Timing Analysis'
spool io_time
select  f.FILE# ,d.name,PHYRDS,PHYWRTS,READTIM/PHYRDS,WRITETIM/PHYWRTS
from v$filestat f, v$datafile d
where f.file#=d.file#
order by readtim/phyrds desc
/
spool off
ttitle off
clear col
```

By analysis of the I/O timing profile, it can be determined if the proper RAID type is being used, which datafiles are under stress, and if any datafile is showing excessive read or write times.

Excessive read or write time determination depends on the type of system being monitoring. While 5-10 milliseconds may be acceptable for a low usage OLTP system, it can be the kiss of death to a high volume DSS or DWH system. Most modern disk arrays, with proper setup of the caching inherent in these systems, should show fractional millisecond read and write times.

This report displays the physical read, physical writes and the time required, on the average, to complete a single read or write.

```
Tue Dec 14                                           page    1
                        IO Timing Analysis

FILE# NAME                       PHYRDS    PHYWRTS READTIM/PHYRDS WRITETIM/PHYWRTS
----- ------------------------------ --------- ---------- --------------- ----------------
   48 /u03/oradata/test/indx02.dbf   242960    132135 .326634014       .038551481
    6 /u03/oradata/test/indx01.dbf   530578    149682 .208246478       .038782218
   37 /u03/oradata/test/test23.dbf  1091065     79533  .04307626       .04663473
   18 /u03/oradata/test/test12.dbf   606694     23945  .04305795       .042848194
   12 /u03/oradata/test/test06.dbf   312113      7358 .042366066       .034792063
   11 /u03/oradata/test/test05.dbf   313332      8533 .041093792       .03668112
   16 /u03/oradata/test/test10.dbf   690730     25095 .040222663       .042637976
   13 /u03/oradata/test/test07.dbf   691412     25523 .040003645       .044195432
    9 /u03/oradata/test/test03.dbf   491937     16034 .039773386       .04091306
   22 /u03/oradata/test/test16.dbf   860536     26111 .039754293       .043774654
   23 /u03/oradata/test/test17.dbf   826277     26888 .038350335       .045894079
    8 /u03/oradata/test/test02.dbf   937230     28027 .037353691       .046383844
   19 /u03/oradata/test/test13.dbf   785076     28655 .036964574       .045820974
   10 /u03/oradata/test/test04.dbf   393073      9081 .035591353       .040524171
   26 /u03/oradata/test/test18.dbf   736361      6036 .035289756       .028164347
   30 /u03/oradata/test/test22.dbf   659906     23790 .034686758       .043926019
   27 /u03/oradata/test/test19.dbf   741042     15088 .034062847       .039634146
```

```
29 /u03/oradata/test/test21.dbf      696834     16406   .033883249   .041204437
28 /u03/oradata/test/test20.dbf      704588     13635   .033405338   .041950862
17 /u03/oradata/test/test11.dbf      819918     18959   .029806639   .041774355
14 /u03/oradata/test/test08.dbf      782111     17235   .029729795   .039860748
21 /u03/oradata/test/test15.dbf      717686     17843   .029568641   .040295914
20 /u03/oradata/test/test14.dbf      771884     18426   .029097636   .040703354
15 /u03/oradata/test/test09.dbf     1010212     13159   .025522366   .038224789
39 /u03/oradata/test/test25.dbf     4175777     80747   .025353365   .045970748
38 /u03/oradata/test/test24.dbf     4217093     89379   .02524891    .045581177
41 /u03/oradata/test/test27.dbf     3485839     80055   .025170985   .047105115
24 /u03/oradata/test/system02.dbf   1046800     13324   .025121322   .034824377
40 /u03/oradata/test/test26.dbf     3533545     81242   .025096327   .045407548
43 /u03/oradata/test/test28.dbf      956177     14803   .024653385   .034587584
44 /u03/oradata/test/test29.dbf      947445     14301   .024372919   .034752814
45 /u03/oradata/test/test30.dbf      931210     14611   .023538192   .035931832
46 /u03/oradata/test/test31.dbf      881485     11499   .023244865   .034437777
 3 /u03/oradata/test/rbs01.dbf        14521    754847   .019144687   .035992724
 7 /u03/oradata/test/test01.dbf    35427079    165822   .018645285   .045096549
47 /u03/oradata/test/system04.dbf   2372756     30354   .018338169   .028694735
```

The next topic covered will illustrate how to investigate File I/O using STATSPACK.

SNAP FILE I/O

The *snapfileio.sql* script provides the capability to calculate the file I/O rates between two STATSPACK runs. This allows the examination of file I/O for a specific SQL statement or application execution. It also allows historical analysis of I/O timing to determine if a disk subsystem is becoming overloaded. The report requires that STATSPACK be installed and that at least two snapshots have been taken covering the time the analysis is for.

🖫 Snapfileio.sql

```
-- *************************************************
-- Copyright © 2005 by Rampant TechPress
-- This script is free for non-commercial purposes
-- with no warranties.  Use at your own risk.
--
-- To license this script for a commercial purpose,
-- contact info@rampant.cc
-- *************************************************

rem
rem NAME: snapfileio.sql
rem
rem FUNCTION: Reports on the file io status of all of the
rem           datafiles in the database.
rem Mike Ault
rem
column sum_io1 new_value st1 noprint
column sum_io2 new_value st2 noprint
column sum_io new_value divide_by noprint
column Percent format 999.999 heading 'Percent|Of IO'
```

```
column brratio format 999.99 heading 'Block|Read|Ratio'
column bwratio format 999.99 heading 'Block|Write|Ratio'
column phyrds heading 'Physical | Reads'
column phywrts heading 'Physical | Writes'
column phyblkrd heading 'Physical|Block|Reads'
column phyblkwrt heading 'Physical|Block|Writes'
column filename format a45 heading 'File|Name'
column file# format 9999 heading 'File'
set feedback off verify off lines 132 pages 60 sqlbl on trims on
rem
select
    nvl(sum(a.phyrds+a.phywrts),0) sum_io1
from
    stats$filestatxs a where snap_id=&&snap;
select nvl(sum(b.phyrds+b.phywrts),0) sum_io2
from
        stats$tempstatxs b where snap_id=&&snap;
select &st1+&st2 sum_io from dual;
rem
ttitle132 'Snap&&snap File IO Statistics Report'
spool fileio&&snap
select
    a.filename, a.phyrds, a.phywrts,
    (100*(a.phyrds+a.phywrts)/&divide_by) Percent,
    a.phyblkrd, a.phyblkwrt, (a.phyblkrd/greatest(a.phyrds,1)) brratio,
     (a.phyblkwrt/greatest(a.phywrts,1)) bwratio
from
    stats$filestatxs a
where
    a.snap_id=&&snap
union
select
    c.filename, c.phyrds, c.phywrts,
    (100*(c.phyrds+c.phywrts)/&divide_by) Percent,
    c.phyblkrd, c.phyblkwrt,(c.phyblkrd/greatest(c.phyrds,1)) brratio,
     (c.phyblkwrt/greatest(c.phywrts,1)) bwratio
from
    stats$tempstatxs c
where
    c.snap_id=&&snap
order by
    1
/
spool off
pause Press enter to continue
set feedback on verify on lines 80 pages 22
clear columns
ttitle off
undef snap
```

The following report displays the file I/O profiles for the delta between two STATSPACK runs:

```
Snap4937 File IO Statistics Report
                                               Physical Physical Block Block
File                       Physical Physical Percent  Block    Block Read  Write
Name                        Reads    Writes   Of IO   Reads   Writes Ratio Ratio
```

```
--------------------------------  ---------  ---------  -------  ---------  --------  -------  ------
/u03/ora/test/PERFSTAT01.dbf        219756      56487     .412     826659     56487     3.76    1.00
/u03/ora/test/test01.dbf           5517891      17408    8.259   25214397     17408     4.57    1.00
/u03/ora/test/test02.dbf            570225       3803     .857    2644848      3803     4.64    1.00
/u03/ora/test/test03.dbf            269048       2022     .404    1296749      2022     4.82    1.00
/u03/ora/test/test04.dbf            193622       1498     .291     988823      1498     5.11    1.00
/u03/ora/test/test05.dbf            152201       1582     .229     711668      1582     4.68    1.00
/u03/ora/test/test06.dbf            133945       1743     .202     699528      1743     5.22    1.00
/u03/ora/test/test07.dbf            420441       3581     .633    1892025      3585     4.50    1.00
/u03/ora/test/test08.dbf            402115       4291     .606    1863824      4298     4.64    1.00
/u03/ora/test/test09.dbf            572794       4420     .861    2656525      4420     4.64    1.00
/u03/ora/test/test10.dbf            402093       3857     .606    1874648      3858     4.66    1.00
/u03/ora/test/test11.dbf            427756       4620     .645    1975145      4620     4.62    1.00
/u03/ora/test/test12.dbf            352769       2726     .530    1592453      2727     4.51    1.00
/u03/ora/test/test13.dbf            469371       3403     .705    2177259      3405     4.64    1.00
/u03/ora/test/test14.dbf            401808       3911     .605    1804736      3912     4.49    1.00
/u03/ora/test/test15.dbf            351103       2813     .528    1638648      2815     4.67    1.00
/u03/ora/test/test16.dbf            529607       2803     .794    2494427      2807     4.71    1.00
/u03/ora/test/test17.dbf            512280       2816     .769    2353612      2818     4.59    1.00
/u03/ora/test/test18.dbf            457229       1667     .685    2196383      1667     4.80    1.00
/u03/ora/test/test19.dbf            460333       2380     .690    2200762      2380     4.78    1.00
/u03/ora/test/test20.dbf            418346       1943     .627    2036327      1943     4.87    1.00
/u03/ora/test/test21.dbf            412864       2583     .620    2041325      2583     4.94    1.00
/u03/ora/test/test22.dbf            393139       2751     .591    1891508      2751     4.81    1.00
/u03/ora/test/test23.dbf            716352      10839    1.085    3145132     10851     4.39    1.00
/u03/ora/test/test24.dbf           2717514      13377    4.075   12626762     13394     4.65    1.00
/u03/ora/test/test25.dbf           2704415       9582    4.050   12567248      9582     4.65    1.00
/u03/ora/test/test26.dbf           2300328      10041    3.447   10611382     10053     4.61    1.00
/u03/ora/test/test27.dbf           2273642       9877    3.407   10610202      9877     4.67    1.00
/u03/ora/test/test28.dbf            556092       4229     .836    2586421      4229     4.65    1.00
/u03/ora/test/test29.dbf            552325       4647     .831    2532729      4647     4.59    1.00
/u03/ora/test/test30.dbf            542029       3054     .813    2496498      3062     4.61    1.00
/u03/ora/test/test31.dbf            516745       3170     .776    2338715      3170     4.53    1.00
/u03/ora/test/test_prd.dbf            1222       1220     .004       1222      1220     1.00    1.00
/u03/ora/test/test_prd01.dbf          1222       1220     .004       1222      1220     1.00    1.00
/u03/ora/test/test_prd02.dbf          1222       1220     .004       1222      1220     1.00    1.00
/u03/ora/test/indx01.dbf            481104      93697     .858     547937     93697     1.14    1.00
/u03/ora/test/indx02.dbf            147209      64355     .316     163323     64355     1.11    1.00
/u03/ora/test/rbs01.dbf               8857     328870     .504       8857    328870     1.00    1.00
/u03/ora/test/system01.dbf         4119727      40297    6.207   21978249     40297     5.33    1.00
/u03/ora/test/system02.dbf          594421       2892     .891    2751097      2893     4.63    1.00
/u03/ora/test/system03.dbf        11577811      39601   17.334   74775020     39601     6.46    1.00
/u03/ora/test/system04.dbf          145128       5379     .225     638060      5379     4.40    1.00
/u03/ora/test/temp01.dbf           1765151     609608    3.543    5382544    555373     3.05    7.47
/u03/ora/test/tools01.dbf             1222       1220     .004       1222      1220     1.00    1.00
/u03/ora/test/users01.dbf             1347       1351     .004       1493      1351     1.11    1.00
```

The next topic will illustrate how I/O can be investigated by session.

Find the Current I/O Session Bandits

If the complaint of poor performance is current, the connected sessions are one of the first things that should be checked to determine which users are impacting the system in undesirable ways. There are a couple of different approaches to this process.

A good place to start is getting an idea of the percentage that each session is or has taken up with respect to I/O. One rule of thumb is that if any session is currently consuming 50% or more of the total I/O, that session and its SQL need to be further investigated to determine what activity it is engaged in.

If physical I/O is a concern, the *physpctio.sql* query will provide the needed information:

📇 physpctio.sql

```
-- *****************************************************
-- Copyright © 2005 by Rampant TechPress
-- This script is free for non-commercial purposes
-- with no warranties.  Use at your own risk.
--
-- To license this script for a commercial purpose,
-- contact info@rampant.cc
-- *****************************************************

select
   sid,
   username,
   round(100 * total_user_io/total_io,2) tot_io_pct
from

(select
     b.sid sid,
     nvl(b.username,p.name) username,
     sum(value) total_user_io
 from
     sys.v_$statname c,
     sys.v_$sesstat a,
     sys.v_$session b,
     sys.v_$bgprocess p
 where
     a.statistic#=c.statistic# and
     p.paddr (+) = b.paddr and
     b.sid=a.sid and
     c.name in ('physical reads',
                'physical writes',
                'physical writes direct',
                'physical reads direct',
                'physical writes direct (lob)',
                'physical reads direct (lob)')
group by
     b.sid, nvl(b.username,p.name)),

(select
     sum(value) total_io
 from
     sys.v_$statname c,
     sys.v_$sesstat a
 where
     a.statistic#=c.statistic# and
     c.name in ('physical reads',
                'physical writes',
                'physical writes direct',
```

```
                 'physical reads direct',
                 'physical writes direct (lob)',
                 'physical reads direct (lob)'))
order by
     3 desc;
```

If the total I/O picture, both logical and physical, is required, the *totpctio.sql* query can be used instead:

🖫 totpctio.sql

```
-- **************************************************
-- Copyright © 2005 by Rampant TechPress
-- This script is free for non-commercial purposes
-- with no warranties.  Use at your own risk.
--
-- To license this script for a commercial purpose,
-- contact info@rampant.cc
-- **************************************************

SELECT
     SID,
     USERNAME,
     ROUND(100 * TOTAL_USER_IO/TOTAL_IO,2) TOT_IO_PCT
FROM
(SELECT
      b.SID SID,
      nvl(b.USERNAME,p.NAME) USERNAME,
      SUM(VALUE) TOTAL_USER_IO
FROM
    sys.V_$STATNAME c,
    sys.V_$SESSTAT a,
    sys.V_$SESSION b,
    sys.v_$bgprocess p
WHERE
    a.STATISTIC#=c.STATISTIC# and
    p.paddr (+) = b.paddr and
    b.SID=a.SID and
    c.NAME in ('physical reads','physical writes',
               'consistent changes','consistent gets',
               'db block gets','db block changes',
               'physical writes direct',
               'physical reads direct',
               'physical writes direct (lob)',
               'physical reads direct (lob)')
GROUP BY
     b.SID, nvl(b.USERNAME,p.name)),
(select
      sum(value) TOTAL_IO
from
      sys.V_$STATNAME c,
      sys.V_$SESSTAT a
WHERE
      a.STATISTIC#=c.STATISTIC# and
      c.NAME in ('physical reads','physical writes',
               'consistent changes',
```

```
                    'consistent gets','db block gets',
                    'db block changes',
                    'physical writes direct',
                    'physical reads direct',
                    'physical writes direct (lob)',
                    'physical reads direct (lob)'))
ORDER BY
          3 DESC;
```

Regardless of the query used, the output would resemble the following:

```
SID  USERNAME        TOT_IO_PCT
--------------------------------
9    USR1                 71.26
20   SYS                  15.76
5    SMON                  7.11
2    DBWR                  4.28
12   SYS                   1.42
6    RECO                   .12
7    SNP0                   .01
10   SNP3                   .01
11   SNP4                   .01
8    SNP1                   .01
1    PMON                     0
3    ARCH                     0
4    LGWR                     0
```

In the above example, it would be prudent for the DBA to examine the USR1 session to see what SQL calls are being made. The SQL chapter will review in detail how to do this; however, for now, consider the above queries as excellent weapons that can be used to quickly pinpoint problem I/O sessions.

If more detail is desired with respect to the top I/O session in a database, use the rather large *topiousers.sql* query to see all the actual I/O numbers:

⊟ topiousers.sql

```
-- ***************************************************
-- Copyright © 2005 by Rampant TechPress
-- This script is free for non-commercial purposes
-- with no warranties.  Use at your own risk.
--
-- To license this script for a commercial purpose,
-- contact info@rampant.cc
-- ***************************************************

select
     b.sid sid,
     decode (b.username,null,e.name,b.username)
     user_name,
     d.spid os_id,
     b.machine machine_name,
     to_char(logon_time,'mm/dd/yy hh:mi:ss pm')
     logon_time,
     (sum(decode(c.name,'physical reads',value,0))
     +
     sum(decode(c.name,'physical writes',value,0))
     +
     sum(decode(c.name,
     'physical writes direct',value,0)) +
     sum(decode(c.name,
     'physical writes direct (lob)',value,0)) +
     sum(decode(c.name,
     'physical reads direct (lob)',value,0)) +
     sum(decode(c.name,
     'physical reads direct',value,0)))
     total_physical_io,
     (sum(decode(c.name,'db block gets',value,0))
     +
     sum(decode(c.name,
     'db block changes',value,0))  +
     sum(decode(c.name,'consistent changes',value,0)) +
     sum(decode(c.name,'consistent gets',value,0)) )
     total_logical_io,
     100 - 100 *(round ((sum (decode
     (c.name, 'physical reads', value, 0)) -
     sum (decode (c.name,
     'physical reads direct', value, 0))) /
     (sum (decode (c.name, 'db block gets',
     value, 1)) +
     sum (decode (c.name, 'consistent gets',
     value, 0))),3)) hit_ratio,
     sum(decode(c.name,'sorts (disk)',value,0))
     disk_sorts,
     sum(decode(c.name,'sorts (memory)',value,0))
     memory_sorts,
     sum(decode(c.name,'sorts (rows)',value,0))
     rows_sorted,
     sum(decode(c.name,'user commits',value,0))
     commits,
     sum(decode(c.name,'user rollbacks',value,0))
     rollbacks,
     sum(decode(c.name,'execute count',value,0))
     executions,
```

```
        sum(decode(c.name,'physical reads',value,0))
        physical_reads,
        sum(decode(c.name,'db block gets',value,0))
        db_block_gets,
        sum(decode(c.name,'consistent gets',value,0))
        consistent_gets,
        sum(decode(c.name,'consistent changes',value,0))
        consistent_changes
from
    sys.v_$sesstat a,
    sys.v_$session b,
    sys.v_$statname c,
    sys.v_$process d,
    sys.v_$bgprocess e
where
    a.statistic#=c.statistic#
and
    b.sid=a.sid
and
    d.addr = b.paddr
and
    e.paddr (+) = b.paddr
and
    c.name in
    ('physical reads',
     'physical writes',
     'physical writes direct',
     'physical reads direct',
     'physical writes direct (lob)',
     'physical reads direct (lob)',
     'db block gets',
     'db block changes',
     'consistent changes',
     'consistent gets',
     'sorts (disk)',
     'sorts (memory)',
     'sorts (rows)',
     'user commits',
     'user rollbacks',
     'execute count'
    )
group by
    b.sid,
    d.spid,
    decode (b.username,null,e.name,b.username),
         b.machine,
         to_char(logon_time,'mm/dd/yy hh:mi:ss pm')
order by
    6 desc;
```

Figure 2.2 represents the results of the above query:

Query | Results

	SID	USER_NAME	OS_ID	MACHINE_NAME	LOGON_TIME	TOTAL_PHYSICAL_IO	TOTAL_LOGICAL_IO	HIT_RATIO	DISK_SORTS	MEMORY_SORTS	ROWS_SORTED	COMMIT
1	2	DBW0	1064	EBT2K11	12/05/02 03:12:10 PM	9982	0	100	0	0	0	
2	12	ORA_MONITOR	2488	EBT2K\EBT2K08	12/12/02 05:28:18 PM	8527	59015775	100	0	269379	126302546	
3	5	SMON	296	EBT2K11	12/05/02 03:12:11 PM	2657	465527	99.4	0	78	175	
4	3	LGWR	980	EBT2K11	12/05/02 03:12:10 PM	34	0	100	0	0	0	
5	6	RECO	1220	EBT2K11	12/05/02 03:12:11 PM	1	1753	99.9	0	8	48	
6	1	PMON	1032	EBT2K11	12/05/02 03:12:09 PM	0	0	100	0	0	0	
7	4	CKPT	1144	EBT2K11	12/05/02 03:12:10 PM	0	0	100	0	0	0	
8	16	SYS	3958	EBT2K\ROBINWS	12/17/02 04:55:29 PM	0	4	100	0	0	0	
9	11	SYS	3096	EBT2K\ROBINWS	12/17/02 05:26:31 PM	0	235	100	0	66	27449	

Figure 2.2: *Sample Top I/O Users detail output*

Such a query can provide details about the actual raw I/O numbers for each connected session. Armed with this information, the DBA can begin to drill down into each heavy-hitting I/O session to determine what SQL calls are being made and which sets of SQL are the I/O hogs.

While information has been provided on how to troubleshoot I/O from a user standpoint, do not forget about all the system activity that Oracle itself generates. One such process is the DBWR which will be covered in the next section.

Report on 9i DBWR Statistics

The *DBWR_STAT.sql* script provides the Database Writer (DBWR) related cumulative statistics. By examining the various DBWR statistics, the DBA can determine if the DBWR process is properly tuned:

DBWR_STAT.sql

```
-- ***********************************************
-- Copyright © 2005 by Rampant TechPress
-- This script is free for non-commercial purposes
-- with no warranties.  Use at your own risk.
--
-- To license this script for a commercial purpose,
-- contact info@rampant.cc
-- ***********************************************

rem
rem dbwr_stat.sql
rem Mike Ault
rem
col name format a46 heading 'DBWR Statistic'
col stat format 9,999,999,999,999 heading 'Statistic Value'
set pages 40
ttitle 'DBWR Statistic Report'
spool dbwr_stat
```

```
select a.name,a.stat
from   (select name, value stat from v$sysstat
         where name not like '%redo%' and name not like '%remote%') a
where (a.name like 'DBWR%' or a.name like '%buffer%' or a.name like
'%write%' or name like '%summed%')
union
select class name, count "value" from v$waitstat where class='data block'
union
select name||' '||to_char(block_size/1024)||' hit ratio' name,
    round(((1 - (physical_reads / (db_block_gets + consistent_gets))) *
100),3) stat
from V$buffer_pool_statistics
union
select name||' '||to_char(block_size/1024)||' free buffer wait'
name,free_buffer_wait stat
from V$buffer_pool_statistics
union
select name||' '||to_char(block_size/1024)||' buffer busy wait'
name,buffer_busy_wait stat
from V$buffer_pool_statistics
union
select name||' '||to_char(block_size/1024)||' write complete wait'
name,write_complete_wait stat
from V$buffer_pool_statistics
/
spool off
set pages 22
ttitle off
```

The following results show the DBWR and physical I/O statistics from
the *v$sysstat* view:

```
Thu Dec 16
page    1
                       DBWR Statistic Report

DBWR Statistic                                 Statistic Value
-------------------------------------------    -----------------
DBWR buffers scanned                                         0
DBWR checkpoint buffers written                        50,131
DBWR checkpoints                                            14
DBWR cross instance writes                                  0
DBWR free buffers found                                     0
DBWR fusion writes                                          0
DBWR lru scans                                              0
DBWR make free requests                                     0
DBWR revisited being-written buffer                         0
DBWR summed scan depth                                      0
DBWR transaction table writes                           2,823
DBWR undo block writes                                 44,313
DEFAULT 4 buffer busy wait                                118
DEFAULT 4 free buffer wait                                  0
DEFAULT 4 hit ratio                                       100
DEFAULT 4 write complete wait                               0
buffer is not pinned count                         26,704,488
buffer is pinned count                             24,711,121
```

```
change write time                                      253
commit cleanout failures: buffer being written           0
commit cleanout failures: write disabled                 0
data block                                             117
dirty buffers inspected                                  0
free buffer inspected                                    4
free buffer requested                              525,286
hot buffers moved to head of LRU                         0
no buffer to keep pinned count                           1
physical writes                                    125,931
physical writes direct                              75,786
physical writes direct (lob)                             0
physical writes non checkpoint                      81,834
pinned buffers inspected                                 4
summed dirty queue length                                0
switch current to new buffer                       487,411

Thu Dec 16
page    2
                        DBWR Statistic Report

DBWR Statistic                             Statistic Value
------------------------------------------ ------------------
write clones created in background                       0
write clones created in foreground                      18

36 rows selected.
```

In the next section will cover what is new and improved for file I/O monitoring and reporting with Oracle 10g.

Oracle 10g FILE I/O

New Analysis Techniques for Oracle10g and Above

Oracle10g has provided new file-related views to help the DBA obtain an even greater understanding of the activity of Oracle datafiles. For starters, there is a new file historical view that allows the DBA to quickly determine when certain datafiles experienced their peak activity.

The *10g_filehist.sql* script shows metrics gathered by Oracle regarding file activity over time:

🖫 10g_filehist.sql

```
-- ****************************************************
-- Copyright © 2005 by Rampant TechPress
-- This script is free for non-commercial purposes
-- with no warranties.  Use at your own risk.
--
-- To license this script for a commercial purpose,
-- contact info@rampant.cc
-- ****************************************************

select
        begin_time,
        end_time,
        a.file_id,
        file_name,
        average_read_time,
        average_write_time,
        physical_reads,
        physical_writes,
        physical_block_reads,
        physical_block_writes
from
        sys.v_$filemetric_history a,
        sys.dba_data_files b
where
        a.file_id = b.file_id
order by
        1,3
```

The *v$file_histogram* view provides a nice breakdown of the occurrences of file read time for each file. The *10g_filehistogram.sql* script provides a quick breakdown of each file histogram:

🖫 10g_filehistogram.sql

```
-- ****************************************************
-- Copyright © 2005 by Rampant TechPress
-- This script is free for non-commercial purposes
-- with no warranties.  Use at your own risk.
--
-- To license this script for a commercial purpose,
-- contact info@rampant.cc
-- ****************************************************

select
        b.file_id,
        file_name,
        singleblkrdtim_milli,
        singleblkrds
from
sys. v_$file_histogram a,
sys.dba_data_files b
where
        a.file# = b.file_id
order by
```

The example output from this query would be similar to the following:

```
FILE_ID FILE_NAME                      SINGLEBLKRDTIM_MILLI SINGLEBLKRDS
------- ------------------------------ -------------------- ------------
      1 C:\ORACLE\PRODUCT\10.1.0\ORADA                    1          838
      1 C:\ORACLE\PRODUCT\10.1.0\ORADA                    2           51
      1 C:\ORACLE\PRODUCT\10.1.0\ORADA                    4           73
      1 C:\ORACLE\PRODUCT\10.1.0\ORADA                    8          235
      1 C:\ORACLE\PRODUCT\10.1.0\ORADA                   16          609
      1 C:\ORACLE\PRODUCT\10.1.0\ORADA                   32          479
      1 C:\ORACLE\PRODUCT\10.1.0\ORADA                   64          350
      1 C:\ORACLE\PRODUCT\10.1.0\ORADA                  128          300
      1 C:\ORACLE\PRODUCT\10.1.0\ORADA                  256           61
      2 C:\ORACLE\PRODUCT\10.1.0\ORADA                    1            1
      2 C:\ORACLE\PRODUCT\10.1.0\ORADA                    2            6
```

In the example, file one had 838 single block reads that took one millisecond, 51 that took two milliseconds and so on. This is useful information to have when trying to determine if certain files are experiencing I/O response time problems.

The *dba_hist_filemetric_history* view collects metric history for datafile input/output related activity such as *average file read/write times*, *number of physical read/write operations*, and *blocks*:

```
SQL> desc DBA_HIST_FILEMETRIC_HISTORY

Name                                      Null?    Type
----------------------------------------- -------- -------
SNAP_ID                                   NOT NULL NUMBER
DBID                                      NOT NULL NUMBER
INSTANCE_NUMBER                           NOT NULL NUMBER
FILEID                                    NOT NULL NUMBER
CREATIONTIME                              NOT NULL NUMBER
BEGIN_TIME                                NOT NULL DATE
END_TIME                                  NOT NULL DATE
INTSIZE                                   NOT NULL NUMBER
GROUP_ID                                  NOT NULL NUMBER
AVGREADTIME                               NOT NULL NUMBER
AVGWRITETIME                              NOT NULL NUMBER
PHYSICALREAD                              NOT NULL NUMBER
PHYSICALWRITE                             NOT NULL NUMBER
PHYBLKREAD                                NOT NULL NUMBER
PHYBLKWRITE                               NOT NULL NUMBER
```

Along with this *dba_hist_filemetric_history* view, there is an AWR data dictionary view called *dba_hist_sysmetric_summary* that contains several useful datafile I/O related metrics:

```
SQL> select metric_name from dba_hist_metric_name where group_name like
'File Metrics%';

METRIC_NAME
------------------------------------
Physical Block Writes (Files-Long)
Physical Block Reads (Files-Long)
Physical Writes (Files-Long)
Physical Reads (Files-Long)
Average File Write Time (Files-Long)
Average File Read Time (Files-Long)
```

The above query output shows all of the metrics available for datafile input/output activity.

Oracle 10g Segment Statistics

The AWR repository also stores a history for a set of segment related statistics such as logical reads, physical reads and writes, buffer busy waits, row lock waits, etc. The kernel AWR view for segment statistics is *dba_hist_seg_stat*:

```
SQL> desc DBA_HIST_SEG_STAT

Name                                     Null?    Type
---------------------------------------- -------- ----------
SNAP_ID                                           NUMBER
DBID                                              NUMBER
INSTANCE_NUMBER                                   NUMBER
TS#                                               NUMBER
OBJ#                                              NUMBER
DATAOBJ#                                          NUMBER
LOGICAL_READS_TOTAL                               NUMBER
LOGICAL_READS_DELTA                               NUMBER
BUFFER_BUSY_WAITS_TOTAL                           NUMBER
BUFFER_BUSY_WAITS_DELTA                           NUMBER
DB_BLOCK_CHANGES_TOTAL                            NUMBER
DB_BLOCK_CHANGES_DELTA                            NUMBER
PHYSICAL_READS_TOTAL                              NUMBER
PHYSICAL_READS_DELTA                              NUMBER
PHYSICAL_WRITES_TOTAL                             NUMBER
PHYSICAL_WRITES_DELTA                             NUMBER
PHYSICAL_READS_DIRECT_TOTAL                       NUMBER
PHYSICAL_READS_DIRECT_DELTA                       NUMBER
PHYSICAL_WRITES_DIRECT_TOTAL                      NUMBER
PHYSICAL_WRITES_DIRECT_DELTA                      NUMBER
ITL_WAITS_TOTAL                                   NUMBER
ITL_WAITS_DELTA                                   NUMBER
ROW_LOCK_WAITS_TOTAL                              NUMBER
ROW_LOCK_WAITS_DELTA                              NUMBER
```

```
GC_CR_BLOCKS_SERVED_TOTAL                              NUMBER
GC_CR_BLOCKS_SERVED_DELTA                              NUMBER
GC_CU_BLOCKS_SERVED_TOTAL                              NUMBER
GC_CU_BLOCKS_SERVED_DELTA                              NUMBER
SPACE_USED_TOTAL                                       NUMBER
SPACE_USED_DELTA                                       NUMBER
SPACE_ALLOCATED_TOTAL                                  NUMBER
SPACE_ALLOCATED_DELTA                                  NUMBER
TABLE_SCANS_TOTAL                                      NUMBER
TABLE_SCANS_DELTA                                      NUMBER
```

This view contains historical snapshots for *v$segstat* dynamic performance view. *The dba_hist_seg_stat* has two columns for each statistic: TOTAL and DELTA. The TOTAL column shows the cumulative value of the statistic, and the DELTA column shows change in the statistic value between *begin_interval_time* and *end_interval_time* in the *dba_hist_snapshot* view for the corresponding *snap_id* in the *dba_hist_seg_stat* view.

Oracle10g also has a more user friendly dynamic view called *v$segment_statistics*, which shows the same statistics along with additional owner and segment names, tablespace name, etc. Available segment level statistics can be selected from *v$segstat_name* view:

```
SQL> select name from V$SEGSTAT_NAME;

NAME
------------------------------------
logical reads
buffer busy waits
gc buffer busy
db block changes
physical reads
physical writes
physical reads direct
physical writes direct
gc cr blocks received
gc current blocks received
ITL waits
row lock waits
space used
space allocated
segment scans
```

Reviewing segment level statistics history helps to identify *hot* segments in the database such as tables and indexes, which possibly play a significant role in performance problems. For example, if the database has a high value of TX enqueue waits, the *dba_hist_seg_stat* view can be queried to find actual segments experiencing high row lock activity.

The *dba_hist_seg_stat* view can be queried using various criteria to identify hot segments. For example, the *seg_top_logreads_10g.sql* script retrieves top segments that have high logical reads activity:

🖫 seg_top_logreads_10g.sql

```
-- ***************************************************
-- Copyright © 2005 by Rampant TechPress
-- This script is free for non-commercial purposes
-- with no warranties.  Use at your own risk.
--
-- To license this script for a commercial purpose,
-- contact info@rampant.cc          .
-- ***************************************************


select
    object_name "Object Name"
  , tablespace_name "Tablespace Name"
  , object_type "Object Type"
  , logical_reads_total "Logical Reads"
  , ratio "%Total"
from(
select
n.owner||'.'||n.object_name||decode(n.subobject_name,null,null,'.'||n.subobj
ect_name) object_name
     , n.tablespace_name
     , case when length(n.subobject_name) < 11 then
              n.subobject_name
            else
              substr(n.subobject_name,length(n.subobject_name)-9)
       end subobject_name
     , n.object_type
     , r.logical_reads_total
     , round(r.ratio * 100, 2) ratio
  from dba_hist_seg_stat_obj  n
     , (select *
          from (select e.dataobj#
                     , e.obj#
                     , e.dbid
                     , e.logical_reads_total - nvl(b.logical_reads_total, 0)
logical_reads_total
                     , ratio_to_report(e.logical_reads_total -
nvl(b.logical_reads_total, 0)) over () ratio
                  from dba_hist_seg_stat  e
                     , dba_hist_seg_stat  b
                 where b.snap_id              = 2694
                   and e.snap_id              = 2707
                   and b.dbid                 = 37933856
                   and e.dbid                 = 37933856
                   and b.instance_number      = 1
                   and e.instance_number      = 1
```

```
                  and e.obj#                            = b.obj#
                  and e.dataobj#                        = b.dataobj#
              and e.logical_reads_total - nvl(b.logical_reads_total, 0)  >
0
                order by logical_reads_total desc) d
         where rownum <= 100) r
 where n.dataobj# = r.dataobj#
   and n.obj#     = r.obj#
   and n.dbid     = r.dbid
)
order by logical_reads_total desc
```

This script allows the identification of *hot* segments which experience
high logical reads activity. This information may help with the selection
of tuning actions such as the optimization of corresponding queries
which access these segments, re-distribute segments across different
disks, etc.

```
SQL> @seg_top_logreads.sql

Object Name                    Tablespace Object Type       Logical Reads    %Total
------------------------------ ---------- ----------------- -------------- ----------
SYSMAN.MGMT_METRICS_RAW_PK     SYSAUX     INDEX                     46272    8,68
SYS.SMON_SCN_TIME              SYSTEM     TABLE                     43840    8,23
SYS.JOB$                       SYSTEM     TABLE                     30640    5,75
SYS.I_SYSAUTH1                 SYSTEM     INDEX                     27120    5,09
PERFSTAT.STATS$EVENT_HISTOGRAM SYSAUX     INDEX                     26912    5,05
```

This report lists the objects in descending order of the percentage of
logical reads to easily identify the objects with the greatest logical read
activity.

The WISE tool has several reports for the retrieval of hot segments that
use the following criteria:

- Top logical reads.

- Top physical reads.

- Top physical writes.

- Top buffer busy waits.

- Top row lock waits.

- Top block changes.

Oracle 10g Datafile I/O Statistics

The Oracle10g database significantly improves the I/O subsystem through the addition of such features as the Automatic Storage Management (ASM) facility. However, it is important to constantly monitor the I/O workload on the database because in a well tuned application, I/O remains a bound factor that can cause significant wait times in data access. I/O layout design is a complex process and includes the consideration of the following points:

- Sufficient disk capacity for business needs.

- Appropriate data protection level using RAID levels, hardware, LVM, etc.

- Sufficient I/O throughput that does not exceed disk I/O bandwidth.

The AWR has several views that can be used to isolate datafile I/O related statistics as well as tablespace space usage statistics.

The dba_hist_filestatxs and dba_hist_tempstatxs views display information about I/O activity for data and temporary database files, respectively:

```
SQL> desc DBA_HIST_FILESTATXS

Name                  Null?     Type
-----------------     --------  -------------
SNAP_ID                         NUMBER
DBID                            NUMBER
INSTANCE_NUMBER                 NUMBER
FILE#                           NUMBER
CREATION_CHANGE#                NUMBER
FILENAME                        VARCHAR2(513)
TS#                             NUMBER
TSNAME                          VARCHAR2(30)
BLOCK_SIZE                      NUMBER
PHYRDS                          NUMBER
PHYWRTS                         NUMBER
SINGLEBLKRDS                    NUMBER
READTIM                         NUMBER
WRITETIM                        NUMBER
SINGLEBLKRDTIM                  NUMBER
PHYBLKRD                        NUMBER
PHYBLKWRT                       NUMBER
WAIT_COUNT                      NUMBER
TIME                            NUMBER
```

The view, *dba_hist_tempstatxs,* has the identical structure. Both views can be queried to monitor overall database I/O activity for a particular snapshot interval grouped by tablespaces using the query *db_tbsp_io_10g.sql:*

🖫 db_tbsp_io_10g.sql

```
-- ***************************************************
-- Copyright © 2005 by Rampant TechPress
-- This script is free for non-commercial purposes
-- with no warranties.  Use at your own risk.
--
-- To license this script for a commercial purpose,
-- contact info@rampant.cc
-- ***************************************************


select tbsp "Tablespace"
     , ios "I/O Activity"
From (
select e.tsname tbsp
     , sum (e.phyrds  - nvl(b.phyrds,0))  +
       sum (e.phywrts - nvl(b.phywrts,0)) ios
  from dba_hist_filestatxs  e
     , dba_hist_filestatxs  b
 where b.snap_id(+)          = &pBgnSnap
   and e.snap_id             = &pEndSnap
   and b.dbid(+)             = &pDbId
   and e.dbid                = &pDbId
   and b.dbid(+)             = e.dbid
   and b.instance_number(+)  = &pInstNum
   and e.instance_number     = &pInstNum
   and b.instance_number(+)  = e.instance_number
   and b.file#               = e.file#
   and ( (e.phyrds  - nvl(b.phyrds,0) ) +
         (e.phywrts - nvl(b.phywrts,0)) ) > 0
 group by e.tsname
union
select e.tsname tbsp
     , sum (e.phyrds  - nvl(b.phyrds,0))  +
       sum (e.phywrts - nvl(b.phywrts,0)) ios
  from dba_hist_tempstatxs  e
     , dba_hist_tempstatxs  b
 where b.snap_id(+)          = &pBgnSnap
   and e.snap_id             = &pEndSnap
   and b.dbid(+)             = &pDbId
   and e.dbid                = &pDbId
   and b.dbid(+)             = e.dbid
   and b.instance_number(+)  = &pInstNum
   and e.instance_number     = &pInstNum
   and b.instance_number(+)  = e.instance_number
   and b.file#               = e.file#
   and ( (e.phyrds  - nvl(b.phyrds,0) ) +
         (e.phywrts - nvl(b.phywrts,0) ) ) > 0
 group by e.tsname
)
```

The script generates a report that shows the I/O activity on a tablespace basis and locates hot tablespaces that experienced a large workload that may be candidates for further tuning consideration:

```
SQL> @db_tbsp_io.sql

Tablespace                    I/O Activity
----------------------------  ------------
SYSAUX                                9630
SYSTEM                                3658
UNDOTBS1                              1104
USERS                                   14
```

The WISE tool offers the following I/O related reports that build time-series charts for I/O database activity:

- I/O by datafiles.

- I/O by tablespaces.

- Total database I/O activity.

- Total tablespace I/O activity.

The screenshots below in Figures 2.3, 2.4 and 2.5, illustrate the sample chart reports available in WISE. These screenshots show database I/O activity by particular datafiles, tablespaces, or total database I/O. WISE also allows the viewing of I/O statistics averaged by hour of day, day of week, or month of year.

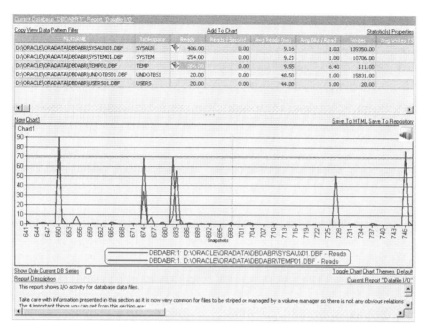

Figure 2.3: *AWR I/O by datafiles chart in WISE.*

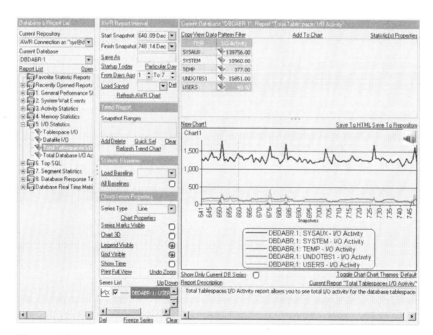

Figure 2.4: *AWR Total Tablespace I/O Activity chart in WISE.*

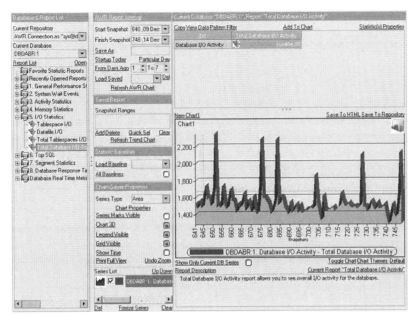

Figure 2.5: *AWR Total Database I/O Activity chart in WISE.*

The following script, *wait_time_detail_10g.sql*, compares the wait event values from *dba_hist_waitstat* and *dba_hist_active_sess_history*. This script quickly allows the identification of the exact objects that are experiencing wait events:

🖫 **wait_time_detail_10g.sql**

```
-- **************************************************
-- Copyright © 2005 by Rampant TechPress
-- This script is free for non-commercial purposes
-- with no warranties.  Use at your own risk.
--
-- To license this script for a commercial purpose,
-- contact info@rampant.cc
-- **************************************************


prompt
prompt  This will compare values from dba_hist_waitstat with
prompt  detail information from dba_hist_active_sess_history.
prompt

set pages 999
set lines 80
```

```
break on snap_time skip 2

col snap_time      heading 'Snap|Time'    format a20
col file_name      heading 'File|Name'    format a40
col object_type    heading 'Object|Type'  format a10
col object_name    heading 'Object|Name'  format a20
col wait_count     heading 'Wait|Count'   format 999,999
col time           heading 'Time'         format 999,999

select
   to_char(begin_interval_time,'yyyy-mm-dd hh24:mi') snap_time,
--   file_name,
   object_type,
   object_name,
   wait_count,
   time
from
   dba_hist_waitstat           wait,
   dba_hist_snapshot           snap,
   dba_hist_active_sess_history ash,
   dba_data_files              df,
   dba_objects                 obj
where
   wait.snap_id = snap.snap_id
and
   wait.snap_id = ash.snap_id
and
   df.file_id = ash.current_file#
and
   obj.object_id = ash.current_obj#
and
   wait_count > 50
order by
   to_char(begin_interval_time,'yyyy-mm-dd hh24:mi'),
   file_name
;
```

This script can also be joined into the *dba_data_files* view to get the file
names associated with the wait event. This is a very powerful script that
can be used to quickly drill-down to find the cause of specific waits. The
following is a sample output from this script:

```
SQL> @wait_time_detail_10g

Copyright 2005 by Donald K. Burleson

This will compare values from dba_hist_waitstat with
detail information from dba_hist_active_sess_hist.


Snap                 Object     Object                    Wait
Time                 Type       Name                      Count       Time
-------------------- ---------- --------------------  --------  --------
2005-02-28 01:00     TABLE      ORDOR                    4,273         67
                     INDEX      PK_CUST_ID              12,373        324
                     INDEX      FK_CUST_NAME             3,883         17
                     INDEX      PK_ITEM_ID               1,256        967
```

2005-02-29 03:00	TABLE	ITEM_DETAIL	83	69
2005-03-01 04:00	TABLE	ITEM_DETAIL	1,246	45
2005-03-01 21:00	TABLE	CUSTOMER_DET	4,381	354
	TABLE	IND_PART	117	15
2005-03-04 01:00	TABLE	MARVIN	41,273	16
	TABLE	FACTOTUM	2,827	43
	TABLE	DOW_KNOB	853	6
	TABLE	ITEM_DETAIL	57	331
	TABLE	HIST_ORD	4,337	176
	TABLE	TAB_HIST	127	66

This example demonstrates how the AWR and ASH data can be used to create an almost infinite number of sophisticated custom performance reports.

A sample custom AWR query can be created by starting with a simple query to plot the *user I/O wait time* statistic for each AWR snapshot. The *phys_disk_reads_10g.sql* script shows that it is easy to extract the physical read counts from the AWR:

⊟ phys_disk_reads_10g.sql

```
-- ***************************************************
-- Copyright © 2005 by Rampant TechPress
-- This script is free for non-commercial purposes
-- with no warranties.  Use at your own risk.
--
-- To license this script for a commercial purpose,
-- contact info@rampant.cc
-- ***************************************************

break on begin_interval_time skip 2

column phyrds              format 999,999,999
column begin_interval_time format a25

select
   begin_interval_time,
   filename,
   phyrds
from
   dba_hist_filestatxs
natural join
   dba_hist_snapshot
;
```

The results below show a running total of Oracle physical reads from *phys_disk_reads_10g.sql*. The snapshots are collected every half-hour in this example, and many DBAs will increase the default collection frequency of AWR snapshots. Starting from this script, a *where* clause criteria could easily be added to create a unique time-series exception report:

```
SQL> @phys_reads

BEGIN_INTERVAL_TIME        FILENAME                                    PHYRDS
------------------------    ----------------------------------------   --------
24-FEB-04 11.00.32.000 PM  E:\ORACLE\ORA92\FSDEV10G\SYSTEM01.DBF       164,700
                           E:\ORACLE\ORA92\FSDEV10G\UNDOTBS01.DBF       26,082
                           E:\ORACLE\ORA92\FSDEV10G\SYSAUX01.DBF       472,008
                           E:\ORACLE\ORA92\FSDEV10G\USERS01.DBF          1,794
                           E:\ORACLE\ORA92\FSDEV10G\T_FS_LSQ.ORA         2,123
```

The simple script called *rpt_10g_sysstat.sql* displays a time-series exception report for any statistic in *dba_hist_sysstat*. This script accepts the statistics number and the value threshold for the exception report as supplied parameters:

🖫 rpt_10g_sysstat.sql

```
-- ***********************************************
-- Copyright © 2005 by Rampant TechPress
-- This script is free for non-commercial purposes
-- with no warranties.  Use at your own risk.
--
-- To license this script for a commercial purpose,
-- contact info@rampant.cc
-- ***********************************************

prompt
prompt  This will query the dba_hist_sysstat view to display all values
prompt  that exceed the value specified in
prompt  the "where" clause of the query.
prompt

set pages 999

break on snap_time skip 2

accept stat_name    char    prompt 'Enter Statistic Name:  ';
accept stat_value   number prompt 'Enter Statistics Threshold value:  ';


col snap_time    format a19
col value        format 999,999,999
```

```
select
   to_char(begin_interval_time,'yyyy-mm-dd hh24:mi') snap_time,
   value
from
   dba_hist_sysstat
  natural join
   dba_hist_snapshot
where
   stat_name = '&stat_name'
and
  value > &stat_value
order by
   to_char(begin_interval_time,'yyyy-mm-dd hh24:mi')
;
```

When the script is run, it will prompt the DBA for the statistic name and threshold value:

```
SQL> @rpt_sysatst

Copyright 2005 by Donald K. Burleson

This will query the dba_hist_sysstat view to display all values
that exceed the value specified in
the "where" clause of the query.

Enter Statistic Name:  physical writes
Enter Statistics Threshold value:  200000

SNAP_TIME                   VALUE
-------------------- ------------
2005-02-21 08:00          200,395
2005-02-27 08:00          342,231
2005-02-29 08:00          476,386
2005-03-01 08:00          277,282
2005-03-02 08:00          252,396
2005-03-04 09:00          203,407
```

The listing above indicates a repeating trend in which physical writes seem to be high at 8:00 a.m. on certain days. This powerful script will allow the DBA to quickly extract exception conditions from any instance-wide Oracle metric and view how the values change over time.

Another example quickly writes a custom exception report. In the following script called *hot_write_files_10g.sql*, the *dba_hist_filestatxs* table can be queried to identify "hot write" datafiles in which the file consumed more than 25% of the total physical writes for the instance.

By taking a closer look at the query, it can be noted that the query compares the physical writes, the *phywrts* column of *dba_hist_filestatxs*, with the instance-wide physical writes, *statistic#* = 55 from *dba_hist_sysstat*.

This simple yet powerful script allows the Oracle professional to track hot-write datafiles over time, thereby gaining important insights into the status of the I/O sub-system.

hot_write_files_10g.sql

```
-- *************************************************
-- Copyright © 2005 by Rampant TechPress
-- This script is free for non-commercial purposes
-- with no warranties.  Use at your own risk.
--
-- To license this script for a commercial purpose,
-- contact info@rampant.cc
-- *************************************************

prompt
prompt  This will identify any single file who's write I/O
prompt  is more than 25% of the total write I/O of the database.
prompt

set pages 999

break on snap_time skip 2

col filename       format a40
col phywrts        format 999,999,999
col snap_time      format a20

select
   to_char(begin_interval_time,'yyyy-mm-dd hh24:mi') snap_time,
   filename,
   phywrts
from
   dba_hist_filestatxs
natural join
   dba_hist_snapshot
where
   phywrts > 0
and
   phywrts * 4 >
(
select
   avg(value)              all_phys_writes
from
   dba_hist_sysstat
 natural join
   dba_hist_snapshot
where
```

```
    stat_name = 'physical writes'
and
  value > 0
)
order by
   to_char(begin_interval_time,'yyyy-mm-dd hh24:mi'),
   phywrts desc
;
```

The sample output from this script is useful because it shows the high-write datafiles and those times when they are hot:

```
SQL> @hot_write_files

This will identify any single file who's write I/O
is more than 25% of the total write I/O of the database.

SNAP_TIME           FILENAME                                PHYWRTS
----------------    ------------------------------------    -------
2005-02-20 23:30    E:\ORACLE\ORA92\FSDEV10G\SYSAUX01.DBF    85,540

2005-02-21 01:00    E:\ORACLE\ORA92\FSDEV10G\SYSAUX01.DBF    88,843

2005-02-21 08:31    E:\ORACLE\ORA92\FSDEV10G\SYSAUX01.DBF    89,463

2005-02-22 02:00    E:\ORACLE\ORA92\FSDEV10G\SYSAUX01.DBF    90,168

2005-02-22 16:30    E:\ORACLE\ORA92\FSDEV10G\SYSAUX01.DBF    143,974
                    E:\ORACLE\ORA92\FSDEV10G\UNDOTBS01.DBF    88,973
```

This type of time-series exception reporting is extremely useful for detecting those times when the Oracle10g database is experiencing I/O related stress. Many Oracle professionals will schedule these types of exception reports using *dbms_scheduler* and send the report via automatic e-mail every day.

The following report called *rpt_sysstat_hr_10g.sql* will show the signature for any Oracle system statistic, averaged by hour of the day:

🖫 rpt_sysstat_hr_10g.sql

```
-- *****************************************************
-- Copyright © 2005 by Rampant TechPress
-- This script is free for non-commercial purposes
-- with no warranties.  Use at your own risk.
--
-- To license this script for a commercial purpose,
-- contact info@rampant.cc
-- *****************************************************
```

```
prompt
prompt
prompt   This will query the dba_hist_sysstat view to
prompt   display average values by hour of the day
prompt

set pages 999

break on snap_time skip 2

accept stat_name char prompt 'Enter Statistics Name:  ';


col snap_time    format a19
col avg_value    format 999,999,999

select
   to_char(begin_interval_time,'hh24') snap_time,
   avg(value)                          avg_value
from
   dba_hist_sysstat
  natural join
   dba_hist_snapshot
where
   stat_name = '&stat_name'
group by
   to_char(begin_interval_time,'hh24')
order by
   to_char(begin_interval_time,'hh24')
;
```

The output shows an average for every hour of the day. This
information can then be easily pasted into an MS-Excel spreadsheet and
plotted with the chart wizard or the WISE tool:

```
SQL> @rpt_sysstat_hr

This will query the dba_hist_sysstat view to
display average values by hour of the day
Enter Statistics Name:  physical reads

SNAP_TIME              AVG_VALUE
-------------------    ------------
00                       120,861
01                       132,492
02                       134,136
03                       137,460
04                       138,944
05                       140,496
06                       141,937
07                       143,191
08                       145,313
09                       135,881
10                       137,031
11                       138,331
12                       139,388
```

```
13                              140,753
14                              128,621
15                              101,683
16                              116,985
17                              118,386
18                              119,463
19                              120,868
20                              121,976
21                              112,906
22                              114,708
23                              116,340
```

Figure 2.6 shows the data after it has been pasted into an MS Excel spreadsheet and plotted with the Excel chart wizard.

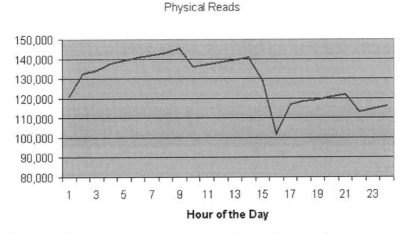

Figure 2.6: *An hourly Signature can show hidden trends.*

For details on the procedure for plotting Oracle performance data, see the OTN article titled, *Perfect Pitch*. Open source products such as RRDtool and WISE can also be used to automate the plotting of data from the AWR and ASH.

The WISE tool is a great way to quickly plot Oracle time series data and gather signatures for Oracle metrics. Figure 2.7 below shows how the WISE tool displays this data. WISE is inexpensive and has the ability to plot performance data on daily or monthly average basis. See www.wise-oracle.com for details.

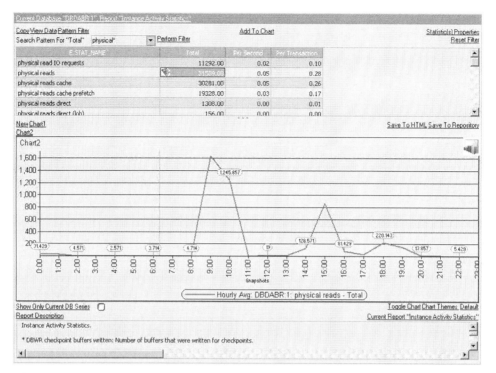

Figure 2.7: *Output from the WISE viewer.*

The same types of reports aggregated by day-of-the week to see ongoing daily trends can also be created. Over long periods of time, almost all Oracle databases will develop distinct signatures that reflect the regular daily processing patterns of the end user community.

The following query, *rpt_sysstat_dy_10g.sql*, will accept any of the values from *dba_hist_sysstat*, and will plot the average values by hour-of-the-day:

rpt_sysstat_dy_10g.sql

```
-- ************************************************
-- Copyright © 2005 by Rampant TechPress
-- This script is free for non-commercial purposes
-- with no warranties.  Use at your own risk.
--
-- To license this script for a commercial purpose,
-- contact info@rampant.cc
-- ************************************************

prompt
```

```
prompt  This will query the dba_hist_sysstat view to display
prompt   average values by day-of-the-week
prompt

set pages 999

accept stat_name char prompt 'Enter Statistic Name:   ';


col snap_time    format a19
col avg_value    format 999,999,999

select
   to_char(begin_interval_time,'day')   snap_time,
   avg(value)                           avg_value
from
   dba_hist_sysstat
natural join
   dba_hist_snapshot
where
   stat_name = '&stat_name'
group by
   to_char(begin_interval_time,'day')
order by
   decode(
   to_char(begin_interval_time,'day'),
   'sunday',1,
   'monday',2,
   'tuesday',3,
   'wednesday',4,
   'thursday',5,
   'friday',6,
   'saturday',7
   )
;
```

The following output is from the script above.

```
SQL> @rpt_sysstat_dy

This will query the dba_hist_sysstat view to display
average values by day-of-the-week

Enter Statistics Name:  physical reads

SNAP_TIME             AVG_VALUE
-------------------  ------------
sunday                  190,185
monday                  135,749
tuesday                  83,313
wednesday               139,627
thursday                105,815
friday                  107,250
saturday                154,279
```

Figure 2.8 shows an average for every day of the week. These types of signatures will stabilize for most Oracle databases, and they can be used to develop a predictive model for proactive tuning activities.

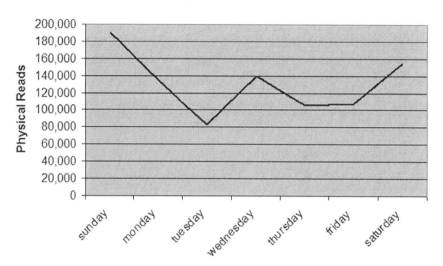

Figure 2.8: *A Signature for average physical reads by day of the week.*

Below is a listing for the *reads_10g.sql* script. This script gathers physical disk read counts, the *phyrds* column of *dba_hist_filestatxs*, and then joins this data into the *dba_hist_snapshot* view to get the *begin_interval_time* column:

⊟ reads_10g.sql

```
-- ***************************************************
-- Copyright © 2005 by Rampant TechPress
-- This script is free for non-commercial purposes
-- with no warranties.  Use at your own risk.
--
-- To license this script for a commercial purpose,
-- contact info@rampant.cc
-- ***************************************************


break on begin_interval_time skip 2

column phyrds  format 999,999,999
column begin_interval_time format a25
```

```
select
   begin_interval_time,
   filename,
   phyrds
from
   dba_hist_filestatxs
 natural join
   dba_hist_snapshot;
```

When the *reads_10g.sql* script is executed, a display of the running total of physical reads organized by datafile can be seen. In this case, the AWR snapshots are collected every half-hour, and the DBA is free to adjust the snapshot collection interval depending on the data needs:

```
SQL> @reads

BEGIN_INTERVAL_TIME          FILENAME                                        PHYRDS
-------------------------    -----------------------------------------       -------
24-FEB-04 11.00.32.000 PM    E:\ORACLE\ORA92\FSDEV10G\SYSTEM01.DBF           164,700
                             E:\ORACLE\ORA92\FSDEV10G\UNDOTBS01.DBF           26,082
                             E:\ORACLE\ORA92\FSDEV10G\SYSAUX01.DBF           472,008
                             E:\ORACLE\ORA92\FSDEV10G\USERS01.DBF              1,794
                             E:\ORACLE\ORA92\FSDEV10G\T_FS_LSQ.ORA            2,123


24-FEB-04 11.30.18.296 PM    E:\ORACLE\ORA92\FSDEV10G\SYSTEM01.DBF           167,809
                             E:\ORACLE\ORA92\FSDEV10G\UNDOTBS01.DBF           26,248
                             E:\ORACLE\ORA92\FSDEV10G\SYSAUX01.DBF           476,616
                             E:\ORACLE\ORA92\FSDEV10G\USERS01.DBF              1,795
                             E:\ORACLE\ORA92\FSDEV10G\T_FS_LSQ.ORA            2,244


25-FEB-04 12.01.06.562 AM    E:\ORACLE\ORA92\FSDEV10G\SYSTEM01.DBF           169,940
                             E:\ORACLE\ORA92\FSDEV10G\UNDOTBS01.DBF           26,946
                             E:\ORACLE\ORA92\FSDEV10G\SYSAUX01.DBF           483,550
                             E:\ORACLE\ORA92\FSDEV10G\USERS01.DBF              1,799
                             E:\ORACLE\ORA92\FSDEV10G\T_FS_LSQ.ORA            2,248
```

Starting from the *reads_10g.sql* script, a *where* clause criteria could easily be added to create a unique time-series exception report on specific data file or specific time periods.

Using just STATSPACK and system utilities holistic data, which provide the status internal to Oracle and external with the various UNIX and Linux commands, the data can then be gathered and analyzed.

The data collected by STATSPACK can be accessed with normal scripts such as the *snapfileio_10g.sql* listed below:

---

snapfileio_10g.sql

```
-- ***************************************************
-- Copyright © 2005 by Rampant TechPress
-- This script is free for non-commercial purposes
-- with no warranties.  Use at your own risk.
--
-- To license this script for a commercial purpose,
-- contact info@rampant.cc
-- ***************************************************
rem
rem NAME: snapfileio.sql

rem FUNCTION: Reports on the file io status of all of the
rem FUNCTION: datafiles in the database for a single snapshot.


column sum_io1 new_value st1 noprint
column sum_io2 new_value st2 noprint
column sum_io new_value divide_by noprint
column Percent format 999.999 heading 'Percent|Of IO'
column brratio format 999.99 heading 'Block|Read|Ratio'
column bwratio format 999.99 heading 'Block|Write|Ratio'
column phyrds heading 'Physical | Reads'
column phywrts heading 'Physical | Writes'
column phyblkrd heading 'Physical|Block|Reads'
column phyblkwrt heading 'Physical|Block|Writes'
column filename format a45 heading 'File|Name'
column file# format 9999 heading 'File'

set feedback off verify off lines 132 pages 60 sqlbl on trims on

select
    nvl(sum(a.phyrds+a.phywrts),0) sum_io1
from
    dba_hist_filestatxs a where snap_id=&&snap;

select nvl(sum(b.phyrds+b.phywrts),0) sum_io2
from
        dba_hist_tempstatxs b where snap_id=&&snap;

select &st1+&st2 sum_io from dual;

rem
@title132 'Snap&&snap File I/O Statistics Report'

spool rep_out\&db\fileio&&snap

select
    a.filename, a.phyrds, a.phywrts,
    (100*(a.phyrds+a.phywrts)/&divide_by) Percent,
    a.phyblkrd, a.phyblkwrt, (a.phyblkrd/greatest(a.phyrds,1)) brratio,
      (a.phyblkwrt/greatest(a.phywrts,1)) bwratio
from
    dba_hist_filestatxs a
where
    a.snap_id=&&snap
union
select
```

```
       c.filename, c.phyrds, c.phywrts,
       (100*(c.phyrds+c.phywrts)/&divide_by) Percent,
       c.phyblkrd, c.phyblkwrt,(c.phyblkrd/greatest(c.phyrds,1)) brratio,
        (c.phyblkwrt/greatest(c.phywrts,1)) bwratio
from
    dba_hist_tempstatxs c
where
    c.snap_id=&&snap
order by
    1
/

spool off
pause Press enter to continue
set feedback on verify on lines 80 pages 22
clear columns
ttitle off
undef snap
```

Of course, a single AWR reading suffers from the same limitations that a single read of the *v$* or *gv$* dynamic performance views. It only gives the cumulative data from when the database was started to the time that the snapshot was taken. A better methodology is shown in *snapdeltafileio_awr.sql*:

🖫 snapdeltafileio_awr.sql

```
--  *********************************************
-- Copyright © 2005 by Rampant TechPress
-- This script is free for non-commercial purposes
-- with no warranties.  Use at your own risk.
--
-- To license this script for a commercial purpose,
-- contact info@rampant.cc
--  *********************************************
rem
rem NAME: snapdeltafileio_awr.sql
rem
rem FUNCTION: Reports on the file io status of all of
rem FUNCTION: the datafiles in the database across
rem FUNCTION: two snapshots.
rem HISTORY:
rem WHO            WHAT          WHEN
rem Mike Ault      Created       11/19/03
rem

column sum_io1 new_value st1 noprint
column sum_io2 new_value st2 noprint
column sum_io new_value divide_by noprint
column Percent format 999.999 heading 'Percent|Of IO'
column brratio format 999.99 heading 'Block|Read|Ratio'
column bwratio format 999.99 heading 'Block|Write|Ratio'
column phyrds heading 'Physical | Reads'
column phywrts heading 'Physical | Writes'
column phyblkrd heading 'Physical|Block|Reads'
```

```
column phyblkwrt heading 'Physical|Block|Writes'
column filename format a45 heading 'File|Name'
column file# format 9999 heading 'File'
set feedback off verify off lines 132 pages 60 sqlbl on trims on

select
    nvl(sum((b.phyrds-a.phyrds)+(b.phywrts-a.phywrts)),0) sum_io1
from
    dba_hist_filestatxs a, dba_hist_filestatxs b
where
        a.snap_id=&&first_snap_id and b.snap_id=&&sec_snap_id
        and a.filename=b.filename;

select
    nvl(sum((b.phyrds-a.phyrds)+(b.phywrts-a.phywrts)),0) sum_io2
from
    dba_hist_tempstatxs a, dba_hist_tempstatxs b
where
        a.snap_id=&&first_snap_id and b.snap_id=&&sec_snap_id
        and a.filename=b.filename;

select &st1+&st2 sum_io from dual;

rem
@title132 'Snap &&first_snap_id to &&sec_snap_id File I/O Statistics Report'
spool rep_out\&db\fileio'&&first_snap_id'_to_'&&sec_snap_id'

select
    a.filename, b.phyrds -a.phyrds phyrds, b.phywrts-a.phywrts phywrts,
    (100*((b.phyrds-a.phyrds)+(b.phywrts-a.phywrts))/&divide_by) Percent,
    b.phyblkrd- a.phyblkrd phyblkrd, b.phyblkwrt-a.phyblkwrt phyblgwrt,
        ((b.phyblkrd-a.phyblkrd)/greatest((b.phyrds-a.phyrds),1)) brratio,
        ((b.phyblkwrt-a.phyblkwrt)/greatest((b.phywrts-a.phywrts),1))
bwratio
from
    dba_hist_filestatxs a, dba_hist_filestatxs b
where
        a.snap_id=&&first_snap_id and b.snap_id=&&sec_snap_id
        and a.filename=b.filename
union
select
    c.filename, d.phyrds-c.phyrds phyrds, d.phywrts-c.phywrts phywrts,
    (100*((d.phyrds-c.phyrds)+(d.phywrts-c.phywrts))/&divide_by) Percent,
    d.phyblkrd-c.phyblkrd phyblkrd, d.phyblkwrt-c.phyblkwrt phyblgwrt,
        ((d.phyblkrd-c.phyblkrd)/greatest((d.phyrds-c.phyrds),1)) brratio,
        ((d.phyblkwrt-c.phyblkwrt)/greatest((d.phywrts-c.phywrts),1))
bwratio
from
    dba_hist_tempstatxs c, dba_hist_tempstatxs d
where
        c.snap_id=&&first_snap_id and d.snap_id=&&sec_snap_id
        and c.filename=d.filename
order by
    1
/
spool off
pause Press enter to continue
set feedback on verify on lines 80 pages 22
clear columns
```

```
ttitle off
undef first_snap_id
undef sec_snap_id
```

This report accepts two snapshot ids and uses them to calculate the delta between the I/O readings. This I/O delta information is vital to help pinpoint real I/O problems for a given time period.

```
Date: 02/25/05                                                   Page:    1
Time: 10:54 AM            Snap 5227 to 5234 File I/O Statistics Report    SYSTEM
                                      DSS database

                                                  Physical   PHY  Block  Block
                                                   Block     BLG   Read  Write
File                     Physical  Physical  Percent  Reads    WRT  Ratio  Ratio
Name                       Reads    Writes    Of IO
------------------------  -------  --------  -------  --------  -----  -----  -----
+DGROUP2/ds/dfile/dss_data.263.1      0         0     .000        0      0    .00    .00
+DGROUP2/ds/dfile/dss_index.264.1     0         0     .000        0      0    .00    .00
+DGROUP2/ds/dfile/perfstat.262.1      0         0     .000        0      0    .00    .00
+DGROUP2/ds/dfile/sys_undts.259.1     0       361    19.253       0   1070    .00   2.96
+DGROUP2/ds/dfile/sysaux.260.1       12      1148    61.867      12   1605   1.00   1.40
+DGROUP2/ds/dfile/system.258.3       22       332    18.880      22    486   1.00   1.46
+DGROUP2/ds/tfile/temp.261.1          0         0     .000        0      0    .00    .00
```

Figure 2.9: *Output from WISE Datafile I/O*

This Wise report also accepts two snapshot ids and uses them to calculate the delta between the I/O readings. The graph allows quick identification of I/O spikes.

The data in the AWR can provide valuable information about cumulative statistics such as file I/O. The following script, *awr_physrds.sql*, provides the physical read statistics gathered for each datafile:

awr_physrds.sql

```
-- ***************************************************
-- Copyright © 2005 by Rampant TechPress
-- This script is free for non-commercial purposes
-- with no warranties.  Use at your own risk.
--
-- To license this script for a commercial purpose,
-- contact info@rampant.cc
-- ***************************************************

break on begin_interval_time skip 1

column phyrds              format 999,999,999
column begin_interval_time format a25
column file_name           format a45

select
   begin_interval_time,
   filename,
   phyrds
from
   dba_hist_filestatxs
  natural join
   dba_hist_snapshot
order by
  begin_interval_time
;
```

The example below shows a running total of physical reads for each datafile. Note that the snapshots are collected every hour with additional ad-hoc snapshots at other times. Starting from this script, a *where* clause could be added to create a unique time-series exception report.

```
BEGIN_INTERVAL_TIME        FILENAME                         PHYRDS
------------------------   ------------------------------   -----
10-NOV-04 09.00.01.000 PM  /oradata/test10g/system01.dbf     3,982
                           /oradata/test10g/undotbs01.dbf       51
                           /oradata/test10g/users01.dbf          7
                           /oradata/test10g/example01.dbf       14
                           /oradata/test10g/sysaux01.dbf       551
                           /oradata/test10g/tbsalert.dbf         7

10-NOV-04 09.11.06.131 PM  /oradata/test10g/system01.dbf     6,120
                           /oradata/test10g/users01.dbf         21
                           /oradata/test10g/tbsalert.dbf        21
                           /oradata/test10g/example01.dbf       28
                           /oradata/test10g/sysaux01.dbf     4,786
                           /oradata/test10g/undotbs01.dbf      231

10-NOV-04 10.00.16.672 PM  /oradata/test10g/system01.dbf    10,950
                           /oradata/test10g/undotbs01.dbf      262
                           /oradata/test10g/users01.dbf         22
                           /oradata/test10g/tbsalert.dbf        22
                           /oradata/test10g/example01.dbf       40
                           /oradata/test10g/sysaux01.dbf     6,320
```

Conclusion

This chapter has provided insightful scripts for monitoring file I/O of Oracle 9i and 10g databases. Through the Oracle 10g AWR and associated views, the DBA has the capability to monitor file I/O at a level of detail never before possible. This arsenal of scripts and reports is useful for many contention situations. This section has included tips and recommendations for reviewing output to isolate the root cause of many I/O related bottlenecks.

Now it is time to move out of the external environment and examine Oracle scripts to monitor and diagnose contention within Oracle's locking, latching, and serialization mechanisms.

Monitoring Locks, Latches, and Waits

In general, Locks protect data while Latches are low level serialization mechanisms that protect memory structures. The set and release of both locks and latches, and the frequency and efficiency under which they are accomplished dramatically affects the performance of an Oracle database. In this chapter, further details regarding monitoring Latches and Locks as well as analyzing Waits will be presented.

Latches

There have been volumes written about Oracle latches. Latches protect the many memory structures in Oracle's SGA. They ensure that one and only one process at a time can run or modify any memory structure at the same instant. Much more restrictive than locks, which at least allow for some collective user interaction, latches have no queuing mechanism.

The latch is either available or it is not. In the event the latch is not available, the only option is to continually retry.

Common indicators of latch contention are the *latch miss ratio*, which records willing-to-wait mode latch requests, and *latch immediate miss ratio*, which records no-wait mode latch requests.

These statistics reflect how often latch requests were made and satisfied without waiting. If either of these exceeds 1%, the DBA can drill down further into latching details to identify which latches are responsible for the contention.

To drill down into latch miss details, use the *latchdet.sql* script:

💾 latchdet.sql

```
-- *************************************************
-- Copyright © 2005 by Rampant TechPress
-- This script is free for non-commercial purposes
-- with no warranties.  Use at your own risk.
--
-- To license this script for a commercial purpose,
-- contact info@rampant.cc
-- *************************************************

select
        name,
        gets,
        round(misses*100/decode(gets,0,1,gets),2) misses,
        round(spin_gets*100/decode(misses,0,1,misses),2) spins,
        immediate_gets igets,
        round(immediate_misses*100/
        decode(immediate_gets,0,1,immediate_gets),2) imisses,
        sleeps
from
        sys.v_$latch
order by
        2 desc;
```

The following listing is the output from the *latchdet.sql* script:

	NAME	GETS	MISSES	SPINS	IGETS	IMISSES	SLEEPS
1	cache buffers chains	44409592	0	0	4724	0	30
2	cache buffers lru chain	2374631	0	0	0	0	0
3	library cache	572680	.01	0	306	0	155
4	row cache objects	399355	0	0	155	0	52
5	session idle bit	198677	0	0	0	0	0
6	shared pool	164652	0	0	0	0	1
7	enqueues	149031	0	0	0	0	0
8	messages	134876	0	0	0	0	0
9	checkpoint queue latch	82846	0	0	0	0	0
10	redo writing	82507	0	0	0	0	7
11	session allocation	66204	0	0	0	0	0
12	enqueue hash chains	63572	0	0	0	0	0
13	undo global data	29407	0	0	0	0	0
14	redo allocation	23957	.01	0	0	0	8
15	active checkpoint queue latch	20344	0	0	0	0	0
16	session timer	20297	0	0	0	0	0
17	sort extent pool	8813	0	0	0	0	0
18	JOX SGA heap latch	3720	0	0	3120	0	0
19	virtual circuit queues	3046	0	0	0	0	0
20	library cache load lock	2526	0	0	0	0	0
21	cache buffer handles	2453	.08	0	0	0	2
22	shared java pool	2289	0	0	0	0	0
23	transaction allocation	1991	.1	0	0	0	2
24	dml lock allocation	1252	0	0	0	0	0
25	longop free list	998	0	0	0	0	0
26	session switching	983	0	0	0	0	0
27	transaction branch allocation	976	0	0	0	0	0

Figure 3.1 – *Output showing latch details*

Monitoring latches in Oracle involves monitoring *sleeps*. A latch can have millions of gets, misses, and other statistics that are related to them, but if it has no sleeps, then it probably isn't a major concern. Therefore, to monitor for latching problems, first look at *sleeps* as is shown in the following *Latch_sleep.sql* script:

🖫 Latch_sleep.sql

```
-- ****************************************************
-- Copyright © 2005 by Rampant TechPress
-- This script is free for non-commercial purposes
-- with no warranties.  Use at your own risk.
--
```

```
-- To license this script for a commercial purpose,
-- contact info@rampant.cc
-- ************************************************

REM
REM Script to determine sleeps for latches
REM M. R. Ault 2005
REM
col name format a30 heading 'Latch Name'
col gets format 99,999,999,999 heading 'Gets'
col misses format 9,999,999,999 heading 'Misses'
col sleeps format 999,999,999 heading 'Sleeps'
set pages 55
ttitle80 'Latches Contention Report'
spool latches_con
select name,gets,misses,sleeps from v$latch where gets>0 and misses>0 order
by gets desc
/
spool off
clear columns
ttitle off
```

The output from the above script should resemble the following:

Latch Name	Gets	Misses	Sleeps
cache buffers chains	668,498,922	16,722	1,576
library cache	57,209,901	87,420	9,747
session idle bit	17,831,191	393	7
row cache objects	16,368,218	2,265	24
enqueues	7,239,390	436	14
checkpoint queue latch	6,741,674	133	55
cache buffers lru chain	5,458,113	134	2
redo allocation	5,321,254	938	105
transaction allocation	5,248,223	458	7
session allocation	4,700,939	1,920	59
shared pool	4,316,720	1,577	991
messages	3,976,313	7,147	200
enqueue hash chains	3,878,828	838	65
redo writing	3,540,931	42,259	679
undo global data	3,374,722	184	1
process queue reference	2,461,595	1,206	2
dml lock allocation	1,370,771	119	1
list of block allocation	1,290,257	45	18
multiblock read objects	639,872	23	9
cache buffer handles	234,148	3	5
latch wait list	6,730	51	4
parallel query stats	22	5	10

This report shows a high number of *sleeps* for the *cache buffer chains* and the *library cache*. These are two areas that should be investigated and possibly tuned.

Locks

It can be a challenge to monitor locks in Oracle. Just for *v$lock_dpt* alone, multiple joins are usually required to get the desired information. The *catblock.sql* script can be used since it creates several useful views for locks, such as the *dba_kgllock*, *dba_lock*, *dba_lock_internaldba_dml_locks*, *dba_ddl_locks*, *dba_waiters*, and *dba_blockers* views.

The *catblock.sql* script is located in the $ORACLE_HOME/ rdbms/admin directory on UNIX or Linux, and in the c:\orant\rdbms\admin directory on NT. It provides access to the *dba_waiters* view.

The *dba_waiters* view gives information on sessions waiting for locks held by other sessions. By joining *v$session* with *dba_waiters*, detailed information can be obtained about the locks and sessions that are waiting. A query on this information is shown below in *waiters.sql*:

🖫 waiters.sql

```
-- ******************************************************
-- Copyright © 2005 by Rampant TechPress
-- This script is free for non-commercial purposes
-- with no warranties.  Use at your own risk.
--
-- To license this script for a commercial purpose,
-- contact info@rampant.cc
-- ******************************************************

COLUMN busername         FORMAT a10      HEADING 'Holding|User'
COLUMN wusername         FORMAT a10      HEADING 'Waiting|User'
COLUMN bsession_id                       HEADING 'Holding|SID'
COLUMN wsession_id                       HEADING 'Waiting|SID'
COLUMN mode_held         FORMAT a10      HEADING 'Mode|Held'
COLUMN mode_requested    FORMAT 999999   HEADING 'Mode|Requested'
COLUMN lock_id1          FORMAT 999999   HEADING 'Lock|ID1'
COLUMN lock_id2          FORMAT a15      HEADING 'Lock|ID2'
COLUMN type                              HEADING 'Lock|Type'

SET LINES 132 PAGES 59 FEEDBACK OFF ECHO OFF
ttitle 'Processes Waiting on Locks Report'
SPOOL waiters

SELECT
   holding_session bsession_id,
   waiting_session wsession_id,
   b.username busername,
```

```
    a.username wusername,
    c.lock_type type,
    mode_held,
    mode_requested,
    lock_id1,
    lock_id2
FROM
    sys.v_$session b,
    sys.dba_waiters c,
    sys.v_$session a
WHERE
    c.holding_session=b.sid
    and
    c.waiting_session=a.sid
;

SPOOL OFF
PAUSE press Enter to continue
CLEAR COLUMNS
SET LINES 80 PAGES 22 FEEDBACK ON
TTITLE OFF
```

In the script above, the lock_id1 and lock_id2 columns map into the object upon which the lock is being held. An example of the outpute is shown below:

```
Holding  Waiting Holding Waiting Lock         Mode      Mode       Lock  Lock
    SID      SID User    User    Type         Held      Requested   ID1   ID2
-------  ------- ------- ------- -----------  --------- ---------  ------ -----
      7       14 DBAUTIL SYSTEM  Transaction  Exclusive Exclusive  65580   279
```

Monitoring Sessions Causing Blocked Locks

The *catblock.sql* script must be run in order to create the *dba_blockers* view. This view indicates all sessions that are currently causing blocks that are not blocked themselves.

The *blockers.sql* script below looks at the other side of the coin. It reports on the sessions that are causing blocks by joining against *v$session* and *dba_locks*:

🖫 blockers.sql

```
-- ************************************************
-- Copyright © 2005 by Rampant TechPress
-- This script is free for non-commercial purposes
-- with no warranties.  Use at your own risk.
--
-- To license this script for a commercial purpose,
-- contact info@rampant.cc
```

```
-- ************************************************
COLUMN username          FORMAT a10      HEADING 'Holding|User'
COLUMN session_id                        HEADING 'SID'
COLUMN mode_held         FORMAT a10      HEADING 'Mode|Held'
COLUMN mode_requested    FORMAT a10      HEADING 'Mode|Requested'
COLUMN lock_id1          FORMAT a10      HEADING 'Lock|ID1'
COLUMN lock_id2          FORMAT a10      HEADING 'Lock|ID2'
COLUMN type                              HEADING 'Lock|Type'

SET LINES 132 PAGES 59 FEEDBACK OFF ECHO OFF
ttitle 'Sessions Blocking Other Sessions Report'
SPOOL blockers

SELECT
   a.session_id,
   username,
   type,
   mode_held,
   mode_requested,
   lock_id1,
   lock_id2
FROM
   sys.v_$session b,
   sys.dba_blockers c,
   sys.dba_lock a
WHERE
   c.holding_session=a.session_id
   AND
   c.holding_session=b.sid
;
SPOOL OFF
PAUSE press Enter to continue
CLEAR COLUMNS
SET LINES 80 PAGES 22 FEEDBACK ON
```

The following is a sample listing of the output from the script above:

```
       Holding    Lock       Mode        Mode        Lock        Lock
  SID  User       Type       Held        Requested   ID1         ID2
------ ---------- ---------- ----------  ----------  ----------  -----
    7  DBAUTIL    USER       Row-S (SS)  None        31299       0
    7  DBAUTIL    USER       Exclusive   None        65580       279
```

Monitoring DDL and DML Locks

Two other types of locks are the Data Definition (DDL) and Data Manipulation (DML) locks. The *dba_dml_locks* and *dba_ddl_locks* views are both created by the catblock.sql script and are used to monitor DML and DDL.

The following two scripts report on DDL and DML locks, respectively:

⊞ ddl_lock.sql

```
-- **************************************************
-- Copyright © 2005 by Rampant TechPress
-- This script is free for non-commercial purposes
-- with no warranties.  Use at your own risk.
--
-- To license this script for a commercial purpose,
-- contact info@rampant.cc
-- **************************************************

COLUMN owner           FORMAT a7    HEADING 'User'
COLUMN session_id      FORMAT 9999 HEADING 'SID'
COLUMN mode_held       FORMAT a7    HEADING 'Lock|Mode|Held'
COLUMN mode_requested FORMAT a7    HEADING 'Lock|Mode|Request'
COLUMN type            FORMAT a20   HEADING 'Type|Object'
COLUMN name            FORMAT a21   HEADING 'Object|Name'

SET FEEDBACK OFF ECHO OFF PAGES 48 LINES 79
ttitle 'Report on All DDL Locks Held'
SPOOL ddl_lock

SELECT
   NVL(owner,'SYS') owner,
   session_id,
   name,
   type,
   mode_held,
   mode_requested
FROM
   sys.dba_ddl_locks
ORDER BY 1,2,3
;
SPOOL OFF
PAUSE press Enter/return to continue
CLEAR COLUMNS
SET FEEDBACK ON PAGES 22 LINES 80
TTITLE OFF
```

The following is a sample listing from the DDL script:

User	SID	Object Name	Type Object	Lock Mode Held	Lock Mode Request
SYS	11	DBMS_SESSION	Body	Null	None
SYS	11	DBMS_STANDARD	Table/Procedure/Type	Null	None
SYS	12	DATABASE	18	Null	None
SYS	12	DBMS_SESSION	Table/Procedure/Type	Null	None
SYS	12	DBMS_SESSION	Body	Null	None
SYS	12	DBMS_STANDARD	Table/Procedure/Type	Null	None
SYS	13	DATABASE	18	Null	None
SYS	13	DBMS_SESSION	Table/Procedure/Type	Null	None
SYS	13	DBMS_SESSION	Body	Null	None

```
SYS          13 DBMS_STANDARD      Table/Procedure/Type Null    None
SYS          14 DATABASE           18                   Null    None
SYS          14 DBMS_APPLICATIO    Body                 Null    None
SYS          14 DBMS_APPLICATION   Table/Procedure/Type Null    None
SYS          14 DBMS_SESSION       Table/Procedure/Type Null    None
SYS          14 DBMS_SESSION       Body                 Null    None
SYS          14 DBMS_STANDARD      Table/Procedure/Type Null    None
SYSTEM        8 SYSTEM             18                   Null    None
SYSTEM       11 SYSTEM             18                   Null    None
SYSTEM       12 SYSTEM             18                   Null    None
SYSTEM       13 SYSTEM             18                   Null    None
SYSTEM       14 SYSTEM             18                   Null    None
```

The following is the DML script:

🖫 dml_lock.sql

```
-- *************************************************
-- Copyright © 2005 by Rampant TechPress
-- This script is free for non-commercial purposes
-- with no warranties.  Use at your own risk.
--
-- To license this script for a commercial purpose,
-- contact info@rampant.cc
-- *************************************************

COLUMN owner             FORMAT a8      HEADING 'User'
COLUMN session_id                       HEADING 'SID'
COLUMN mode_held         FORMAT a10     HEADING 'Mode|Held'
COLUMN mode_requested    FORMAT a10     HEADING 'Mode|Requested'

SET FEEDBACK OFF ECHO OFF PAGES 59 LINES 80
ttitle 'Report on All DML Locks Held'
SPOOL dml_lock

SELECT
   NVL(owner,'SYS') owner,
   session_id,
   name,
   mode_held,
   mode_requested
FROM
   sys.dba_dml_locks
ORDER BY 2
;

SPOOL OFF
PAUSE press Enter to continue
CLEAR COLUMNS
SET FEEDBACK ON PAGES 22 LINES 80
TTITLE OFF
```

When contention is suspected, a quick look at the DDL and DML reports can tell the DBA if a session is holding a lock on the table or object involved. Be cautious, these reports contain volatile information and are useful only for pinpoint monitoring of a specific problem.

Monitoring Internal Locks

The internal lock is the final lock that will be covered. The database's internal processes generate internal locks. The *catblock.sql* script creates the *dba_internal_locks* view. The following script, *int_lock.sql*, can be used for monitoring the internal lock:

🖫 **int_lock.sql**

```
-- *************************************************
-- Copyright © 2005 by Rampant TechPress
-- This script is free for non-commercial purposes
-- with no warranties.  Use at your own risk.
--
-- To license this script for a commercial purpose,
-- contact info@rampant.cc
-- *************************************************

COLUMN username          FORMAT a10      HEADING 'Lock|Holder'
COLUMN session_id                        HEADING 'User|SID'
COLUMN lock_type         FORMAT a27      HEADING 'Lock Type'
COLUMN mode_held         FORMAT a10      HEADING 'Mode|Held'
COLUMN mode_requested    FORMAT a10      HEADING 'Mode|Requested'
COLUMN lock_id1          FORMAT a30      HEADING 'Lock/Cursor|ID1'
COLUMN lock_id2          FORMAT a10      HEADING 'Lock|ID2'

PROMPT 'ALL is all types or modes'
ACCEPT lock PROMPT 'Enter Desired Lock Type: '
ACCEPT mode PROMPT 'Enter Lock Mode: '
SET LINES 132 PAGES 59 FEEDBACK OFF ECHO OFF VERIFY OFF
BREAK ON username
ttitle 'Report on Internal Locks Mode: &mode Type: &lock'
SPOOL int_locks

SELECT
   NVL(b.username,'SYS') username,
   session_id,lock_type,mode_held,
   mode_requested,lock_id1,lock_id2
FROM
   sys.dba_lock_internal a,
   sys.v_$session b
WHERE
   UPPER(mode_held) like UPPER('%&mode%')
OR
   UPPER('&mode')='ALL'
AND
   UPPER(lock_type) like UPPER('%&lock%')
OR
   UPPER(mode_held) like UPPER('%&mode%')
OR
```

```
    UPPER('&mode')='ALL'
AND
    UPPER('&lock')='ALL'
AND
    a.session_id=b.sid
ORDER BY 1,2
;
SPOOL OFF
PAUSE press Enter to continue
SET LINES 80 PAGES 22 FEEDBACK ON VERIFY ON
CLEAR COLUMNS
CLEAR BREAKS
UNDEF LOCK
UNDEF MODE
```

It is wise to remain cautious here too. The report can be several pages long in an idle instance. An excerpt from the report is shown on the next page:

Lock Holder	User SID	Lock Type	Mode Held	Mode Requested	Lock/Cursor ID1	Lock ID2
DBAUTIL	7	Cursor Definition Pin	Share	None	table_1_0_139_0_0_	57BFE99C
	7	Cursor Definition Lock	Null	None	table_1_0_139_0_0_	57BFE99C
	7	Cursor Definition Lock	Null	None	SELECT ATTRIBUTE FROM V$CONT EXT WHERE NAMESPACE = 'LBAC$L ABELS'	57B96CF0
	7	Cursor Definition Lock	Null	None	SELECT POL#, PACKAGE FROM LBA C$POL WHERE BITAND(FLAGS,1) = 1 ORDER BY PACKAGE	57B7E728
	7	Cursor Definition Lock	Null	None	commit	57B5ABC0
	7	Cursor Definition Lock	Null	None	SELECT POL#, PACKAGE FROM LBA C$POL WHERE BITAND(FLAGS,1) = 1 ORDER BY PACKAGE	57B96EE4
	7	Body Definition Lock	Null	None	SYS.DBMS_SESSION	57B879E8
	7	Body Definition Lock	Null	None	LBACSYS.LBAC_CACHE	57BA1D8C
	7	Cursor Definition Lock	Null	None	SELECT MAX(TAG#) FROM LBAC$L AB	57B7C038
	7	Cursor Definition Lock	Null	None	select pol#, usr_name, usr_lab els, package, privs from lbac$ user_logon where usr_name = :u sername	57B91108

Monitoring Waits

Waits occur when Oracle experiences contention for a specific resource. Tuning should involve monitoring waits, latches, and locks. Since latches and locks have already been covered, the third member of this trio, waits, can now be explored. The *v$waitstat* DPT is the place to begin looking at this process.

The *v$waitstat* table is the usual source of wait information for the average tuner. This table has a very basic structure noted as follows:

```
EXADB>DESC v$waitstat

 Name                            Null?    Type
 -------------------------------- -------- -----------
 CLASS                                    VARCHAR2(18)
 COUNT                                    NUMBER
 TIME                                     NUMBER
```

The class column contains the name of the particular type of wait. The count column gives the total number of these types of waits that have occurred since the last database startup. The final column, time, gives the total elapsed time, in centiseconds, that the waits have consumed according to Oracle's internal determinations.

A typical select on a large instance may look like the following:

```
EXADB>SELECT * FROM v$waitstat WHERE count>0;

CLASS                  COUNT       TIME
----------------- ---------- ----------
data block            101069     123495
segment header            70         55
unused                   241         21
undo header            10012       6678
undo block               191         51
```

Unfortunately, without a bit of decryption these numbers don't really give much information. Admittedly, a number like 101069 tends to boggle one's mind; however, when placed in the proper context it may not be as bad as it initially appears. These 101069 waits generated only 123495 centiseconds of wait time or 1.22 centiseconds per wait event.

To put these waits in context, one must understand to what the CLASS column is actually referring. Table 3.1 defines what the CLASS column is referencing.

CLASS	DEFINITION
bitmap block	This tells how many bitmap block waits have happened. Bitmap blocks are used in locally managed tablespaces and for locally managed space management in Oracle9i (automated freelist and pctfree/pctuser initrans/maxtrans management).
bitmap index block	This tells how many waits happened in bitmap index blocks.
data block	This tells how many data blocks themselves experienced waits.
extent map	For locally managed tablespaces, this tells how many extant map waits have occurred.
free list	This tells how many waits there have been on free lists in the database.
save undo block	A save undo segment is generated when a tablespace is taken offline in an emergency situation, this tells how many waits have occurred on a save undo segment block (undo means rollback).
save undo header	This tells how many waits have occurred in a save undo header.
segment header	A database segment corresponds to a table, index, cluster, etc. This wait tells how many waits there have been on a segment header entry.
sort block	This wait is for sort blocks.
system undo block	A system undo segment is the SYSTEM rollback segment in the SYSTEM tablespace. This shows waits on the system rollback segment blocks.
system undo header	This shows waits on the system rollback segment header.
undo block	This one statistics carries the load for all normal rollback segment block waits.
undo header	This one statistic carries the load for all normal rollback segment header blocks.
unused	This statistic carries information on waits on unused blocks.

Table 3.1: *Wait Classes and Their Definitions.*

Table 3.2 shows the actions that are used to rectify block waits based on block types.

BLOCK TYPE	POSSIBLE ACTIONS
Segment header	Increase of number of FREELISTs. Use FREELIST GROUPs (even in single instance this can make a difference).

freelist blocks	Add more FREELISTS. In case of Parallel Server make sure that each instance has its own FREELIST GROUP(s).
undo waits	Generally speaking most of these waits are self-explanatory. For example, if there are block waits for undo segments, larger rollback segments may be needed. If header waits for rollback segments are experienced, more rollback segments may be needed. This takes care of six of the waits shown above.
sort waits	Waits for sort blocks could indicate insufficient sort area size or sort segments in the sort tablespace.

Table 3.2: *Block Type and Action List.*

Generally, it is rare to see waits on any of the bitmap statistics, segment statistics, unused statistics or extent statistics. If they do show up in the statistics, they are usually of a small number and of such short duration that they have little if any meaning to overall tuning.

Following this explanation of how waits are monitored, data block waits can now be explained.

Data Block Waits

Data block waits are caused by a number of conditions such as:

- Insufficient freelists or freelist groups.

- Bad *initrans* value.

- Bad settings for PCTFREE/PCTUSED (continued rows).

- Too many rows per block.

- Unselective indexes.

- Right-hand indexes.

How can the DBA determine which object is experiencing which problems? First, the DBA needs to find out specifically where the blocks are that are having the problems. This can be done by using the *x$kcbfwait* and *v$datafile* tables in a report that is run from the sys user. The *Waits_file.sql* is one approach to the solution: such as:

⊟ Waits_file.sql

```
-- **************************************************
-- Copyright © 2005 by Rampant TechPress
-- This script is free for non-commercial purposes
-- with no warranties.  Use at your own risk.
--
-- To license this script for a commercial purpose,
-- contact info@rampant.cc
-- **************************************************

REM
REM Waits per Datafile report
REM M. Ault 2005
REM

col name format a66 heading 'Data File Name'
col count format 999,999,999 heading 'Wait|Count'
col file# heading 'File#' format 9,999
col wait_time heading 'Time'
col ratio heading 'Time|Count' format 999.99

set pages 47
compute sum of count on report
break on report
ttitle 'Waits Per Datafile'
set lines 132
spool waits_file

SELECT file#, name, count, time wait_time,
time/count ratio
FROM x$kcbfwait, v$datafile
WHERE indx + 1 = file#
AND time>0
Order By count DESC
/
spool off
clear columns
clear computes
ttitle off
set pages 22 lines 80
```

An example output from the above query is shown below:

File#	Data File Name	Wait Count	Time	Time Count
67	/data/EXADB/oradata02/dimension.dbf	12,867	82558	6.42
158	/data/EXADB/oradata06/dimension2.dbf	12,508	99476	7.95
209	/data/EXADB/oradata07/dimension3.dbf	12,193	91256	7.48
1	/data/EXADB/oradata01/PRDsystem.dbf	8,880	3183	.36
203	/data/EXADB/oradata0a/rbs_all_08.rbs	6,310	4340	.69
68	/data/EXADB/oradata0b/btr_u128m_2002.dbf	722	16456	22.79
182	/data/EXADB/oradata06/km_u128m_D008.dbf	694	2291	3.30
79	/data/EXADB/oradata06/btr_trn.dbf	628	864	1.38

The report shown above was shortened to show only the heavy hitters. Once the data file names have been noted, the objects located in each file can be found by using a query such as the following against the *dba_extents* view:

```
SELECT distinct owner, segment_name, segment_type
   FROM dba_extents
  WHERE file_id= &FILE_ID
 ;
```

From the report results, file number 67 is the heaviest hitter and would logically be the first file reviewed:

```
EXADB>col segment_name format a30
EXADB>col owner format a10
EXADB>/
Enter value for file_id: 67

OWNER       SEGMENT_NAME                      SEGMENT_TYPE
----------  -------------------------------  ----------------
DIMENSION   AUD_FACTOR_CHANGES               TABLE
DIMENSION   DIM_BRAND                        TABLE
DIMENSION   DIM_CARRIER                      TABLE
DIMENSION   DIM_COMMITMENT                   TABLE
DIMENSION   DIM_CONSUMING_ACCOUNT            TABLE
DIMENSION   DIM_CONTRACT                     TABLE
DIMENSION   DIM_CUSTOMER                     TABLE
DIMENSION   DIM_DAILY_CALENDAR               TABLE
DIMENSION   DIM_DAILY_CALENDAR_BKUP          TABLE
DIMENSION   DIM_GL_ACCOUNT                   TABLE
...
DIMENSION   VALIDATE_DIM_TABLE_XWALK_TB      TABLE
DIMENSION   VALIDATE_HIERARCHY_TB            TABLE
DIMENSION   VALIDATE_HIERARCHY_TMP_TB        TABLE
103 rows selected.
```

The possible candidates have been reduced to 103 from a database with 2221 tables. By knowing the application, the high activity tables such as DIM_CUSTOMER can be chosen from this list and perhaps a concentrated study conducted there.

Another way to identify objects with high data block counts would be to look at the items *initrans*, freelists and continued rows to see which ones have default settings or are experiencing row or block chaining. The following is an example query to show this information:

```
SELECT DISTINCT a.table_name,a.ini_trans, a.freelists, a.pct_free,
a.pct_used, a.chain_cnt
```

```
FROM dba_tables a, dba_extents b
WHERE a.table_name=b.segment_name AND
b.file_id=&file_id;
```

This query may not be of any assistance if all the tables have default settings. The next avenue to pursue would be to determine which of the objects are using the most SGA space. If they are being used a majority of the time, the chances are that they are the cause of most of the problems experienced. This will require a join against the *obj* and *x$bh* views. Using these SYSTEM tables and views requires the use of the SYS user. An example query is shown:

```
SELECT
b.name object,
a.dbarfil file#,
COUNT(a.dbablk) "Num blocks",
SUM(a.tch) "Touches"
FROM x$bh a, obj$ b
WHERE a.obj=b.dataobj#
AND a.tch>0
AND a.file#=&file_no
GROUP BY b.name,a.dbarfil
ORDER BY 4 desc
```

An example output for troubled file number 67 is shown below:

OBJECT	FILE#	Num blocks	Touches
DIM_CUSTOMER	67	589	3955
DIM_PRODUCT	67	401	1372
DIM_DAILY_CALENDAR	67	98	1055
DIM_MSA	67	48	48
DIM_LOCATION	67	1	39
DIM_HIST_RPTLOC	67	1	14
DIM_ITEM_LOCATION	67	1	4

As expected, the DIM_CUSTOMER table has the most blocks and the most touches. The candidates have been reduced from 103 to 6. In Oracle versions 8i and above, the *tch*, or *touch*, column in the *x$bh* table indicates how many times a buffer has been touched by a user process. By seeing how many blocks and how many block touches a particular table has for a specific file, the hot objects in that file that may require additional tuning efforts can be located.

The block level storage values for the candidate tables using a select on *dba_tables* can be identified with the following query:

```
SELECT
table_name,ini_trans, freelists, freelist_groups, chain_cnt
FROM dba_tables
WHERE table_name IN
('DIM_CUSTOMER',
'DIM_PRODUCT',
'DIM_DAILY_CALENDAR',
'DIM_MSA',
'DIM_LOCATION',
'DIM_HIST_RPTLOC',
'DIM_ITEM_LOCATION')
/
```

The results of the above query show that all of the tables in question have default values:

TABLE_NAME	INI_TRANS	FREELISTS	FREELIST_GROUPS	CHAIN_CNT
DIM_CUSTOMER	1	1	1	0
DIM_DAILY_CALENDAR	1	1	1	0
DIM_LOCATION	1	1	1	0
DIM_HIST_RPTLOC	1	1	1	0
DIM_MSA	1	1	1	71
DIM_PRODUCT	1	1	1	0
DIM_ITEM_LOCATION	1	1	1	0

The next step would be to determine which of the above six tables undergoes the most Insert Update and Delete (IUD) activities and the number of simultaneous transactions per block.

This database happens to be a 16K block size data warehouse so the DBA can expect that some of these tables could have a significant number of rows per block. A look at *dba_tables* for the information on rows per block can be accomplished with the following:

```
SELECT
table_name,value/avg_row_len RPB
FROM dba_tables, v$parameter
WHERE table_name IN
('DIM_CUSTOMER',
'DIM_PRODUCT',
'DIM_DAILY_CALENDAR',
'DIM_MSA',
'DIM_LOCATION',
'DIM_HIST_RPTLOC',
'DIM_ITEM_LOCATION')
```

```
AND name='db_block_size'
/

TABLE_NAME                          RPB
-------------------------------     ----------
DIM_CUSTOMER                        12.7007752
DIM_DAILY_CALENDAR                  25.1674347
DIM_LOCATION                        125.068702
DIM_HIST_RPTLOC                     36.2477876
DIM_MSA                             86.2315789
DIM_PRODUCT                         12.8501961
DIM_ITEM_LOCATION                   62.5343511
```

Based on the above information, the DBA should examine the DIM_LOCATION, DIM_MSA and DIM_ITEM_LOCATION tables with the idea of reducing their rows per block. The other tables to look at are *ini_trans* and *freelists*; however, they are not always the solution as is shown in the next phase of this investigation.

What about the case in which there are a large number of waits, but the wait time is not much of an issue? For example the following script, *wait_file.sql*, generates a waits per file report:

🖫 Waits_file.sql

```
-- *****************************************************
-- Copyright © 2005 by Rampant TechPress
-- This script is free for non-commercial purposes
-- with no warranties.  Use at your own risk.
--
-- To license this script for a commercial purpose,
-- contact info@rampant.cc
-- *****************************************************

col name format a50 heading 'Data File Name'
col count format 999,999,999 heading 'Wait|Count'
col file# heading 'File#' format 9,999
col wait_time heading 'Time'
col ratio heading 'Time|Count' format 999.99
set pages 47
compute sum of count on report
break on report
ttitle 'Waits Per Datafile'
set lines 132
spool waits_file
SELECT file#, name, count, time wait_time,
time/count ratio
FROM x$kcbfwait, v$datafile
WHERE indx + 1 = file#
AND time>0
Order By count DESC
/
```

```
spool off
clear columns
clear computes
ttitle off
set pages 22 lines 80
```

From the example database, the results look like the following:

```
                                         Wait          Time
   File# Data File Name            Wait  Count  Time   Count
   ------ ------------------------------- ------- ------ -----
      67 /data/EXADB/oradata02/dimension.dbf  43,346  114829  2.65
     209 /data/EXADB/oradata07/dimension3.dbf 42,950  449439 10.46
     158 /data/EXADB/oradata06/dimension2.dbf 40,677  240046  5.90
```

In the above situation, calculate the standard deviation to determine if the time spent per wait, the last column, is abnormal. This can be accomplished by cutting and pasting the data into Excel and running the Excel *stdev* and *avg* functions. In the case of the above files, when the values for the other datafiles are taken into account the average wait is 3.74 centiseconds, the standard deviation is +/- 5.14 centiseconds for a range of 0-8.89 centiseconds per wait. Of the three files in the example, only file 209 shows a large deviation from this range.

By using this query to find the SGA data buffers used by objects in file 209 the result is the following:

```
                                    File
   Object Name                   Number Num blocks   Touches
   ------------------------------ ---------- ---------- ----------
   DIM_PRODUCT                       209        932     117845
   DIM_CUSTOMER                      209       1452      73385
   DIM_DAILY_CALENDAR                209         26         85
   DIM_LOCATION                      209          1         73
   DIM_FUND_CATEGORY                 209          1         34
   DIM_HIST_STOCK_NUMBER             209          1         28
   DIM_OWNER                         209          1         24
   MTV_DIM_REPORT_ON_DATE            209          1          3
   DIM_HIST_RPTLOC                   209          1          2
   DIM_SHIPPING_METHOD               209          1          2
```

Given this data, the DBA would examine DIM_PRODUCT and DIM_CUSTOMER to attempt to locate problems. Further investigation would show that these tables undergo few INSERT or DELETE operations, but do undergo numerous UPDATEs. These UPDATE activities rarely actually change data, driving the touch count way up and possibly causing the high wait counts.

In addition, the process is not doing multiple simultaneous inserts into a single block, but may be doing multiple serial inserts that should not cause *freelist* or *ini_trans* contention. The solution in this case is to rewrite the application code to only update what is needed.

When monitoring waits, not only should the counts of waits be examined. The time spent in a wait condition should also be investigated. Information has been presented on how to drill down from the basic I/O wait indications to the file and ultimately to the table or object to see the actual object that may be causing the problem. Once the objects that may be the cause of high wait counts are identified, the various causes of the waits and example analysis for each cause can be investigated. In this way, the DBA can gain a better understanding of how to isolate I/O wait problems and resolve them using database statistics instead of guesswork. The next section will explore the new monitoring capabilities of Oracle 10g.

Monitoring Oracle 10g

With Oracle10g, it became easier to filter out wait events and identify wait behavior through the use of the new wait class identifier. DBAs have struggled with wait events in the past due to the fact that wait events can be cryptic to decipher at times. The new 10g wait class identifier makes the identification of wait behavior much easier as wait events are grouped into different classes that are much easier to understandable. As of this writing, the different classes include:

- Administrative

- Application

- Cluster

- Commit

- Concurrency

- Configuration

- Idle

- Network

- Other

- Scheduler

- System I/O

- User I/O

It is easier to pinpoint that the majority of waits in a database can be attributed to User I/O than trying to mentally group together a listing of individual wait events. It is possible to drill down into specific wait events from the wait classes to get to the heart of any bottleneck issue.

A nice query to use in Oracle10g to see a summary of wait activity based on wait class on a database is the *10g_sysclasssum.sql* script:

10g_sysclasssum.sql

```
-- ****************************************************
-- Copyright © 2005 by Rampant TechPress
-- This script is free for non-commercial purposes
-- with no warranties.  Use at your own risk.
--
-- To license this script for a commercial purpose,
-- contact info@rampant.cc
-- ****************************************************

select
        wait_class,
        total_waits,
        round(100 * (total_waits / sum_waits),2) pct_waits,
        round((time_waited / 100),2) time_waited_secs,
        round(100 * (time_waited / sum_time),2) pct_time
from
(select
        wait_class,
        total_waits,
        time_waited
from
        v$system_wait_class
where
        wait_class != 'Idle'),
(select
        sum(total_waits) sum_waits,
        sum(time_waited) sum_time
from
```

```
        v$system_wait_class
where
        wait_class != 'Idle')
order by
        5 desc
```

Figure 3.2 is a sample output showing Oracle10g wait activity by wait class:

	WAIT_CLASS	TOTAL_WAITS	PCT_WAITS	TIME_WAITED_SECS	PCT_TIME
1	User I/O	50454498	64.39	6660	46.59
2	System I/O	2509549	3.2	2548.18	17.82
3	Network	24254066	30.95	2503.96	17.52
4	Application	363882	.46	1355.71	9.48
5	Other	44853	.06	469.15	3.28
6	Commit	208998	.27	397.22	2.78
7	Concurrency	12905	.02	278.22	1.95
8	Configuration	508119	.65	83.22	.58

Figure 3.2 – *Sample output showing Oracle10g wait activity by wait class.*

In Oracle10g, the wait class activity over time can be viewed through the *v$waitclassmetric_history* view. The *10g_sysclasshist.sql* script is a good one to use to see wait times over time in each of the various wait classes:

10g_sysclasshist.sql

```
-- *************************************************
-- Copyright © 2005 by Rampant TechPress
-- This script is free for non-commercial purposes
-- with no warranties.  Use at your own risk.
--
-- To license this script for a commercial purpose,
-- contact info@rampant.cc
-- *************************************************

col Time         format a20              HEADING 'Time'
col wait_class   format a20              HEADING 'Wait Class'
col time_waited  format 999,999,999.99 HEADING 'Time Waited'
select  b.wait_class,
        to_char(a.end_time,'YYYY-MON-DD HH') Time,
        sum(round((a.time_waited / 100),2)) time_waited
from
        sys.v_$waitclassmetric_history a,
        sys.v_$system_wait_class b
```

```
where
        a.wait_class# = b.wait_class# and
        b.wait_class != 'Idle'
group by  wait_class, to_char(a.end_time,'YYYY-MON-DD HH')
order by 1,2
```

The following is an example from this script.

```
Wait Class            Time                   Time Waited
-------------------   --------------------   ---------------
Administrative        2005-MAR-04 10                    .00
Administrative        2005-MAR-04 11                    .00
Application           2005-MAR-04 10                  30.97
Application           2005-MAR-04 11                  20.64
Cluster               2005-MAR-04 10                   6.87
Cluster               2005-MAR-04 11                   7.39
Commit                2005-MAR-04 10                  10.04
Commit                2005-MAR-04 11                  10.12
Concurrency           2005-MAR-04 10                   1.33
Concurrency           2005-MAR-04 11                   1.48
Configuration         2005-MAR-04 10                    .31
Configuration         2005-MAR-04 11                    .26
Network               2005-MAR-04 10                    .60
Network               2005-MAR-04 11                    .70
Other                 2005-MAR-04 10               1,522.02
Other                 2005-MAR-04 11               2,204.08
System I/O            2005-MAR-04 10                  34.31
System I/O            2005-MAR-04 11                  40.02
User I/O              2005-MAR-04 10                  59.71
User I/O              2005-MAR-04 11                  67.59

20 rows selected.
```

By changing the *end_time* date format in the script, one can drill into more detailed time spans as needed.

One new wait enhancement in Oracle10g deals with wait histograms. Assume that table scans, often identified by the *db file scattered read* wait event, may be slowing the system down. There are a lot of them, but are they really causing an issue? The *10g_waithist.sql* query, which uses the *v$event_histogram* view can provide the answer:

🖫 10g_waithist.sql

```
-- *****************************************************
-- Copyright © 2005 by Rampant TechPress
-- This script is free for non-commercial purposes
-- with no warranties.  Use at your own risk.
--
-- To license this script for a commercial purpose,
-- contact info@rampant.cc
```

```
-- **************************************************
select
        round((wait_time_milli / 1000),4) wait_time_secs,
        wait_count
from
        sys.v_$event_histogram
where
        event = 'db file scattered read'
order by
        2
```

Figure 3.3 shows an example of a wait histogram for the *db file scattered read* event:

	WAIT_TIME_SECS	WAIT_COUNT
1	4.096	1
2	2.048	6
3	1.024	125
4	.512	346
5	.256	1136
6	.128	3294
7	.064	6071
8	.002	6458
9	.004	11716
10	.032	13454
11	.008	14688
12	.016	26534
13	.001	187342

Figure 3.3 – *Example wait histogram for the db file scattered read event.*

In the above example, the system has only experienced one *db file scattered read* wait that lasted approximately four seconds, with all others experiencing much less time consumption. It would be up to the DBA to decide if this is a problem.

There is a standard AWR report containing a Wait Events section that displays top wait events. The following query, *wt_events_int_10g.sql*, can also be used to allow retrieval of top wait events for a particular AWR snapshot interval:

🖫 wt_events_int_10g.sql

```
-- ****************************************************
-- Copyright © 2005 by Rampant TechPress
-- This script is free for non-commercial purposes
-- with no warranties.  Use at your own risk.
--
-- To license this script for a commercial purpose,
-- contact info@rampant.cc
-- ****************************************************

select event
    , waits "Waits"
    , time "Wait Time (s)"
    , pct*100 "Percent of Total"
    , waitclass "Wait Class"
from (select e.event_name event
                    , e.total_waits - nvl(b.total_waits,0)  waits
                    , (e.time_waited_micro -
nvl(b.time_waited_micro,0))/1000000  time
                    , (e.time_waited_micro - nvl(b.time_waited_micro,0))/
                    (select sum(e1.time_waited_micro -
nvl(b1.time_waited_micro,0)) from dba_hist_system_event b1 ,
dba_hist_system_event e1
                        where b1.snap_id(+)         = b.snap_id
                            and e1.snap_id          = e.snap_id
                            and b1.dbid(+)          = b.dbid
                            and e1.dbid             = e.dbid
                            and b1.instance_number(+) = b.instance_number
                            and e1.instance_number  = e.instance_number
                            and b1.event_id(+)      = e1.event_id
                            and e1.total_waits      > nvl(b1.total_waits,0)
                            and e1.wait_class       <> 'Idle'
    ) pct
                    , e.wait_class waitclass
                from
                    dba_hist_system_event b ,
                    dba_hist_system_event e
                where b.snap_id(+)          = &pBgnSnap
                    and e.snap_id           = &pEndSnap
                    and b.dbid(+)           = &pDbId
                    and e.dbid              = &pDbId
                    and b.instance_number(+) = &pInstNum
                    and e.instance_number   = &pInstNum
                    and b.event_id(+)       = e.event_id
                    and e.total_waits       > nvl(b.total_waits,0)
                    and e.wait_class        <> 'Idle'
        order by time desc, waits desc
    )
```

The sample output of the above query looks like the following:

```
SQL> @ wt_events_int_10g.sql

EVENT                          Waits  Wait Time (s)  Percent of Total  Wait Class
------------------------------ ------ -------------- ----------------- ------------
control file parallel write    11719         119.13  34,1611762        System I/O
class slave wait                  20         102.46  29,3801623        Other
Queue Monitor Task Wait           74          66.74  19,1371008        Other
log file sync                    733          20.60   5,90795938       Commit
db file sequential read         1403          14.27   4,09060416       User I/O
log buffer space                 178          10.17   2,91745801       Configuration
process startup                  114           7.65   2,19243344       Other
db file scattered read           311           2.14    ,612767501      User I/O
control file sequential read    7906           1.33    ,380047642      System I/O
latch free                       254           1.13    ,324271668      Other
log file switch completion        20           1.11    ,319292495      Configuration
```

The output of *wt_events_int_10g.sql* script displays the wait events ordered by wait times in seconds.

The WISE tool has a report name Top Wait Events that yields a chart for the top wait events that occurred for the particular snapshot interval as shown in Figure 3.4.

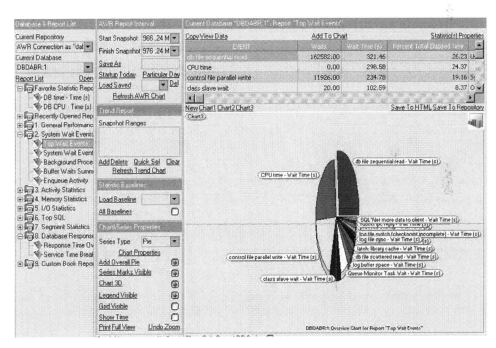

Figure 3.4: *AWR Top Wait Events chart in WISE.*

The following *dba_hist* views are available to access wait events statistics in the AWR repository.

dba_hist_system_event

The *dba_hist_system_event* view displays information about the count of total waits and time waited in microseconds:

```
SQL> desc DBA_HIST_SYSTEM_EVENT

Name                                      Null?    Type
----------------------------------------- -------- ----------------
SNAP_ID                                            NUMBER
DBID                                               NUMBER
INSTANCE_NUMBER                                    NUMBER
EVENT_ID                                           NUMBER
EVENT_NAME                                         VARCHAR2(64)
WAIT_CLASS_ID                                      NUMBER
WAIT_CLASS                                         VARCHAR2(64)
TOTAL_WAITS                                        NUMBER
TOTAL_TIMEOUTS                                     NUMBER
TIME_WAITED_MICRO                                  NUMBER
```

This view stores snapshots of the *v$system_event* system dynamic view. The *sys_event_int_10g.sql* query can be used to retrieve wait events data for a particular snapshot interval:

🖫 sys_event_int_10g.sql

```
-- ***************************************************
-- Copyright © 2005 by Rampant TechPress
-- This script is free for non-commercial purposes
-- with no warranties.  Use at your own risk.
--
-- To license this script for a commercial purpose,
-- contact info@rampant.cc
-- ***************************************************

select
    event "Event Name",
    waits "Waits",
    timeouts "Timeouts",
    time "Wait Time (s)",
    avgwait "Avg Wait (ms)",
    waitclass "Wait Class"
from
    (select e.event_name event
        , e.total_waits - nvl(b.total_waits,0)  waits
        , e.total_timeouts - nvl(b.total_timeouts,0) timeouts
        , (e.time_waited_micro - nvl(b.time_waited_micro,0))/1000000  time
```

```
            ,  decode ((e.total_waits - nvl(b.total_waits, 0)), 0,
to_number(NULL),
            ((e.time_waited_micro - nvl(b.time_waited_micro,0))/1000) /
(e.total_waits - nvl(b.total_waits,0)) ) avgwait
            , e.wait_class waitclass
    from
        dba_hist_system_event b ,
        dba_hist_system_event e
    where
                        b.snap_id(+)              = &pBgnSnap
            and e.snap_id                         = &pEndSnap
            and b.dbid(+)                         = &pDbId
            and e.dbid                            = &pDbId
            and b.instance_number(+)              = &pInstNum
            and e.instance_number                 = &pInstNum
            and b.event_id(+)                     = e.event_id
            and e.total_waits                     > nvl(b.total_waits,0)
            and e.wait_class                      <> 'Idle' )
order by time desc, waits desc
```

In the above and some subsequent queries the following parameters need to have appropriate values substituted for them:

- *&pBgnSnap* – The start snapshot number for the AWR snapshot interval of interest.

- *&pEndSnap* – The finish snapshot number for the AWR snapshot interval of interest.

- *&pDbId* – The database identified of the target database.

- *&pInstNum* – The instance number of the target database.

The sample output for the above query is:

```
SQL> @ Sys_event_int_10g.sql

Event Name                   Waits   Timeouts Wait Time (s) Avg Wait (ms) Wait Class
---------------------------- ------- -------- ------------- ------------- -------------
control file parallel write  11719          0        119.13         10.17 System I/O
class slave wait                20         20        102.46      5,122.91 Other
Queue Monitor Task Wait         74          0         66.74        901.86 Other
log file sync                  733          6         20.60         28.11 Commit
db file sequential read       1403          0         14.27         10.17 User I/O
log buffer space               178          0         10.17         57.16 Configuration
process startup                114          0          7.65         67.07 Other
db file scattered read         311          0          2.14          6.87 User I/O
control file sequential read  7906          0          1.33           .17 System I/O
latch free                     254          0          1.13          4.45 Other
log file switch completion      20          0          1.11         55.67 Configuration
```

The WISE tool has a report named System Wait Events that runs the above query with some additional information as shown in the chart in Figure 3.5.

---

dba_hist_system_event

Using this chart it becomes a quick task to identify instances when the database spent the most wait time and what particular wait events caused the wait.

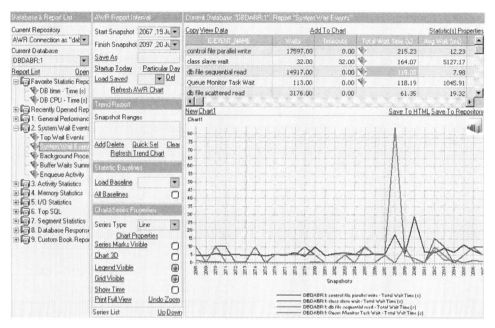

Figure 3.5: *AWR System Wait Events chart in WISE.*

Knowing that the *dba_hist_system_event* view displays information about the count of total waits and time waited in microseconds, the next section will now show how the *dba_hist_event_name* view can be used to help tune Oracle.

dba_hist_event_name

The *dba_hist_event_name* view shows information about all wait events available in the database. This view contains the history of snapshots for *v$event_name* view:

```
SQL> desc DBA_HIST_EVENT_NAME
 Name                                     Null?    Type
 ---------------------------------------- -------- ---------------
```

```
DBID                                     NOT NULL NUMBER
EVENT_ID                                 NOT NULL NUMBER
EVENT_NAME                               NOT NULL VARCHAR2(64)
WAIT_CLASS_ID                                     NUMBER
WAIT_CLASS                                        VARCHAR2(64)
```

This view allows users to find the wait class to which every wait event belongs.

dba_hist_waitstat

The *dba_hist_waitstat* view displays historical statistical information about block contention. The AWR stores this information from the *v$waitstat* dynamic view:

```
SQL> desc DBA_HIST_WAITSTAT
 Name                                    Null?    Type
 --------------------------------------- -------- -------------
 SNAP_ID                                          NUMBER
 DBID                                             NUMBER
 INSTANCE_NUMBER                                  NUMBER
 CLASS                                            VARCHAR2(18)
 WAIT_COUNT                                       NUMBER
 TIME                                             NUMBER
```

This view is useful in the following situation. If the top wait events query as described above reveals the fact that the wait event buffer busy waits has a large wait time, then the *dba_hist_waitstat* view can be queried to investigate what particular type of block caused this situation. After that, other *dba_hist* specific views described below can be used to drill down to locate additional information.

For example, the *dba_hist_active_sess_history* view can be queried to identify particular sessions and objects that caused the high contention. The datafile and objects ids can be found in the *v$session_wait* dynamic view. The *wait_stat_int_10g.sql* query can be used to retrieve historical block contention statistics:

🖫 wait_stat_int_10g.sql

```
-- ***************************************************
-- Copyright © 2005 by Rampant TechPress
-- This script is free for non-commercial purposes
-- with no warranties.  Use at your own risk.
```

```
--
-- To license this script for a commercial purpose,
-- contact info@rampant.cc
-- ***************************************************

select e.class "E.CLASS"
     , e.wait_count  - nvl(b.wait_count,0)    "Waits"
     , e.time        - nvl(b.time,0)          "Total Wait Time (cs)"
     , (e.time       - nvl(b.time,0)) /
       (e.wait_count - nvl(b.wait_count,0)) "Avg Time (cs)"
  from dba_hist_waitstat b
     , dba_hist_waitstat e
 where b.snap_id          = &pBgnSnap
   and e.snap_id          = &pEndSnap
   and b.dbid             = &pDbId
   and e.dbid             = &pDbId
   and b.dbid             = e.dbid
   and b.instance_number  = &pInstNum
   and e.instance_number  = &pInstNum
   and b.instance_number  = e.instance_number
   and b.class            = e.class
   and b.wait_count       < e.wait_count
 order by 3 desc, 2 desc
```

The sample query output looks like the following:

```
SQL> @Wait_stat_int_10g.sql

E.CLASS              Waits Total Wait Time (cs) Avg Time (cs)
------------------   ----------  -------------------- -------------
undo header             97                   121   1,24742268
file header block        2                   114            57
```

The output of the *wait_stat_int_10g.sql* script shows which particular buffer wait events play a significant role.

The WISE tool has a corresponding report named Buffer Waits Summary that generates time-series charts for the block contention statistics as shown in Figure 3.6.

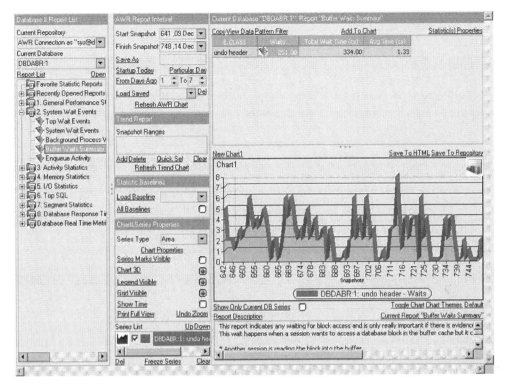

Figure 3.6: *AWR Buffer Waits Summary chart in WISE.*

dba_hist_waitclassmet_history

The *dba_hist_waitclassmet_history* view displays the metric history for wait event classes such as Application, Commit, Concurrency, Configuration, and Other:

```
SQL> desc  DBA_HIST_WAITCLASSMET_HISTORY

Name                                     Null?    Type
---------------------------------------- -------- ----------
SNAP_ID                                  NOT NULL NUMBER
DBID                                     NOT NULL NUMBER
INSTANCE_NUMBER                          NOT NULL NUMBER
WAIT_CLASS_ID                            NOT NULL NUMBER
WAIT_CLASS                                        VARCHAR2(64)
BEGIN_TIME                               NOT NULL DATE
END_TIME                                 NOT NULL DATE
INTSIZE                                  NOT NULL NUMBER
GROUP_ID                                 NOT NULL NUMBER
```

```
AVERAGE_WAITER_COUNT                         NOT NULL NUMBER
DBTIME_IN_WAIT                               NOT NULL NUMBER
TIME_WAITED                                  NOT NULL NUMBER
WAIT_COUNT                                   NOT NULL NUMBER
```

The metrics stored in this view include average waiter count, database time spent in the wait, time waited, and number of wait times.

The *dba_hist_waitclassmet_history* table contains summary information for these categories. There are times when summary information may provide clues as to the nature of the performance problem.

The *ash_waitclass_waits.sql* script provides one way to look at this summary-level data grouped by the AWR snapshot and wait class:

🖫 ash_waitclass_waits.sql

```
-- ***************************************************
-- Copyright © 2005 by Rampant TechPress
-- This script is free for non-commercial purposes
-- with no warranties.  Use at your own risk.
--
-- To license this script for a commercial purpose,
-- contact info@rampant.cc
-- ***************************************************

break on begin_time skip 1

column wait_class format a15

select
  begin_time,
  wait_class,
  average_waiter_count,
  dbtime_in_wait
from
  dba_hist_waitclassmet_history
where
  dbtime_in_wait >10
order by
  begin_time,
  wait_class,
  average_waiter_count DESC;
```

The following is a sample output:

```
                            AVERAGE        DBTIME
BEGIN_TIM WAIT_CLASS     WAITER COUNT    IN WAIT
--------- --------------- ------------   ------------
12-NOV-04 Commit               0             18
```

```
Other            0        100
Commit           0         17
Other            0        100
Other            0        100
Commit           0         17
Commit           0         14
Commit           0         18
Other            0        100
```

dba_hist_latch

The *dba_hist_latch* view contains historical latch statistics from the *v$latch* dynamic performance view. The statistics in the *dba_hist_latch* view are grouped by latch names and allow users to tune applications if wait events show a significant latch contention. For example, latch resource usage is greatly reduced if the application is properly tuned and shared pool is used.

```
SQL> desc DBA_HIST_LATCH

Name                 Null?      Type
-----------------    --------   -----------
SNAP_ID                         NUMBER
DBID                            NUMBER
INSTANCE_NUMBER                 NUMBER
LATCH_HASH                      NUMBER
LATCH_NAME                      VARCHAR2(64)
LEVEL#                          NUMBER
GETS                            NUMBER
MISSES                          NUMBER
SLEEPS                          NUMBER
IMMEDIATE_GETS                  NUMBER
IMMEDIATE_MISSES                NUMBER
SPIN_GETS                       NUMBER
SLEEP1                          NUMBER
SLEEP2                          NUMBER
SLEEP3                          NUMBER
SLEEP4                          NUMBER
WAIT_TIME                       NUMBER
```

This view is used in the following query which can be used to retrieve historical data about latches from AWR:

🖫 latch_int_10g.sql

```
-- *************************************************
-- Copyright © 2005 by Rampant TechPress
-- This script is free for non-commercial purposes
-- with no warranties.  Use at your own risk.
--
-- To license this script for a commercial purpose,
-- contact info@rampant.cc
-- *************************************************

select e.latch_name "Latch Name"
    , e.gets    - b.gets  "Get Requests"
    , to_number(decode(e.gets, b.gets, null,
       (e.misses - b.misses) * 100/(e.gets - b.gets)))   "Percent Get
Misses"
    , to_number(decode(e.misses, b.misses, null,
       (e.sleeps - b.sleeps)/(e.misses - b.misses)))     "Avg Sleeps / Miss"
    , (e.wait_time - b.wait_time)/1000000 "Wait Time (s)"
    , e.immediate_gets - b.immediate_gets "No Wait Requests"
    , to_number(decode(e.immediate_gets,
                 b.immediate_gets, null,
                  (e.immediate_misses - b.immediate_misses) * 100 /
                  (e.immediate_gets    - b.immediate_gets)))   "Percent
No Wait Miss"
 from  dba_hist_latch  b
    , dba_hist_latch  e
 where b.snap_id          = &pBgnSnap
   and e.snap_id          = &pEndSnap
   and b.dbid             = &pDbId
   and e.dbid             = &pDbId
   and b.dbid             = e.dbid
   and b.instance_number  = &pInstNum
   and e.instance_number  = &pInstNum
   and b.instance_number  = e.instance_number
   and b.latch_hash       = e.latch_hash
   and e.gets - b.gets    > 0
 order by 1, 4
```

The results of the query show latch activity statistics and identifies the particular type of latch that produces miss events that cause processes to wait:

```
SQL> @latch_int_10g.sql

Latch Name                                                    Get Requests
-------------------------------------------------------- ------------
Percent Get Misses Avg Sleeps / Miss Wait Time (s) No Wait Requests
------------------ ------------------ ------------- ----------------
Percent No Wait Miss
--------------------
Consistent RBA                                                        5670
                    0                          0                  0

FOB s.o list latch                                                    203
                    0                          0                  0

In memory undo latch                                                 22929
                    0                          0               5163
                    0

JOX SGA heap latch                                                   1173
                    0                          0                  0
```

The following is a graphical representation using the WISE tool.

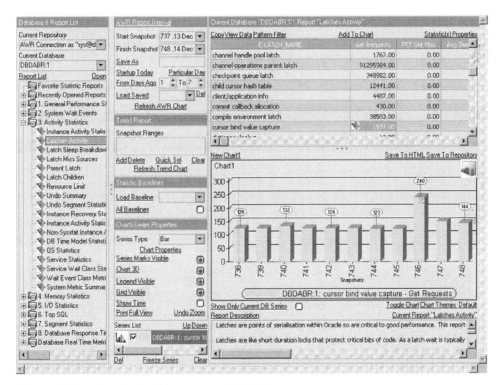

Figure 3.7: *Latch Activity chart in WISE.*

The next section goes into more specific detail concerning latches.

dba_hist_latch_misses_summary

The *dba_hist_latch_misses_summary* view displays historical summary statistics about missed attempts to get latches:

```
SQL> desc DBA_HIST_LATCH_MISSES_SUMMARY

Name                 Null?     Type
-----------------    --------  ------------
SNAP_ID                        NUMBER
DBID                           NUMBER
INSTANCE_NUMBER                NUMBER
PARENT_NAME                    VARCHAR2(50)
WHERE_IN_CODE                  VARCHAR2(64)
NWFAIL_COUNT                   NUMBER
SLEEP_COUNT                    NUMBER
WTR_SLP_COUNT                  NUMBER
```

The *latch_miss_int_10g.sql* query can be used to get statistics on latch misses for a particular snapshot interval:

🖫 latch_miss_int_10g.sql

```
-- *************************************************
-- Copyright © 2005 by Rampant TechPress
-- This script is free for non-commercial purposes
-- with no warranties.  Use at your own risk.
--
-- To license this script for a commercial purpose,
-- contact info@rampant.cc
-- *************************************************

select    latchname "Latch Name",
          nwmisses "No Wait Misses",
          sleeps "Sleeps",
              waiter_sleeps "Waiter Sleeps"
From (
select e.parent_name||' '||e.where_in_code  latchname
    , e.nwfail_count - nvl(b.nwfail_count,0) nwmisses
    , e.sleep_count  - nvl(b.sleep_count,0)  sleeps
    , e.wtr_slp_count - nvl(b.wtr_slp_count,0)   waiter_sleeps
  from dba_hist_latch_misses_summary  b
    , dba_hist_latch_misses_summary  e
 where b.snap_id(+)            = &pBgnSnap
   and e.snap_id              = &pEndSnap
   and b.dbid(+)              = &pDbId
   and e.dbid                 = &pDbId
   and b.dbid(+)              = e.dbid
   and b.instance_number(+)   = &pInstNum
   and e.instance_number      = &pInstNum
   and b.instance_number(+)   = e.instance_number
   and b.parent_name(+)       = e.parent_name
```

```
    and b.where_in_code(+)      = e.where_in_code
    and e.sleep_count           > nvl(b.sleep_count,0)
)
 order by 1, 3 desc
```

The output of the *latch_miss_int_10g.sql* query provides additional details about *sleeps* that occur while the database attempts to acquire a particular latch:

```
SQL> @latch_miss_int_10g.sql

Latch Name                            No Wait Misses     Sleeps Waiter Sleeps
------------------------------------------------------ --- ---------- -----
KWQMN job cache list latch kwqmnuji: update job it     0          8          0
cache buffers chains kcbgcur: kslbegin                 0          2          0
cache buffers chains kcbgtcr: fast path                0          2          0
cache buffers lru chain kcbzgws_1                      0          1          1
latch wait list No latch                               0       1163       1163
library cache kgldti: 2child                           0          3          0
library cache kglhdgc: child:                          0          1          0
library cache kglic                                    0          3          0
library cache kglobld                                  0          1          2
library cache kglobpn: child:                          0         11         15
library cache kglpin                                   0          4          0
library cache kglpnc: child                            0         51       1606
library cache kglpndl: child: after processing         0          7          0
library cache kglpndl: child: before processing        0       1016         40
```

The WISE tool contains several reports for analyzing latch related statistics such as Latches Activity, Latch Sleep Breakdown, Parent Latch, Latch Children, and Latch Miss Sources. Latch Miss Sources is shown in charted form in Figure 3.8.

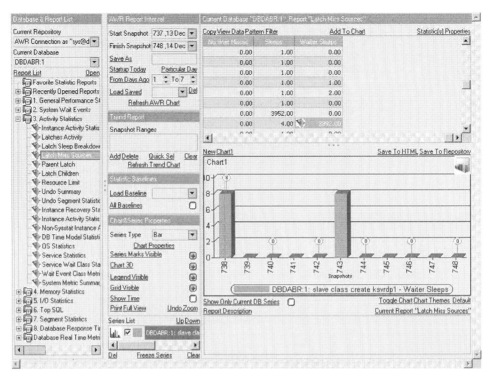

Figure 3.8: *AWR Latch Miss Sources chart in WISE.*

The script *wait_time_detail_10g.sql* compares the wait event values of *dba_hist_waitstat* and *dba_hist_active_sess_history*. This comparison allows the identification of the exact objects that are experiencing wait events:

⊟ wait_time_detail_10g.sql

```
-- ***************************************************
-- Copyright © 2005 by Rampant TechPress
-- This script is free for non-commercial purposes
-- with no warranties.  Use at your own risk.
--
-- To license this script for a commercial purpose,
-- contact info@rampant.cc
-- ***************************************************

prompt
prompt  This will compare values from dba_hist_waitstat with
prompt  detail information from dba_hist_active_sess_history.
prompt

set pages 999
set lines 80
```

```
break on snap_time skip 2

col snap_time      heading 'Snap|Time'    format a20
col file_name      heading 'File|Name'    format a40
col object_type    heading 'Object|Type'  format a10
col object_name    heading 'Object|Name'  format a20
col wait_count     heading 'Wait|Count'   format 999,999
col time           heading 'Time'         format 999,999

select
   to_char(begin_interval_time,'yyyy-mm-dd hh24:mi') snap_time,
--   file_name,
   object_type,
   object_name,
   wait_count,
   time
from
   dba_hist_waitstat            wait,
   dba_hist_snapshot            snap,
   dba_hist_active_sess_history ash,
   dba_data_files               df,
   dba_objects                  obj
where
   wait.snap_id = snap.snap_id
and
   wait.snap_id = ash.snap_id
and
   df.file_id = ash.current_file#
and
   obj.object_id = ash.current_obj#
and
   wait_count > 50
order by
   to_char(begin_interval_time,'yyyy-mm-dd hh24:mi'),
   file_name
;
```

If the file names associated with the wait event need to be obtained, this script can also be joined into the *dba_data_files* view. This is a very powerful script that can be used to quickly drill-in to find the cause of specific waits. Below is a sample output from *wait_time_detail*:

```
SQL> @wait_time_detail
```

Copyright 2005 by Donald K. Burleson

```
This will compare values from dba_hist_waitstat with
detail information from dba_hist_active_sess_hist.

Snap                    Object      Object          Wait
Time                    Type        Name            Count       Time
--------------------    ----------  --------------- --------  --------
2005-02-28 01:00        TABLE       ORDOR            4,273         67
                        INDEX       PK_CUST_ID      12,373        324
                        INDEX       FK_CUST_NAME     3,883         17
                        INDEX       PK_ITEM_ID       1,256        967


2005-02-29 03:00        TABLE       ITEM_DETAIL         83         69


2005-03-01 04:00        TABLE       ITEM_DETAIL      1,246         45


2005-03-01 21:00        TABLE       CUSTOMER_DET     4,381        354
                        TABLE       IND_PART           117         15


2005-03-04 01:00        TABLE       MARVIN          41,273         16
                        TABLE       FACTOTUM         2,827         43
                        TABLE       DOW_KNOB           853          6
                        TABLE       ITEM_DETAIL         57        331
                        TABLE       HIST_ORD         4,337        176
                        TABLE       TAB_HIST           127         66
```

This simple example should demonstrate how the AWR and ASH data
can be used to create an almost infinite number of sophisticated custom
performance reports.

Oracle 10g Instance Wait Tuning

The use of the Active Session History (ASH) data collection within
Oracle 10g provides a wealth of excellent instance tuning opportunities.
The *dba_hist_sys_time_model* table can be queried to locate aggregate
information on where Oracle sessions are spending most of their time.

resource_waits.sql uses the *v$active_session_history* table to view specific
events with the highest resource waits:

🖫 resource_waits.sql

```
-- *************************************************
-- Copyright © 2005 by Rampant TechPress
-- This script is free for non-commercial purposes
-- with no warranties.  Use at your own risk.
--
-- To license this script for a commercial purpose,
-- contact info@rampant.cc
-- *************************************************

select
   ash.event,
   sum(ash.wait_time +
   ash.time_waited) ttl_wait_time
from
   v$active_session_history ash
where
   ash.sample_time between sysdate - 60/2880 and sysdate
group by
   ash.event
order by 2;
```

The following is a sample output from this script:

```
EVENT                                              TTL_WAIT_TIME
-------------------------------------------------- -------------
SQL*Net message from client                                  218
db file sequential read                                    37080
control file parallel write                               156462
jobq slave wait                                          3078166
Queue Monitor Task Wait                                  5107697
rdbms ipc message                                       44100787
class slave wait                                       271136729
```

The code, *user_waiting.sql*, uses the *v$active_session_history* table to view users and identify which users are waiting the most time for database resources:

🖫 user_waiting.sql

```
-- *************************************************
-- Copyright © 2005 by Rampant TechPress
-- This script is free for non-commercial purposes
-- with no warranties.  Use at your own risk.
--
-- To license this script for a commercial purpose,
-- contact info@rampant.cc
-- *************************************************

select
   sess.sid,
   sess.username,
   sum(ash.wait_time + ash.time_waited) wait_time
```

```
from
   v$active_session_history ash,
   v$session sess
where
   ash.sample_time > sysdate-1
and
   ash.session_id = sess.sid
group by
   sess.sid,
   sess.username
order by 3;
```

The following is a sample output from this script:

```
   SID USERNAME                                 WAIT_TIME
---------- ------------------------------- ----------
   140 OPUS                                         30055
   165                                              30504
   169                                            9234463
   167                                           27089994
   160                                           34145401
   168                                           40033486
   152                                           45162031
   159                                           81921987
   144 OPUS                                     129249875
   150 SYS                                      134263687
   142                                          163752689
   166                                          170700889
   149 OPUS                                     195664013
   163                                          199860105
   170                                          383992930
```

Oracle10g Wait Event Tuning

Not all Events are Created Equal

The information contained in the AWR is substantial since over 800 distinct wait events are tracked. To facilitate the use of these events, they have been grouped into 12 areas called Wait Classes. These classes are listed in Table 3.3.

Wait Classes	
Administrative	Application
Cluster	Commit
Concurrency	Configuration
Idle	Network
Other	Scheduler
System I/O	User I/O

Table 3.3: *Oracle 10g wait event classes.*

More detailed ASH information on waits that are occurring in a specific wait class is available in other areas of the repository. The script, *ash_list_events.sql*, lists the specific wait events that are part of each wait class:

🖫 ash_list_events.sql

```
-- *************************************************
-- Copyright © 2005 by Rampant TechPress
-- This script is free for non-commercial purposes
-- with no warranties.  Use at your own risk.
--
-- To license this script for a commercial purpose,
-- contact info@rampant.cc
-- *************************************************

break on wait_class skip 1

column event_name format a40
column wait_class format a20

select
  wait_class,
  event_name
from
  dba_hist_event_name
order by
  wait_class,
  event_name;
```

With over 800 events, this could be a bit overwhelming, so it may be advisable to filter this query with a where clause to restrict the output to the wait class that is most needed. Some of the events that would be revealed are shown below for the System I/O and User I/O as an example:

```
WAIT_CLASS     EVENT_NAME
----------     ----------------------------
System I/O     db file parallel write
               io done
               kfk: async disk IO
               ksfd: async disk IO
               log file parallel write
               log file sequential read
               log file single write
               recovery read

User I/O       BFILE read
               buffer read retry
               db file parallel read
               db file scattered read
               db file sequential read
               db file single write
```

The listing above is useful if the AWR top-5 timed events report indicates a significant amount of time spent on I/O related waits.

Event Wait Analysis with ASH

With ASH tables, a snapshot of Oracle wait events can be obtained every hour. The changes in wait behavior can then be plotted over time. Thresholds can also be set and reported only on wait events that exceed the pre-defined threshold. The *ash_event_rollup.sql* is a script that can commonly be used for exception reporting of wait events:

🖫 **ash_event_rollup.sql**

```
-- ***************************************************
-- Copyright © 2005 by Rampant TechPress
-- This script is free for non-commercial purposes
-- with no warranties.  Use at your own risk.
--
-- To license this script for a commercial purpose,
-- contact info@rampant.cc
-- ***************************************************

ttitle 'High waits on events|Rollup by hour'


column mydate heading 'Yr.  Mo Dy Hr'      format a13;
column event                               format a30;
column total_waits     heading 'tot waits' format 999,999;
column time_waited     heading 'time wait' format 999,999;
column total_timeouts heading 'timeouts'  format 9,999;
```

```
break on to_char(snap_time,'yyyy-mm-dd') skip 1;

 select
   to_char(e.sample_time,'yyyy-mm-dd HH24')   mydate,
   e.event,
   count(e.event)                             total_waits,
   sum(e.time_waited)                         time_waited
from
   v$active_session_history e
where
   e.event not like '%timer'
and
   e.event not like '%message%'
and
   e.event not like '%slave wait%'
having
   count(e.event) > 100
group by
   to_char(e.sample_time,'yyyy-mm-dd HH24'),
   e.event
order by 1
;
```

The following list is the output from this script. A time-series result showing the days and hours when the thresholds are exceeded can be seen. Looking at this listing, it is apparent that every evening between 10:00 p.m. and 11:00 p.m., high waits are experienced on the redo logs:

```
Wed Aug 21                                       page    1
                      High waits on events
                       Rollup by hour

Yr.  Mo Dy Hr EVENT                     tot waits time wait
------------ -------------------------- --------- ---------
2002-08-18 22 LGWR wait for redo copy       9,326     1,109
2002-08-18 23 LGWR wait for redo copy       8,506       316
2002-08-18 23 buffer busy waits              214     21,388
2002-08-19 00 LGWR wait for redo copy        498         5
2002-08-19 01 LGWR wait for redo copy        497        15
2002-08-19 22 LGWR wait for redo copy       9,207     1,433
2002-08-19 22 buffer busy waits              529     53,412
2002-08-19 23 LGWR wait for redo copy       9,066       367
2002-08-19 23 buffer busy waits              250     24,479
2002-08-20 00 LGWR wait for redo copy        771        16
2002-08-20 22 LGWR wait for redo copy       8,030     2,013
2002-08-20 22 buffer busy waits              356     35,583
2002-08-20 23 LGWR wait for redo copy       8,021       579
2002-08-20 23 buffer busy waits              441     44,677
2002-08-21 00 LGWR wait for redo copy       1,013        26
2002-08-21 00 rdbms ipc reply                160     30,986
2002-08-21 01 LGWR wait for redo copy        541        17
```

The Oracle Wait Event Interface within Oracle10g OEM gives the DBA the ability to monitor database bottlenecks in real time.

This tool becomes even more powerful when used together with the AWR tables. The following section will take a closer look at ASH scripts.

Inside the Active Session History Tables

Prior to Oracle 10g, there was no standard way to keep and analyze the history for a session's wait events in the Oracle database kernel. As a result, custom code was written to vacuum wait information from the *v$* views to store them inside STATSPACK extension tables. Before the release of 10g, Oracle's inherent inability to capture information was crucial because most of the wait events that occurred in real time were not caught using manual queries.

This issue caused many database specialists to develop custom tools to monitor wait events in an automated manner; however, this approach had a downside of placing additional overhead on the system. Oracle10g relieves the DBA from this problem through the introduction of the ASH. The ASH dynamic performance views contain history for wait events that occurred during recent sessions.

The first component of ASH is the *v$session_wait_history* view. This view contains the last ten wait events for every current database session:

```
SQL> desc v$session_wait_history

Name                    Null?    Type
----------------------- -------- ------------
SID                              NUMBER
SEQ#                             NUMBER
EVENT#                           NUMBER
EVENT                            VARCHAR2(64)
P1TEXT                           VARCHAR2(64)
P1                               NUMBER
P2TEXT                           VARCHAR2(64)
P2                               NUMBER
P3TEXT                           VARCHAR2(64)
P3                               NUMBER
WAIT_TIME                        NUMBER
```

WAIT_COUNT   NUMBER

If this ASH dynamic view is queried for a particular session, as in the following script, it becomes apparent that this session waited for some additional latch events:

🖫 ash_event_hist.sql

```
-- *************************************************
-- Copyright © 2005 by Rampant TechPress
-- This script is free for non-commercial purposes
-- with no warranties.  Use at your own risk.
--
-- To license this script for a commercial purpose,
-- contact info@rampant.cc
-- *************************************************

select
   swh.seq#,
   sess.sid,
   sess.username username,
   swh.event     event,
   swh.p1,
   swh.p2
from
   v$session                sess,
   v$session_wait_history swh
where
   sess.sid = 74
and
   sess.sid = swh.sid
order by
   swh.seq#;
```

```
SEQ# SID USERNAME EVENT                          P1          P2
---- --- -------- -------------------------- ---------- ----------
   1  74 PCS      buffer busy waits                   3      21277
   2  74 PCS      latch: cache buffers chains 1556332118        172
   3  74 PCS      latch: cache buffers chains 1556332118        172
   4  74 PCS      buffer busy waits                   4        155
```

So, by querying the *v$session_wait_history* view, it becomes clear that the user associated with session id 74, was faced with some additional waits including buffer busy waits for UNDO segment determined by P1=3 and P2=21277. Also, it appears that the session had many waits for cache buffer chain latch. This contention has two likely causes: very long buffer chains or very heavy access to the same data blocks.

Due to the volume of data that can be found in *v$active_session_history* during times of heavy activity, not all of the data is stored in the AWR tables. This is because of the "dirty read" mechanism which reads data even though it may belong to an in-process transaction. This allows the impact on the database to be negligible. Yet, in spite of this limitation, enough data is kept to allow the ASH information to be statistically accurate and useful for historical review.

For example, using the *ash_sql.sql* query below, the DBA is able to identify SQL statements that accessed the orders table for session number 74 today:

🖫 ash_sql.sql

```
-- *****************************************************
-- Copyright © 2005 by Rampant TechPress
-- This script is free for non-commercial purposes
-- with no warranties.  Use at your own risk.
--
-- To license this script for a commercial purpose,
-- contact info@rampant.cc
-- *****************************************************

select
   h.sql_id,
   s.sql_text
from
   dba_hist_active_sess_history h,
   v$sql                        s
where
   h.session_id = 74
AND
   h.sql_id = s.sql_id
AND
   TRUNC(h.sample_time) = TRUNC(SYSDATE)
AND
   s.sql_fulltext like '%orders%';
```

The output of this query shows the actual SQL statements executed against the orders table. This output is truncated to only one record that was retrieved due the large amount of data available:

```
SQL_ID        SQL_TEXT
------------- ----------------------------------------------------
4g5qdabvfumhc select c.c_day wrk_date, c.day_type, nvl(c.rl_day, 'N')
              rl_day, nvl(c.short_day,'N') short_day, c.week_day,
                 p.id ewp_id, p.emp_id, p.dep_id, p.flag_main, p.ec
              a_id, p.emp_sal, p.sal_prc,        nvl(d.start_date, p.
              start_date) start_date, nvl(nvl(d.finish_date, p.finish
```

```
_date), to_date('9999', 'yyyy')) finish_date, d.id wpd_
id, d.wsc_id, d.team_num, d.ept_id,        (select deco
de(c.day_type, 'W',
```

The output above shows the SQL that was issued against the orders table. Since end users run the application on database account PCS and this application produces the same set of SQL statements against the database, the DBA can go further and determine what SQL statements issued against the orders table were issued most frequently in the recent past.

These SQL statements are the most likely candidates for further investigations in order to find an effective way to reduce buffer busy waits events. *ash_event_count.sql* is a query that retrieves the most frequent SQL statements identifiers against the orders table:

🖫 ash_event_count.sql

```
-- ***************************************************
-- Copyright © 2005 by Rampant TechPress
-- This script is free for non-commercial purposes
-- with no warranties.  Use at your own risk.
--
-- To license this script for a commercial purpose,
-- contact info@rampant.cc
-- ***************************************************

select
   h.sql_id,
   count(*)
from
   dba_hist_active_sess_history h,
   v$sql                        s
where
   h.sql_id = s.sql_id
and
   s.sql_fulltext like '%orders%'
having
   count(*) > 1
group by
   h.sql_id
order by
   2 DESC;
```

The output of the above query yields the following results:

```
SQL_ID          COUNT(*)
------------- ----------
3ta4tz9xbn4gf    2,678
```

The DBA can now retrieve actual SQL statements from the *v$sql* view using the SQL identifiers retrieved above. Then, a deeper investigation can be conducted of those suspect SQL statements.

Signature Analysis of Wait Events

There are many more benefits that can be achieved using information provided by ASH. The ASH is a useful tool for database activity analysis and performance tuning. The two sample analytical reports below make use of the ASH *v$active_session_history* view.

Signature analysis is an important area of Oracle tuning and one that especially applies to time-series wait event analysis. Just as Socrates said "Know Thy Self," the Oracle DBA must "Know thy Database." Signature analysis is ideal for wait event tuning:

- Spotting hidden trends.

- Allowing holistic tuning.

- Allowing just-in-time anticipation and self-tuning using the *dbms_scheduler* package.

- Allows adjusting of object characteristics such as freelists, file placement, caching, block population.

The script *wait_time_detail.sql* compares the wait event values from *dba_hist_waitstat* and *dba_hist_active_sess_history*. This allows the DBA to identify the exact objects that are experiencing wait events.

🖫 wait_time_detail.sql

```
-- ***************************************************
-- Copyright © 2005 by Rampant TechPress
-- This script is free for non-commercial purposes
-- with no warranties.  Use at your own risk.
--
-- To license this script for a commercial purpose,
-- contact info@rampant.cc
-- ***************************************************

set pages 999
```

```
set lines 80

break on snap_time skip 2

col snap_time      heading 'Snap|Time'    format a20
col file_name      heading 'File|Name'    format a40
col object_type    heading 'Object|Type'  format a10
col object_name    heading 'Object|Name'  format a20
col wait_count     heading 'Wait|Count'   format 999,999
col time           heading 'Time'         format 999,999

select
   to_char(begin_interval_time,'yyyy-mm-dd hh24:mi') snap_time,
--   file_name,
   object_type,
   object_name,
   wait_count,
   time
from
   dba_hist_waitstat              wait,
   dba_hist_snapshot              snap,
   dba_hist_active_sess_history   ash,
   dba_data_files                 df,
   dba_objects                    obj
where
   wait.snap_id = snap.snap_id
and
   wait.snap_id = ash.snap_id
and
   df.file_id = ash.current_file#
and
   obj.object_id = ash.current_obj#
and
   wait_count > 50
order by
   to_char(begin_interval_time,'yyyy-mm-dd hh24:mi'),
   file_name
;
```

This script is enabled to join into the *dba_data_files* view to get the file names associated with the wait event. This is a very powerful script that can be used to quickly drill-in to find the cause of specific waits. Below is a sample output from this script:

```
SQL> @wait_time_detail
```

This will compare values from dba_hist_waitstat with detail information from dba_hist_active_sess_history.

Snap Time	Object Type	Object Name	Wait Count	Time
2005-02-28 01:00	TABLE	ORDOR	4,273	67
	INDEX	PK_CUST_ID	12,373	324

```
               INDEX      FK_CUST_NAME   3,883      17
               INDEX      PK_ITEM_ID     1,256     967

2005-02-29 03:00   TABLE      ITEM_DETAIL       83      69

2005-03-01 04:00   TABLE      ITEM_DETAIL    1,246      45

2005-03-01 21:00   TABLE      CUSTOMER_DET   4,381     354
               TABLE      IND_PART         117      15

2005-03-04 01:00   TABLE      MARVIN        41,273      16
               TABLE      FACTOTUM       2,827      43
               TABLE      DOW_KNOB         853       6
               TABLE      ITEM_DETAIL       57     331
               TABLE      HIST_ORD       4,337     176
               TABLE      TAB_HIST         127      66
```

The first analytic trend report yields total wait times by the hour of a day. The *ash_wait_time.sql* report shows when database sessions have to wait for resources that decrease response time:

🖫 ash_wait_time.sql

```
-- *************************************************
-- Copyright © 2005 by Rampant TechPress
-- This script is free for non-commercial purposes
-- with no warranties.  Use at your own risk.
--
-- To license this script for a commercial purpose,
-- contact info@rampant.cc
-- *************************************************

select
   TO_CHAR(h.sample_time,'HH24') "Hour",
   Sum(h.wait_time/100) "Total Wait Time (Sec)"
from
   v$active_session_history    h,
   v$event_name                n
where
   h.session_state = 'ON CPU'
and
   h.session_type = 'FOREGROUND'
and
   h.event_id = n.EVENT_ID
and
   n.wait_class <> 'Idle'
group by
   TO_CHAR(h.sample_time,'HH24');
```

The output of this query might look like the results listed below. It shows a distinct signature, or repeating wait event pattern, within the database.

This signature will be valid for the entire range of ASH snapshots that the DBA chooses to retain, and many DBAs will retain several months worth of ASH data so that they can perform system-wide wait event tuning.

```
Hr Total Wait Time (Sec)
-- --------------------
11                   219
12               302,998
13                60,982
14               169,716
15                39,593
16               299,953
17               122,933
18                 5,147
```

From the above listing, it appears that the database had the most wait times at 12:00 a.m. and 4:00 p.m. as charted in Figure 3.9.

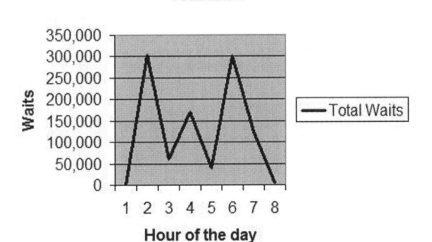

Figure 3.9: *Aggregate total waits by hour of the day.*

Most Oracle databases have daily signatures with regularly repeating trends in wait events. In the same manner, the *ash_total_wait_time_dy.sql* query that reports total wait times by the day of the week could be run:

🖬 **ash_total_wait_time_dy.sql**

```
-- ***************************************************
-- Copyright © 2005 by Rampant TechPress
-- This script is free for non-commercial purposes
-- with no warranties.  Use at your own risk.
--
-- To license this script for a commercial purpose,
-- contact info@rampant.cc
-- ***************************************************

select
   TO_CHAR(h.sample_time,'Day') "Hour",
   sum(h.wait_time/100) "Total Wait Time (Sec)"
from
   v$active_session_history      h,
   v$event_name                  n
where
   h.session_state = 'ON CPU'
and
   h.session_type = 'FOREGROUND'
and
   h.event_id = n.EVENT_ID
and
   n.wait_class <> 'Idle'
group by
   TO_CHAR(h.sample_time,'Day');
```

This query produces a listing that looks like the one shown below:

```
Hour        Total Wait Time (Sec)
---------   ---------------------
Monday                    679,089
Tuesday                   141,142
Wednesday                 181,226
Thursday                  241,711
Friday                    319,023
Saturday                   93,362
Sunday                     81,086
```

From this output, it is clear that the database is most stressed on Monday, and the numbers can be visualized by pasting them into a spreadsheet and plotting them with the chart wizard as shown in Figure 3.10.

Total Waits

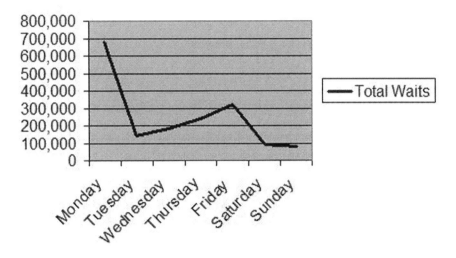

Figure 3.10: *Wait signature by Day of the week.*

The results from the two above trend reports allow the DBA to further investigate ASH data in order to get more detailed information. The *ash_total_wait_time.sql* query below retrieves a list of wait events, which had high wait time from 12:00 a.m. to 1:00 p.m. This time period was selected because one previous report showed that sessions experienced high wait times during this time period.

🖫 ash_total_wait_time.sql

```
-- ********************************************
-- Copyright © 2005 by Rampant TechPress
-- This script is free for non-commercial purposes
-- with no warranties.  Use at your own risk.
--
-- To license this script for a commercial purpose,
-- contact info@rampant.cc
-- ********************************************

select
   h.event "Wait Event",
   SUM(h.wait_time/100) "Wait Time (Sec)"
from
   v$active_session_history      h,
   v$event_name                  n
where
   h.session_state = 'ON CPU'
```

```
and
   h.session_type = 'FOREGROUND'
and
   h.event_id = n.EVENT_ID
and
   to_char(h.sample_time,'HH24') = '12'
and
   n.wait_class <> 'Idle'
group by
   h.event
order by
  2 DESC;
```

This query returns results that look like the following, showing aggregate totals for important wait events:

```
Wait Event                    Wait Time (Sec)
----------------------------- ---------------
buffer busy waits                     522,152
db file sequential read               299,572
SQL*Net more data to client               317
SQL*Net more data from client             201
SQL*Net message to client                  55
```

From the listing above, the DBA can conclude that between 12:00 a.m. and 1:00 p.m., the database sessions waited most for buffer busy waits and *db file sequential read* events with table access by index.

After these results are acquired, the DBA can determine what SQL statements were issued during this time period and probably find ones that may cause buffer cache contention or heavy disk read access.

The ASH provides the Oracle DBA with the ability to build different trend reports in order to observe database activity from various points of view.

The AWR stores snapshots for the ASH view called *v$active_session_history* in its internal table *wrh$_active_session_history*. This table is available to DBAs through the *dba_hist_active_sess_history* view. The AWR does not store snapshots of ASH activity on a continuous basis. This means that the *wrh$_active_session_history* table stores sessions' activity records that were in the SGA circular buffer at the time the AWR snapshot was taken.

This data archiving approach does not allow the DBA to monitor activity for particular sessions because the AWR misses all the activity that occurred in the session in the time period between two AWR snapshots.

However, trend reports based on data exposed by the *dba_hist_active_sess_history* view can be built. The following is a presentation of information on valuable trend analysis that can be performed against the AWR concerning ASH activity.

It is possible to identify hot datafiles or database objects that are accessed by sessions more frequently than others are, and thus could be candidates for additional tuning investigations. The *ash_file_wait_time_dy.sql* query shows hot datafiles that caused the most wait times while accessing:

💾 ash_file_wait_time_dy.sql

```
-- *************************************************
-- Copyright © 2005 by Rampant TechPress
-- This script is free for non-commercial purposes
-- with no warranties.  Use at your own risk.
--
-- To license this script for a commercial purpose,
-- contact info@rampant.cc
-- *************************************************

select
   f.file_name         "Data File",
   COUNT(*)            "Wait Number",
   SUM(h.time_waited) "Total Time Waited"
from
   v$active_session_history    h,
   dba_data_files              f
where
   h.current_file# = f.file_id
group by
   f.file_name
order by 3 DESC;
```

This query produces output like the one below:

```
Data File                               Wait Number Total Time Waited
------------------------------------    ----------- -----------------
D:\ORACLE\ORADATA\DBDABR\SYSAUX01.DBF           153        11,169,771
D:\ORACLE\ORADATA\DBDABR\SYSTEM01.DBF           222         6,997,212
D:\ORACLE\ORADATA\DBDABR\UNDOTBS01.DBF           45         1,758,065
```

The datafile named *d:\oracle\oradata\dbdabr\sysaux01.dbf* had the highest wait time during access to its data. This might indicate the need to further investigate SQL statements that are accessing data within this datafile or the need to spread its content (hot table rows or indexes) between several datafiles, thus eliminating a possible hot spot.

The Oracle multiple data buffers or the KEEP pool could also be used to reduce waits on these objects by caching them in the data buffers. If high waits on in-buffer reads (consistent get waits) are seen, the SQL that accesses the hot object needs to be tuned to reduce the amount of logical I/O.

The next query against the *dba_hist_active_sess_history* view reports a list of resources that were in high demand in the last hour. The *ash_wait_time_sum.sql* query does not reflect Idle wait events:

🖫 ash_wait_time_sum.sql

```
-- ***************************************************
-- Copyright © 2005 by Rampant TechPress
-- This script is free for non-commercial purposes
-- with no warranties.  Use at your own risk.
--
-- To license this script for a commercial purpose,
-- contact info@rampant.cc
-- ***************************************************

select
   e.name                          "Wait Event",
   SUM(h.wait_time + h.time_waited) "Total Wait Time"
from
   v$active_session_history        h,
   v$event_name                    e
where
   h.event_id = e.event_id
and
   e.wait_class <> 'Idle'
group by
   e.name
order by 2 DESC;
```

This query produces a listing like the one below, showing the aggregate wait time for each event:

```
Wait Event                      Total Wait Time
----------------------------    ---------------
log buffer space                      9,638,484
db file sequential read               8,442,918
log file switch completion            5,231,711
write complete waits                  5,200,368
db file scattered read                4452,153
process startup                       3623,464
rdbms ipc reply                         917,765
log file sync                           662,224
latch free                              550,241
latch: library cache                    370,696
db file parallel write                  364,641
free buffer waits                       319,151
latch: redo allocation                   64,984
LGWR wait for redo copy                  63,647
read by other session                    52,757
log file sequential read                 46,126
null event                               33,011
log file parallel write                  26,280
SQL*Net more data to client               8,894
latch: cache buffers chains               7,005
control file sequential read              3,966
direct path read temp                       395
direct path write temp                      229
SQL*Net message to client                    74
```

From the listing above, the DBA should take issue with the log buffer space wait event that may indicate the need to increase the *log_buffer* parameter to increase the cache in order to minimize this possible bottleneck.

Using the AWR's ASH view, the DBA can also retrieve a list of database users who have experienced high wait times during the time period between any two snapshots. The *ash_total_wait_time_dy.sql* query can be used to identify these target users:

ash_total_wait_time_dy.sql

```
-- *****************************************************
-- Copyright © 2005 by Rampant TechPress
-- This script is free for non-commercial purposes
-- with no warranties.  Use at your own risk.
--
-- To license this script for a commercial purpose,
-- contact info@rampant.cc
-- *****************************************************
```

```
select
   s.sid,
   s.username,
   sum(h.wait_time + h.time_waited) "total wait time"
from
   v$active_session_history       h,
   v$session                      s,
   v$event_name                   e
where
   h.session_id = s.sid
and
   e.event_id = h.event_id
and
   e.wait_class <> 'Idle'
and
   s.username IS NOT NULL
group by
   s.sid, s.username
order by 3;
```

In this sample output the total wait time can be viewed, both by process SID and by individual users:

```
      SID    USERNAME            total wait time
---------    ---------------     ---------------
      261    SYS                       1,537,288
      259    SYS                      12,247,007
      254    SYS                      18,640,736
```

The next sample query against the AWR ASH table shows a list of database objects that caused the most wait times during time interval stored in AWR. Note that idle wait times are not included in the output.

🖫 ash_hot_objects.sql

```
-- ***************************************************
-- Copyright © 2005 by Rampant TechPress
-- This script is free for non-commercial purposes
-- with no warranties.  Use at your own risk.
--
-- To license this script for a commercial purpose,
-- contact info@rampant.cc
-- ***************************************************

select
   o.owner,
   o.object_name,
   o.object_type,
   SUM(h.wait_time + h.time_waited) "total wait time"
from
   v$active_session_history       h,
   dba_objects                    o,
```

```
   v$event_name                    e
where
   h.current_obj# = o.object_id
and
   e.event_id = h.event_id
and
   e.wait_class <> 'Idle'
group by
   o.owner,
   o.object_name,
   o.object_type
order by 4 DESC;
```

The report produces a list of hot objects which might be candidates for further tuning investigations:

OWNER	Object Name	Object Type	total wait time
SYSMAN	MGMT_OMS_PARAMETERS	TABLE	1,1232E+10
SYS	SCHEDULER$_WINDOW_DE TAILS	TABLE	2989867
SYSMAN	MPVV_PK	INDEX	1333198
SYSMAN	MGMT_DELTA_ENTRY_SHO ULD_BE_UK	INDEX	835641
SYSMAN	MGMT_DB_LATEST_HDM_F INDINGS	TABLE	397504
SYS	CDEF$	TABLE	116853
SYS	I_LINK1	INDEX	46922
SYS	SYS_IOT_TOP_8542	INDEX	25469
SYS	I_COM1	INDEX	24908
SYS	I_CDEF3	INDEX	23125
SYSMAN	MGMT_DB_LATEST_HDM_F INDINGS	INDEX	11325
SYS	I_OBJ2	INDEX	5953
SYS	WRH$_ACTIVE_SESSION_ HISTORY_BL	TABLE	304
SYSTEM	SQLPLUS_PRODUCT_PROF ILE	TABLE	3

The example below shows a running total of physical reads for each datafile. The snapshots are collected every hour with additional ad-hoc snapshots at other times. Starting from this script, a where clause criteria could easily be added and a unique time-series exception report could be created.

BEGIN_INTERVAL_TIME	FILENAME	PHYRDS
10-NOV-04 09.00.01.000 PM	/oradata/test10g/system01.dbf	3,982
	/oradata/test10g/undotbs01.dbf	51

```
                              /oradata/test10g/users01.dbf         7
                              /oradata/test10g/example01.dbf       14
                              /oradata/test10g/sysaux01.dbf       551
                              /oradata/test10g/tbsalert.dbf         7

10-NOV-04 09.11.06.131 PM /oradata/test10g/system01.dbf      6,120
                          /oradata/test10g/users01.dbf          21
                          /oradata/test10g/tbsalert.dbf         21
                          /oradata/test10g/example01.dbf        28
                          /oradata/test10g/sysaux01.dbf      4,786
                          /oradata/test10g/undotbs01.dbf       231

10-NOV-04 10.00.16.672 PM /oradata/test10g/system01.dbf     10,950
                          /oradata/test10g/undotbs01.dbf       262
                          /oradata/test10g/users01.dbf          22
                          /oradata/test10g/tbsalert.dbf         22
                          /oradata/test10g/example01.dbf        40
                          /oradata/test10g/sysaux01.dbf      6,320
```

Latch contention can be a source of performance problems. When faced with latch issues, *ash_latch.sql* can help to identify the biggest latch issues from this repository. Rather than transient data, this will allow the DBA to examine recent data and determine trend information as well as data from a point in the recent past. How far in the past depends on the settings that have been used for the database.

🖫 ash_latch.sql

```
-- *************************************************
-- Copyright © 2005 by Rampant TechPress
-- This script is free for non-commercial purposes
-- with no warranties.  Use at your own risk.
--
-- To license this script for a commercial purpose,
-- contact info@rampant.cc
-- *************************************************

break on begin_interval_time skip 1

column begin_interval_time format a25
column latch_name             format a40

select
   begin_interval_time,
   latch_name,
   gets,
   misses,
   sleeps
from
   dba_hist_latch
natural join
   dba_hist_snapshot
where
   (misses + sleeps ) > 0
```

```
order by
  begin_interval_time,
  misses DESC,
  sleeps DESC
;
```

The listing below is important because latch misses can be tracked over time. Oracle is very dynamic and latch-related performance problems are often so sporadic that they disappear before anyone is aware of them.

```
BEGIN LATCH
TIME  NAME                          GETS        MISSES        SLEEPS
----- -------------------------     ----------  ----------    -------
6 AM  library cache                 4,451,177         856        943
      shared pool                   3,510,651         482        611
      redo allocation                 146,500         139        139
      cache buffers chains         13,050,732          52        104
      session allocation            8,176,366          43         43
      slave class create                2,534          41         41
      cache buffers lru chain         347,142          33         33
      row cache objects             2,556,877          24         26
      library cache pin             2,611,493           8          8
      messages                      1,056,963           7          5
      library cache lock            1,483,983           4          4
      object queue header operation 1,386,809           3          3
      enqueue hash chains           2,915,290           3          3
      enqueues                      2,693,816           2          2
      client/application info          11,578           1          3
      JOX SGA heap latch               43,033           1          2
      simulator lru latch              17,806           1          1
      JS slv state obj latch               85           1          1

7 AM  library cache                 4,540,521         862        950
      shared pool                   3,582,239         485        614
      redo allocation                 149,434         140        140
      cache buffers chains         13,214,066          53        105
      session allocation            8,342,651          43         43
      slave class create                2,590          42         42
      cache buffers lru chain         352,002          33         33
      row cache objects             2,606,652          24         26
      library cache pin             2,663,535           8          8
      messages                      1,079,305           7          5
      library cache lock            1,514,016           4          4
      object queue header operation 1,412,733           3
```

Comparing data from these two snapshots can help identify latch-related performance problems.

These trends can also be expanded on by examining the delta values (e.g. changes) between ASH statistics using the new *dba_hist_sys_time_model* table in the *ash_trend.sql* script:

🖫 ash_trend.sql

```
-- ************************************************
-- Copyright © 2005 by Rampant TechPress
-- This script is free for non-commercial purposes
-- with no warranties.  Use at your own risk.
--
-- To license this script for a commercial purpose,
-- contact info@rampant.cc
-- ************************************************

break on begin_interval_time skip 0

column stat_name format a25

select
  begin_interval_time,
  new.stat_name,
  (new.value - old.value) "Difference"
from
   dba_hist_sys_time_model old,
   dba_hist_sys_time_model new,
   dba_hist_snapshot        ss
where
   new.stat_name = old.stat_name
and
   new.snap_id = ss.snap_id
and
   old.snap_id = ss.snap_id - 1
and
   new.stat_name like '%&stat_name%'
order by
   begin_interval_time;
```

This produces a report similar to the one below. This report was run for the event *hard parse elapsed time*. The output can be analyzed to detect repeating patterns of specific wait events.

The results show a huge increase at 11:00 p.m. when the wait time delta nearly doubled from the previous hour. This is an important clue for further investigation.

```
BEGIN_INTERVAL_TIME        STAT_NAME                  Difference
------------------------   ------------------------   ----------
12-NOV-04 08.00.20.745 PM  hard parse elapsed time     10,605,028
12-NOV-04 09.00.48.205 PM  hard parse elapsed time     15,628,615
12-NOV-04 10.00.13.470 PM  hard parse elapsed time     54,707,455
12-NOV-04 11.00.41.412 PM  hard parse elapsed time     96,643,842
13-NOV-04 12.00.06.899 AM  hard parse elapsed time     16,890,047
```

This section has demonstrated several instances where the ASH is a useful tool for database activity analysis and performance tuning.

Conclusion

This chapter has presented scripts and techniques that can be used to monitor Locks, Latches and Waits. Also presented are new AWR and ASH views now available in Oracle 10g.

By following the guidelines in this chapter, the detection and correction of many latch or lock issues can be accomplished.

Monitoring Users and Processes

Users and processes are the mechanisms that Oracle uses to communicate with the outside world. The way that users are configured, with temporary and default tablespaces and permissions and grants, determine how efficiently they process data. The processes within Oracle can also be configured and tuned to operate more efficiently. This chapter will provide the tools necessary to ensure that database users and processes are configured properly.

Monitoring Currently Logged-in User Processes

For monitoring purposes, a useful report should list currently logged-in processes, their user IDs and operating system IDs, as well as any programs they are currently running. Using the following script, called *pid.sql*, should prove helpful:

🖫 pid.sql

```
-- ***************************************************
-- Copyright © 2005 by Rampant TechPress
-- This script is free for non-commercial purposes
-- with no warranties.  Use at your own risk.
--
-- To license this script for a commercial purpose,
-- contact info@rampant.cc
-- ***************************************************

COLUMN terminal FORMAT a10   HEADING 'Terminal'
COLUMN program FORMAT  a30   HEADING 'Program'
COLUMN pid      FORMAT  9999  HEADING 'Process|ID'
COLUMN sid      FORMAT  9999  HEADING 'Session|ID'
COLUMN osuser  FORMAT  A15   HEADING 'Operating|System|User'
COLUMN spid     FORMAT  A7    HEADING 'OS|Process|ID'
COLUMN serial# FORMAT  99999 HEADING 'Serial|Number'
SET LINES 132 PAGES 58
BREAK ON username
COMPUTE COUNT OF pid ON username
ttitle "Oracle Processes"
SPOOL cur_proc
SELECT
   NVL(a.username,'Null') username,
   b.pid,
   a.sid,
   DECODE(a.terminal,'?','Detached',a.terminal) terminal,
   b.program,
   b.spid,
   a.osuser,
   a.serial#
 FROM
   v$session a,
   v$process b
WHERE
   a.PADDR = b.ADDR
ORDER by
   a.username,
   b.pid
;
SPOOL OFF
CLEAR BREAKS
CLEAR COLUMNS
SET PAGES 22
TTITLE OFF
PAUSE Press Enter to continue
```

The following is a sample listing from this script:

```
OS       Operating                        Process System         Serial
Process  Session                                                                  User
USERNAME              ID  ID Terminal     Program               ID          ID          Number
-------------------   --  -- --------     -------------------   --------    --------    ------
DBAUTIL               12   7 pts/1        oracle (TNS V1-V3)    1182        oracle      46
****************************   ------
count                  1
SYSTEM                13   8 pts/3        oracle@diogenes (TNS V1-V3) 15885 oracle      3146
         14 MRAMOBILE oracle@diogenes (TNS V1-V3) 19156
************************   ------
count                  2
Null                   2   1 UNKNOWN      oracle@diogenes (PMON)      147   oracle      1
         3  2 UNKNOWN oracle@diogenes (DBW0)      149
         4  3 UNKNOWN oracle@diogenes (LGWR)      151
         5  4 UNKNOWN oracle@diogenes (CKPT)      153
         6  5 UNKNOWN oracle@diogenes (SMON)      155
         7  6 UNKNOWN oracle@diogenes (RECO)      157
****************************   ------
count                  6
```

Locating Top Resource Sessions

When the phone starts ringing with complaints of performance slow-downs, one of the first things to do is perform a cursory examination of the workload that exists on the database. To do this examination, check the following:

- The sessions that are connected to the database.

- What and how much resources each session is using.

- What the resource-heavy sessions are or have been executing.

There are a number of database monitors on the market that give a 'Top Sessions' view of things. Even if a third-party monitor is not available, it is possible to quickly pinpoint all the various metrics needed with just a few queries.

To get a bird's eye view of the top resource users with respect to physical I/O, logical I/O, memory, and CPU, execute the rather large *topsess.sql* query on Oracle8i and above:

🖫 topsess.sql

```
-- *************************************************
-- Copyright © 2005 by Rampant TechPress
-- This script is free for non-commercial purposes
-- with no warranties.  Use at your own risk.
--
-- To license this script for a commercial purpose,
-- contact info@rampant.cc
-- *************************************************

select
       'top physical i/o process' category,
       sid,
       username,
       total_user_io amt_used,
       round(100 * total_user_io/total_io,2) pct_used
from
(select
       b.sid sid,
       nvl(b.username,p.name) username,
       sum(value) total_user_io
from
    sys.v_$statname c,
    sys.v_$sesstat a,
    sys.v_$session b,
    sys.v_$bgprocess p
```

```
where
      a.statistic#=c.statistic# and
      p.paddr (+) = b.paddr and
      b.sid=a.sid and
      c.name in ('physical reads','physical writes',
                 'physical reads direct',
                 'physical reads direct (lob)',
                 'physical writes direct',
                 'physical writes direct (lob)')
group by
      b.sid, nvl(b.username,p.name)
order by
      3 desc),
(select
      sum(value) total_io
from
      sys.v_$statname c,
      sys.v_$sesstat a
where
      a.statistic#=c.statistic# and
      c.name in ('physical reads','physical writes',
                 'physical reads direct',
                 'physical reads direct (lob)',
                 'physical writes direct',
                 'physical writes direct (lob)'))
where
      rownum < 2
union all
select
      'top logical i/o process',
      sid,
      username,
      total_user_io amt_used,
      round(100 * total_user_io/total_io,2) pct_used
from
(select
        b.sid sid,
       nvl(b.username,p.name) username,
       sum(value) total_user_io
from
      sys.v_$statname c,
      sys.v_$sesstat a,
      sys.v_$session b,
      sys.v_$bgprocess p
where
      a.statistic#=c.statistic# and
      p.paddr (+) = b.paddr and
      b.sid=a.sid and
      c.name in ('consistent gets','db block gets')
group by
      b.sid, nvl(b.username,p.name)
order by
      3 desc),
(select
      sum(value) total_io
from
      sys.v_$statname c,
      sys.v_$sesstat a
where
```

```
        a.statistic#=c.statistic# and
        c.name in ('consistent gets','db block gets'))
where
        rownum < 2
union all
select
        'top memory process',
        sid,
        username,
        total_user_mem,
        round(100 * total_user_mem/total_mem,2)
from
(select
        b.sid sid,
        nvl(b.username,p.name) username,
        sum(value) total_user_mem
from
        sys.v_$statname c,
        sys.v_$sesstat a,
        sys.v_$session b,
        sys.v_$bgprocess p
where
        a.statistic#=c.statistic# and
        p.paddr (+) = b.paddr and
        b.sid=a.sid and
        c.name in ('session pga memory','session uga memory')
group by
        b.sid, nvl(b.username,p.name)
order by
        3 desc),
(select
        sum(value) total_mem
from
        sys.v_$statname c,
        sys.v_$sesstat a
where
        a.statistic#=c.statistic# and
        c.name in ('session pga memory','session uga memory') )
where
        rownum < 2
union all
select
        'top cpu process',
        sid,
        username,
        total_user_cpu,
        round(100 * total_user_cpu/greatest(total_cpu,1),2)
from
(select
        b.sid sid,
        nvl(b.username,p.name) username,
        sum(value) total_user_cpu
from
        sys.v_$statname c,
        sys.v_$sesstat a,
        sys.v_$session b,
        sys.v_$bgprocess p
where
        a.statistic#=c.statistic# and
```

```
     p.paddr (+) = b.paddr and
     b.sid=a.sid and
     c.name = 'CPU used by this session'
group by
     b.sid, nvl(b.username,p.name)
order by
     3 desc),
(select
     sum(value) total_cpu
from
     sys.v_$statname c,
     sys.v_$sesstat a
where
     a.statistic#=c.statistic# and
     c.name = 'CPU used by this session'  )
where
     rownum < 2;
```

The output from this query might look like the following:

```
CATEGORY                   SID USERNAME    AMT_USED    PCT_USED
-------------------------------------------------------------
Top Physical I/O Process   19 ORA_USR1    120423120      99.68
Top Logical I/O Process     5      SMON      2774880      25.50
Top Memory Process         19 ORA_USR1      6198492      27.83
Top CPU Process            19 ORA_USR1     15435557      99.75
```

In the above example, a DBA should focus on SID 19, as it seems to have a stranglehold on the system in terms of overall resource consumption. A rule of thumb is that no session should consume more than 25-50% of the overall resources in a particular category. If such is not the case, examine each session in more detail to gain insight into what each session might be doing.

To drill down and get more detail on across-the-board resource consumption, run a query such as the *topsessdet.sql* script:

🖫 topsessdet.sql

```
-- ***********************************************
-- Copyright © 2005 by Rampant TechPress
-- This script is free for non-commercial purposes
-- with no warranties.  Use at your own risk.
--
-- To license this script for a commercial purpose,
-- contact info@rampant.cc
-- ***********************************************
select *
       from
(select
```

```
        b.sid sid,
        decode (b.username,null,e.name,b.username) user_name,
        d.spid os_id,
        b.machine machine_name,
        to_char(logon_time,'mm/dd/yy hh:mi:ss pm') logon_time,
        (sum(decode(c.name,'physical reads',value,0)) +
        sum(decode(c.name,'physical writes',value,0)) +
        sum(decode(c.name,'physical writes direct',value,0)) +
        sum(decode(c.name,'physical writes direct (lob)',value,0))
        +
        sum(decode(c.name,'physical reads direct (lob)',value,0))
        +
        sum(decode(c.name,'physical reads direct',value,0)))
        total_physical_io,
        (sum(decode(c.name,'db block gets',value,0))  +
        sum(decode(c.name,'db block changes',value,0))  +
        sum(decode(c.name,'consistent changes',value,0)) +
        sum(decode(c.name,'consistent gets',value,0))  )
        total_logical_io,
        100 -
        100 *
        (round ((sum (decode (c.name, 'physical reads', value,
        0)) -
        sum (decode (c.name, 'physical reads direct', value,
        0))) /
        (sum (decode (c.name, 'db block gets', value, 1)) +
        sum (decode (c.name, 'consistent gets', value, 0))
        ),3)) hit_ratio,
        (sum(decode(c.name,'session pga memory',value,0))+
        sum(decode(c.name,'session uga memory',value,0)) )
        total_memory_usage,
        sum(decode(c.name,'parse count (total)',value,0)) parses,
        sum(decode(c.name,'CPU used by this session',value,0))
        total_cpu,
        sum(decode(c.name,'parse time cpu',value,0)) parse_cpu,
        sum(decode(c.name,'recursive cpu usage',value,0))
        recursive_cpu,
        sum(decode(c.name,'CPU used by this session',value,0)) -
        sum(decode(c.name,'parse time cpu',value,0)) -
        sum(decode(c.name,'recursive cpu usage',value,0))
        other_cpu,
        sum(decode(c.name,'sorts (disk)',value,0)) disk_sorts,
        sum(decode(c.name,'sorts (memory)',value,0)) memory_sorts,
        sum(decode(c.name,'sorts (rows)',value,0)) rows_sorted,
        sum(decode(c.name,'user commits',value,0)) commits,
        sum(decode(c.name,'user rollbacks',value,0)) rollbacks,
        sum(decode(c.name,'execute count',value,0)) executions,
        sum(decode(c.name,'physical reads',value,0))
        physical_reads,
        sum(decode(c.name,'db block gets',value,0)) db_block_gets,
        sum(decode(c.name,'consistent gets',value,0))
        consistent_gets,
        sum(decode(c.name,'consistent changes',value,0))
        consistent_changes
from
        sys.v_$sesstat a,
        sys.v_$session b,
        sys.v_$statname c,
        sys.v_$process d,
```

```
        sys.v_$bgprocess e
where
        a.statistic#=c.statistic# and
        b.sid=a.sid  and
        d.addr = b.paddr and
        e.paddr (+) = b.paddr  and
        c.name in ('physical reads',
                'physical writes',
                'physical writes direct',
                'physical reads direct',
                'physical writes direct (lob)',
                'physical reads direct (lob)',
                'db block gets',
                'db block changes',
                'consistent changes',
                'consistent gets',
                'session pga memory',
                'session uga memory',
                'parse count (total)',
                'CPU used by this session',
                'parse time cpu',
                'recursive cpu usage',
                'sorts (disk)',
                'sorts (memory)',
                'sorts (rows)',
                'user commits',
                'user rollbacks',
                'execute count'
)
group by
        b.sid,
        d.spid,
        decode (b.username,null,e.name,b.username),
        b.machine,
        to_char(logon_time,'mm/dd/yy hh:mi:ss pm')
order by
        6 desc);
```

The output from this query is pretty large, but as the selected columns indicate, much more detail can be obtained from this query than the top session's summary query. For example, the CPU usage is broken down by parse, recursive, and other CPU usage:

	SID	USER_NAME	OS_ID	MACHINE_NAME	LOGON_TIME	TOTAL_PHYSICAL_IO	TOTAL_LOGICAL_IO	HIT_RATIO	TOTAL_MEMORY_USAGE	PARSES	TOTAL_CPU	PARSE_
1	13	USR1	344	EBT2K\EBT2K08	12/17/02 11:12:45 PM	7209	26147989	100	1646676	39406	52671	
2	2	DBW0	1484	EBT2K04	12/17/02 11:10:30 PM	762	0	100	758700	0	0	
3	5	SMON	2316	EBT2K04	12/17/02 11:10:31 PM	731	38035	98.1	282028	437	0	
4	18	SYS	2512	EBT2K\ROBINWS	12/18/02 01:44:59 PM	343	32345	100	541740	48	112	
5	3	LGWR	2492	EBT2K04	12/17/02 11:10:30 PM	66	0	100	302300	0	0	
6	4	CKPT	2580	EBT2K04	12/17/02 11:10:30 PM	64	0	100	358424	0	0	
7	15	DBSNMP	2304	EBT2K\EBT2K04	12/17/02 11:10:57 PM	37	349	89.9	192968	53	0	
8	12	SYS	2240	EBT2K\ROBINWS	12/18/02 04:26:29 PM	19	101	99.2	434232	20	5	
9	6	RECO	2404	EBT2K04	12/17/02 11:10:31 PM	1	162	99.5	154576	41	0	
10	1	PMON	2628	EBT2K04	12/17/02 11:10:29 PM	0	0	100	78220	0	0	
11	7	SNP0	2416	[NULL]	12/18/02 04:26:17 PM	0	0	100	367832	0	20	
12	8	SNP1	2040	[NULL]	12/18/02 04:26:16 PM	0	0	100	361780	0	14	
13	9	SNP2	2368	[NULL]	12/18/02 04:26:16 PM	0	0	100	214108	0	19	
14	10	SNP3	1668	[NULL]	12/18/02 04:26:17 PM	0	0	100	138300	0	6	
15	11	SNP4	2500	[NULL]	12/18/02 04:26:18 PM	0	0	100	138300	0	6	

Figure 4.1: *Partial top sessions detail output*

The next topic will examine how to analyze wait response problems by drilling deeper to find session bottlenecks.

Session Bottleneck Analysis

After looking at system-level wait activity, the DBA can drill down further to discover which current connections may be responsible for any reported waits that are being observed at the system level. One query that can be used to collect such data is the *sesswaits.sql* script, which filters out some common idle wait events:

sesswaits.sql

```
-- *************************************************
-- Copyright © 2005 by Rampant TechPress
-- This script is free for non-commercial purposes
-- with no warranties.  Use at your own risk.
--
-- To license this script for a commercial purpose,
-- contact info@rampant.cc
-- *************************************************

SELECT
       b.sid,
       decode(b.username,NULL,c.name,b.username) process_name,
       event,
       a.total_waits,
       round((a.time_waited / 100),2)
       time_wait_sec,a.total_timeouts,
       round((average_wait / 100),2)
       average_wait_sec,
       round((a.max_wait / 100),2) max_wait_sec
  FROM
       sys.v_$session_event a,
       sys.v_$session b,
       sys.v_$bgprocess c
```

```
WHERE
       event NOT IN
          ('lock element cleanup',
          'pmon timer',
          'rdbms ipc message',
          'smon timer',
          'SQL*Net message from client',
          'SQL*Net break/reset to client',
          'SQL*Net message to client',
          'SQL*Net more data to client',
          'dispatcher timer',
          'Null event',
          'parallel query dequeue wait',
          'parallel query idle wait - Slaves',
          'pipe get',
          'PL/SQL lock timer',
          'slave wait',
          'virtual circuit status',
          'WMON goes to sleep'
          )
   and event NOT LIKE 'DFS%'
   and event NOT LIKE 'KXFX%'
   and a.sid = b.sid
   and b.paddr = c.paddr (+)
order by
    4 desc;
```

The following is a sample historical wait output at the session level:

	SID	PROCESS_NAME	EVENT	TOTAL_WAITS	TIME_WAIT_SEC	TOTAL_TIMEOUTS	AVERAGE_WAIT_SEC	MAX_WAIT_SEC
1	4	CKPT	control file parallel write	729	8.77	0	.01	.86
2	11	SYS	control file sequential read	262	2.54	0	.01	.14
3	4	CKPT	control file sequential read	228	10.31	0	.05	.23
4	5	SMON	db file scattered read	124	13.08	0	.11	.22
5	9	SCHED	db file sequential read	111	8.84	0	.08	.19
6	11	SYS	db file sequential read	73	3.69	0	.05	.15
7	3	LGWR	log file parallel write	69	1.92	64	.03	.13
8	5	SMON	db file sequential read	68	6.13	0	.09	.19
9	2	DBW0	control file sequential read	35	1.74	0	.05	.25
10	3	LGWR	control file sequential read	30	1.91	0	.06	.16
11	2	DBW0	direct path read	18	.22	0	.01	.15
12	2	DBW0	db file parallel write	16	.22	16	.01	.08
13	3	LGWR	control file parallel write	14	1.43	0	.1	.26
14	3	LGWR	direct path read	9	0	0	0	0
15	8	SYS	db file sequential read	8	.25	0	.03	.08
16	3	LGWR	direct path write	8	.17	0	.02	.17
17	3	LGWR	log file single write	7	.33	0	.05	.07
18	3	LGWR	log file sequential read	6	.22	0	.04	.07
19	9	SCHED	log file sync	3	.08	0	.03	.03
20	11	SYS	library cache pin	3	.12	0	.04	.12
21	2	DBW0	async disk IO	2	.22	0	.11	.15
22	3	LGWR	async disk IO	2	.17	0	.09	.17
23	11	SYS	buffer busy waits	1	.01	0	.01	.01
24	6	RECO	db file sequential read	1	.12	0	.12	.12

Figure 4.2: *Sample historical wait output at the session level.*

Such a query could indicate which Oracle processes were responsible for most of the *db file sequential waits* that were reported in the global system overview query.

Like the system-level query, the above query shows cumulative wait statistics for each session since it has been connected. All data for that session is lost once it disconnects from the database.

A final level of detail can be obtained by checking for any active Oracle processes that are currently waiting. One query that can be used to uncover such data is the *csesswaits.sql* script:

csesswaits.sql

```
-- ***************************************************
-- Copyright © 2005 by Rampant TechPress
-- This script is free for non-commercial purposes
-- with no warranties.  Use at your own risk.
--
-- To license this script for a commercial purpose,
-- contact info@rampant.cc
-- ***************************************************

SELECT
        a.sid,
        decode(b.username,NULL,c.name,b.username) process_name,
        a.event,
        a.seconds_in_wait,
        a.wait_time,
        a.state,
        a.p1text,
        a.p1,
        a.p1raw,
        a.p2text,
        a.p2,
        a.p2raw,
        a.p3text,
        a.p3,
        a.p3raw
  FROM
        sys.v_$session_wait a,
        sys.v_$session b,
        sys.v_$bgprocess c
  WHERE
        event NOT IN
          ('lock element cleanup',
          'pmon timer',
          'rdbms ipc message',
          'smon timer',
          'SQL*Net message from client',
          'SQL*Net break/reset to client',
          'SQL*Net message to client',
```

```
        'SQL*Net more data to client',
        'dispatcher timer',
        'Null event',
        'parallel query dequeue wait',
        'parallel query idle wait - Slaves',
        'pipe get',
        'PL/SQL lock timer',
        'slave wait',
        'virtual circuit status',
        'WMON goes to sleep'
        )
   and event NOT LIKE 'DFS%'
   and event NOT LIKE 'KXFX%'
   and a.sid = b.sid
   and b.paddr = c.paddr (+)
order by
      4 desc;
```

The following is the output showing a session currently waiting on a resource:

Figure 4.3: *Output showing a session currently waiting on a resource.*

The *sesshitrate.sql* script below will provide a *buffer cache hit ratio* for all currently connected sessions:

sesshitrate.sql

```
-- ****************************************************
-- Copyright © 2005 by Rampant TechPress
-- This script is free for non-commercial purposes
-- with no warranties.  Use at your own risk.
--
-- To license this script for a commercial purpose,
-- contact info@rampant.cc
-- ****************************************************

select
        b.sid sid,
        decode (b.username,null,e.name,b.username)
        user_name,
        d.spid os_id,
        b.machine machine_name,
        to_char(logon_time,'mm/dd/yy hh:mi:ss pm')
        logon_time,
        100 - 100 *
        (round ((sum (decode (c.name,
        'physical reads', value, 0)) -
        sum (decode (c.name,
```

```
        'physical reads direct', value, 0)) -
        sum(decode (c.name,
        'physical reads direct (lob)', value, 0))) /
        (sum (decode (c.name,
        'db block gets', value, 1)) +
        sum (decode (c.name,
        'consistent gets', value, 0))),3)) hit_ratio
from
        sys.v_$sesstat a,
        sys.v_$session b,
        sys.v_$statname c,
        sys.v_$process d,
        sys.v_$bgprocess e
where
        a.statistic#=c.statistic# and
        b.sid=a.sid   and
        d.addr = b.paddr and
        e.paddr (+) = b.paddr   and
        c.name in ('physical reads',
                   'physical reads direct',
                   'physical writes direct (lob)',
                   'physical reads direct (lob)',
                   'db block gets',
                   'consistent gets')
group by

        b.sid,
        d.spid,
        decode (b.username,null,e.name,b.username),
        b.machine,
        to_char(logon_time,'mm/dd/yy hh:mi:ss pm')
order by
        6 desc;
```

The following is sample output showing session hit ratio information:

	SID	USER_NAME	OS_ID	MACHINE_NAME	LOGON_TIME	HIT_RATIO
1	1	PMON	292	EBT2K11	01/03/03 01:01:16 pm	100
2	2	DBW0	1148	EBT2K11	01/03/03 01:01:16 pm	100
3	3	LGWR	304	EBT2K11	01/03/03 01:01:16 pm	100
4	6	RECO	1136	EBT2K11	01/03/03 01:01:17 pm	100
5	8	SYS	2552	EBT2K\BILLYWS	01/17/03 02:59:01 pm	100
6	9	QVIN	2420	EBT2K\BILLYWS	01/17/03 02:39:55 pm	100
7	12	SYSMAN	2948	EBT2K\EBT2K11	01/07/03 10:29:04 am	100
8	14	SYSMAN	2800	EBT2K\EBT2K11	01/07/03 10:29:05 am	100
9	15	SYSMAN	1424	EBT2K\EBT2K11	01/07/03 10:29:05 am	100
10	24	ERADMIN	452	EBT2K\ROBINWS	01/16/03 10:27:14 am	100
11	23	USER21|	3176	EBT2K\EBT2K12	01/17/03 03:59:10 pm	100
12	22	SYS	2312	EBT2K\BILLYWS	01/17/03 03:32:51 pm	100
13	21	USER21	2136	EBT2K\EBT2K12	01/14/03 11:12:56 am	100
14	19	SYSMAN	1560	EBT2K\EBT2K11	01/07/03 10:29:05 am	100
15	18	SYS	3972	EBT2K\BILLYWS	01/17/03 03:02:23 pm	100
16	17	SYSMAN	2000	EBT2K\EBT2K11	01/07/03 10:29:05 am	100
17	13	SYSMAN	236	EBT2K\EBT2K11	01/07/03 10:29:05 am	100
18	30	SYS	3752	EBT2K\ROBINWS	01/16/03 09:27:38 am	100
19	29	SYS	3620	EBT2K\BILLYWS	01/17/03 02:57:11 pm	100
20	27	SYS	1884	EBT2K\ROBINWS	01/17/03 03:55:18 pm	100
21	26	SYS	3128	EBT2K\ROBINWS	01/17/03 03:59:45 pm	100
22	11	SYSMAN	2952	EBT2K\EBT2K11	01/07/03 10:29:04 am	100
23	4	CKPT	1176	EBT2K11	01/03/03 01:01:17 pm	100
24	5	SMON	1236	EBT2K11	01/03/03 01:01:17 pm	99.8
25	25	SYSTEM	612	EBT2K\EBT2K11	01/07/03 10:29:44 am	99.5

Figure 4.4: *Sample output showing session hit ratio information*

After examining the session hit ratio information, move into SQL statement analysis using the *sqlhitrate.sql* script:

🖫 sqlhitrate.sql

```
-- ***************************************************
-- Copyright © 2005 by Rampant TechPress
-- This script is free for non-commercial purposes
-- with no warranties.  Use at your own risk.
--
-- To license this script for a commercial purpose,
-- contact info@rampant.cc
-- ***************************************************
select
        sql_text ,
        b.username ,
        100 - round(100 *
        a.disk_reads/greatest(a.buffer_gets,1),2) hit_ratio
from
        sys.v_$sqlarea a,
        sys.all_users b
where
        a.parsing_user_id=b.user_id and
        b.username not in ('SYS','SYSTEM')
order by
        3 desc;
```

The following is a sample output showing the SQL statement hit ratio analysis:

	SQL_TEXT	USERNAME	HIT_RATIO
1	SELECT 1035, COUNT(*) FROM SYS.SEG$ S,SYS.TS$ TS WHERE S.TS# = TS.TS# AND DECODE(BITAND(TS.FLAGS, 3), 1, TO_NUMBER(NULL),S.EXTSIZE	USER1	100
2	COMMIT	QVIN	100
3	SELECT 980, CHAINEDFETCHES,TOTALFETCHES FROM (SELECT VALUE AS CHAINEDFETCHES FROM SYS.V_$SYSSTAT A WHERE NAME='table fetch	USER1	100
4	SELECT 1036, COUNT(*) FROM (SELECT ROUND((100*Sum_Free_Blocks / Sum_Alloc_Blocks),2) PCT_FREE FROM (SELECT Tablespace_Name,SUM(Blocks) Sum_Alloc_Blocks,SUM(bytes) AS Total_space FROM SYS.DBA_DATA_FILES GROUP BY Tablespace_Name), (SELECT	USER1	100
5	SELECT /*+ ALL_ROWS IGNORE_WHERE_CLAUSE */ NVL(SUM(C1),0), NVL(SUM(C2),0), COUNT(DISTINCT C3) FROM (SELECT /*+	QVIN	100
6	COMMIT WORK	QVIN	100
7	/* OracleOEM */ UPDATE smp_vdp_node_info SET status = 'N', DOWN_TIME = :1, DOWN_TIMEZONE = :2 WHERE (status = 'Y') AND (node = :3) AND	SYSMAN	100
8	begin PERFCNTR_DRILLDOWN_QUERIES.fetchcursor_10(QUERY_LIST_IN=>'914',MAX_ROWS_IN=>500,VAR1_OUT=>:R001C001,VAR2_OUT=>:R001C002,VAR3_OU	USER1	100
9	SELECT 976, ROUND(A.VALUE/1048576,2) DB,ROUND(B.VALUE/1048576,2) FS,ROUND(C.VALUE/1048576,2) RB,ROUND(D.VALUE/1048576,2) VS FROM	USER1	100
10	LOCK TABLE smp_vdp_node_oms_map IN EXCLUSIVE MODE	SYSMAN	100
11	LOCK TABLE smp_vdg_gateway_map in EXCLUSIVE MODE	SYSMAN	100
12	SELECT 1033, b.USERNAME,b.SID,b.SERIAL#,B.STATUS,DECODE((SUBSTR(B.MACHINE,LENGTH(B.MACHINE),1)),CHR(0),(SUBSTR(B.MACHINE,1,LENGTH(B.MACHINE)-1)),RTRIM(B.MACHINE)) MACHINE,ROUND(SUM(DECODE(c.NAME,'session pga memory',VALUE,0))/1024,2) pga_memory,ROUND(SUM(DECODE(c.NAME,'session uga memory',VALUE,0))/1024,2) uga_memory,ROUND(SUM(DECODE(c.NAME, 'sorts	USER1	100

Figure 4.5: *Sample output showing SQL statement hit ratio analysis*

One nuance to be aware of in the SQL hit ratio script as well as the buffer pool script, which calculates hit rates for the different buffer pools, is that the Oracle *v$sqlarea* view does not provide a way to filter direct reads. These are physical reads that do not pass through the buffer cache, and consequently do not increment any logical I/O counters. This means it is possible to have an SQL statement that prompts a lot of direct reads, while the hit ratio shows *negative*.

Investigating Session Memory Usage

It is not uncommon for one or two users to cause runtime problems that plague an entire database. The problem could be a runaway process, an un-tuned batch procedure, or other user-initiated operations.

User connection memory consumption can get out of hand, and extreme cases can cause headaches at both the database and operating system level (ORA-4030 errors).

The session memory issue only applies when the Oracle Multi-threaded Server (MTS) is not being used. If the MTS is implemented, Oracle will allocate all SGA sort areas to the large pool and the sessions will not have external PGA memory regions.

If the database server does not have an overabundance of memory, periodically check to identify the heavy memory users, along with the total percentage of memory each user consumes.

If there are one or two users who have more than 15%-50% of the total memory usage, the sessions should be investigated more closely to see the kind of activities they are performing.

To find the sessions that use the most memory in a database, the *memhog.sql* script can be used:

🖫 memhog.sql

```
-- ****************************************************
-- Copyright © 2005 by Rampant TechPress
-- This script is free for non-commercial purposes
-- with no warranties.  Use at your own risk.
--
-- To license this script for a commercial purpose,
-- contact info@rampant.cc
-- ****************************************************

select
      sid,
      username,
      round(total_user_mem/1024,2) mem_used_in_kb,
      round(100 * total_user_mem/total_mem,2) mem_percent
from
(select
    b.sid sid,
    nvl(b.username,p.name) username,
    sum(value) total_user_mem
from
    sys.v_$statname c,
    sys.v_$sesstat a,
    sys.v_$session b,
    sys.v_$bgprocess p
where
```

```
      a.statistic#=c.statistic# and
      p.paddr (+) = b.paddr and
      b.sid=a.sid and
      c.name in ('session pga memory','session uga memory')
group by
      b.sid, nvl(b.username,p.name)),
(select
      sum(value) total_mem
from
      sys.v_$statname c,
      sys.v_$sesstat a
where
      a.statistic#=c.statistic# and
      c.name in ('session pga memory','session uga memory'))
order by
      3 desc;
```

The following sample output shows the top memory users in a database:

	SID	USERNAME	MEM_USED_IN_KB	MEM_PERCENT
1	2	DBW0	740.92	18.28
2	14	SYS	685.63	16.91
3	7	SNP0	417.76	10.31
4	3	LGWR	295.21	7.28
5	5	SMON	275.42	6.79
6	13	SYS	232.14	5.73
7	8	SNP1	217.38	5.36
8	11	SNP4	216.77	5.35
9	9	SNP2	200.73	4.95
10	10	SNP3	200.73	4.95
11	12	DBSNMP	188.45	4.65
12	4	CKPT	172.29	4.25
13	6	RECO	150.95	3.72
14	22	SYS	86.88	2.14
15	1	PMON	76.39	1.88

Figure 4.6: *Sample output showing the top memory users in a database*

Examining Background Processes

How can the DBA determine if Oracle's DBWR, LGWR, ARCH or other background processes are experiencing I/O bottlenecks? First, the *bgact.sql* query can be issued to get a general handle on DBWR and LGWR activity:

🖫 bgact.sql

```
-- ***************************************************
-- Copyright © 2005 by Rampant TechPress
-- This script is free for non-commercial purposes
-- with no warranties.  Use at your own risk.
--
-- To license this script for a commercial purpose,
-- contact info@rampant.cc
-- ***************************************************

select
   name,
   value
from
   sys.v_$sysstat
where
   (name like '%DBWR%'
or
     name in
       ('dirty buffers inspected',
        'summed dirty queue length',
        'write requests'))
or
       (name like '%redo%')
order by
     1;
```

The output from the above query might look like the following:

```
NAME                              VALUE
---------------------------------------
DBWR buffers scanned                  0
DBWR checkpoint buffers written     438
DBWR checkpoints                      0
DBWR cross instance writes            0
DBWR free buffers found               0
DBWR lru scans                        0
DBWR make free requests               0
DBWR revisited being-written buffer   0
DBWR summed scan depth                0
DBWR transaction table writes       151
DBWR undo block writes              154
dirty buffers inspected               0
redo blocks written                 804
redo buffer allocation retries        0
redo entries                       1297
redo log space requests               0
redo log space wait time              0
redo log switch interrupts            0
redo ordering marks                   0
redo size                        329192
redo synch time                      54
```

```
redo synch writes                        116
redo wastage                           69528
redo write time                           79
redo writer latching time                  0
redo writes                              237
summed dirty queue length                  0
```

Seeing non-zero values for the DBWR, summed dirty queue length typically indicates that buffers are being left in the write queue after a write request. This could signal that the DBWR process is falling behind and that more DBWR processes should be added to the system. Non-zero values for the redo log space wait requests and redo log space wait time statistics could indicate a too-low setting for the log buffer.

Archive log I/O problems can usually be viewed in the form of entries in the Oracle alert log. Entries in the alert log are messages indicating waits for the archive log files to complete.

To get an idea of how many logs the archive process writes per day, a query like the *archhist.sql* script can be issued. The query shows the number of logs written per day for the last 30 days:

🖫 archhist.sql

```
-- ************************************************
-- Copyright © 2005 by Rampant TechPress
-- This script is free for non-commercial purposes
-- with no warranties.  Use at your own risk.
--
-- To license this script for a commercial purpose,
-- contact info@rampant.cc
-- ************************************************

select
   to_char(completion_time,'mm/dd/yy') completion_time,
   count(*)                            log_count
from
   sys.v_$archived_log
where
   sysdate - completion_time < 31
group by
   to_char(completion_time,'mm/dd/yy')
order by
   1 desc;
```

The output from the above query might look like the following:

```
COMPLETI  LOG_COUNT
--------  ----------
04/21/05          8
04/20/05         10
04/19/05          8
04/18/05          9
04/17/05          3
04/16/05          4
04/15/05         10
04/14/05         11
04/13/05         10
04/12/05          8
04/11/05         10
```

Once the overall I/O picture of Oracle's background processes has been examined, specific areas, such as rollback segments, can then be reviewed.

Monitoring Rollback Activity

If a lot of DML activity is occurring in the database, rollback segments can become hotspots for I/O activity. This is especially true for versions 8i and below. Oracle writes data to individual rollback segments to undo changes made to the Oracle database from within a transaction. Rollbacks are also used to maintain read consistency for multiple users of modified data.

To check the amount of rollback I/O the database is experiencing, *rolldet.sql* query can be used:

🖫 **rolldet.sql**

```
-- ***************************************************
-- Copyright © 2005 by Rampant TechPress
-- This script is free for non-commercial purposes
-- with no warranties.  Use at your own risk.
--
-- To license this script for a commercial purpose,
-- contact info@rampant.cc
-- ***************************************************
select
   name,
   round ((rssize / 1024), 2) size_kb,
   shrinks,
   extends,
   gets,
   waits,
   writes,
   xacts,
```

```
  status,
  round ((hwmsize / 1024), 2) hw_kb
from
  sys.v_$rollstat a,
  sys.v_$rollname b
where
  (a.usn = b.usn)
order by
  name;
```

Here is a sample output of rollback activity:

	NAME	SIZE_KB	SHRINKS	EXTENDS	GETS	WAITS	WRITES	XACTS	STATUS	HW_KB
1	RBS0	4088	0	0	3572	0	3624	0	ONLINE	4088
2	RBS1	4088	0	0	3573	0	6194	0	ONLINE	4088
3	RBS10	4088	0	0	3569	0	8252	0	ONLINE	4088
4	RBS11	4088	0	0	3568	0	1650	0	ONLINE	4088
5	RBS12	4088	0	0	3566	0	1266	0	ONLINE	4088
6	RBS13	4088	0	0	3566	0	1150	0	ONLINE	4088
7	RBS14	4088	0	0	3566	0	1420	0	ONLINE	4088
8	RBS15	4088	0	0	3566	0	1152	0	ONLINE	4088
9	RBS16	4088	0	0	3566	0	1480	0	ONLINE	4088
10	RBS17	4088	0	0	3566	0	4448	0	ONLINE	4088
11	RBS18	4088	0	0	3566	0	1436	0	ONLINE	4088
12	RBS19	4088	0	0	3567	0	4266	0	ONLINE	4088
13	RBS2	4088	0	0	3575	0	3874	0	ONLINE	4088
14	RBS20	4088	0	0	3566	0	994	0	ONLINE	4088
15	RBS21	4088	0	0	3566	0	1054	0	ONLINE	4088
16	RBS22	4088	0	0	3566	0	1044	0	ONLINE	4088
17	RBS23	4088	0	0	3566	0	1214	0	ONLINE	4088
18	RBS24	4088	0	0	3568	0	1556	0	ONLINE	4088
19	RBS25	4088	0	0	3568	0	1528	0	ONLINE	4088

Figure 4.7: *Rollback activity details*

To properly tune rollback I/O, the first step is to ensure that there are enough segments to accommodate the workload of the database. A count of active rollback segments that is consistently equal to or near the number of rollbacks defined for the database is an indicator that more should be created.

An overall rollback contention ratio of 1% or higher is an indicator of too few rollbacks, as well. Wait counts greater than zero for each rollback segment are further evidence that more rollback segments should be created.

If Oracle9i or above is in use, the new UNDO tablespace feature that allows Oracle to automatically manage all rollback activity should be used. It is possible to include dynamic allocation of more rollback segments when it becomes necessary.

After ensuring that enough rollback segments exist in the database, attention should shift to the question of sizing. Dynamic rollback extension can take a toll on performance if a DBA is consistently enlarging segments to accommodate heavy transaction loads.

The presence of rollback segments undergoing numerous extends and shrinks such as Oracle returning a segment back to its OPTIMAL setting, as well as rollback segments with current or high-water mark sizes greater than their OPTIMAL setting, is usually a good indicator that they should be permanently enlarged.

Oracle 10g

Session Wait Analysis in Oracle10g

As it does with system wait activity, Oracle10g provides improved metrics when it comes to analyzing session wait and other activity. When it comes to wait activity, the DBA can look at session wait activities in summary form through wait classes, as well as obtain enhanced drill down information for each session.

To examine session wait activity via the new Oracle10g wait classes, the *10g_sesswaitclass.sql* script can be used:

10g_sesswaitclass.sql

```
-- ****************************************************
-- Copyright © 2005 by Rampant TechPress
-- This script is free for non-commercial purposes
-- with no warranties.  Use at your own risk.
--
-- To license this script for a commercial purpose,
-- contact info@rampant.cc
-- ****************************************************

select
        a.sid,
        b.username,
        a.wait_class,
        a.total_waits,
        round((a.time_waited / 100),2) time_waited_secs
from
        sys.v_$session_wait_class a,
        sys.v_$session b
where
        b.sid = a.sid and
        b.username is not null and
        a.wait_class != 'Idle'
order by
        1,2,5 desc
```

The following output shows the analyzing of session waits at the wait class level:

	SID	USERNAME	WAIT_CLASS	TOTAL_WAITS	TIME_WAITED_SECS
14	249	SYSMAN	User I/O	86607	71.31
15	249	SYSMAN	Commit	2312	3.88
16	249	SYSMAN	Concurrency	74	.52
17	249	SYSMAN	Configuration	35	.22
18	249	SYSMAN	Application	622	.21
19	249	SYSMAN	Network	18638	.07
20	249	SYSMAN	Other	29	.02
21	250	DBSNMP	User I/O	20545	46.89
22	250	DBSNMP	Commit	10712	23.01
23	250	DBSNMP	Network	381278	5.59
24	250	DBSNMP	System I/O	69663	2.78
25	250	DBSNMP	Concurrency	114	1.35

Figure 4.8: *Analyzing session waits at the wait class level.*

Adding a specific SID to the query filter shown above will result in data for only that specific SID.

It is possible to drill down to find new information on session wait and execution activity in Oracle10g as well. New performance views allow the DBA to obtain the last ten wait events that a session has experienced along with the time spent performing certain functions like parse time.

To acquire the last ten wait events for a session, use the *10g_last10waits.sql* script. For this example, a SID of 249 was used:

🖫 10g_last10waits.sql

```
-- ****************************************************
-- Copyright © 2005 by Rampant TechPress
-- This script is free for non-commercial purposes
-- with no warranties.  Use at your own risk.
--
-- To license this script for a commercial purpose,
-- contact info@rampant.cc
-- ****************************************************

select
        a.seq# wait_number,
        a.event,
        c.wait_class wait_class,
        round((a.wait_time / 100),2) wait_time_secs,
        a.p1text,
        a.p1,
        a.p2text,
        a.p2,
        a.p3text,
        a.p3
from
        sys.v_$session_wait_history a,
        sys.v_$session b,
        sys.v_$event_name c
where
        a.sid = b.sid and
        a.event# = c.event# and
        b.sid = 249
order by
        1,3
```

In Oracle10g and above, the *10g_usertime.sql* script can be used to determine the amount of time each user session has spent executing user based calls, running SQL and PL/SQL, parsing SQL, and more:

10g_usertime.sql

```
-- ***************************************************
-- Copyright © 2005 by Rampant TechPress
-- This script is free for non-commercial purposes
-- with no warranties.  Use at your own risk.
--
-- To license this script for a commercial purpose,
-- contact info@rampant.cc
-- ***************************************************

select
        a.sid,
        b.username,
        a.stat_name,
        round((a.value / 1000000),3) time_secs
from
        sys.v_$sess_time_model a,
        sys.v_$session b
where
        a.sid = b.sid and
        b.sid = < enter SID >
order by
        4 desc
```

An example output for a session might look like the following:

```
SID USERNAME STAT_NAME                            TIME_SECS
---- -------- ----------------------------------- ----------
 154 SYS      DB time                                  1.003
 154 SYS      sql execute elapsed time                  .837
 154 SYS      parse time elapsed                         .382
 154 SYS      hard parse elapsed time                    .38
 154 SYS      DB CPU                                     .22
 154 SYS      connection management call elapsed        .039
 154 SYS      PL/SQL compilation elapsed time           .003
 154 SYS      background elapsed time                       0
 154 SYS      PL/SQL execution elapsed time                0
 154 SYS      Java execution elapsed time                  0
 154 SYS      inbound PL/SQL rpc elapsed time              0
 154 SYS      hard parse (bind mismatch) elapsed           0
 154 SYS      background cpu time                           0
 154 SYS      failed parse elapsed time                    0
 154 SYS      hard parse (sharing criteria) elaps          0
 154 SYS      failed parse (out of shared memory)          0
 154 SYS      sequence load elapsed time                   0
```

These details can help determine the exact nature of work each session has been doing. Once the top sessions have been located, the next step is to locate the SQL calls they have made and determine what killer queries each session has submitted. It may be a case of un-tuned SQL or inappropriately submitted SQL, such as SQL used for a report that should be run during off hours.

The *histsesstime.sql* script for Oracle 10g can be used for assistance in understanding what sessions were logged on for a particular time period and the amount of session time and wait percentage each experienced:

🖫 histsesstime.sql

```
-- ****************************************************
-- Copyright © 2005 by Rampant TechPress
-- This script is free for non-commercial purposes
-- with no warranties.  Use at your own risk.
--
-- To license this script for a commercial purpose,
-- contact info@rampant.cc
-- ****************************************************

select
        sess_id,
        username,
        program,
        sess_time,
        round(100 * (sess_time / total_time),2) pct_time_waited
from
(select
        a.session_id sess_id,
        decode(session_type,'BACKGROUND',session_type,c.username) username,
        a.program program,
        sum(a.time_waited) sess_time
from
        sys.v_$active_session_history a,
        sys.v_$event_name b,
        sys.dba_users c
where
        a.event# = b.event# and
        a.user_id = c.user_id and
        sample_time > '23-SEP-04 12:00:00 AM' and
        sample_time < '25-SEP-04 12:00:00 AM'
group by
        a.session_id,
        decode(session_type,'BACKGROUND',session_type,c.username),
        a.program),
(select
        sum(a.time_waited) total_time
from
        sys.v_$active_session_history a,
        sys.v_$event_name b
where
        a.event# = b.event# and
        sample_time > '23-SEP-04 12:00:00 AM' and
        sample_time < '25-SEP-04 12:10:00 AM' )
order by 5 desc
```

Different timeframes can be substituted where necessary. The output might look like the following:

```
SESS_ID USERNAME    PROGRAM          SESS_TIME PCT_TIME_WAITED
------- ---------- ---------------- ---------- ---------------
    159 BACKGROUND ORACLE.EXE (QMN    5126682           22.67
    147 BACKGROUND ORACLE.EXE (q00    5125630           22.66
    152 BACKGROUND ORACLE.EXE (m00    5125241           22.66
    153 ERADMIN                       3950017           17.47
    155 SYSMAN                        1946696            8.61
    166 BACKGROUND ORACLE.EXE (CKP     456499            2.02
    152 BACKGROUND ORACLE.EXE (m00     313561            1.39
    165 BACKGROUND ORACLE.EXE (SMO     250101            1.11
    151 SYS                           118730             .52
```

This listing is in descending order of the percentage of wait time for a given session. The next topic covers historical information for sessions in 10g.

dba_hist_sessmetric_history

The *dba_hist_sessmetric_history* view collects history information for important session related metrics such as:

```
SQL> select metric_name from dba_hist_metric_name where group_name like
'Session Metrics%';

METRIC_NAME
--------------------------------------
Blocked User Session Count
Logical Reads Ratio (Sess/Sys) %
Physical Reads Ratio (Sess/Sys) %
Total Parse Count (Session)
Hard Parse Count (Session)
PGA Memory (Session)
Physical Reads (Session)
CPU Time (Session)
User Transaction Count (Session)
```

The *dba_hist_sessmetric_history* view can be queried to find additional metric details about particular sessions of interest:

```
SQL> desc DBA_HIST_SESSMETRIC_HISTORY

Name                                    Null?    Type
--------------------------------------- -------- ----------
SNAP_ID                                 NOT NULL NUMBER
DBID                                    NOT NULL NUMBER
```

```
INSTANCE_NUMBER                              NOT NULL NUMBER
BEGIN_TIME                                   NOT NULL DATE
END_TIME                                     NOT NULL DATE
SESSID                                       NOT NULL NUMBER
SERIAL#                                      NOT NULL NUMBER
INTSIZE                                      NOT NULL NUMBER
GROUP_ID                                     NOT NULL NUMBER
METRIC_ID                                    NOT NULL NUMBER
METRIC_NAME                                  NOT NULL VARCHAR2(64)
VALUE                                        NOT NULL NUMBER
METRIC_UNIT                                  NOT NULL VARCHAR2(64)
```

This view contains a *metric_unit* column that helps identify measure units for every metric.

This wraps up an examination of how to view Oracle 10g session information. The next section explores Background Process*es* in 10g

dba_hist_bg_event_summary

The *dba_hist_bg_event_summary* data dictionary view is very similar to the *dba_hist_system_event* view. The difference is that the *dba_hist_bg_event_summary* view displays historical information about wait events caused by Oracle background processes activities. Oracle background processes form a kernel Oracle instance with an SGA memory region and perform many types of important jobs.

During their job in a concurrent access environment, these kernel Oracle processes cause some contention for system resources in much the same way as do the foreground user processes serving end users. Oracle DBAs may want to know what part of database waits are caused by background Oracle processes so that corresponding tuning actions related to those background Oracle processes can be taken.

```
SQL> desc DBA_HIST_BG_EVENT_SUMMARY
 Name                                      Null?    Type
 ----------------------------------------- -------- ----------------
 SNAP_ID                                   NOT NULL NUMBER
 DBID                                      NOT NULL NUMBER
 INSTANCE_NUMBER                           NOT NULL NUMBER
 EVENT_ID                                  NOT NULL NUMBER
 EVENT_NAME                                NOT NULL VARCHAR2(64)
 WAIT_CLASS_ID                                      NUMBER
 WAIT_CLASS                                         VARCHAR2(64)
```

```
TOTAL_WAITS                                        NUMBER
TOTAL_TIMEOUTS                                     NUMBER
TIME_WAITED_MICRO                                  NUMBER
```

The *bg_event_int_10g.sql* query can be used to retrieve background wait event data for a particular snapshot interval:

🖫 bg_event_int_10g.sql

```
-- *************************************************
-- Copyright © 2005 by Rampant TechPress
-- This script is free for non-commercial purposes
-- with no warranties.  Use at your own risk.
--
-- To license this script for a commercial purpose,
-- contact info@rampant.cc
-- *************************************************

select
    event "Event Name",
    waits "Waits",
    timeouts "Timeouts",
    time "Wait Time (s)",
    avgwait "Avg Wait (ms)",
    waitclass "Wait Class"
from
    (select e.event_name event
         , e.total_waits - nvl(b.total_waits,0)  waits
         , e.total_timeouts - nvl(b.total_timeouts,0) timeouts
         , (e.time_waited_micro - nvl(b.time_waited_micro,0))/1000000  time
         ,  decode ((e.total_waits - nvl(b.total_waits, 0)), 0,
to_number(NULL),
           ((e.time_waited_micro - nvl(b.time_waited_micro,0))/1000) /
(e.total_waits - nvl(b.total_waits,0)) ) avgwait
         , e.wait_class waitclass
      from
         dba_hist_bg_event_summary b ,
         dba_hist_bg_event_summary e
      where
                   b.snap_id(+)          = &pBgnSnap
             and e.snap_id               = &pEndSnap
             and b.dbid(+)               = &pDbId
             and e.dbid                  = &pDbId
             and b.instance_number(+)    = &pInstNum
             and e.instance_number       = &pInstNum
             and b.event_id(+)           = e.event_id
             and e.total_waits           > nvl(b.total_waits,0)
             and e.wait_class            <> 'Idle' )
order by time desc, waits desc
```

The WISE tool has a corresponding report named Background Process Wait Events that allows users to build time-series charts for background wait events as shown in Figure 4.9.

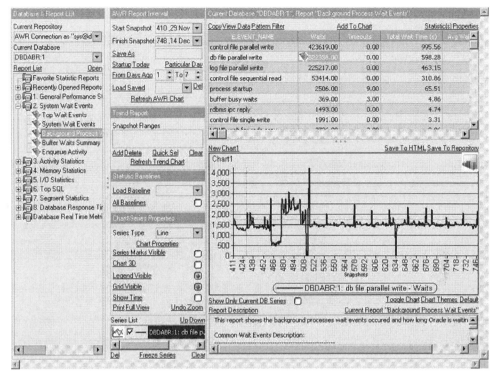

Figure 4.9: *AWR Background Process Wait Events chart in WISE.*

The output of *bg_event_int_10g.sql* script looks similar to the output of the *sys_event_int_10g.sql* script with the exception that wait events are displayed for background processes.

Conclusion

This chapter examined the monitoring of users and processes. Hopefully the DBA now has the means to examine how users are set up and processes tuned on in the system, and thus can use this data to ensure they access Oracle efficiently and with low system impact.

Objects

This chapter will introduce ways the various objects in a database are accessed. By understanding how objects such as tables and indexes are accessed, the DBA can then determine if the access is correct or if actions need to be taken to optimize this critical component of Oracle tuning and monitoring.

Determine Global Object Access Patterns

Oracle has come a long way in helping the database professional determine how objects in the database are being accessed. Oracle9i, in particular, introduced a number of statistical views that can be queried to get a handle on object access patterns. For those who have not upgraded to 9i or 10g yet, there are still methods that can be used to understand the I/O occurring against the database.

The first step is a global sweep of access pattern activity. A query such as the *globaccpatt.sql* script can be used for that:

🖫 globaccpatt.sql

```
-- *****************************************************
-- Copyright © 2005 by Rampant TechPress
-- This script is free for non-commercial purposes
-- with no warranties.  Use at your own risk.
--
-- To license this script for a commercial purpose,
-- contact info@rampant.cc
-- *****************************************************

select
   name,
   value
from
   sys.v_$sysstat
where
   name in
   ('table scans (cache partitions)',
    'table scans (direct read)',
    'table scans (long tables)',
    'table scans (rowid ranges)',
    'table scans (short tables)',
    'table fetch by rowid',
    'table fetch continued row')
order by
   1;
```

Results from such a query might look like the following:

```
NAME                              VALUE
------------------------------------ ------
table fetch by rowid              146540
table fetch continued row            698
table scans (cache partitions)         0
table scans (direct read)              0
table scans (long tables)              0
table scans (rowid ranges)             0
table scans (short tables)           262
```

When reviewing the output from the above query, the following items should be the focus:

- Long table scans are typically an activity that should be avoided. They have the capability to cause needless physical and logical I/O as well as flood the buffer cache with seldom-referenced blocks of data. A script that will reveal the large tables that are being scanned will be presented later is this chapter.

- The *table fetch continued row* statistic is indicative of chained/migrated row I/O. Such activity is not desirable because chained/migrated row access can cause twice the I/O needed to access a table. This is because Oracle must do two or more I/Os to read a chained/migrated row in a table.

To get a quick idea of how many tables in the database suffer from such a condition, the very simplistic *chaincnt.sql* script can be used:

🖫 chaincnt.sql

```
-- ************************************************
-- Copyright © 2005 by Rampant TechPress
-- This script is free for non-commercial purposes
-- with no warranties.  Use at your own risk.
--
-- To license this script for a commercial purpose,
-- contact info@rampant.cc
-- ************************************************

select
        count(*)
from
        sys.tab$
where
        chncnt > 0;
```

The output from this script looks like this;

```
  COUNT(*)
----------
         6
```

- If high numbers in the *table fetch continued row* statistic are present in the previous global access report, the *chainpct.sql* script can be used to determine the percentage of such activity in the overall I/O of the database:

🖫 chainpct.sql

```
-- ************************************************
-- Copyright © 2005 by Rampant TechPress
-- This script is free for non-commercial purposes
-- with no warranties.  Use at your own risk.
```

```
--
-- To license this script for a commercial purpose,
-- contact info@rampant.cc
-- ****************************************************

select
   round(100 * (chained_row_fetches /
   total_fetches),2) pct_chain_access
from
   (select
      value as chained_row_fetches
   from
      sys.v_$sysstat a
   where
      name = 'table fetch continued row'),
   (select
      sum(value) as total_fetches
   from
      sys.v_$sysstat
   where
      name in ('table fetch by rowid',
               'table scan rows gotten'));
```

The output from this script looks like this.

```
PCT_CHAIN_ACCESS
----------------
               1
```

Should this query return anything over 25%, the database is likely suffering from a bad case of chained/migrated rows or perhaps a very hot chained/migrated row table is being accessed repeatedly.

The next report shows tables with chained rows as reported by the analysis process of the Oracle database. If the analyze routines have not been run against the database or are not current, then the data from this report will not be accurate.

The actual tables that contain chained rows can be found by using the *chaintables.sql* query:

🖫 chaintables.sql

```
-- ****************************************************
-- Copyright © 2005 by Rampant TechPress
-- This script is free for non-commercial purposes
-- with no warranties.  Use at your own risk.
--
-- To license this script for a commercial purpose,
```

```
-- contact info@rampant.cc
-- ****************************************************
-- chained_rows.sql
-- FUNCTION: Show percentage of chained rows
-- tables must have been analyzed
-- MRA
--
column "Chain Percent" format 999.99
column table_name heading 'Table|Name'
column chain_cnt heading 'Chained|Rows'
column num_rows heading 'Row|Count'
set pages 47
set feedback off
ttitle 'Chained Rows Report'
spool chained_rows
select table_name,chain_cnt, num_rows, chain_cnt/num_rows*100 "Chain
Percent" from dba_tables
where
chain_cnt>1
and owner not in ('SYS','SYSTEM');
spool off
ttitle off
```

```
Date: 11/30/04    Tables With Chained Rows      Page:   1

OWNER     TABLE_NAME           CHAIN_CNT NUM_ROWS     CHN_PCT TABLESPACE_NAME
--------  -------------------- --------- -------- ----------- ---------------
AK        AK_FLOW_PAGES               13      606  2.14521452             AKD
AK        AK_REGIONS                 265   11,341  2.33665462             AKD
ALR       ALR_ALERT_CHECKS         1,222   15,437  7.91604586            ALRD
AMS       AMS_SETUP_TYPES             10    1,001  .999000999            AMSD
AMS       AMS_CUSTOM_SETUP_ATTR       83    1,085  7.64976959            AMSD
AP        AP_BANK_ACCOUNTS_ALL       515    8,966  5.74392148             APD
AP        AP_INVOICE_PAYMENTS_ALL     43  324,290  .013259737             APD
APPLSYS   FND_PERFORMANCE_DATA        20       20         100            FNDD
APPLSYS   AD_PATCH_HIST_TEMP          30      180  16.6666667        APPLSYSD
APPLSYS   FND_TERRITORIES             11      244  4.50819672            FNDD
```

Detecting Object Fragmentation

Object fragmentation can damage performance in one of two ways:

- If there are objects in dictionary-managed tablespaces that have a maximum extent limit set to something other than unlimited, the objects could run out of space.

- A result of repeated insert and delete activity is that tables can become internally fragmented and contain much wasted space. In the same way, indexes can become fragmented so that their depth reaches unacceptable levels. This predicament will be covered in the next section.

How can a DBA tell if the objects are getting close to hitting their maximum extent limit? This is actually quite easy to accomplish.

If version 8 or higher of Oracle is in use, the *maxext8.sql* script can be employed:

🖫 maxext8.sql

```
-- ***************************************************
-- Copyright © 2005 by Rampant TechPress
-- This script is free for non-commercial purposes
-- with no warranties.  Use at your own risk.
--
-- To license this script for a commercial purpose,
-- contact info@rampant.cc
-- ***************************************************

select
        owner,
        decode(partition_name,NULL,segment_name,segment_name ||
        '.' || partition_name) segment_name,
        segment_type,
        extents,
        max_extents,
        initial_extent,
        next_extent,
        tablespace_name
from
        sys.dba_segments
where
        max_extents - extents <= 5 and
        segment_type <> 'CACHE'
order by
        1,2,3;
```

The following output shows objects nearing their maximum extent limit:

	OWNER	SEGMENT_NAME	SEGMENT_TYPE	EXTENTS	MAX_EXTENTS	INITIAL_EXTENT	NEXT_EXTENT	TABLESPACE_NAME
1	ERADMIN	CANT_EXTEND	TABLE	3	4	131072	131072	USER_DATA
2	USER21	TABLE1	TABLE	1	1	16384	6144000	USER_DATA
3	USER21	TABLE2	TABLE	1	1	106496	8192	USER_DATA
4	USER21	TABLE3	TABLE	1	1	106496	8192	USER_DATA

Figure 5.1: *Output showing objects nearing their maximum extent limit*

Another extent problem arises when an object in a dictionary-managed tablespace cannot extend because of a lack of contiguous free space.

To uncover this type of problem, the *objdef.sql* script can be used:

🖫 objdef.sql

```
-- **************************************************
-- Copyright © 2005 by Rampant TechPress
-- This script is free for non-commercial purposes
-- with no warranties.  Use at your own risk.
--
-- To license this script for a commercial purpose,
-- contact info@rampant.cc
-- **************************************************

select
    a.owner,
    a.segment_name,
    a.segment_type,
    a.tablespace_name,
    a.next_extent,
    max(c.bytes) max_contig_space
from
    sys.dba_segments a,
    sys.dba_free_space c
where
    a.tablespace_name = c.tablespace_name and
    a.next_extent >
        (select
             max(bytes)
         from
             sys.dba_free_space b
         where
             a.tablespace_name = b.tablespace_name and
             b.tablespace_name = c.tablespace_name)
group by
        a.owner,
        a.segment_name,
        a.tablespace_name,
        a.segment_type,
        a.next_extent
```

The following output shows the objects that have a space deficit in their parent tablespace:

	OWNER	SEGMENT_NAME	SEGMENT_TYPE	TABLESPACE_NAME	NEXT_EXTENT	MAX_CONTIG_SPACE
1	BAD_GUY	ADMISSION	TABLE PARTITION	USER_DATA	104857600	64749568
2	ERADMIN	ADMISSION	TABLE PARTITION	USER_DATA	104857600	64749568
3	ERADMIN	REF440	INDEX	USER_DATA	102400000	64749568
4	USER21	TABLE1	TABLE	USER_DATA	6144000	4767744
5	SYS	C_FILE#_BLOCK#	CLUSTER	SYSTEM	335872	245760
6	SYS	EMBARCADERO_EXPLAIN_PLAN	TABLE	SYSTEM	507904	245760
7	SYS	I_IDL_SB41	INDEX	SYSTEM	335872	245760
8	SYS	I_IDL_UB11	INDEX	SYSTEM	1146880	245760
9	SYS	I_IDL_UB21	INDEX	SYSTEM	335872	245760
10	SYS	JAVASNM$	TABLE	SYSTEM	507904	245760

Figure 5.2: *Output showing objects that have a space deficit in their parent tablespace*

Correcting Object Fragmentation

The prescription for correcting object fragmentation is generally total object reorganization. Such a procedure used to be fraught with errors and fear, even when third party software products were used. Fortunately, this is not the case any longer as Oracle has provided more built-in reorganization capabilities with each new release, and has even gone so far as to grant online reorganization abilities for certain object types.

The next section will cover, in detail, the reorganization techniques and methods that can be used to fix objects when they need to be reorganized.

Removing Storage-Related Performance Vampires

While storage-related problems can cause an instant hang in an otherwise smoothly running database, they can also slowly rob a system of its good performance over time. This happens when once well organized objects become not so well-organized. Such situations are not always difficult to diagnose if the DBA is looking in the right place.

Detecting Space-Related Object Performance Problems

What are some of the space-related object problems to be on the lookout for? With respect to tables, there are at least two different anomalies that can cause problems.

Table Diagnostics

Tables that suffer from high levels of wasted space could definitely be causing the database to spin in undesirable ways. The other problem that might exist is one of chained or migrated rows. Row chaining has already been covered to some degree while reviewing object access patterns. Now row chaining will be explored from a space management point of view.

Under normal circumstances, a row of data should fit completely inside one Oracle block. Sometimes, however, this is not the case, and the table suddenly finds itself containing chained or migrated rows, which are rows that span more than one data block.

Chaining occurs when a row is initially too large to fit inside one block. Two or more blocks are used by Oracle to hold the row. Migration deals with rows that have grown so big that they can no longer be contained within their original block. When this occurs, Oracle relocates the row out of its original block into another block but leaves a pointer behind to indicate the relocation.

Both chaining and migration force Oracle to perform more than one I/O to retrieve data that could normally be obtained with a single I/O operation. The end result is degraded performance.

How can a DBA determine the levels of wasted space in tables, plus find out if they suffer from a chained or migrated row problem? The scripts below will provide all the answers. They will locate tables that contain 25% or more wasted space.

As a bonus, the scripts also calculate the chained row ratio for a table, the percentage of used extents to maximum extents, and determine if the object can extend into its next block of free space. In other words, these are nice reorganization diagnostic scripts.

If Oracle8 or higher is in use, the *tabreorg8.sql* script can be employed:

🖫 tabreorg8.sql

```
-- **************************************************
-- Copyright © 2005 by Rampant TechPress
-- This script is free for non-commercial purposes
-- with no warranties.  Use at your own risk.
--
-- To license this script for a commercial purpose,
-- contact info@rampant.cc
-- **************************************************

select
        /*+ RULE */
        owner,
```

```
        segment_name table_name,
        segment_type,
        round(bytes/1024,2) table_kb,
        num_rows,
        blocks,
        empty_blocks,
        hwm highwater_mark,
        avg_used_blocks,
        greatest(round(100 * (nvl(hwm - avg_used_blocks,0) /
        greatest(nvl(hwm,1),1) ),2),0) block_inefficiency,
        chain_pct,
        max_extent_pct,
        extents,
        max_extents,
        decode(greatest(max_free_space -
        next_extent,0),0,'n','y') can_extend_space,
        next_extent,
        max_free_space,
        o_tablespace_name tablespace_name
from
(select
        a.owner owner,
        segment_name,
        segment_type,
        bytes,
        num_rows,
        a.blocks blocks,
        b.empty_blocks empty_blocks,
        a.blocks - b.empty_blocks - 1 hwm,
        decode(round((b.avg_row_len * num_rows *
        (1 + (pct_free/100))) /
        c.blocksize,0),0,1,round((b.avg_row_len * num_rows *
        (1 + (pct_free/100))) / c.blocksize,0)) + 2
        avg_used_blocks,
        round(100 * (nvl(b.chain_cnt,0) /
        greatest(nvl(b.num_rows,1),1)),2)
        chain_pct,
        a.extents extents,
        round(100 * (a.extents / a.max_extents),2) max_extent_pct,
        a.max_extents max_extents,
        b.next_extent next_extent,
        b.tablespace_name o_tablespace_name
    from
        sys.dba_segments a,
        sys.dba_all_tables b,
        sys.ts$ c
  where
        ( a.owner = b.owner ) and
        ( segment_name = table_name ) and
        ( ( segment_type = 'TABLE ) ) and
        b.tablespace_name = c.name
union all
select
        a.owner owner,
        segment_name || '.' || b.partition_name,
        segment_type,
        bytes,
        b.num_rows,
        a.blocks blocks,
```

```
           b.empty_blocks empty_blocks,
           a.blocks - b.empty_blocks - 1 hwm,
           decode(round((b.avg_row_len * b.num_rows * (1 +
           (b.pct_free/100))) /
           c.blocksize,0),0,1,round((b.avg_row_len * b.num_rows *
           (1 + (b.pct_free/100))) / c.blocksize,0)) + 2
           avg_used_blocks,
           round(100 * (nvl(b.chain_cnt,0) /
           greatest(nvl(b.num_rows,1),1)),2)
           chain_pct,
           a.extents extents,
           round(100 * (a.extents / a.max_extents),2) max_extent_pct,
           a.max_extents max_extents,
           b.next_extent,
           b.tablespace_name o_tablespace_name
    from
           sys.dba_segments a,
           sys.dba_tab_partitions b,
           sys.ts$ c,
           sys.dba_tables d
    where
           ( a.owner = b.table_owner ) and
           ( segment_name = b.table_name ) and
           ( ( segment_type = TABLE PARTITION' ) ) and
           b.tablespace_name = c.name and
           d.owner = b.table_owner and
           d.table_name = b.table_name and
           a.partition_name = b.partition_name),
(   select
           tablespace_name f_tablespace_name,
           max(bytes) max_free_space
    from
           sys.dba_free_space
    group by tablespace_name)
    where
           f_tablespace_name = o_tablespace_name and
           greatest(round(100 * (nvl(hwm - avg_used_blocks,0) /
           greatest(nvl(hwm,1),1) ),2),0) > 25
order by 10 desc, 1 asc,2 asc
```

The following partial output shows the wasted space amounts and chained row percentage of database tables:

	OWNER	TABLE_NAME	SEGMENT_TYPE	TABLE_KB	NUM_ROWS	BLOCKS	EMPTY_BLOCKS	HIGHWATER_MARK	AVG_USED_BLOCKS	BLOCK_INEFFICIENCY	CHAIN_PCT
1	ERADMIN	EMP	TABLE	19072	0	2384	120	2263	3	99.87	0
2	SYS	OBJ$	TABLE	2440	4387	305	1	303	43	85.61	0
3	SYS	ADMISSION_NO	TABLE	256	1520	32	0	31	5	83.87	0
4	USER21	TABLE1	TABLE	256	0	32	15	16	3	81.25	0
5	USER21	TABLE2	TABLE	256	130	32	12	19	4	78.95	0
6	USER21	TABLE3	TABLE	176	40	22	0	21	11	47.62	82.5
7	ERADMIN	EMBARCADERO	TABLE	384	2217	48	6	41	27	34.15	0
8	SYS	PROCEDURE$	TABLE	80	418	10	3	6	4	33.33	0
9	BRKADMIN	INVESTMENT	TABLE	64	412	8	0	7	5	28.57	0

Figure 5.3: *Wasted space amounts and chained row percentage of tables*

To see the shape that all database tables are in, remove the *where* clause that restricts the output to only those tables having a block efficiency ranking of 25% or higher.

There are a couple of columns to hone in on. The block inefficiency ranking will highlight any table that suffers from a lot of wasted space. For example, the ERADMIN.EMP table has no rows in it but sports a large high-water mark. Therefore, it tops the list in terms of tables with high amounts of wasted space.

The chain percent column is also of interest. This column indicates how badly the table suffers from chained or migrated rows. The USER21.TABLE3 table appears to be in bad shape with respect to chained/migrated rows. Generally, if a table appears to have a chain percent of 25% or more, the DBA should look into reorganizing it.

Like tables, indexes can become disorganized due to heavy DML activity. In the next section, diagnosing index performance problems will be covered.

Index Diagnostics

There has been much debate in the DBA world as to what to look for when determining if an index is in poor shape, but the *idxreorg8.sql* script below should help.

This script displays the level and clustering factor of the index, calculates the percentage of used extents to maximum extents, and determines if the index can extend into its next block of free space.

For Oracle8 and higher, the *idxreorg8.sql* script can be used:

🖫 idxreorg8.sql

```
-- ***************************************************
-- Copyright © 2005 by Rampant TechPress
-- This script is free for non-commercial purposes
-- with no warranties.  Use at your own risk.
--
-- To license this script for a commercial purpose,
```

```
-- contact info@rampant.cc
-- *************************************************
select
        /*+ RULE */
        owner,
        segment_name index_name,
        segment_type,
        round(bytes/1024,2) index_kb,
        num_rows,
        clustering_factor,
        blevel,
        blocks,
        max_extent_pct,
        extents,
        max_extents,
        decode(greatest(max_free_space -
        next_extent,0),0,'n','y') can_extend_space,
        next_extent,
        max_free_space,
        o_tablespace_name
from
(select
        a.owner owner,
        segment_name,
        segment_type,
        bytes,
        num_rows,
        b.clustering_factor,
        b.blevel,
        a.blocks blocks,
        a.extents extents,
        round(100 * (a.extents / a.max_extents),2)
        max_extent_pct,
        a.max_extents max_extents,
        b.next_extent next_extent,
        b.tablespace_name o_tablespace_name
    from
        sys.dba_segments a,
        sys.dba_indexes b,
        sys.ts$ c
  where
        ( a.owner = b.owner ) and
        ( segment_name = index_name ) and
        ( ( segment_type = 'INDEX' ) ) and
        b.tablespace_name = c.name
 union all
 select
        a.owner owner,
        segment_name || '.' || b.partition_name,
        segment_type,
        bytes,
        b.num_rows,
        b.clustering_factor,
        b.blevel,
        a.blocks blocks,
        a.extents extents,
        round(100 * (a.extents / a.max_extents),2)
        max_extent_pct,
        a.max_extents max_extents,
```

```
        b.next_extent,
        b.tablespace_name o_tablespace_name
    from
        sys.dba_segments a,
        sys.dba_ind_partitions b,
        sys.ts$ c,
        sys.dba_indexes d
    where
        ( a.owner = b.index_owner ) and
        ( segment_name = b.index_name ) and
        ( ( segment_type = INDEX PARTITION' ) ) and
        b.tablespace_name = c.name and
        d.owner = b.index_owner and
        d.index_name = b.index_name and
        a.partition_name = b.partition_name),
(  select
        tablespace_name f_tablespace_name,
        max(bytes) max_free_space
    from
        sys.dba_free_space
    group by tablespace_name)
where
    f_tablespace_name = o_tablespace_name
order
    by 1,2;
```

The following partial output shows the index reorganization diagnostics:

OWNER	INDEX_NAME	SEGMENT_TYPE	INDEX_KB	NUM_ROWS	CLUSTERING_FACTOR	BLEVEL	BLOCKS	MAX_EXTENT_PCT	EXTI
7	AURORAJISUTILITY$ SNS$NODE_INDEX	INDEX	64	84	10	0	8	0	
8	AURORAJISUTILITY$ SNS$PERM_INDEX	INDEX	64	312	1	0	8	0	
9	AURORAJISUTILITY$ SNS$REFADDR_INDEX	INDEX	64	291	5	0	8	0	
10	AURORAJISUTILITY$ SNS$SHARED$OBJ_INDEX	INDEX	64	0	0	0	8	0	
11	AURORAJISUTILITY$ SYS_C0011031	INDEX	64	117	1	0	8	0	
12	AURORAJISUTILITY$ SYS_C0011032	INDEX	64	0	0	0	8	0	
13	BILLY	SYS_C0011859	INDEX	128	0	0	0	16	.02	
14	BILLY	SYS_C0011860	INDEX	128	1	1	0	16	.02	
15	BRKADMIN	BROKER_COMMISSION_N1	INDEX	32	0	0	0	4	0	
16	BRKADMIN	BROKER_N1	INDEX	32	20	1	0	4	0	
17	BRKADMIN	CLIENT_N1	INDEX	32	500	8	0	4	0	

Figure 5.4: *Partial output showing index reorganization diagnostics*

The presence of index levels beyond four, or bad clustering factors for indexes with supposed high cardinality, should lead a DBA to investigate whether the index should be reorganized or even maintained in the system.

The following script can used to evaluate the clustering factors and index levels of appropriate indexes.

cfb_ratio.sql

```
-- *****************************************************
-- Copyright © 2005 by Rampant TechPress
-- This script is free for non-commercial purposes
-- with no warranties.  Use at your own risk.
--
-- To license this script for a commercial purpose,
-- contact info@rampant.cc
-- *****************************************************

-- Mike Ault
--
column table_name format a20 heading 'Table|Name'
column index_name format a20 heading 'Index|Name'
column dirty_blocks heading 'Dirty|Blocks'
column clustering_factor heading 'Clustering|Factor'
column cfb_ratio heading 'Clustering Factor|To Blocks Ratio' format
99,999.99
column owner format a15 heading 'Owner'
ttitle 'Clustering Factor to Block Ratio Report'
set lines 132 verify off pages 55 feedback off
break on owner on table_name
spool rep_out\&&database\cfb_ratio
select t.owner,t.table_name,i.index_name, t.num_rows, t.blocks
dirty_blocks,i.clustering_factor,
i.clustering_factor/decode(t.blocks,0,decode(i.clustering_factor,0,1,i.clust
ering_factor),t.blocks) cfb_ratio, i.blevel
from dba_tables t, dba_indexes i
where t.owner=i.table_owner and t.table_name=i.table_name
and t.owner not in
('SYS','SYSTEM','DBAUTIL','OUTLN','DBSNMP','SPOTLIGHT','PERFSTAT','RMAN','IW
ATCH')
order by
t.owner,i.clustering_factor/decode(t.blocks,0,decode(i.clustering_factor,0,1
,i.clustering_factor),t.blocks) desc,t.table_name,i.index_name
/
spool off
set lines 80 pages 22 feedback on verify on
clear columns
ttitle off

rem and
i.clustering_factor/decode(t.blocks,0,decode(i.clustering_factor,0,1,i.clust
ering_factor),t.blocks)>10
```

This report displays the indexes that may have statistics that indicate they need reorganization, rebuilding, or need to have their columns re-ordered.

```
Wed Jun 16                                                    page    1
                   Clustering Factor to Block Ratio Report

                                                          Cluster
                                                        Factor to
          Table               Index            NUM   Dirty  Cluster   Blocks
Owner Name                     Name            ROWS  Blocks  Factor  Ratio LEVEL
----- -------------------- -------------------- ------- -------- ---------- --------- -----
```

AK	AK_ATTRIBUTES_TL	AK_ATTRIBUTES_TL_U1	71800	995	33272	33.44	2
	AK_ATTRIBUTES	AK_ATTRIBUTES_U1	70060	1150	33872	29.45	1
	AK_REGIONS_TL	AK_REGIONS_TL_U1	15877	215	5520	25.67	1
	AK_FOREIGN_KEYS	AK_FOREIGN_KEYS_N1	1256	30	569	18.97	1
	AK_REGIONS	AK_REGIONS_U1	15877	350	6132	17.52	1
	AK_OBJECTS	AK_OBJECTS_U1	934	25	363	14.52	1
	AK_OBJECTS_TL	AK_OBJECTS_TL_U1	934	25	345	13.80	1
	AK_FOREIGN_KEYS	AK_FOREIGN_KEYS_U1	1256	30	406	13.53	1
	AK_FOREIGN_KEYS_TL	AK_FOREIGN_KEYS_TL_U1	1256	30	382	12.73	1
	AK_REGION_ITEMS_TL	AK_REGION_ITEMS_TL_U1	72520	2435	29295	12.03	2
	AK_WEB_USER_SEC_ATTR _VALUES	AK_WEB_USER_SEC_ATTR _VALUES_N1	314	5	54	10.80	1
	AK_UNIQUE_KEYS	AK_UNIQUE_KEYS_U1	728	25	261	10.44	1
	AK_CUSTOM_REGION_ITE MS	AK_CUSTOM_REGION_ITE MS_U1	9850	195	2018	10.35	2
	AK_CUSTOM_REGION_ITE MS_TL	AK_CUSTOM_REGION_ITE MS_TL_N1	9850	195	2014	10.33	2
	AK_CUSTOM_REGION_ITE MS	AK_CUSTOM_REGION_ITE MS_N2	9850	195	1957	10.04	2
AMS	AMS_LIST_SRC_FIELDS_ TL	AMS_LIST_SRC_FIELDS_ TL_N1	978	25	644	25.76	1
	AMS_CUSTOM_SETUP_ATT R	AMS_CUSTOM_SETUP_ATT R_N2	1072	25	514	20.56	1
		AMS_CUSTOM_SETUP_ATT R_U2	1072	25	407	16.28	1
	AMS_STATUS_ORDER_RUL	AMS_STATUS_ORDER_RUL	298	10	119	11.90	1

Locating Hot I/O Objects

Once the locations of the hotspots in the database are known with respect to storage structures, it is time to drill down and locate the objects that are most in demand. There is no doubt that hub tables in a system can cause a major I/O bottleneck if they are not correctly designed and implemented.

To get an idea of which objects have been the favorite of a database's SQL calls, the following *toptables.sql* query can be run. This query returns the top 100 objects as determined by SQL statement execution:

🖫 **toptables.sql**

```
-- ***************************************************
-- Copyright © 2005 by Rampant TechPress
-- This script is free for non-commercial purposes
-- with no warranties.  Use at your own risk.
--
-- To license this script for a commercial purpose,
-- contact info@rampant.cc
-- ***************************************************

select
   table_owner "table owner",
   table_name "table name",
   command "command issued",
   0 - executions    "executions",
   disk_reads "disk reads",
   gets "buffer gets",
```

```
    rows_processed "rows processed"
from
(select
        distinct executions,
                command,
                table_owner,
                table_name,
                gets,
                rows_processed,
                disk_reads
 from
(select
        decode (a.command_type ,
                2, 'insert ' ,
                3,'select ',
                6, 'update  ' ,
                7, 'delete ' ,
                26,'table lock  ') command ,
                c.owner table_owner,
                c.name table_name ,
                sum(a.disk_reads) disk_reads  ,
                sum(0 - a.executions) executions ,
                sum(a.buffer_gets) gets  ,
                sum(a.rows_processed) rows_processed
 from
        sys.v_$sql  a ,
        sys.v_$object_dependency b ,
        sys.v_$db_object_cache   c
 where
        a.command_type in (2,3,6,7,26)and
        b.from_address = a.address and
        b.to_owner = c.owner and
        b.to_name= c.name and
        c.type = 'table' and
        c.owner not in ('SYS','SYSTEM')
 group by
        a.command_type , c.owner  , c.name )  )
where
        rownum <= 100;
```

Output from the above query might look like the following:

	TABLE OWNER	TABLE NAME	COMMAND ISSUED	EXECUTIONS	DISK READS	BUFFER GETS	ROWS PROCESSED
1	ERADMIN	TESTXML_927	SELECT	13	2	131	0
2	ERADMIN	ADMISSION	SELECT	7	13	184	2508
3	ERADMIN	TESTXML_927NEW2	SELECT	4	0	94	0
4	ERADMIN	TESTLOB_NEW	SELECT	2	5	127	2
5	ERADMIN	ADMISSION_TEST	SELECT	1	1	111	0
6	ERADMIN	MEDICATION_DISP	SELECT	1	1	32	0
7	ERADMIN	PATIENT_PROCEDURE	SELECT	1	5	23	0
8	ERADMIN	TESTXML_927NEW	SELECT	1	0	53	3
9	WMSYS	WM$ENV_VARS	SELECT	1	8	403	1
10	WMSYS	WM$VERSIONED_TABLES	SELECT	1	8	403	1
11	WMSYS	WM$VERSION_HIERARCHY_TABLE	SELECT	1	8	403	1

Figure 5.5: *Top tables query output*

The observation of a single table with a lot of DML activity provides a clue that it may be a potential bottleneck for the system. Other things to consider when reviewing output from this query include:

- Small frequently-accessed tables should be considered candidates for the Oracle KEEP buffer pool in Oracle8i and higher or be set to CACHE in Oracle7 and higher.

- Large tables that are frequently accessed and scanned should be reviewed to determine if they could be partitioned. Partitioning can reduce scan times if only one or a handful of partitions can be scanned instead of the entire table. High amounts of disk reads for tables in the above query are red flags that can help identify partitioning possibilities.

- If it is possible that large tables are being scanned and Oracle9i is being used, the new *v_$sql_plan* view can be implemented to validate those suspicions.

The *largescan9i.sql* query uses this new view to show which large tables, defined in the query as tables over 1MB, are being scanned in the database:

🖫 largescan9i.sql

```
-- *************************************************
-- Copyright © 2005 by Rampant TechPress
-- This script is free for non-commercial purposes
-- with no warranties.  Use at your own risk.
--
-- To license this script for a commercial purpose,
-- contact info@rampant.cc
-- *************************************************

select
   table_owner,
   table_name,
   table_type,
   size_kb,
   statement_count,
   reference_count,
   executions,
   executions * reference_count total_scans
from
   (select
       a.object_owner table_owner,
       a.object_name table_name,
```

```
      b.segment_type table_type,
      b.bytes / 1024 size_kb,
      sum(c.executions ) executions,
      count( distinct a.hash_value ) statement_count,
      count( * ) reference_count
   from
      sys.v_$sql_plan a,
      sys.dba_segments b,
      sys.v_$sql c
   where
      a.object_owner (+) = b.owner
   and
         a.object_name (+) = b.segment_name
and
         b.segment_type IN ('TABLE', 'TABLE PARTITION')
and
         a.operation LIKE '%TABLE%'
and
         a.options = 'FULL'
and
         a.hash_value = c.hash_value
and
         b.bytes / 1024 > 1024
group by
   a.object_owner,
   a.object_name,
   a.operation,
   b.bytes / 1024,
   b.segment_type
order by
   4 desc, 1, 2 );
```

The following output is from the 9i large table scan query:

	TABLE_OWNER	TABLE_NAME	TABLE_TYPE	SIZE_KB	STATEMENT_COUNT	REFERENCE_COUNT	EXECUTIONS	TOTAL_SCANS
1	ERADMIN	EMP	TABLE	19456	2	2	2	4
2	SYS	DEPENDENCY$	TABLE	3496	1	1	1	1
3	SYS	OBJ$	TABLE	3136	4	7	25	175

Figure 5.6: *Output from the 9i large table scan query*

After finding what is being accessed the most, the next step might be to find what SQL statement(s) are causing all the activity. Please refer to the chapter on SQL to investigate further.

The powerful reporting capabilities for objects in 10g will be covered next.

Oracle10g

The query below will extract important costing information for all objects involved in each query. In this situation, SYS objects are not counted:

🖫 **awr_sql_object_char.sql**

```
-- ***************************************************
-- Copyright © 2005 by Rampant TechPress
-- This script is free for non-commercial purposes
-- with no warranties.  Use at your own risk.
--
-- To license this script for a commercial purpose,
-- contact info@rampant.cc
-- ***************************************************

col c1 heading 'Owner'            format a13
col c2 heading 'Object|Type'      format a15

col c3 heading 'Object|Name'      format a25
col c4 heading 'Average|CPU|Cost' format 9,999,999
col c5 heading 'Average|IO|Cost'  format 9,999,999


break on c1 skip 2
break on c2 skip 2


select
  p.object_owner    c1,
  p.object_type     c2,
  p.object_name     c3,
  avg(p.cpu_cost)   c4,
  avg(p.io_cost)    c5
from
  dba_hist_sql_plan p
where
      p.object_name is not null
   and
      p.object_owner <> 'SYS'
group by
  p.object_owner,
  p.object_type,
  p.object_name
order by
  1,2,4 desc
;
```

The following is a sample of the output. It shows the average CPU and I/O costs for all objects that participate in queries, over time periods:

Owner	Object Type	Object Name	Average CPU Cost	Average IO Cost
OLAPSYS	INDEX	CWM$CUBEDIMENSIONUSE_IDX	200	0
OLAPSYS	INDEX (UNIQUE)	CWM$DIMENSION_PK		
OLAPSYS		CWM$CUBE_PK	7,321	0
OLAPSYS		CWM$MODEL_PK	7,321	0
OLAPSYS	TABLE	CWM$CUBE	7,911	0
OLAPSYS		CWM$MODEL	7,321	0
OLAPSYS		CWM2$CUBE	7,121	2
OLAPSYS		CWM$CUBEDIMENSIONUSE	730	0
MYSCHEMA	INDEX (UNIQUE)	STATS$TIME_MODEL_STATNAME_PK	39,242	2
MYSCHEMA		CUSTOMER_DETS_PK	21,564	2
MYSCHEMA		STATS$SGASTAT_U	21,442	2
MYSCHEMA		STATS$SQL_SUMMARY_PK	16,842	2
MYSCHEMA		STATS$SQLTEXT_PK	14,442	1
MYSCHEMA		STATS$IDLE_EVENT_PK	8,171	0
MYSCHEMA	TABLE	CUSTOMER_DETS	5,571,375	24
MYSCHEMA		STATS$FILE_HISTOGRAM	1,373,396	5
MYSCHEMA		STATS$SYSTEM_EVENT	996,571	6
MYSCHEMA		STATS$LATCH	462,161	5
MYSCHEMA		STATS$SQL_SUMMARY	440,038	7
MYSCHEMA		STATS$PARAMETER	361,439	5
MYSCHEMA		STATS$FILESTATXS	224,227	3
MYSCHEMA		STATS$WAITSTAT	144,554	3
MYSCHEMA		STATS$TEMP_HISTOGRAM	126,304	3
MYSCHEMA		STATS$LIBRARYCACHE	102,846	3
MYSCHEMA		STATS$TEMPSTATXS	82,762	3
MYSCHEMA		STATS$SGASTAT	51,807	5
MYSCHEMA		STATS$SQLTEXT	17,781	2
MYSCHEMA		STATS$SQL_PLAN_USAGE	0	2
SPV	INDEX (UNIQUE)	WSPV_REP_PK	7,321	0
SPV		SPV_ALERT_DEF_PK	7,321	0
SPV	TABLE	WSPV_REPORTS	789,052	28
SPV		SPV_MONITOR	54,092	3
SPV		SPV_SAVED_CHARTS	38,337	3
SPV		SPV_DB_LIST	37,487	3
SPV		SPV_SCHED	35,607	3
SPV		SPV_FV_STAT	35,607	3
SPV		SPV_ALERT_DEF	15,868	1
SPV		SPV_BASELINES	7,121	2
SPV		SPV_ALERT_HISTORY	7,121	2
SPV		SPV_STORED_SNAP_RANGES	7,121	2

This script can be easily changed to allow a table name to be entered and the changes in access details seen over a period of time:

🖬 awr_sql_object_char_detail.sql

```
-- ****************************************************
-- Copyright © 2005 by Rampant TechPress
-- This script is free for non-commercial purposes
-- with no warranties.  Use at your own risk.
--
-- To license this script for a commercial purpose,
-- contact info@rampant.cc
-- ****************************************************

accept tabname prompt 'Enter Table Name:'

col c0 heading 'Begin|Interval|time' format a8
col c1 heading 'Owner'               format a10
col c2 heading 'Object|Type'         format a10
col c3 heading 'Object|Name'         format a15
col c4 heading 'Average|CPU|Cost'    format 9,999,999
col c5 heading 'Average|IO|Cost'     format 9,999,999


break on c1 skip 2
break on c2 skip 2

select
  to_char(sn.begin_interval_time,'mm-dd hh24') c0,
  p.object_owner                               c1,
  p.object_type                                c2,
  p.object_name                                c3,
  avg(p.cpu_cost)                              c4,
  avg(p.io_cost)                               c5
from
  dba_hist_sql_plan p,
  dba_hist_sqlstat  st,
  dba_hist_snapshot sn
where
  p.object_name is not null
and
   p.object_owner <> 'SYS'
and
   p.object_name = 'CUSTOMER_DETS'
and
  p.sql_id = st.sql_id
and
  st.snap_id = sn.snap_id
group by
  to_char(sn.begin_interval_time,'mm-dd hh24'),
  p.object_owner,
  p.object_type,
  p.object_name
order by
  1,2,3 desc
;
```

This script is extremely useful because the changes to the table's access patterns can be seen over time:

```
Begin                                           Average    Average
Interval            Object     Object               CPU         IO
time      Owner     Type       Name               Cost       Cost
--------  --------- ---------  ---------------- ---------- ----------
10-25 17  MYSCHEMA  TABLE      CUSTOMER_DETS      28,935          3
10-26 15  MYSCHEMA             CUSTOMER_DETS      28,935          3
10-27 18  MYSCHEMA             CUSTOMER_DETS   5,571,375         24
10-28 12  MYSCHEMA             CUSTOMER_DETS      28,935          3
```

The time-series plot for the table access pattern shown in Figure 5.7 was produced by the WISE tool:

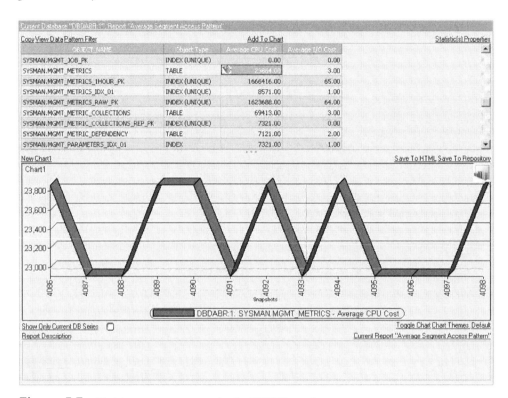

Figure 5.7: *Table access pattern plot in WISE tool.*

Now that the important table structures have been examined, information on how to obtain spectacular reports from this AWR data to reveal hidden bottlenecks and how the database is performing can be introduced.

Viewing Table and Index Access with AWR

One of the problems in Oracle9i was the single bit-flag that was used to monitor index usage. The flag could be set with the "alter index xxx monitoring usage" command. To see if the index was accessed, the *v$object_usage* view needs to be queried.

The goal of any index access is to use the most selective index for a query, which would be the one that produces the smallest number of rows. The Oracle data dictionary is usually quite good at this, but it is up to the DBA to define the index. Missing function-based indexes are a common source of sub-optimal SQL execution because Oracle will not use an indexed column unless the WHERE clause matches the index column exactly.

Tracking SQL Nested Loop Joins

Nested loop joins are the most common method utilized by Oracle to match rows in multiple tables. Nested loop joins always invoke an index, and they are never parallelized.

The *awr_nested_join_alert.sql* script can be used to count nested loop joins per hour:

🖫 awr_nested_join_alert.sql

```
-- *************************************************
-- Copyright © 2005 by Rampant TechPress
-- This script is free for non-commercial purposes
-- with no warranties.  Use at your own risk.
--
-- To license this script for a commercial purpose,
-- contact info@rampant.cc
-- *************************************************

col c1 heading 'Date'                 format a20
col c2 heading 'Nested|Loops|Count'   format 99,999,999
col c3 heading 'Rows|Processed'       format 99,999,999
col c4 heading 'Disk|Reads'           format 99,999,999
col c5 heading 'CPU|Time'             format 99,999,999


accept nested_thr char prompt 'Enter Nested Join Threshold: '
```

```
ttitle 'Nested Join Threshold|&nested_thr'

select
   to_char(sn.begin_interval_time,'yy-mm-dd hh24')  c1,
   count(*)                                          c2,
   sum(st.rows_processed_delta)                      c3,
   sum(st.disk_reads_delta)                          c4,
   sum(st.cpu_time_delta)                            c5
from
   dba_hist_snapshot sn,
   dba_hist_sql_plan  p,
   dba_hist_sqlstat   st
where
   st.sql_id = p.sql_id
and
   sn.snap_id = st.snap_id
and
   p.operation = 'NESTED LOOPS'
having
   count(*) > &hash_thr
group by
   begin_interval_time;
```

The output follows below. The number of total nested loop joins during the snapshot period along with a count of the rows processed and the associated disk I/O can be seen. This report is useful when the DBA needs to know if increasing *pga_aggregate_target* will improve performance.

```
              Nested Loop Join Thresholds

              Nested
              Loops        Rows         Disk         CPU
Date          Count     Processed       Reads        Time
------------------  ---------  -----------  -----------  -----------
04-10-10 16        22          750          796      4,017,301
04-10-10 17        25          846            6      3,903,560
04-10-10 19        26          751        1,430      4,165,270
04-10-10 20        24          920            3      3,940,002
04-10-10 21        25          782            5      3,816,152
04-10-11 02        26          905            0      3,935,547
04-10-11 03        22        1,001            0      3,918,891
04-10-11 04        29          757            8      3,939,071
04-10-11 05        28          757          745      4,395,197
04-10-11 06        24          839            4      4,010,775
```

In the report above, nested loops are favored by SQL that returns a smaller number of *rows_processed* than hash joins, which tend to return larger result sets.

The *awr_sql_index.sql* script exposes the cumulative usage of database indexes:

🖫 awr_sql_index.sql

```
-- ****************************************************
-- Copyright © 2005 by Rampant TechPress
-- This script is free for non-commercial purposes
-- with no warranties.  Use at your own risk.
--
-- To license this script for a commercial purpose,
-- contact info@rampant.cc
-- ****************************************************

col c0 heading 'Begin|Interval|time'  format a8
col c1 heading 'Index|Name'           format a20
col c2 heading 'Disk|Reads'           format 99,999,999
col c3 heading 'Rows|Processed'       format 99,999,999
select
  to_char(s.begin_interval_time,'mm-dd hh24')  c0,
  p.object_name              c1,
  sum(t.disk_reads_total)    c2,
  sum(t.rows_processed_total) c3
from
      dba_hist_sql_plan p,
      dba_hist_sqlstat  t,
      dba_hist_snapshot s
where
      p.sql_id = t.sql_id
   and
      t.snap_id = s.snap_id
   and
      p.object_type like '%INDEX%'
group by
      to_char(s.begin_interval_time,'mm-dd hh24'),
      p.object_name
order by
      c0,c1,c2 desc
;
```

The following listing is a sample of the output in which the stress on every important index over time can be seen. This information is important for placing index blocks into the KEEP pool to reduce disk reads and for determining the optimal setting for the all important *optimizer_index_caching* parameter.

```
Begin
Interval Index                        Disk         Rows
time     Name                        Reads    Processed
-------- -------------------- ----------- -----------
10-14 12 I_CACHE_STATS_1                         114
10-14 12 I_COL_USAGE$                 201       8,984
10-14 12 I_FILE1                        2           0
```

```
10-14 12 I_IND1                          93          604
10-14 12 I_JOB_NEXT                       1      247,816
10-14 11 I_KOPM1                          4        2,935
10-14 11 I_MON_MODS$_OBJ                 12       28,498
10-14 11 I_OBJ1                      72,852          604
10-14 11 I_PARTOBJ$                      93          604
10-14 11 I_SCHEDULER_JOB2                 4            0
10-14 11 SYS_C002433                    302        4,629
10-14 11 SYS_IOT_TOP_8540                 0       75,544
10-14 11 SYS_IOT_TOP_8542                 1        4,629
10-14 11 WRH$_DATAFILE_PK                 2            0
10-14 10 WRH$_SEG_STAT_OBJ_PK           93          604
10-14 10 WRH$_TEMPFILE_PK                              0
10-14 10 WRI$_ADV_ACTIONS_PK            38        1,760
```

The above report quickly reveals the highest impact tables.

The *awr_sql_index_access.sql* script is one that will summarize index access by snapshot period:

🖫 awr_sql_index_access.sql

```
-- *****************************************************
--    Copyright © 2005 by Rampant TechPress Inc.
--    Free for non-commercial use!
--    To license, e-mail info@rampant.cc
-- *****************************************************

col c1 heading 'Begin|Interval|Time'    format a20
col c2 heading 'Index|Range|Scans' format 999,999
col c3 heading 'Index|Unique|Scans' format 999,999
col c4 heading 'Index|Full|Scans' format 999,999

select
  r.c1  c1,
  r.c2  c2,
  u.c2  c3,
  f.c2  c4
from
(
select
  to_char(sn.begin_interval_time,'yy-mm-dd hh24')  c1,
  count(1)                        c2
from
   dba_hist_sql_plan p,
   dba_hist_sqlstat  s,
   dba_hist_snapshot sn
where
   p.object_owner <> 'SYS'
and
   p.operation like '%INDEX%'
and
   p.options like '%RANGE%'
and
   p.sql_id = s.sql_id
```

```
and
  s.snap_id = sn.snap_id
group by
  to_char(sn.begin_interval_time,'yy-mm-dd hh24')
order by
1 ) r,
(
select
  to_char(sn.begin_interval_time,'yy-mm-dd hh24')  c1,
  count(1)                          c2
from
  dba_hist_sql_plan p,
  dba_hist_sqlstat  s,
  dba_hist_snapshot sn
where
  p.object_owner <> 'SYS'
and
  p.operation like '%INDEX%'
and
  p.options like '%UNIQUE%'
and
  p.sql_id = s.sql_id
and
  s.snap_id = sn.snap_id
group by
  to_char(sn.begin_interval_time,'yy-mm-dd hh24')
order by
1 ) u,
(
select
  to_char(sn.begin_interval_time,'yy-mm-dd hh24')  c1,
  count(1)                          c2
from
  dba_hist_sql_plan p,
  dba_hist_sqlstat  s,
  dba_hist_snapshot sn
where
  p.object_owner <> 'SYS'
and
  p.operation like '%INDEX%'
and
  p.options like '%FULL%'
and
  p.sql_id = s.sql_id
and
  s.snap_id = sn.snap_id
group by
  to_char(sn.begin_interval_time,'yy-mm-dd hh24')
order by
1 ) f
where
      r.c1 = u.c1
  and
      r.c1 = f.c1
;
```

The following sample output shows those specific times at which the database performs unique scans, index range scans, and index fast full scans:

Begin Interval Time	Index Range Scans	Index Unique Scans	Index Full Scans
04-10-21 15	36	35	2
04-10-21 19	10	8	2
04-10-21 20		8	2
04-10-21 21		8	2
04-10-21 22	11	8	3
04-10-21 23	16	11	3
04-10-22 00	10	9	1
04-10-22 01	11	8	3
04-10-22 02	12	8	1
04-10-22 03	10	8	3
04-10-22 04	11	8	2
04-10-22 05		8	3
04-10-22 06		8	2
04-10-22 07	10	8	3
04-10-22 08		8	2
04-10-22 09		8	2
04-10-22 10		10	4
04-10-22 11	11	8	1
04-10-22 12	9	7	3
04-10-22 13		7	2
04-10-22 14		8	2
04-10-22 15	10	8	3
04-10-22 17		9	3
04-10-22 18	11	9	3
04-10-22 19	10	9	3
04-10-22 20	11	9	2
04-10-22 21	10	8	3
04-10-22 22	11	8	1
04-10-22 23		9	3

SQL object usage can also be summarized by day of the week using the *awr_sql_object_avg_dy.sql* script:

🖫 awr_sql_object_avg_dy.sql

```
-- ***************************************************
-- Copyright © 2005 by Rampant TechPress
-- This script is free for non-commercial purposes
-- with no warranties.  Use at your own risk.
--
-- To license this script for a commercial purpose,
-- contact info@rampant.cc
-- ***************************************************

col c1 heading 'Object|Name'        format a30
col c2 heading 'Week Day'           format a15
```

```
col c3     heading 'Invocation|Count'     format 99,999,999

break on c1 skip 2
break on c2 skip 2

select

decode(c2,1,'Monday',2,'Tuesday',3,'Wednesday',4,'Thursday',5,'Friday',6,'Sa
turday',7,'Sunday') c2,
   c1,
   c3
from
(
select
   p.object_name               c1,
   to_char(sn.end_interval_time,'d')   c2,
   count(1)                    c3
from
   dba_hist_sql_plan   p,
   dba_hist_sqlstat    s,
   dba_hist_snapshot   sn
where
   p.object_owner <> 'SYS'
and
   p.sql_id = s.sql_id
and
   s.snap_id = sn.snap_id
group by
   p.object_name,
   to_char(sn.end_interval_time,'d')
order by
   c2,c1
)
;
```

The following output shows the top objects within the database during each snapshot period:

```
                  Object                          Invocation
Week Day          Name                               Count
---------------   ------------------------------   -----------
Monday            CUSTOMER                              44
                  CUSTOMER_ORDERS                       44
                  CUSTOMER_ORDERS_PRIMARY               44
                  MGMT_CURRENT_METRICS_PK               43
                  MGMT_FAILOVER_TABLE                   47
                  MGMT_JOB                             235
                  MGMT_JOB_EMD_STATUS_QUEUE             91
                  MGMT_JOB_EXECUTION                   235
                  MGMT_JOB_EXEC_IDX01                  235
                  MGMT_JOB_EXEC_SUMMARY                 94
                  MGMT_JOB_EXEC_SUMM_IDX04              94
                  MGMT_JOB_PK                          235
                  MGMT_METRICS                          65
                  MGMT_METRICS_1HOUR_PK                 43
Tuesday           CUSTOMER                              40
```

```
              CUSTOMER   _CHECK                      2
              CUSTOMER  _PRIMARY                     1
              CUSTOMER_ORDERS                       46
              CUSTOMER_ORDERS_PRIMARY               46
              LOGMNR_LOG$                            3
              LOGMNR_LOG$_PK                         3
              LOGSTDBY$PARAMETERS                    2
              MGMT_CURRENT_METRICS_PK               31
              MGMT_FAILOVER_TABLE                   42
              MGMT_JOB                             200
              MGMT_JOB_EMD_STATUS_QUEUE             78
              MGMT_JOB_EXECUTION                   200
              MGMT_JOB_EXEC_IDX01                  200
              MGMT_JOB_EXEC_SUMMARY                 80
              MGMT_JOB_EXEC_SUMM_IDX04              80
              MGMT_JOB_PK                          200
              MGMT_METRICS                          48
Wednesday     CURRENT_SEVERITY_PRIMARY_KEY           1
              MGMT_CURRENT_METRICS_PK               17
              MGMT_CURRENT_SEVERITY                  1
              MGMT_FAILOVER_TABLE                   24
              MGMT_JOB                             120
              MGMT_JOB_EMD_STATUS_QUEUE             46
              MGMT_JOB_EXECUTION                   120
              MGMT_JOB_EXEC_IDX01                  120
              MGMT_JOB_EXEC_SUMMARY                 48
              MGMT_JOB_EXEC_SUMM_IDX04              48
              MGMT_JOB_PK                          120
              MGMT_METRICS                          36
              MGMT_METRICS_1HOUR_PK                 14
              MGMT_METRICS_IDX_01                   24
              MGMT_METRICS_IDX_03                    1
              MGMT_METRICS_PK                       11
```

When these examples are plotted, well-defined signatures emerge for particular tables, access plans and SQL statements. Most Oracle databases are remarkably predictable, with the exception of DSS and ad-hoc query systems, and the DBA can quickly track the usage of all SQL components.

An understanding of the SQL signature can be extremely useful for determining which objects to place in the KEEP pool and determining the most active tables and indexes in the database.

The next section will present information on how to count the frequency in which indexes are used within Oracle.

Counting Index Usage Inside SQL

Prior to Oracle9i, it was very difficult to see if an index was being used by the SQL in a database. It required *explaining* all of the SQL in the library cache into a holding area and then parsing through the execution plans for the index name. The process was simplified slightly in Oracle9i when the primitive *alter index xxx monitoring usage* command was introduced. With it came the ability to see if the index was invoked.

The problem has always been that it is very difficult to know what indexes are the most popular. In Oracle10g, the DBA can easily see what indexes are used, when they are used, and the context in which they are used.

index_usage_hr.sql is a simple AWR query that can be used to plot index usage:

🖫 index_usage_hr.sql

```
-- ****************************************************
-- Copyright © 2005 by Rampant TechPress
-- This script is free for non-commercial purposes
-- with no warranties.  Use at your own risk.
--
-- To license this script for a commercial purpose,
-- contact info@rampant.cc
-- ****************************************************

col c1 heading 'Begin|Interval|time'  format a20
col c2 heading 'Search Columns'       format 999
col c3 heading 'Invocation|Count'     format 99,999,999


break on c1 skip 2

accept idxname char prompt 'Enter Index Name: '

ttitle 'Invocation Counts for index|&idxname'

select
   to_char(sn.begin_interval_time,'yy-mm-dd hh24')  c1,
   p.search_columns                                 c2,
   count(*)                                         c3
from
   dba_hist_snapshot   sn,
   dba_hist_sql_plan   p,
   dba_hist_sqlstat    st
where
```

```
   st.sql_id = p.sql_id
and
   sn.snap_id = st.snap_id
and
   p.object_name = '&idxname'
group by
   begin_interval_time,search_columns;
```

This query will produce output showing a summary count of the index specified during the snapshot interval. This can be compared to the number of times that a table was invoked from SQL.

The following is sample output from this script:

```
Invocation Counts for cust_index

Begin
Interval                                Invocation
time                 Search Columns          Count
-------------------- --------------- -----------
04-10-21 15                        1           3
04-10-10 16                        0           1
04-10-10 19                        1           1
04-10-11 02                        0           2
04-10-11 04                        2           1
04-10-11 06                        3           1
04-10-11 11                        0           1
04-10-11 12                        0           2
04-10-11 13                        2           1
04-10-11 15                        0           3
04-10-11 17                        0          14
04-10-11 18                        4           1
04-10-11 19                        0           1
04-10-11 20                        3           7
04-10-11 21                        0           1
```

Figure 5.8 below is a sample screenshot of a time-series plot for index access produced by the WISE tool:

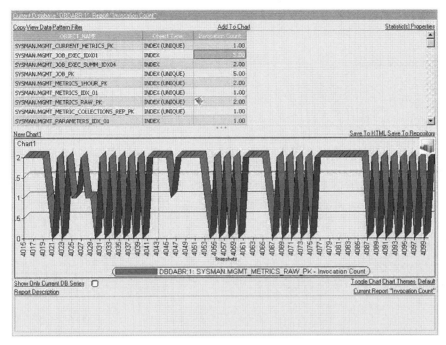

Figure 5.8: *Index invocation count time-series plot in WISE tool.*

The AWR SQL tuning tables offer a wealth of important time metrics. This data can be summarized by a snapshot period providing an overall view of how Oracle is accessing the table data. The *awr_access_counts.sql* script will yield this type of information:

🖫 **awr_access_counts.sql**

```
-- ************************************************
-- Copyright © 2005 by Rampant TechPress
-- This script is free for non-commercial purposes
-- with no warranties.  Use at your own risk.
--
-- To license this script for a commercial purpose,
-- contact info@rampant.cc
-- ************************************************

ttile 'Table Access|Operation Counts|Per Snapshot Period'

col c1 heading 'Begin|Interval|time'  format a20
col c2 heading 'Operation'            format a15
col c3 heading 'Option'               format a15
col c4 heading 'Object|Count'         format 999,999

break on c1 skip 2
```

```
break on c2 skip 2

select
  to_char(sn.begin_interval_time,'yy-mm-dd hh24')  c1,
  p.operation     c2,
  p.options       c3,
  count(1)        c4
from
  dba_hist_sql_plan p,
  dba_hist_sqlstat  s,
  dba_hist_snapshot sn
where
  p.object_owner <> 'SYS'
and
  p.sql_id = s.sql_id
and
  s.snap_id = sn.snap_id
group by
  to_char(sn.begin_interval_time,'yy-mm-dd hh24'),
  p.operation,
  p.options
order by
  1,2,3;
```

The following output shows the overall total counts for each object and table access method:

Begin Interval time	Operation	Option	Object Count
04-10-15 16	INDEX	UNIQUE SCAN	1
04-10-15 16	TABLE ACCESS	BY INDEX ROWID	1
04-10-15 16		FULL	2
04-10-15 17	INDEX	UNIQUE SCAN	1
04-10-15 17	TABLE ACCESS	BY INDEX ROWID	1
04-10-15 17		FULL	2
04-10-15 18	INDEX	UNIQUE SCAN	1
04-10-15 18	TABLE ACCESS	BY INDEX ROWID	1
04-10-15 18		FULL	2
04-10-15 19	INDEX	UNIQUE SCAN	1
04-10-15 19	TABLE ACCESS	BY INDEX ROWID	1
04-10-15 19		FULL	2
04-10-15 20	INDEX	UNIQUE SCAN	1
04-10-15 20	TABLE ACCESS	BY INDEX ROWID	1
04-10-15 20		FULL	2

```
04-10-15 21          INDEX          UNIQUE SCAN          1

04-10-15 21          TABLE ACCESS   BY INDEX ROWID       1
04-10-15 21                         FULL                 2
```

For non-OLTP databases that regularly perform large full-table and full-index scans, it is helpful to know those times when the full scan activity is high. The *awr_sql_full_scans.sql* will yield this type of information:

awr_sql_full_scans.sql

```
-- ************************************************
-- Copyright © 2005 by Rampant TechPress
-- This script is free for non-commercial purposes
-- with no warranties.  Use at your own risk.
--
-- To license this script for a commercial purpose,
-- contact info@rampant.cc
-- ************************************************

col c1 heading 'Begin|Interval|Time'   format a20
col c2 heading 'Index|Table|Scans' format 999,999
col c3 heading 'Full|Table|Scans' format 999,999

select
  i.c1   c1,
  i.c2   c2,
  f.c2   c3
from
(
select
  to_char(sn.begin_interval_time,'yy-mm-dd hh24')  c1,
  count(1)                              c2
from
   dba_hist_sql_plan p,
   dba_hist_sqlstat  s,
   dba_hist_snapshot sn
where
   p.object_owner <> 'SYS'
and
   p.operation like '%TABLE ACCESS%'
and
   p.options like '%INDEX%'
and
   p.sql_id = s.sql_id
and
   s.snap_id = sn.snap_id
group by
  to_char(sn.begin_interval_time,'yy-mm-dd hh24')
order by
1 ) i,
(
select
  to_char(sn.begin_interval_time,'yy-mm-dd hh24')  c1,
  count(1)                              c2
```

```
from
   dba_hist_sql_plan p,
   dba_hist_sqlstat  s,
   dba_hist_snapshot sn
where
   p.object_owner <> 'SYS'
and
   p.operation like '%TABLE ACCESS%'
and
   p.options = 'FULL'
and
   p.sql_id = s.sql_id
and
   s.snap_id = sn.snap_id
group by
  to_char(sn.begin_interval_time,'yy-mm-dd hh24')
order by
1 ) f
where
     i.c1 = f.c1
;
```

The following output shows a comparison of index-full scans vs. full-table scans:

Begin Interval Time	Index Table Scans	Full Table Scans
04-10-21 15	53	18
04-10-21 17	3	3
04-10-21 18	1	2
04-10-21 19	15	6
04-10-21 20		6
04-10-21 21		6
04-10-21 22	16	6
04-10-21 23	21	9
04-10-22 00	16	6
04-10-22 01		6
04-10-22 02	17	6
04-10-22 03	15	6
04-10-22 04	16	6
04-10-22 05		6
04-10-22 06		6
04-10-22 07	15	6
04-10-22 08		6
04-10-22 09		6
04-10-22 10	18	8
04-10-22 11	16	6
04-10-22 12	14	6
04-10-22 13		6
04-10-22 14		6
04-10-22 15	15	11
04-10-22 16	1	7
04-10-22 17	15	6
04-10-22 18	16	6

This information is the signature for large-table full-table scans and can help the DBA in both SQL tuning and instance tuning. For SQL tuning, this report will dictate when to drill down to verify that all of the large-table full-table scans are legitimate. Once verified, this same data can be used to dynamically reconfigure the Oracle instance to accommodate the large scans.

Now that the indexing component has been presented, methods for using the AWR data to track full-scan behavior over time can be explained.

Tracking Full Scan Access

Since large-table full-table scans are a common symptom of sub-optimal execution plans (i.e. missing indexes), it is especially important for the DBA to know how to count all of the specific SQL access methods and understand how they change over time.

Once there is assurance that the large-table full-table scans are legitimate, those times when they are executed must be identified so that the DBA can implement a selective parallel query, depending on the existing CPU consumption on the server. Oracle Parallel Query drives up CPU consumption and should be invoked when the server can handle the additional load.

The following script will report overall counts of full table scans by hour.

🖫 **awr_full_table_scans.sql**

```
-- ************************************************
-- Copyright © 2005 by Rampant TechPress
-- This script is free for non-commercial purposes
-- with no warranties.  Use at your own risk.
--
-- To license this script for a commercial purpose,
-- contact info@rampant.cc
-- ************************************************
```

```
ttile 'Large Full-table scans|Per Snapshot Period'

col c1 heading 'Begin|Interval|time' format a20
col c4 heading 'FTS|Count'             format 999,999

break on c1 skip 2
break on c2 skip 2

select
  to_char(sn.begin_interval_time,'yy-mm-dd hh24')   c1,
  count(1)                                           c4
from
   dba_hist_sql_plan p,
   dba_hist_sqlstat  s,
   dba_hist_snapshot sn,
   dba_segments      o
where
   p.object_owner <> 'SYS'
and
   p.object_owner = o.owner
and
   p.object_name = o.segment_name
and
   o.blocks > 1000
and
   p.operation like '%TABLE ACCESS%'
and
   p.options like '%FULL%'
and
   p.sql_id = s.sql_id
and
   s.snap_id = sn.snap_id
group by
  to_char(sn.begin_interval_time,'yy-mm-dd hh24')
order by
  1;
```

The following output shows the overall total counts for tables
experiencing large-table full-table scans because the scans may be due to
a missing index:

```
     Large Full-table scans
       Per Snapshot Period

Begin
Interval              FTS
time                  Count
-------------------- --------
04-10-18 11                 4
04-10-21 17                 1
04-10-21 23                 2
04-10-22 15                 2
04-10-22 16                 2
04-10-22 23                 2
04-10-24 00                 2
04-10-25 00                 2
```

```
04-10-25 10                2
04-10-25 17                9
04-10-25 18                1
04-10-25 21                1
04-10-26 12                1
04-10-26 13                3
04-10-26 14                3
04-10-26 15               11
04-10-26 16                4
04-10-26 17                4
04-10-26 18                3
04-10-26 23                2
04-10-27 13                2
04-10-27 14                3
04-10-27 15                4
04-10-27 16                4
04-10-27 17                3
04-10-27 18               17
04-10-27 19                1
04-10-28 12               22
04-10-28 13                2
04-10-29 13                9
```

Figure 5.9 shows that this data can easily be plotted and the trend for the database easily seen:

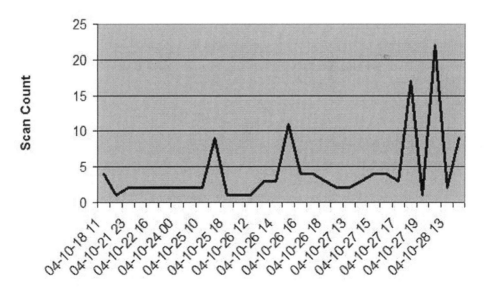

Figure 5.9: *Trends of large-table full-table scans.*

Search for Symptoms! One of the most common manifestations of sub-optimal SQL execution is a large-table full-table scan.

Whenever an index is missing, Oracle may be forced to read every row in the table when an index might be faster.

If the large-table full-table scans are legitimate, the DBA will want to know the periods in which they are invoked so that the OPQ can be invoked to speed-up the scans.

The following script will report an average number of full-table scans by hour of the day.

💾 awr_sql_access_hr.sql

```
-- ***************************************************
-- Copyright © 2005 by Rampant TechPress
-- This script is free for non-commercial purposes
-- with no warranties.  Use at your own risk.
--
-- To license this script for a commercial purpose,
-- contact info@rampant.cc
-- ***************************************************

ttile 'Large Tabe Full-table scans|Averages per Hour'

col c1 heading 'Day|Hour'          format a20
col c2 heading 'FTS|Count'         format 999,999

break on c1 skip 2
break on c2 skip 2

select
  to_char(sn.begin_interval_time,'hh24')  c1,
  count(1)                         c2
from
   dba_hist_sql_plan p,
   dba_hist_sqlstat  s,
   dba_hist_snapshot sn,
   dba_segments      o
where
   p.object_owner <> 'SYS'
and
   p.object_owner = o.owner
```

```
and
   p.object_name = o.segment_name
and
   o.blocks > 1000
and
   p.operation like '%TABLE ACCESS%'
and
   p.options like '%FULL%'
and
   p.sql_id = s.sql_id
and
   s.snap_id = sn.snap_id
group by
  to_char(sn.begin_interval_time,'hh24')
order by
  1;
```

The following output shows the average number of large-table full-table scans per hour:

```
Large Table Full-table scans
Averages per Hour

Day                             FTS
Hour                          Count
-------------------- --------
00                                4
10                                2
11                                4
12                               23
13                               16
14                                6
15                               17
16                               10
17                               17
18                               21
19                                1
23                                6
```

The *awr_sql_access_day.sql* script below shows the same data for day of the week:

🖫 awr_sql_access_day.sql

```
-- ****************************************************
-- Copyright © 2005 by Rampant TechPress
-- This script is free for non-commercial purposes
-- with no warranties.  Use at your own risk.
--
-- To license this script for a commercial purpose,
-- contact info@rampant.cc
-- ****************************************************

ttile 'Large Table Full-table scans|Averages per Week Day'
```

```
col c1 heading 'Week|Day'            format a20
col c2 heading 'FTS|Count'           format 999,999

break on c1 skip 2
break on c2 skip 2

select
  to_char(sn.begin_interval_time,'day')  c1,
  count(1)                               c2
from
  dba_hist_sql_plan p,
  dba_hist_sqlstat  s,
  dba_hist_snapshot sn,
  dba_segments      o
where
  p.object_owner <> 'SYS'
and
  p.object_owner = o.owner
and
  p.object_name = o.segment_name
and
  o.blocks > 1000
and
  p.operation like '%TABLE ACCESS%'
and
  p.options like '%FULL%'
and
  p.sql_id = s.sql_id
and
  s.snap_id = sn.snap_id
group by
  to_char(sn.begin_interval_time,'day')
order by
1;
```

The following sample query output shows the specific times when the database experienced large table scans:

```
Large Table Full-table scans
Averages per Week Day


Week                     FTS
Day                    Count
-------------------- --------
sunday                     2
monday                    19
tuesday                   31
wednesday                 34
thursday                  27
friday                    15
Saturday                   2
```

The *awr_sql_scan_sums.sql* code below is an amazing script that will show access patterns of usage over time. To really know a system, gaining an understanding of how SQL accesses the tables and indexes in a database can provide incredible insight. The optimal instance configuration for large-table full-table scans is quite different than the configuration for an OLTP databases. This handy report will quickly identify changes in table access patterns:

🖫 awr_sql_scan_sums.sql

```
-- *************************************************
-- Copyright © 2005 by Rampant TechPress
-- This script is free for non-commercial purposes
-- with no warranties.  Use at your own risk.
--
-- To license this script for a commercial purpose,
-- contact info@rampant.cc
-- *************************************************

col c1 heading 'Begin|Interval|Time'          format a20
col c2 heading 'Large|Table|Full Table|Scans' format 999,999
col c3 heading 'Small|Table|Full Table|Scans' format 999,999
col c4 heading 'Total|Index|Scans'            format 999,999


select
  f.c1   c1,
  f.c2   c2,
  s.c2   c3,
  i.c2   c4
from
(
select
  to_char(sn.begin_interval_time,'yy-mm-dd hh24')  c1,
  count(1)                           c2
from
   dba_hist_sql_plan p,
   dba_hist_sqlstat  s,
   dba_hist_snapshot sn,
   dba_segments      o
where
   p.object_owner <> 'SYS'
and
   p.object_owner = o.owner
and
   p.object_name = o.segment_name
and
   o.blocks > 1000
and
   p.operation like '%TABLE ACCESS%'
and
   p.options like '%FULL%'
and
   p.sql_id = s.sql_id
```

```
and
   s.snap_id = sn.snap_id
group by
   to_char(sn.begin_interval_time,'yy-mm-dd hh24')
order by
1 ) f,
(
select
   to_char(sn.begin_interval_time,'yy-mm-dd hh24')  c1,
   count(1)                                 c2
from
   dba_hist_sql_plan p,
   dba_hist_sqlstat  s,
   dba_hist_snapshot sn,
   dba_segments      o
where
   p.object_owner <> 'SYS'
and
   p.object_owner = o.owner
and
   p.object_name = o.segment_name
and
   o.blocks < 1000
and
   p.operation like '%INDEX%'
and
   p.sql_id = s.sql_id
and
   s.snap_id = sn.snap_id
group by
   to_char(sn.begin_interval_time,'yy-mm-dd hh24')
order by
1 ) s,
(
select
   to_char(sn.begin_interval_time,'yy-mm-dd hh24')  c1,
   count(1)                                 c2
from
   dba_hist_sql_plan p,
   dba_hist_sqlstat  s,
   dba_hist_snapshot sn
where
   p.object_owner <> 'SYS'
and
   p.operation like '%INDEX%'
and
   p.sql_id = s.sql_id
and
   s.snap_id = sn.snap_id
group by
   to_char(sn.begin_interval_time,'yy-mm-dd hh24')
order by
1 ) i
where
      f.c1 = s.c1
   and
      f.c1 = i.c1
;
```

The sample output looks like the following, in which a comparison of index vs. table scan access is shown. This is a very important signature for any database because it reveals, at a glance, the balance between OLTP index and data warehouse type access:

Begin Interval Time	Large Table Full Table Scans	Small Table Full Table Scans	Total Index Scans
04-10-22 15	2	19	21
04-10-22 16		1	1
04-10-25 10		18	20
04-10-25 17	9	15	17
04-10-25 18	1	19	22
04-10-25 21		19	24
04-10-26 12		23	28
04-10-26 13	3	17	19
04-10-26 14		18	19
04-10-26 15	11	4	7
04-10-26 16	4	18	18
04-10-26 17		17	19
04-10-26 18	3	17	17
04-10-27 13	2	17	19
04-10-27 14	3	17	19
04-10-27 15	4	17	18
04-10-27 16		17	17
04-10-27 17	3	17	20
04-10-27 18	17	20	22
04-10-27 19	1	20	26
04-10-28 12	22	17	20
04-10-28 13	2	17	17
04-10-29 13	9	18	19

This is a very important report because it demonstrates the way that Oracle is accessing data over time periods. This is especially important because it shows when the database processing modality shifts between OLTP (*first_rows* index access) to a batch reporting mode (*all_rows* full scans) as shown in Figure 5.10.

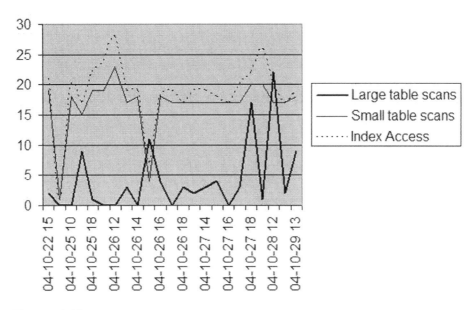

Figure 5.10: *Plot of full scans vs. index access.*

The example in Figure 5.4 is typical of an OLTP database with the majority of access being via small-table full-table scans and index access. In this case, the DBA should carefully check the large-table full-table scans, verify their legitimacy (i.e. no missing indexes), and adjust them to maximize their throughput.

Of course, in a really busy database there may be concurrent OLTP index access and full-table scans for reports and it is the job of the DBA to know the specific times at which to shift table access modes and those tables that experience the changes.

The *awr_sql_full_scans_avg_dy.sql* code is a script that functions to roll-up average scans into daily averages:

🖫 **awr_sql_full_scans_avg_dy.sql**
```
-- ***************************************************
-- Copyright © 2005 by Rampant TechPress
-- This script is free for non-commercial purposes
-- with no warranties.  Use at your own risk.
--
```

```
-- To license this script for a commercial purpose,
-- contact info@rampant.cc
-- *************************************************

col c1 heading 'Begin|Interval|Time'    format a20
col c2 heading 'Index|Table|Scans' format 999,999
col c3 heading 'Full|Table|Scans' format 999,999

select
  i.c1   c1,
  i.c2   c2,
  f.c2   c3
from
(
select
  to_char(sn.begin_interval_time,'day')   c1,
  count(1)                                 c2
from
   dba_hist_sql_plan p,
   dba_hist_sqlstat  s,
   dba_hist_snapshot sn
where
  p.object_owner <> 'SYS'
and
   p.operation like '%TABLE ACCESS%'
and
   p.options like '%INDEX%'
and
   p.sql_id = s.sql_id
and
   s.snap_id = sn.snap_id
group by
  to_char(sn.begin_interval_time,'day')
order by
1 ) i,
(
select
  to_char(sn.begin_interval_time,'day')   c1,
  count(1)                                 c2
from
   dba_hist_sql_plan p,
   dba_hist_sqlstat  s,
   dba_hist_snapshot sn
where
  p.object_owner <> 'SYS'
and
   p.operation like '%TABLE ACCESS%'
and
   p.options = 'FULL'
and
   p.sql_id = s.sql_id
and
   s.snap_id = sn.snap_id
group by
  to_char(sn.begin_interval_time,'day')
order by
1 ) f
where
     i.c1 = f.c1
```

The following is the sample output:

```
Begin                   Index      Full
Interval                Table      Table
Time                    Scans      Scans
-------------------- -------- --------
sunday                    393        189
monday                    383        216
tuesday                   353        206
wednesday                 357        178
thursday                  488        219
friday                    618        285
saturday                  400        189
```

Once plotted, as shown in Figure 5.11, the signature shows that Fridays are very high in full-table scans, probably as the result of weekly reporting. If the hourly signature is compared with the daily signature for LTFTS, the DBA can quickly see the hourly signature and can infer that the period of LTFTS is on Fridays between 3:00 p.m. and 5:00 p.m.:

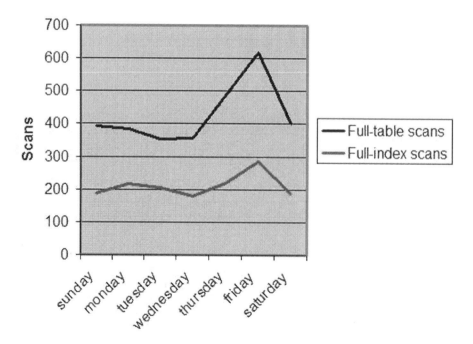

Figure 5.11: *Plot of full scans.*

With this knowledge the DBA can anticipate the changes in processing from index access to LTFTS access by adjusting the instance configurations. Whenever the database changes into a mode dominated by LTFTS, the DBA can decrease the data buffer sizes (*db_cache_size*, *db_nk_cache_size*). When parallel LTFTS bypass the data buffers, the intermediate rows are kept in the *pga_aggregate_target* region. Therefore, it is wise to use *dbms_scheduler* to anticipate this change and resize the SGA in time to accommodate the regularly repeating change in access patterns.

The *ash_hot_objects.sql* query against the AWR ASH table shows a list of database objects that caused the most wait times during time interval stored in AWR. Idle wait times are not included in the output:

ash_hot_objects.sql

```
--  ****************************************************
--  Copyright © 2005 by Rampant TechPress
--  This script is free for non-commercial purposes
--  with no warranties.  Use at your own risk.
--
--  To license this script for a commercial purpose,
--  contact info@rampant.cc
--  ****************************************************

select
   o.owner,
   o.object_name,
   o.object_type,
   SUM(h.wait_time + h.time_waited) "total wait time"
from
   v$active_session_history      h,
   dba_objects                   o,
   v$event_name                  e
where
   h.current_obj# = o.object_id
and
   e.event_id = h.event_id
and
   e.wait_class <> 'Idle'
group by
   o.owner,
   o.object_name,
   o.object_type
order by 4 DESC;
```

This report produces a list of hot objects which might be candidates for further tuning investigations:

```
                            Object          Object
OWNER                       Name            Type       total wait time
--------------------------- --------------- ---------- ----------------
SYSMAN                      MGMT_OMS_PARAMETERS  TABLE        1,1232E+10
SYS                         SCHEDULER$_WINDOW_DE TABLE          2989867
                            TAILS

SYSMAN                      MPVV_PK              INDEX          1333198
SYSMAN                      MGMT_DELTA_ENTRY_SHO INDEX           835641
                            ULD_BE_UK

SYSMAN                      MGMT_DB_LATEST_HDM_F TABLE           397504
                            INDINGS

SYS                         CDEF$                TABLE           116853
SYS                         I_LINK1              INDEX            46922
SYS                         SYS_IOT_TOP_8542     INDEX            25469
SYS                         I_COM1               INDEX            24908
SYS                         I_CDEF3              INDEX            23125
SYSMAN                      MGMT_DB_LATEST_HDM_F INDEX            11325
                            INDINGS

SYS                         I_OBJ2               INDEX             5953
SYS                         WRH$_ACTIVE_SESSION_ TABLE              304
                            HISTORY_BL

SYSTEM                      SQLPLUS_PRODUCT_PROF TABLE               3
                            ILE
```

Conclusion

In this chapter, object access and status monitoring were explained. Scripts that allow the DBA to determine object health were presented and guidelines were given for maintaining database objects in optimal form.

SGA Monitoring

The database Shared Global Area (SGA) is the most critical aspect of the Oracle database system. The SGA provides buffers and control structures that, if not properly tuned and maintained, will cause significant performance issues. This chapter provides the tools needed to monitor and maintain the SGA components of Oracle instances.

Importance of Proper Configuration

When the subject of Oracle performance tuning is raised almost every database professional thinks of tweaking the RAM memory settings. After all, don't servers with more RAM run faster than comparable servers with less memory? Shouldn't databases work the same?

Not surprisingly, the general answer is, yes. Databases operating with more memory will usually run hundreds of times faster than those whose RAM allocations are rationed out in smaller portions. There are, of course, exceptions to every rule, and those exceptions will be covered in this chapter.

Those who think that throwing memory at a database is always going to solve serious performance problems are setting themselves up for a rude awakening. It takes a careful blend of balance and investigation to determine exactly how much memory a database needs and where those allocations should be made.

It is also critically important not to over allocate a database's memory allotment. Doing so can cause a server to page swap and thrash to the point at which all operations will come to a complete standstill.

Without a doubt, a separate book could be written on the subject of memory concepts and tuning within Oracle. Instead of trying to cover every minute detail with respect to memory optimization, this chapter will focus on getting the most bang for the buck when turning Oracle's memory knobs.

There is nothing more irritating than spending an hour and a half reading an in-depth white paper on something like Oracle latch analysis only to discover that following the author's advice yields no noticeable benefit on the database.

This chapter has been designed to provide what is needed to maximize memory inside and outside the database by focusing on the following topics:

- How to determine if the right amount of memory is being given to Oracle.

- What new memory options in Oracle offer the most potential for improving performance.

- How to keep data, code, and object definitions in memory so response times are the fastest possible.

- How to quickly pinpoint user sessions that degrade response times by using excessive memory resources.

Once a DBA has a handle on these issues, it will be easier to ensure that the Oracle database is properly configured from a memory standpoint. To begin this process, the current memory configuration and usage of the database must be analyzed.

Getting a Handle on Memory Usage

Not surprisingly, each release of Oracle has featured additional memory parameters that can be tweaked to create an optimal memory configuration for a database. In trained hands, these parameters can make a dramatic difference in how well the database runs.

Happily, Oracle has now made these key memory settings dynamic in version 9i and above, meaning that DBAs can now size the SGA without having to start and stop the database.

The starting point with an existing database is to understand how much RAM the database server offers, and then determine the current settings of the Oracle SGA. This provides a basis for judging whether Oracle can benefit from adding or manipulating memory and how much headroom exists.

The method used to obtain the memory configuration of the server will depend on the hardware and operating system platform. Most operating systems have decent GUI interfaces that allow for such configuration information to be obtained through pointing and clicking.

Once the memory configuration for the server is known, diagnostics should be performed to investigate the metrics of the paging/swapping situation on the server. Again, the method for obtaining such information will depend on the hardware platform. Regardless of the platform, excessive paging and swapping should be avoided. These activities tend to degrade the overall performance of anything that runs on the server since data is constantly transferred from RAM to physical swap files and then back again.

Once a moderate comfort level with the memory behavior on the database server is reached, it is time to focus attention on Oracle. The first step is to find the size of the current SGA that controls the database. To get such information, the *sgasize.sql* script can be used. This script can be used on all Oracle versions; however, some of the columns may be NULL or zero because certain memory regions are not available in all versions.

🖫 sgasize.sql

```
-- ****************************************************
-- Copyright © 2005 by Rampant TechPress
-- This script is free for non-commercial purposes
-- with no warranties.  Use at your own risk.
--
-- To license this script for a commercial purpose,
-- contact info@rampant.cc
-- ****************************************************

select
      db_size_in_mb - db_caches db_buffers_in_mb,
      db_caches db_caches_mb,
      fixed_size_in_mb,
      lb_size_in_mb,
      sp_size_in_mb,
      lp_size_in_mb,
      jp_size_in_mb
from
(select
      round (max(a.bytes) / 1024 / 1024, 2)  db_size_in_mb
  from
      sys.v_$sgastat a
 where
      (a.name = 'db_block_buffers' or a.name = 'buffer_cache')),
(select
      nvl(round (sum (b.value) / 1024 / 1024, 2),0) db_caches
  from
      sys.v_$parameter b
 where
      b.name like '%k_cache_size'),
(select
      round (sum (b.bytes) / 1024 / 1024, 2) fixed_size_in_mb
  from
      sys.v_$sgastat b
 where
       b.name = 'fixed_sga'),
```

```
(select
        round (sum (c.bytes) / 1024 / 1024, 2) lb_size_in_mb
  from
        sys.v_$sgastat c
where
        c.name=  'log_buffer' ),
(select
        round (sum (d.value) / 1024 / 1024, 2) sp_size_in_mb
  from
        sys.v_$parameter d
where
        d.name = 'shared_pool_size'),
(select
        round (sum (e.value) / 1024 / 1024, 2) lp_size_in_mb
  from
        sys.v_$parameter e
where
        e.name = 'large_pool_size' ),
(select
        round (sum (f.value) / 1024 / 1024, 2) jp_size_in_mb
  from
        sys.v_$parameter f
where
        f.name = 'java_pool_size');
```

The following output shows a summary of Oracle SGA settings:

	DB_BUFFERS_IN_MB	DB_CACHES	FIXED_SIZE_IN_MB	LB_SIZE_IN_MB	SP_SIZE_IN_MB	LP_SIZE_IN_MB	JP_SIZE_IN_MB
1	56	16	.43	.63	48	8	32

Figure 6.1: *Getting a summary of Oracle SGA settings*

This script delivers more detailed information than the standard *show sga* command in the server manager or SQL*Plus because it breaks down the standard buffer cache, showing the total amount of memory given to the special 9i and above data caches, and displaying information for the large and java pools.

Exactly what each of these areas is and how Oracle uses them are the topics of the next section.

Understanding the SGA

Most DBAs know all about the Oracle Shared Global Area (SGA). The SGA is Oracle's structural memory area that facilitates the transfer of data and information between clients and the Oracle database. Long gone are the days when only four main tunable components existed. If Oracle9i or above is in use, expect to deal with the following memory regions:

- **Default Buffer Cache** - This is the default memory cache that stores data blocks when they are read from the database. If the DBA does not specifically place objects in another data cache, any data requested by clients from the database will be placed into this cache. This memory area is controlled by the *db_block_buffers* parameter in Oracle8 and below, and *db_cache_size* in Oracle9i and above.

- **Keep Buffer Cache** - Beginning with Oracle8, a DBA can assign objects to a special cache that will retain those object's requested blocks in RAM for as long as the database is up. The keep cache's main function is to hold frequently referenced lookup tables that should always be kept in memory for quick access. The *buffer_pool_keep* parameter controls the size of this cache in Oracle8, while the *db_keep_cache_size* parameter handles the cache in Oracle9i and above. The keep pool is a sub-pool of the default buffer cache.

- **Recycle Buffer Cache** - The opposite of the keep cache is the recycle cache. When large table scans occur, the data filling a memory cache is unlikely to be needed again and should be quickly discarded from RAM. By placing this data into the recycle cache, it will neither occupy valuable memory space nor prevent blocks that are needed from being placed in a buffer. Should it be requested again, the discarded data is quickly available. The *buffer_pool_recycle* parameter controls the size of this cache in Oracle8 and below, while the *db_recycle_cache_size* parameter handles the cache in Oracle9i and above.

- **Specific Blocksize Caches** - Beginning in Oracle9i, a DBA can create tablespaces with blocksizes that differs from the overall database blocksize. When data is read into the SGA from these tablespaces, the data has to be placed into memory regions that can accommodate their special blocksize. Oracle9i and above has memory settings for 2K, 4K, 8K, 16K, and 32K caches. The configuration parameter names are in the pattern of *db_nk_cache_size*.

- **Shared Pool** - This familiar area holds object structures and code definitions, as well as other metadata. Setting the proper amount of memory in the shared pool assists a great deal in improving overall performance with respect to code execution and object references. The *shared_pool_size* parameter controls this memory region.

- **Large Pool** - Starting in Oracle8, a DBA can configure an optional, specialized memory region called the *large pool* that holds items for shared server operations, backup and restore tasks, and other miscellaneous tasks. The *large_pool_size* parameter controls this memory region. The large pool is also used for sorting when the multi-threaded server (MTS) is implemented.

- **Java Pool** - This area handles the memory for Java methods, class definitions, etc. The *java_pool_size* parameter controls the amount of memory for this area.

- **Redo Log Buffer** - This area buffers modifications that are made to the database before they are physically written to the redo log files. The *log_buffer* configuration parameter controls this memory area.

Oracle also maintains a fixed area in the SGA that contains a number of atomic variables, pointers, and other miscellaneous structures that reference areas of the SGA.

Once the current settings of the SGA are understood, attention should be focused on how well it is being utilized.

Gaining Insight into Memory Use

There are a number of key ratios and wait metrics that can be used to assemble a global picture of SGA performance.

Before using the scripts below to obtain key memory metrics, the DBA should be aware that some database professionals passionately believe that ratio-based analysis is a worthless endeavor. These database professionals favor a wait-based or bottleneck approach instead. There are certainly valid reasons for not relying solely on ratios to determine if the database is functioning properly; however, when practiced correctly, ratio-based analysis is indeed worthwhile and can contribute to understanding system performance.

What are some of the key indicators of memory efficiency and usage? Rather than list each metric in a single script, the *memsnap.sql* script below obtains many key memory metrics in a single query and presents them all at once:

🔲 memsnap.sql

```
-- ************************************************
-- Copyright © 2005 by Rampant TechPress
-- This script is free for non-commercial purposes
-- with no warranties.  Use at your own risk.
--
-- To license this script for a commercial purpose,
-- contact info@rampant.cc
-- ************************************************

select
       buffer_hit_ratio,
       percent_shared_pool_free,
       lib_cache_hit_ratio,
       object_reloads,
       dd_cache_hit_ratio,
       redo_log_space_waits,
       redo_log_space_wait_time,
       mem_sort_ratio,
       parse_execute_ratio,
       buffer_busy_waits,
       latch_miss_ratio
from
(select
       100 -
       100 *
       (round ((sum (decode (name, 'physical reads', value, 0)) -
        sum (decode (name, 'physical reads direct', value, 0)) -
        sum (decode (name,
        'physical reads direct (lob)', value, 0))) /
        (sum (decode (name,
        'session logical reads', value, 1))),3)) buffer_hit_ratio
 from
       sys.v_$sysstat
 where
       name in ('session logical reads',
                'physical reads direct (lob)',
                'physical reads', 'physical reads direct')),
(select
       round (100 * (free_bytes / shared_pool_size), 2)
```

```
          percent_shared_pool_free
  from
       (select
               sum (bytes) free_bytes
          from
               sys.v_$sgastat
          where
               name = 'free memory'
            and
               pool = 'shared pool'),
       (select
               value shared_pool_size
          from
               sys.v_$parameter
          where
               name = 'shared_pool_size')),
(select
       100 - round ((sum (reloads) /
       sum (pins)) * 100, 2) lib_cache_hit_ratio
  from
       sys.v_$librarycache),
(select
       100 - round ((sum (getmisses) /
       (sum (gets) + sum (getmisses)) * 100), 2) dd_cache_hit_ratio
from    sys.v_$rowcache),
(select round (
          (100 * b.value) /
          decode ((a.value + b.value), 0, 1, (a.value + b.value)),
          2)mem_sort_ratio
  from
       v$sysstat a,
       v$sysstat b
 where
       a.name = 'sorts (disk)'
   and b.name = 'sorts (memory)'),
(select
       round(100 * (sum (sys.v_$latch.misses) /
       sum (sys.v_$latch.gets)),2) latch_miss_ratio
  from
       sys.v_$latch),
(select
       round (100 * (a.value - b.value) /
       decode (a.value, 0, 1, a.value), 2) parse_execute_ratio
  from
       sys.v_$sysstat a,
       sys.v_$sysstat b
 where
       a.name = 'execute count'
   and b.name = 'parse count (hard)'),
(select
       nvl(sum(total_waits),0) buffer_busy_waits
from
       sys.v_$system_event a,
       sys.v_$event_name b
where
       a.event = 'buffer busy waits' and
       a.event (+) = b.name),
(select
       sum(reloads) object_reloads
```

```
  from
      sys.v_$librarycache),
(select
      value redo_log_space_waits
  from
      sys.v_$sysstat
where
      name = 'redo log space requests'),
(select
      value redo_log_space_wait_time
  from
      sys.v_$sysstat
where
      name = 'redo log space wait time');
```

The following partial output shows key memory usage metrics:

BUFFER_HIT_RATIO	LIB_CACHE_HIT_RATIO	OBJECT_RELOADS	DD_CACHE_HIT_RATIO	MEM_SORT_RATIO	PARSE_EXECUTE_RATIO	PERCENT_SHARED_POOL_FREE
99.9	99.99	9	94.93	99.89	98.12	69.33

Figure 6.2: *Partial output showing key memory usage metrics*

The buffer cache hit ratio is the first statistic shown in the above output. As mentioned, many DBAs today maintain that this measure is not a good indicator of performance, but is this actually true?

The Buffer Cache Hit Ratio: Still Worthwhile?

The buffer cache hit ratio indicates how often data is found in memory versus disk. Critics of this ratio complain that it is not a good indicator of performance because:

- Many analysts use cumulative numbers for the computations, which can artificially inflate the value to a meaningless measure.

- It does not negatively reflect excessive logical I/O activity, although faster than disk I/O, can certainly suppress performance on any database.

While these complaints have some merit, one must use delta statistics over time to come up with a meaningful value for the ratio, and high logical I/O values can definitely be a leading cause of bad execution times. When properly computed, the buffer cache hit ratio is an excellent indicator of how often the data requested by users is found in RAM instead of disk; a fact of no small importance.

More on Memory Ratios

The global statistic shown above is a good place to start, but one does not have to stop the analysis there. It is possible to penetrate deeper to find cache hit ratios at the buffer pool, session, and SQL statement level.

If using a *keep* and *recycle* buffer pool in addition to the default buffer cache, the *poolhit.sql* script can be used to find the hit rates in each pool:

🖫 **poolhit.sql**

```
-- *************************************************
-- Copyright © 2005 by Rampant TechPress
-- This script is free for non-commercial purposes
-- with no warranties.  Use at your own risk.
--
-- To license this script for a commercial purpose,
-- contact info@rampant.cc
-- *************************************************

select
        name,
        100 * (1 - (physical_reads / (db_block_gets +
        consistent_gets))) hit_ratio
from
        sys.v$buffer_pool_statistics
where
        db_block_gets + consistent_gets > 0;
```

Output from the above query might look like the following as it displays the various memory cache hit ratios:

```
NAME        HIT_RATIO
----------  ---------
DEFAULT         92.82
KEEP            93.98
RECYCLE         85.05
```

Getting Advice on the Buffer Cache

The old rule of thumb was that if the buffer cache hit ratios were depressed, typically below 90%, the *db_block_buffer/db_cache_size* parameter would be increased until the ratio improved. This practice

---

may not yield better overall performance as it will not help excessive logical I/O caused by inefficient SQL calls, but increasing the cache memory can indeed improve response times for many databases suffering from improper cache sizes.

It stands to reason that memory should be added to Oracle intelligently, which means keeping an eye on server page and swap activity. How will the amount of extra memory that the cache needs be determined? If the truth were known, most DBAs simply begin edging the memory setting higher with no rhyme or reason, and hope to stop the dial on just the right amount.

With Oracle9i and above, the *db_cache_advice* parameter can be used to help predict the benefit of adding additional memory to the buffer/data cache. Setting this value to ON instructs Oracle to begin collecting I/O statistics that can be used to assist in intelligently assigning additional RAM to Oracle, while not giving more than is actually needed. The technique generally involves setting the *db_cache_advice* parameter to ON during a time that represents the normal workload for the database.

Once the database has been stressed, the prediction results can be examined by using the *cacheadvice.sql* script:

⊟ cacheadvice.sql

```
-- ***************************************************
-- Copyright © 2005 by Rampant TechPress
-- This script is free for non-commercial purposes
-- with no warranties.  Use at your own risk.
--
-- To license this script for a commercial purpose,
-- contact info@rampant.cc
-- ***************************************************

select
        size_for_estimate,
        buffers_for_estimate,
        estd_physical_read_factor,
        estd_physical_reads
from
        sys.v_$db_cache_advice
where
        name = 'DEFAULT'and
        block_size = (select
                             value
```

```
        from
            sys.v_$parameter
        where
            name = 'db_block_size') and
    advice_status = 'ON';
```

The following output examines Oracle's prediction for adding or subtracting RAM from the data cache:

	SIZE_FOR_ESTIMATE	BUFFERS_FOR_ESTIMATE	ESTD_PHYSICAL_READ_FACTOR	ESTD_PHYSICAL_READS
1	8	1001	315.959	2718195
2	16	2002	1.6436	14140
3	24	3003	1.2744	10963
4	32	4004	1.0872	9353
5	40	5005	1.0333	8890
6	48	6006	1	8603
7	56	7007	1	8603
8	64	8008	1	8603
9	72	9009	1	8603
10	80	10010	1	8603
11	88	11011	1	8603
12	96	12012	1	8603
13	104	13013	1	8603
14	112	14014	1	8603
15	120	15015	1	8603
16	128	16016	1	8603
17	136	17017	1	8603
18	144	18018	1	8603
19	152	19019	1	8603
20	160	20020	1	8603

Figure 6.3: *Examining Oracle's prediction for adding or subtracting RAM from the data cache*

In the above example, for this small 9.2 instance, anything above 16MB for the buffer cache will be wasted RAM.

As a general guideline, all memory available on the host should be tuned, and the *db_cache_size* should be allocating RAM resources up to the point of diminishing returns as shown in Figure 6.4. This is the point at which additional buffer blocks do not significantly improve the buffer hit ratio.

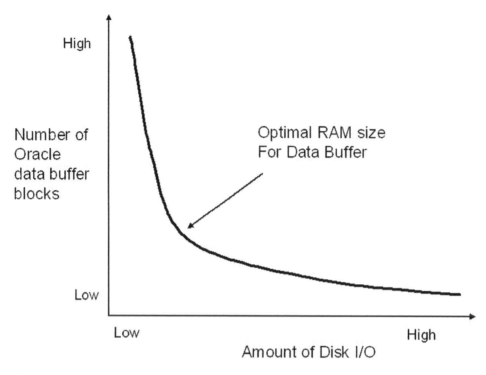

Figure 6.4: *The optimal size of the RAM data buffer.*

The *v$db_cache_advice* view is similar to an Oracle7 utility that also predicted the benefit of adding data buffers. The Oracle7 utility used the *x$kcbrbh* view to track buffer hits and the *x$kcbcbh* view to track buffer misses.

How to Keep Data Where It Belongs

It is definitely desirable to keep frequently accessed data in the buffer and data cache so that queries needing that data have the fastest possible access to it. How can this be accomplished?

Exploiting the 9i and Above Data Caches

In Oracle9i and above, tablespaces can be created with blocksizes that differ from the overall database blocksize. If this is done, it is also necessary to enable one or more of the new *db_nk_cache_size* parameters so that blocks read in from tablespaces that have a different blocksize than the regular database blocksize have a cache to reside.

For example, for a tablespace created with a 16K blocksize, there must also be RAM for those blocks set aside using the *db_16k_cache_size* parameter. Such allocations are in addition to the memory allotments specified by the *db_cache_size* parameter.

This feature allows tuning of the database in ways that were impossible in earlier versions of Oracle. For example, it is possible to use the large (16-32K) blocksize data caches to store data from indexes or tables that are the object of repeated large scans. Does such a thing really help performance? A small, but revealing, test can answer that question.

For the test, the following query will be used against a 9i database that has a database blocksize of 8K, but also has the 16K cache enabled along with a 16K tablespace:

```
select
      count(*)
from
      eradmin.admission
where
      patient_id between 1 and 40000;
```

The ERADMIN.ADMISSION table has 150,000 rows in it and has an index build on the *patient_id* column. An EXPLAIN of the query reveals that it uses an index range scan to produce the desired end result:

```
Execution Plan
----------------------------------------------------------
   0      SELECT STATEMENT Optimizer=CHOOSE
   1      (Cost=41 Card=1 Bytes=4)
   1    0   SORT (AGGREGATE)
   2    1     INDEX (FAST FULL SCAN) OF 'ADMISSION_PATIENT_ID'
              (NON-UNIQUE) (Cost=41 Card=120002 Bytes=480008)
```

Executing the query twice to eliminate parse activity and to cache any data with the index residing in a standard 8K tablespace, produces these runtime statistics:

```
Statistics
-------------------------------------------------
        0  recursive calls
        0  db block gets
      421  consistent gets
        0  physical reads
        0  redo size
      371  bytes sent via SQL*Net to client
      430  bytes received via SQL*Net from client
        2  SQL*Net roundtrips to/from client
        0  sorts (memory)
        0  sorts (disk)
        1  rows processed
```

To test the effectiveness of the new 16K cache and 16K tablespace, the index used by the query will be rebuilt into the larger tablespace, while everything else remains the same:

```
alter index
    eradmin.admission_patient_id
    rebuild nologging noreverse tablespace indx_16k;
```

Once the index is nestled firmly into the 16K tablespace, the query is re-executed (again, twice) with the following runtime statistics being produced:

```
Statistics
-------------------------------------------------
        0  recursive calls
        0  db block gets
      211  consistent gets
        0  physical reads
        0  redo size
      371  bytes sent via SQL*Net to client
      430  bytes received via SQL*Net from client
        2  SQL*Net roundtrips to/from client
        0  sorts (memory)
        0  sorts (disk)
        1  rows processed
```

The amount of logical reads has been cut in half simply by using the new 16K tablespace and accompanying 16K data cache. Clearly, the benefits of the proper use of the new data caches and multi-block tablespace features of Oracle9i are worth investigating and testing.

Other Interesting Buffer Cache Metrics

For a deeper understanding of how the buffer cache is being utilized, there are a few additional queries that can be run to gain such insight. If the *keep* and *recycle* buffer caches are being used, the *cacheobjcnt.sql* query can be used to get an idea of how many objects have been assigned to each cache:

🖫 cacheobjcnt.sql

```
-- **************************************************
-- Copyright © 2005 by Rampant TechPress
-- This script is free for non-commercial purposes
-- with no warranties.  Use at your own risk.
--
-- To license this script for a commercial purpose,
-- contact info@rampant.cc
-- **************************************************

select
      decode(cachehint, 0, 'default', 1,
      'keep', 2, 'recycle', null) cache,
      count(*) objects
from
      sys.seg$ s
where
      s.user#  in
      (select
          user#
       from
          sys.user$
       where
          name not in ('sys','system'))
group by
      decode(cachehint, 0, 'default', 1,
      'keep', 2, 'recycle', null)
order by
    1;
```

The output should resemble the following:

```
CACHE       OBJECTS
----------------
default       2023
keep             5
```

Finally, in order to analyze the buffer cache activity from time to time to see how it is being utilized, the *buffutl.sql* script can be used. It will show

how full the cache currently is along with the state of the buffers in the cache:

🖫 buffutl.sql

```
-- ***************************************************
-- Copyright © 2005 by Rampant TechPress
-- This script is free for non-commercial purposes
-- with no warranties.  Use at your own risk.
--
-- To license this script for a commercial purpose,
-- contact info@rampant.cc
-- ***************************************************

select
      'free' buffer_state,
      nvl(sum(blocksize) / 1024 ,0) amt_kb
from
      sys.x$bh a,
      sys.ts$ b
where
      state = 0  and
      a.ts#  =  b.ts#
union all
select
      'read/mod' buffer_state,
      nvl(sum(blocksize) / 1024 ,0) amt_kb
from
      sys.x$bh a,
      sys.ts$ b
where
      state = 1  and
      a.ts#  =  b.ts#
union all
select
      'read/notmod',
      nvl(sum(blocksize) / 1024 ,0) amt_kb
from
      sys.x$bh a,
      sys.ts$ b
where
      state = 2  and
      a.ts#  =  b.ts#
union all
select
      'being read' buffer_state,
      nvl(sum(blocksize) / 1024 ,0) amt_kb
from
      sys.x$bh a,
      sys.ts$ b
where
      state = 3  and
      a.ts#  =  b.ts#
order by
      1;
```

The output from the above query would be similar to this:

```
BUFFER_STATE      AMT_KB
----------------------
being read          5920
free               23568
read/mod           47952
read/notmod            0
```

Now that ways to interrogate the buffer cache have been explored, the next area to examine is the shared pool.

Structure of the Shared Pool

Tuning the shared pool is one of the least understood features of the Oracle Shared Global Area (SGA). The generally accepted approach to tuning involves throwing memory into the pool until the problem either goes away or is masked. This section will examine the shared pool and will outline a method for tuning it that uses measurement, instead of guesswork, to drive the tuning methodology. Numerous scripts for examining the shared pool are also provided.

Many people know little more about the shared pool than it is a part of the Oracle shared global area. What exactly is the shared pool? The shared pool contains several key performance-related memory areas. If the shared pool is improperly sized, overall database performance will suffer, sometimes dramatically. Figure 6.5 diagrams the shared pool structure located inside the various Oracle SGAs.

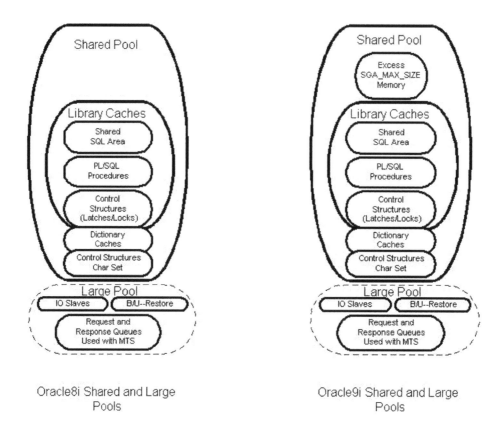

Figure 6.5: *Oracle 8i and Oracle 9i Shared Pool Structures.*

An examination of these structures reveals that the shared pool is separated into many substructures. The substructures of the shared pool fall into two broad areas: the fixed-size areas that stay relatively constant in size; and the variable-size areas that grow and shrink according to user and program requirements. The 10g shared pool structure is similar to the 9i structure.

In the figure, the areas inside the *library cache's* substructure are variable in size, while those outside the library caches, with the exception of the request and response queues used with MTS, stay relatively fixed in size. The sizes are determined by an Oracle internal algorithm that calculates a ratio from the fixed areas, based on the overall shared pool size, a few of the initialization parameters, and empirical determinations from previous versions.

In early versions of Oracle, notably 6.2 and lower, the dictionary caches could be sized individually, allowing finer control of this aspect of the shared pool. With Oracle 7 and all future releases, the internal algorithm for sizing the data dictionary caches took that fine control out of the hands of the DBA.

The shared pool is used for objects that can be shared among all users, such as table definitions, reusable SQL even though non-reusable SQL is also stored there, PL/SQL packages, procedures, and functions. Cursor information is also stored in the shared pool. At a minimum, the shared pool must be sized to accommodate the needs of the fixed areas plus a small amount of memory reserved for use in parsing SQL and PL/SQL statements. Otherwise, ORA-07445 errors will result. This concludes the review of how the shared pool is structured. The next topic to explore is how to properly configure the shared pool.

Monitoring and Tuning the Shared Pool

From experience, it has been determined that the default values for the shared pool size initialization parameters are almost always too small by at least a factor of four. Unless the database is limited to the basic scott/tiger type schema and the overall physical data size is less than a couple of hundred Megabytes, even the large parameters are far too small. What parameters control the size of the shared pool? Essentially, there is only one; the *shared_pool_size*. The other shared pool parameters control how the variable-size areas in the shared pool are parsed out, but they do not affect overall shared pool size.

Oracle8 introduced a new area, the *large pool*, controlled by the *large_pool_size* parameter. In general, it is suggested that the shared pool size start at 40 megabytes and increase from there. The large pool size will depend on the number of concurrent users, the number of multi-threaded servers, and the dispatchers and sort requirements for the application.

Looking into the Shared Pool

The four metrics below are revealed by the *memsnap.sql* query and concern the shared pool. Execution response times can be adversely affected if Oracle has to handle parse activity, perform object definition lookups, or manage other code-related or reference tasks. The shared pool helps Oracle keep these reference-related activities to a minimum by holding SQL statements along with code and object definitions in memory.

As with the data cache, properly sizing the shared pool can be tricky and often involves trial and error. The *memsnap.sql* query reveals that a shared pool that is sized too small has the following characteristics:

- Zero or near-zero percent free in the pool after the database has only been up a short while.

- A library cache hit ratio that is below average; 95% or below.

- Many object reloads due to definitions being forced from the pool prematurely.

- A below average data dictionary cache hit ratio; 95% or below.

The last three metrics mentioned above should be viewed in the same light as the buffer cache hit ratio in that delta measurements often produce more meaningful results than cumulative measurements, and some databases will perform quite well with measures that appear non-optimal.

With respect to the percent free in the shared pool, a near zero reading after the database has been up for some time is probably fine. But, if the pool drops to zero percent free shortly after Oracle is started, that is a strong indication that it may be sized too small.

When Does Less Become More?

So, why not just size the shared pool to some huge number and be done? First, as with sizing the data cache, this requires that the DBA keep an eye on available memory at the server level so that paging or swapping is not induced when RAM is added to the shared pool.

However, the second and main reason one should not oversize the shared pool is that sometimes a large pool actually causes reduced response times. How can this happen? The simple explanation is that it takes Oracle longer to search for object definitions or SQL statements in a shared pool that is excessively large.

Oracle will always try to reuse SQL statements to keep from re-parsing a query. While this can certainly reduce execution times when a shared pool is sized correctly, it can actually hinder progress when the pool is so large that Oracle wastes time interrogating it.

Getting More Details on Shared Pool Usage

While the global ratios and metrics can provide a rough idea of how efficient the shared pool is, probing deeper will provide more details on how the pool is being utilized and whether it is sized correctly.

The two main areas of the shared pool are the library and data dictionary caches. The library cache holds commonly used SQL statements, basically database code objects. One excellent method of improving performance in Oracle is to encourage the reuse of SQL statements so that expensive parse operations are avoided. The library cache assists this tuning effort.

The data dictionary cache enables the sharing of object definition information. The dictionary cache stores the description of database structures so that needed structure references can be resolved as quickly as possible.

There are three queries that can be used to extract the details of library cache usage. The *libdet.sql* script will show which object types are taking longer than others to find:

🖫 libdet.sql

```
-- *****************************************************
-- Copyright © 2005 by Rampant TechPress
-- This script is free for non-commercial purposes
-- with no warranties.  Use at your own risk.
--
-- To license this script for a commercial purpose,
-- contact info@rampant.cc
-- *****************************************************

select
        namespace,
        gets,
        round(gethitratio*100,2) gethitratio,
        pins,
        round(pinhitratio*100,2) pinhitratio,
        reloads,
        invalidations
from
        sys.v_$librarycache
order by
        1;
```

The following output shows the extraction of the library cache details:

	NAMESPACE	GETS	GETHITRATIO	PINS	PINHITRATIO	RELOADS	INVALIDATIONS
1	BODY	7755	99.47	7761	99.34	0	0
2	CLUSTER	9962	99.84	6838	99.62	0	0
3	INDEX	682	54.99	408	20.34	0	0
4	JAVA DATA	16	62.5	61	73.77	2	0
5	JAVA RESOURCE	0	100	0	100	0	0
6	JAVA SOURCE	16	81.25	22	50	2	0
7	OBJECT	0	100	0	100	0	0
8	PIPE	0	100	0	100	0	0
9	SQL AREA	2491828	99.56	11586427	99.8	1039	5494
10	TABLE/PROCEDURE	499978	99	3052161	99.64	1338	0
11	TRIGGER	44032	99.92	44039	99.91	0	0

Figure 6.6: *Extracting the library cache details*

Use bottleneck or wait-based analysis in addition to ratios and drill down queries to get an idea of overall library cache health. The *libwait.sql* query provides clues about whether Oracle has been waiting for library cache activities:

🖫 libwait.sql

```
-- *************************************************
-- Copyright © 2005 by Rampant TechPress
-- This script is free for non-commercial purposes
-- with no warranties.  Use at your own risk.
--
-- To license this script for a commercial purpose,
-- contact info@rampant.cc
-- *************************************************

select
       b.name,
       nvl(max(a.total_waits),0)
from
       sys.v_$system_event a,
       sys.v_$event_name b
where
       a.event (+)  = b.name and
       b.name in ('latch free','library cache load lock',
                  'library cache lock','library cache pin')
group by
       b.name
```

Output from the above script might resemble the following:

```
NAME                        WAITS
-------------------------   -----
latch free                     16
library cache load lock         2
library cache lock              0
library cache pin               0
```

Increasing numbers of waits for the above events could indicate an undersized shared pool. The *libobj.sql* script will dig even deeper into the *library cache* and uncover exactly which objects currently reside in the cache. This script can return large amounts of data in databases with large shared pools and many references to code and data objects:

🖫 libobj.sql

```
-- *************************************************
-- Copyright © 2005 by Rampant TechPress
-- This script is free for non-commercial purposes
-- with no warranties.  Use at your own risk.
--
-- To license this script for a commercial purpose,
-- contact info@rampant.cc
```

```
-- *****************************************************
select
        owner,
        name,
        type,
        sharable_mem,
        loads,
        executions,
        locks,
        pins,
        kept
from    sys.v_$db_object_cache
order by
        type asc;
```

The following output shows the results from drilling down into the *library cache*:

	OWNER	NAME	TYPE	SHARABLE_MEM	LOADS
8	[NULL]	select i.obj#, i.flags, u.name, o.name from sys.obj$ o, sys.user$ u, ind$ idx, sys.indpart$ i	CURSOR	11416	1
9	[NULL]	select /*+ rule */ bucket_cnt, row_cnt, cache_cnt, null_cnt, timestamp#, sample_size, minimum,	CURSOR	10468	1
10	[NULL]	select i.obj#, i.flags, u.name, o.name from sys.obj$ o, sys.user$ u, ind$ idx, sys.indpart$ i	CURSOR	1064	1
11	[NULL]	select /*+ rule */ bucket_cnt, row_cnt, cache_cnt, null_cnt, timestamp#, sample_size, minimum,	CURSOR	1068	1
12	[NULL]	select grantee#,privilege#,nvl(col#,0),max(nvl(opti	CURSOR	1003	1
13	[NULL]	SELECT 1 FROM SYS.OBJ$ WHERE OWNER# =1	CURSOR	920	1
14	[NULL]	select privilege#,nvl(col#,0),max(nvl(option$,0))fro	CURSOR	982	1
15	[NULL]	select signature from triggerjavas$ where obj#=:1	CURSOR	4224	1
16	[NULL]	select class_name, class_factory, class_factory_	CURSOR	966	1
17	[NULL]	select class_name, class_factory, class_factory_	CURSOR	5516	1
18	[NULL]	select flags from triggerjavaf$ where obj#=:1	CURSOR	903	1
19	[NULL]	select flags from triggerjavaf$ where obj#=:1	CURSOR	4524	1
20	[NULL]	select text from view$ where rowid=:1	CURSOR	895	1
21	[NULL]	select text from view$ where rowid=:1	CURSOR	4252	1
22	[NULL]	select privilege#,nvl(col#,0),max(nvl(option$,0))fro	CURSOR	6848	1
23	[NULL]	SELECT 1 FROM SYS.OBJ$ WHERE OWNER# =1	CURSOR	6960	1
24	[NULL]	insert into uet$ (segfile#,segblock#,ext#,ts#,file#,b	CURSOR	5756	1
25	[NULL]	select count (*), state from SYSTEM.DEF$_AQER	CURSOR	940	1

Figure 6.7: *Drilling down into the library cache*

Is there anything else that should be reviewed with respect to the shared pool? One other area of interest is the data dictionary cache.

More Shared Pool Metrics

To see how often Oracle is finding the system references it needs in the data dictionary; the *dictdet.sql* script, which is sorted from the best-hit ratios to the worst can be invoked:

🖫 dictdet.sql

```
-- ****************************************************
-- Copyright © 2005 by Rampant TechPress
-- This script is free for non-commercial purposes
-- with no warranties.  Use at your own risk.
--
-- To license this script for a commercial purpose,
-- contact info@rampant.cc
-- ****************************************************

select
      parameter,
      usage,
      gets,
      getmisses,
      100 - round((getmisses/
      (gets + getmisses) * 100),2) hit_ratio
from
      sys.v_$rowcache
where
      gets + getmisses <> 0
order by
      5 desc;
```

The following output shows the results from drilling down into the dictionary cache:

	PARAMETER	USAGE	GETS	GETMISSES	HIT_RATIO
1	dc_profiles	1	37318	1	100
2	dc_tablespaces	20	287977	20	99.99
3	dc_users	39	393939	42	99.99
4	dc_rollback_segments	12	106272	11	99.99
5	dc_user_grants	36	172771	48	99.97
6	dc_files	14	35355	14	99.96
7	dc_usernames	18	94137	35	99.96
8	dc_sequences	5	3426	18	99.48
9	dc_global_oids	19	1477	19	98.73
10	dc_tablespace_quotas	14	974	16	98.38
11	dc_object_ids	1037	82692	1521	98.19
12	dc_segments	629	41262	916	97.83
13	dc_objects	1638	77893	4367	94.69
14	dc_histogram_defs	1262	19592	2241	89.74
15	dc_constraints	1	1482	748	66.46
16	dc_table_scns	0	6	6	50

Figure 6.8: *Drilling down into the dictionary cache*

Just as with the *library cache*, a high *data dictionary cache hit ratio* is desirable. Strive for a hit ratio between 90% and 100%, with 95% being a good rule-of-thumb benchmark.

When a database is first started, the overall *data dictionary cache hit ratio*, as well as the individual hit ratios in the above query, will not be at an optimal level. This is because all references to object definitions will be relatively new, and as such, must be placed into the shared pool. In this situation, the DBA should expect hit ratios between 80% and 90% for new database startups.

If, however, after a solid hour or two of steady database time the *data dictionary cache hit ratio* has not increased to desirable levels, the DBA should consider the possibility of increasing the *shared_pool_size* parameter. The following script will show how much of the shared pool is actually being used.

🖫 shared_pool.sql

```
-- *****************************************************
-- Copyright © 2005 by Rampant TechPress
-- This script is free for non-commercial purposes
-- with no warranties.  Use at your own risk.
--
-- To license this script for a commercial purpose,
-- contact info@rampant.cc
-- *****************************************************

select
   sum(a.bytes)/(1024*1024) shared_pool_used,
   max(b.value)/(1024*1024) shared_pool_size,
   max(b.value)/(1024*1024))-((sum(a.bytes)/(1024*1024))
shared_pool_avail,
   (sum(a.bytes)/max(b.value))*100 shared_pool_pct
from
   v$sgastat a,
   v$parameter b
where
   a.pool = 'shared pool'
and
   a.name != 'free memory'
and
   b.name='shared_pool_size';
```

The results from the above query will be similar to the following. This output indicates that only about 10 percent of the shared pool is being utilized:

```
SHARED_POOL_USED SHARED_POOL_SIZE SHARED_POOL_AVAIL SHARED_POOL_PCT
---------------- ---------------- ----------------- ---------------
            3.66            38.15             34.49            9.60
```

All too often, the only thing monitored is the amount of the shared pool that is filled. It is important to know how it is filled; with good reusable SQL or bad throw away SQL. It is also important to know how the space is being used before deciding whether the shared pool should be increased in size, decreased in size, or kept the same with a periodic flush schedule. How can the contents of the shared pool and whether it is being properly reused or not be determined? The following few reports can help provide an answer.

The first report shows how individual users are utilizing the shared pool. Before the report can be run, a summary view of the *v$sqlarea* view must be created. The code for the *sql_summary* view is shown in below:

🔲 sql_summary.sql

```
-- *************************************************
-- Copyright © 2005 by Rampant TechPress
-- This script is free for non-commercial purposes
-- with no warranties.  Use at your own risk.
--
-- To license this script for a commercial purpose,
-- contact info@rampant.cc
-- *************************************************

create or replace view
   sql_summary
as
select
   username,
   sharable_mem,
   persistent_mem,
   runtime_mem
from
   sys.v_$sqlarea a,
   dba_users b
where
  a.parsing_user_id = b.user_id;
```

Once the *sql_summary* view is created, the following *sqlsum.sql* script is used to generate a summary report of the SQL areas in use by the connections. The report shows the distribution of SQL areas and can indicate whether users are hogging a disproportionate amount of the shared pool area. Usually, a user that is hogging a large volume of the shared pool is not using good SQL coding techniques, thereby generating a large number of non-reusable SQL areas.

🔲 sqlsum.sql

```
-- *************************************************
-- Copyright © 2005 by Rampant TechPress
-- This script is free for non-commercial purposes
-- with no warranties.  Use at your own risk.
--
-- To license this script for a commercial purpose,
-- contact info@rampant.cc
-- *************************************************

column areas                             heading Used|Areas
column sharable    format 999,999,999     heading Shared|Bytes
column persistent  format 999,999,999     heading Persistent|Bytes
```

```
column runtime      format 999,999,999    heading Runtime|Bytes
column username     format a15            heading "User"
column mem_sum      format 999,999,999    heading Mem|Sum

ttitle "Users SQL Area Memory Use"
spool sqlsum
set pages 59 lines 80
break on report

compute sum of sharable on report
compute sum of persistent on report
compute sum of runtime on report
compute sum of mem_sum on report

select
   username,
   sum(sharable_mem) Sharable,
   sum( persistent_mem) Persistent,
   sum( runtime_mem) Runtime ,
   count(*) Areas,
   sum(sharable_mem+persistent_mem+runtime_mem) Mem_sum
from
   sql_summary
group by username
order by 2;

spool off
pause Press enter to continue
clear columns
clear breaks
set pages 22 lines 80
ttitle off
```

A sample output from the script is shown below. If a particular user is hogging an SQL area, the script will show which areas they are and what is in them. This report on the actual SQL area contents can then be used to help teach the user how to better construct reusable SQL statements.

User	Shared Bytes	Persistent Bytes	Runtime Bytes	Used Areas	Mem Sum
AJONES	408,211,332	12,876,752	58,737,832	13814	479,825,916
PRECISE	45,392,274	1,155,440	12,562,016	322	59,109,730
SYS	7,458,619	86,912	350,088	2791	7,895,619
DWPROC	6,710,324	239,128	1,194,792	205	8,144,244
NETSPO	5,907,293	86,032	657,384	51	6,650,709
DSSUSER	4,985,220	174,304	742,136	97	5,901,660
...					
DEMERY	59,205	1,752	6,760	1	67,717
DBSNMP	14,416	816	5,840	1	21,072
sum	489,039,559	14,826,608	75,968,544	17427	579,834,711

In the sample output, it is noted that the *ajones* user holds the most SQL areas. The application DBA user, *dwproc*, holds a great deal less. Usually, the application owner will hold the largest section of memory in a well-designed system, followed by ad-hoc users using properly designed SQL.

In a situation where users aren't using properly designed SQL statements, the ad-hoc users will usually have the largest number of SQL areas and hog the most memory. This is the case in the sample report. Practice has shown that if a shared pool contains greater than 7,000 to 10,000 SQL areas, the pool latch has difficulty in keeping up and performance suffers. Again, the script shows the actual in-memory SQL areas for a specific user.

The *sqlmem.sql* script below shows the sample output from a report run against a user on the test system, *graphics_dba:*

🖫 sqlmem.sql

```
-- ***************************************************
-- Copyright © 2005 by Rampant TechPress
-- This script is free for non-commercial purposes
-- with no warranties.  Use at your own risk.
--
-- To license this script for a commercial purpose,
-- contact info@rampant.cc
-- ***************************************************
column sql_text         format a60   heading Text word_wrapped
column sharable_mem                  heading Shared|Bytes
column persistent_mem                heading Persistent|Bytes
column loads                         heading Loads
column users            format a15   heading "User"
column executions                      heading "Executions"
column users_executing                 heading "Used By"

ttitle "Users SQL Area Memory Use"
spool sqlmem
set long 2000 pages 59 lines 132
break on users

compute sum of sharable_mem on users
compute sum of persistent_mem on users
compute sum of runtime_mem on users

select username users, sql_text, Executions, loads, users_executing,
 sharable_mem, persistent_mem
from   sys.v_$sqlarea a, dba_users b
where  a.parsing_user_id = b.user_id
 and b.username like upper('%&user_name%')
order by 3 desc,1;
```

```
spool off
pause Press enter to continue
clear columns
clear computes
clear breaks
set pages 22 lines 80
```

The following page shows a sample listing:

Shared Per. User	Text	Executions	Loads	Used By	Bytes	Bytes
GRAPHICS_DBA	BEGIN dbms_lob.read (:1, :2, :3, :4); END;	2121	1	0	10251	488
	alter session set nls_language= 'AMERICAN' nls_territory= 'AMERICA' nls_currency= '$' nls_iso_currency= 'AMERICA' nls_numeric_characters= '.,' nls_calENDar= 'GREGORIAN' nls_date_format= 'DD-MON-YY' nls_date_language= 'AMERICAN' nls_sort= 'BINARY',	7	1	0	3975	408
	BEGIN :1 := dbms_lob.getLength (:2); END;	6	1	0	9290	448
	SELECT TO_CHAR(image_seq.nextval) FROM dual	6	1	0	6532	484
	SELECT graphic_blob FROM internal_graphics WHERE graphic_id=10	2	1	0	5863	468
	SELECT RPAD(TO_CHAR(graphic_id),5)||':'||RPAD(graphic_desc,30)||':'||RPAD(graphic_type,10) FROM internal_graphics ORDER BY graphic_id	1	1	0	7101	472
	SELECT graphic_blob FROM internal_graphics WHERE graphic_id=12	1	1	0	6099	468
	SELECT graphic_blob FROM internal_graphics WHERE graphic_id=32	1	1	0	6079	468
	SELECT graphic_blob FROM internal_graphics WHERE graphic_id=4	1	1	0	6074	468
	SELECT graphic_blob FROM internal_graphics WHERE graphic_id=8	1	1	0	5962	468
************** sum					67226	4640

Be warned that the script can generate a report of several hundred pages for a user with a large number of SQL areas (e.g., the *ajones* user in the previous report). What are the specific things that can be checked in a user's SQL areas? First, check whether bind variables are used. Bind variable usage is shown by the inclusion of variables such as ":1" or ":B" in the SQL text.

Notice how the first four statements in the sample report use bind variables and are consequently reusable. Non-bind variables mean hard-coded values such as "Missing" or "10" are used. Also, most of the remaining statements in the report do not use bind variables, even though many of the SQL statements are nearly identical. This is one of the leading causes of shared pool misuse and results in useful SQL being drowned in tons of non-reusable garbage SQL.

The problem with non-reusable SQL is that it must still be checked by any new SQL inserted into the pool. To be technically correct, its hash value is scanned. While a hash value scan may seem trivial, if the shared pool contains tens of thousands of SQL areas, it can cause a performance bottleneck. Without running a report for each of possibly hundreds of users, how can it be determined if there is garbage SQL in the shared pool?

The *sql_garbage* script below provides details on reuse of the SQL area by individual users. The view can be tailored to individual environments if the limit on reuse, currently set at one, is too restrictive. For example, in a recent tuning assignment, resetting the value to 12 resulted in nearly 70 percent of the SQL being rejected as garbage. In DSS or data warehouse systems, in which rollups are performed by the month, bi-monthly, or weekly values of 12, 24, or 52 might be advisable.

sql_garbage.sql

```
-- *****************************************************
-- Copyright © 2005 by Rampant TechPress
-- This script is free for non-commercial purposes
-- with no warranties.  Use at your own risk.
--
-- To license this script for a commercial purpose,
-- contact info@rampant.cc
```

```
-- **************************************************
REM View to sort SQL into GOOD and GARBAGE
REM
CREATE OR REPLACE VIEW sql_garbage AS
SELECT  b.username users,
        SUM(a.sharable_mem+a.persistent_mem) Garbage,
        TO_NUMBER(null) good
FROM    sys.v_$sqlarea a, dba_users b
WHERE   (a.parsing_user_id = b.user_id and a.executions<=1)
GROUP BY b.username
  UNION
SELECT DISTINCT b.username users,
        TO_NUMBER(null) garbage,
        SUM(c.sharable_mem+c.persistent_mem) Good
FROM    dba_users b, sys.v_$sqlarea c
WHERE   (b.user_id = c.parsing_user_id and c.executions>1)
GROUP BY b.username;

column garbage format a14 heading 'Non-Shared SQL'
column good format a14 heading 'Shared SQL'
column good_percent format a14 heading 'Percent Shared'
column users format a14 heading users
column nopr noprint
set feedback off
ttitle 'Shared Pool Utilization'
spool sql_garbage

select 1 nopr, a.users users,
      to_char(a.garbage,'9,999,999,999') garbage,
      to_char(b.good,'9,999,999,999') good,
      to_char((b.good/(b.good+a.garbage))*100,'9,999,999.999')
       good_percent
from  sql_garbage a, sql_garbage b
where a.users=b.users
      and a.garbage is not null and b.good is not null
union
select 2 nopr, '-------------' users,
      '-------------' garbage,
      '-------------' good,
      '-------------' good_percent
from  dual
union
select 3 nopr, to_char(count(a.users)) users,
      to_char(sum(a.garbage),'9,999,999,999') garbage,
      to_char(sum(b.good),'9,999,999,999') good,
      to_char(((sum(b.good)/(sum(b.good)+sum(a.garbage)))*100),
       '9,999,999.999') good_percent
from  sql_garbage a, sql_garbage b
where  a.users=b.users
and    a.garbage is not null and b.good is not null
order by 1,3 desc
/
spool off
```

The following result indicates which users are not making good use of reusable SQL:

---

users	Non-Shared SQL	Shared SQL	Percent Shared
AJONES	371,387,006	1,007,366	.271
NETSPO	10,603,456	659,999	5.860
DCHUN	6,363,158	151,141	2.320
DSSUSER	5,363,057	824,865	13.330
MRCHDXD	4,305,330	600,824	12.246
DWPROC	2,690,086	4,901,400	64.564
CWOOD	946,199	239,604	20.206
TMANCEOR	877,644	93,323	9.611
GCMATCH	604,369	1,637,788	73.045
MAULT	445,566	3,737,984	89.350
PRECISE	205,564	46,342,150	99.558
BKUEHNE	154,754	35,858	18.812
SYS	146,811	9,420,434	98.465
SMANN	102,460	8,523,746	98.812
MRCHPHP	56,954	59,069	50.911
MRCHAEM	42,465	65,017	60.491
16	404,553,888	78,358,468	16.226

In this result, the *ajones* user only shows 0.271% shared SQL use, based on memory footprints. From the report, a low reuse value for *ajones* based on the information provided in earlier reports would be expected.

A final report, *similar_sql.sql*, shows SQL that is being generated over and over again, based on the first 90 characters. Of course, longer or shorter pieces of code can be viewed by simply changing the call to the *substr()* function.

💾 similar_sql.sql

```
-- *************************************************
-- Copyright © 2005 by Rampant TechPress
-- This script is free for non-commercial purposes
-- with no warranties.  Use at your own risk.
--
-- To license this script for a commercial purpose,
-- contact info@rampant.cc
-- *************************************************

set lines 140 pages 55 verify off feedback off
col num_of_times heading 'Number|Of|Repeats'
col SQL heading 'SubString width - &&chars Characters'
col username format a15 heading 'User'
ttitle 'Similar SQL'
spool similar_sql&&chars
select b.username,substr(a.sql_text,1,&&chars) SQL, count(a.sql_text)
num_of_times from v$sqlarea a, dba_users b
where a.parsing_user_id=b.user_id
```

```
group by b.username,substr(a.sql_text,1,&&chars) having
count(a.sql_text)>&&num_repeats
order by count(a.sql_text) desc
/
spool off
undef chars
undef num_repeats
clear columns
set lines 80 pages 22 verify on feedback on
ttitle off
```

An example report generated by this script is shown on the next page:

User	SubString - 90 Characters	Repeats
SYS	INSERT INTO MONT3_TBL_SLA_FAILURES_LOG (ERROR_CODE,ERROR_TEXT,ERROR_FIELDS,ERROR_DATE) VAL	142
BO	update OBJ_M_TIMESTAMP set M_TMS_N_ENTITYTYPE = 2 , M_TMS_N_ENTITYID = 16 , M_TMS_N_BEGINT	91
BO	select pj.BATCH_ID, pj.DOCUMENT_ID, pj.USER_SUBMIT_ID, pj.PRIORITY, pj.FREQUENCY, pj.BEGIN	83
DWOWNER	SELECT ds.segment_name, ds.segment type, ds.tablespace name, ds.owner, f.file#, e.block#	21
SYS	INSERT INTO FTIN1_TBL_PMC_DATA_LOG (ERROR_CODE,ERROR_TEXT,ERROR_FIELDS,ERROR_DATE) VALUES(	21
DWOWNER	select fe.ts#, fs.file_id, fe.block#, fe.length FROM sys.dba_free space fs, sys.fet$ fe, s	21
DWOWNER	SELECT tablespace_name, initial_extent, next_extent, min_extents, max extents, pct	14
DWOWNER	INSERT INTO FTIN1_TBL_SLA_FAILURES_LOG (ERROR_CODE,ERROR_TEXT,ERROR_FIELDS,ERROR_DATE) VAL	12
SYS	INSERT INTO FTIN1_TBL_NPO_DATA_LOG (ERROR_CODE,ERROR_TEXT,ERROR_FIELDS,ERROR_DATE) VALUES(	11
BO	select M_GENPAR_N_ID from OBJ_M_GENPAR where M_GENPAR_N_ID = 500 and M_GENPAR_N_APPLID = 9	8
SYS	GRANT SELECT ON DBA_	7
BO	select M_ACTL_N_ID, M_ACTOR_N_ID, M_ACTL_N_FATLINKID, M_ACTL_N_ACTORTYPE, M_ACTL_N_INFO, M	6
SYS	GRANT SELECT ON V_$S	5
BO	select M_ACTOR_N_ID, M_ACTOR_N_STATUS, M_ACTOR_N_LEVEL, M_ACTOR_N_AUTID, M_ACTOR_N_ENDING,	4
SYS	SELECT tablespace_name, initial_extent, next_extent, min_extent, max_extent, pct_i	4
DWOWNER	GRANT SELECT ON V_$I	4
SYS	alter session set nls_language= 'AMERICAN' nls_territory= 'AMERICA' nls_currency= '$' nls	4
SYS	INSERT INTO MES_TRANSACTION_LOG_INTERIM (TRANSACTION_KEY,LOT_KEY,PLANT_LOCATION,ACTUAL_DAT	4
SYS	GRANT SELECT ON dba_	4
GTRMAP1	select decode(transaction_name,'START',operation_name,'COMPLETE',from operation name) oper	4
BO	select M_DOC_N_ID, M_RES_N_STATUS, M_DOC_N_REPOID, M_DOC_C_NAME, M_ACTOR_C_NAME, M_DOC_N_D	4

Conclusions about the Shared Pool

Reports have been examined that show both gross and detailed shared pool usage and whether shared areas are being reused. What can be done with this data? Ideally, the results will be used to size the shared pool properly. The following are a few general guidelines for shared pool sizing:

Shared Pool Sizing: Guideline 1

If gross usage of the shared pool in a non-ad-hoc environment rises to 95% or greater and stays there, a shared pool size large enough to hold the fixed size portions should be established. Reusable packages and procedures should be pinned and the shared pool increased by 20% increments, until usage drops below 90% on average.

Shared Pool Sizing: Guideline 2

If the shared pool shows a mixed ad-hoc and reuse environment, a shared pool size large enough to hold the fixed size portions should be established. The reusable packages should be pinned and a comfort level above this required pool fill level established. Then a routine flush cycle should be established to filter non-reusable code from the pool.

Shared Pool Sizing: Guideline 3

If the shared pool shows that no reusable SQL is being used, a shared pool large enough to hold the fixed size portions, plus a few Megabytes, should be established. The few extra Megabytes should usually not exceed 40. The least recently used (LRU) algorithm should be allowed to manage the shared pool.

Using guidelines one, two, and three, a standard-sized system should start at around 40 megabytes. Guideline two recommends a routine flush cycle be instituted. This is counter to the Oracle Support recommendation in their shared pool white papers; however, Oracle works from the questionable assumption that proper SQL is being generated and that the SQL present in the shared pool is going to be reused.

In an environment in which there is a mixture of reusable and non-reusable SQL, the non-reusable SQL will act as a drag against the other SQL unless it is periodically removed by flushing.

The following code, *Flush_it_proc.sql*, is a PL/SQL package that can be used by the *dbms_job* job queues to periodically flush the shared pool when it exceeds a specified percentage:

🖫 Flush_it_proc.sql

```
-- ******************************************************
-- Copyright © 2005 by Rampant TechPress
-- This script is free for non-commercial purposes
-- with no warranties.  Use at your own risk.
--
-- To license this script for a commercial purpose,
-- contact info@rampant.cc
-- ******************************************************
CREATE OR REPLACE PROCEDURE flush_it(
    p_free IN NUMBER, num_runs IN NUMBER) IS
--
CURSOR get_share IS
SELECT
  LEAST(MAX(b.value)/(1024*1024),SUM(a.bytes)/(1024*1024))
   FROM v$sgastat a, v$parameter b
 WHERE (a.pool='shared pool'
 AND a.name <> ('free memory'))
 AND b.name = 'shared_pool_size';
--
CURSOR get_var IS
 SELECT   value/(1024*1024)
 FROM v$parameter
 WHERE name = 'shared_pool_size';
--
CURSOR get_time IS
 SELECT sysdate FROM dual;
--
-- Following cursors from Steve Adams Nice_flush
--
  CURSOR reused_cursors IS
    SELECT address || ',' || hash_value
    FROM sys.v_$sqlarea
    WHERE executions > num_runs;
  cursor_string varchar2(30);
--
  CURSOR cached_sequences IS
    SELECT  sequence_owner, sequence_name
    FROM  sys.dba_sequences
```

```
    WHERE cache_size > 0;
  sequence_owner varchar2(30);
  sequence_name varchar2(30);
--
  CURSOR candidate_objects IS
    SELECT kglnaobj, decode(kglobtyp, 6, 'Q', 'P')
    FROM sys.x_$kglob
    WHERE inst_id = userenv('Instance') AND
      kglnaown = 'SYS' AND kglobtyp in (6, 7, 8, 9);
  object_name varchar2(128);
  object_type char(1);
--
-- end of Steve Adams Cursors
--
  todays_date      DATE;
  mem_ratio        NUMBER;
  share_mem        NUMBER;
  variable_mem     NUMBER;
  cur              INTEGER;
  sql_com   VARCHAR2(60);
  row_proc  NUMBER;
--
BEGIN
 OPEN get_share;
 OPEN get_var;
 FETCH get_share INTO share_mem;
 FETCH get_var INTO variable_mem;
 mem_ratio:=share_mem/variable_mem;
 IF mem_ratio>p_free/100 THEN
 --
 -- Following keep sections from Steve Adams nice_flush
 --
 BEGIN
  OPEN reused_cursors;
  LOOP
    FETCH reused_cursors INTO cursor_string;
    EXIT WHEN reused_cursors%notfound;
    sys.dbms_shared_pool.keep(cursor_string, 'C');
  END LOOP;
 END;
 BEGIN
  OPEN cached_sequences;
  LOOP
    FETCH cached_sequences INTO sequence_owner, sequence_name;
    EXIT WHEN cached_sequences%notfound;
    sys.dbms_shared_pool.keep(sequence_owner || '.' || sequence_name, 'Q');
  END LOOP;
 END;
 BEGIN
  OPEN candidate_objects;
  LOOP
    FETCH candidate_objects INTO object_name, object_type;
    EXIT WHEN candidate_objects%notfound;
    sys.dbms_shared_pool.keep('SYS.' || object_name, object_type);
  END LOOP;
 END;
 --
 -- end of Steve Adams section
 --
```

```
 cur:=DBMS_SQL.OPEN_CURSOR;
 sql_com:='ALTER SYSTEM FLUSH SHARED_POOL';
 DBMS_SQL.PARSE(cur,sql_com,dbms_sql.v7);
 row_proc:=DBMS_SQL.EXECUTE(cur);
 DBMS_SQL.CLOSE_CURSOR(cur);
 OPEN get_time;
 FETCH get_time INTO todays_date;
 INSERT INTO dba_running_stats VALUES
    (
    'Flush of Shared Pool',1,35,todays_date,0
    );
 COMMIT;
 END IF;
END flush_it;
```

An example of a command that can be used to perform a flush once every 30 minutes, but only when the pool reaches 95% full, would be:

```
VARIABLE x NUMBER;
BEGIN
dbms_job.submit(
:X,'BEGIN flush_it(95,24); END;',SYSDATE,'SYSDATE+(30/1440)');
END;
/
COMMIT;
(Always commit after assigning a job or the job will not be run and queued)
```

There has been some discussion whether this really does help performance. A test on a production instance was run. On day 1 there was no automated flushing and on day 2 automated flushing was utilized. Observe Figure 6.9 in which a series of graphs of performance indicators, flush cycles, and users are shown:

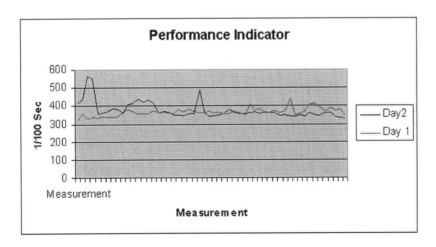

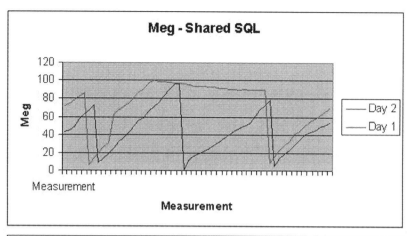

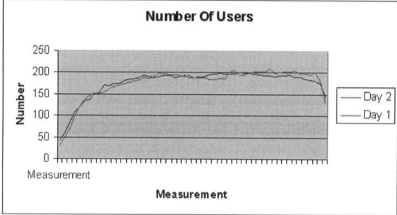

Figure 6.9: *Graphs Showing Effects of Flushing.*

Notice the overall trend of the performance indicator between day 1 and day 2 in the graphs. On day 1, the day with an initial flush, as indicated by the steep plunge on the pool utilization graph, followed by the buildup to maximum and the flattening of the graph, the performance indicator shows an upward trend.

The performance indicator is a measure of how long the database takes to do a specific set of tasks. An increase in the performance indicator shows a net decrease in performance.

However, on day 2, the overall trend is downward, with the average value less than the average value from day 1. Overall, flushing improved the performance by 10 to 20 percent, as indicated by the performance indicator. Depending on the environment, improvements of 40 to 50 percent have been observed.

One factor complicating the analysis was several large batch jobs run on day 2 were not run on day 1. The results still show that flushing has a positive effect on performance when the database is in a mixed SQL environment with a large percentage of non-reusable SQL areas.

If the shared pool has already been over-allocated, guideline three may actually result in a decrease in the size of the shared pool. In this situation, the shared pool has become a cesspool filled with garbage SQL. After allocating enough memory for dictionary objects and other fixed areas and ensuring that the standard packages and such are pinned, only a few megabytes beyond this amount of memory are maintained for SQL statements.

Since none of the code is being reused, the hash search overhead should be reduced as much as possible. This can be accomplished by reducing the size of the available SQL area memory so that the number of kept statements is as small as possible.

Shared Pool Sizing:Guideline 4

The usage patterns of packages, procedures, functions, triggers, and cursors should be determined. Those that are frequently used should be pinned.

How to Keep Code Where It Belongs

Many loads could indicate that the object is continuously being forced from the cache, which would potentially degrade performance.

If the object is a code object such as a procedure, package, etc., the code should be pinned in the cache to stop it from being removed. In the *libobj.sql* query that was listed previously, refer to the *kept* column to see which code objects, if any, have already been pinned.

The *dbms_shared_pool* package is used to pin or unpin code objects to and from the *library cache*. For example, in order to assure that a frequently referenced procedure called *eradmin.add_admission* was always available in the library cache for quick reference, execute the following:

```
exec sys.dbms_shared_pool.keep('ERADMIN.ADD_ADMISSION','P');
```

Performing a pin keeps the code available at all times. Pinned objects are also impervious to an *alter system flush shared_pool* command.

The following script, *Gen_keep.sql,* which generates a script to pin appropriate objects can be run:

⌸ Gen_keep.sql

```
--  *************************************************
-- Copyright © 2005 by Rampant TechPress
-- This script is free for non-commercial purposes
-- with no warranties.  Use at your own risk.
--
-- To license this script for a commercial purpose,
-- contact info@rampant.cc
--  *************************************************

set lines 132 feedback off verify off
set pages 0
spool keep_them.sql
select  'execute
dbms_shared_pool.keep('||chr(39)||OWNER||'.'||name||chr(39)||','|| chr(39)||
decode(type,'PACKAGE','P','PROCEDURE','P','FUNCTION','P','SEQUENCE','Q',
                        'TRIGGER','R')||chr(39)||')'
from
 v$db_object_cache
where
 type not in ('NOT LOADED','NON-EXISTENT','VIEW','TABLE',
  'INVALID TYPE','CURSOR','PACKAGE BODY')
 and executions>loads and executions>1 and kept='NO'
order by owner,namespace,type,executions desc
/
spool off
```

The following output, *keep_them.sql,* is a set of pinning commands:

keep_them.sql

```
--  ****************************************************
-- Copyright © 2005 by Rampant TechPress
-- This script is free for non-commercial purposes
-- with no warranties.  Use at your own risk.
--
-- To license this script for a commercial purpose,
-- contact info@rampant.cc
--  ****************************************************

execute dbms_shared_pool.keep('APPS.WF_PARAMETER_T','')
execute dbms_shared_pool.keep('APPS.WF_EVENT_T','')
execute dbms_shared_pool.keep('APPS.WF_AGENT_T','')
execute dbms_shared_pool.keep('APPS.BOSS_GET_EMP_NAME','P')
execute dbms_shared_pool.keep('APPS.BEN_PEN_BUS','P')
execute dbms_shared_pool.keep('APPS.PAY_ELE_SHD','P')
execute dbms_shared_pool.keep('APPS.PSB_HR_POPULATE_DATA_PVT','P')
execute dbms_shared_pool.keep('APPS.BEN_ENROLLMENT_ACTION_ITEMS','P')
execute dbms_shared_pool.keep('APPS.FND_REQUEST_SET','P')
execute dbms_shared_pool.keep('APPS.BOSS_RECEIPT','P')
execute dbms_shared_pool.keep('APPS.BEN_ELIG_DPNT_WHO','R')
execute dbms_shared_pool.keep('APPS.BEN_ELIG_PER_ELCTBL_CHC_WHO','R')
execute dbms_shared_pool.keep('APPS.BEN_ELIG_PER_OPT_F_WHO','R')
execute dbms_shared_pool.keep('APPS.GHR_PAY_ELEMENT_ENTVAL_F_AFIUD','R')
execute dbms_shared_pool.keep('APPS.BEN_ENRT_RT_WHO','R')
execute dbms_shared_pool.keep('APPS.BEN_ELIG_PER_F_WHO','R')
```

While this technique works well for code objects, what about regular SQL statements? What procedure would be used to keep them in the shared pool so that parse operations are minimized? The easiest method is to ensure that user sessions are launching identical SQL statements, which allows reuse to occur in the cache.

If Oracle detects that a user process has launched an identical SQL statement that is already present in the cache, it will reuse the statement rather than parse and load it into memory. Using literals in SQL statements instead of bind variables can greatly hinder this process. The key to statement reuse is that the SQL has to be identical, and the use of literals in SQL statements can entirely negate this.

If it is not possible to encase a user's SQL in applications or stored code objects to ensure bind variables are being used instead of literals, what can be done? In version 8.1.6, Oracle quietly introduced the *cursor_sharing* parameter, which deals with the problem of literals in otherwise identical SQL statements in a hurry.

If the parameter is set to FORCE, Oracle will substitute bind variables in the place of literals in any SQL statement and place it into the *library cache*. This permits any statement submitted subsequently to be reused, so long as the only difference is its bind variable(s).

Shared Pool Sizing: Guideline 5

The Shared Pool and the MTS

Using the Oracle multi-threaded server option (MTS) may require a dramatic increase in the size of the shared pool. This increase is due to the addition of the user global areas required for sorting and message queues. When using MTS, the *v$sgastat* values for MTS-related memory areas should be monitored, and the shared pool memory allocations adjusted accordingly.

Shared Pool Sizing: Guideline 6

Bind variables, PL/SQL (procedures or functions), and views should be used to reduce the size of large SQL statements in order to prevent hashing problems.

Are there any other SGA issues that should be checked periodically? One area is the redo log buffer.

Shared Pool Sizing: Guideline 7

If no flushing is used, the shared pool size should be increased in order to reduce reloads and invalidations and increase hit ratios.

The data dictionary caches used to be tuned individually through several initialization parameters. Now, they are internally controlled. The *ddcache.sql* script below can be used to monitor the overall hit ratio for the data dictionary caches:

ddcache.sql

```
-- ***************************************************
-- Copyright © 2005 by Rampant TechPress
-- This script is free for non-commercial purposes
-- with no warranties.  Use at your own risk.
--
-- To license this script for a commercial purpose,
-- contact info@rampant.cc
-- ***************************************************

ttitle "DD Cache Hit Ratio"
spool ddcache
SELECT
   (SUM(getmisses)/SUM(gets))*100 RATIO
FROM
   v$rowcache;
spool off
pause Press enter to continue
ttitle off
```

Here is the output from the script above:

```
   RATIO
---------
 1.273172
```

The reported ratio should always be less than one. The ratio corresponds to the number of times out of 100 that the database engine searched the cache without finding anything. A dictionary cache miss is more expensive than a data block buffer miss, so if the ratio approaches one, the size of the shared pool should be increased. If the ratio is close to one, the internal algorithm isn't allocating enough memory to the data dictionary caches.

Guideline 8

If the data dictionary cache ratio is greater than 1.0, the size of the shared pool should be increased.

Examining the Log Buffer

Sometimes a user process must wait for space in the redo log buffer. Oracle uses the log buffer to cache redo entries prior to writing them to disk, and if the buffer area is not large enough for the redo entry load, waits can occur.

The log buffer is normally small in comparison with other regions of the SGA, and a small increase in size can significantly enhance throughput.

The *memsnap.sql* script, provided near the beginning of this chapter, contains two main numbers to watch for the log buffer; redo log space requests and, perhaps more importantly, redo log wait time.

If either statistic strays too far from zero, consider increasing the *log_buffer* parameter and adding more memory to the redo log buffer.

With a better understanding of how the SGA is performing globally, this might be a good time to look into memory usage at the session level to see which processes are consuming the most resources and making life miserable for everyone.

Miscellaneous Memory Issues

Buffer Busy Waits

Buffer busy waits occur when a process needs to access a data block in the buffer cache but cannot because it is being used by another process. So, it must wait. Buffer busy waits normally center around contention for rollback segments, too small an *initrans* setting for tables, or insufficient *freelists* for tables.

The remedy for each situation would be to increase the number of rollback segments, to alter tables for larger *initrans* settings to allow for more transactions per data block, or add more *freelists*. The automatic segment management feature in Oracle9i locally-managed tablespaces can make the *freelist* problem a thing of the past, while the UNDO tablespace feature of 9i can help remedy any rollback contention problem.

However, segment header contention will still occur when concurrent tasks attempt to INSERT into the same table, and multiple *freelists* are required to remove these sources of buffer busy waits.

If using Oracle9i and above, the *bufobjwaits.sql* will find which objects have been the sources of buffer busy waits:

🖫 bufobjwaits.sql

```
-- ***************************************************
-- Copyright © 2005 by Rampant TechPress
-- This script is free for non-commercial purposes
-- with no warranties.  Use at your own risk.
--
-- To license this script for a commercial purpose,
-- contact info@rampant.cc
-- ***************************************************

select
        owner,
        object_name,
        object_type,
        value waits
from
        sys.v_$segment_statistics
where
        (statistic_name = 'buffer busy waits' and value > 0)
order by
        1,2;
```

The output is noted as follows and displays the objects that have waited and the number of times:

```
OWNER       OBJECT_NAME    OBJECT_TYPE    WAITS
---------------------------------------------
USR1        TAB1           TABLE              3
USR1        TAB2           TABLE              2
USR1        TAB3           TABLE              2
```

Oracle 10g

Oracle10g Automatic Memory Management

In Oracle10g, it is possible to follow the progress of various memory ratios, as well as other performance metrics, over time through the *v$sysmetric_history* view. The nice thing is that the computational work of producing delta-based statistics has already been done, so no special scripts or STATSPACK are needed to do the job.

Ratio Coverage in Oracle10g

The following is a quick examination of how Oracle10g enables the historical analysis of ratios in newly introduced performance views.

If the DBA wants to look at the library cache hit ratio over the last hour, the *libcachhist.sql* script can be used:

🖫 libcachhist.sql

```
-- *************************************************
-- Copyright © 2005 by Rampant TechPress
-- This script is free for non-commercial purposes
-- with no warranties.  Use at your own risk.
--
-- To license this script for a commercial purpose,
-- contact info@rampant.cc
-- *************************************************

select
        to_char(end_time, 'YYYY-MON-DD HH:MI:SS') end_time,
        value,
        metric_unit
from
        sys.v_$sysmetric_history
where
        metric_name = 'Library Cache Hit Ratio'
order by
        1
```

The truncated output from the above SQL script looks like this:

```
END TIME                      VALUE METRIC_UNIT
--------------------      ---------- ----------------------
2004-MAY-03 04:03:25         100 % Hits/Pins
2004-MAY-03 04:04:24         100 % Hits/Pins
2004-MAY-03 04:05:25          99 % Hits/Pins
2004-MAY-03 04:06:27          99 % Hits/Pins
2004-MAY-03 04:07:25          99 % Hits/Pins
2004-MAY-03 04:08:26          99 % Hits/Pins
2004-MAY-03 04:09:24          99 % Hits/Pins
2004-MAY-03 04:10:25          99 % Hits/Pins
2004-MAY-03 04:11:27          99 % Hits/Pins
2004-MAY-03 04:12:26          99 % Hits/Pins
2004-MAY-03 04:13:26          98 % Hits/Pins
2004-MAY-03 04:14:24         100 % Hits/Pins
2004-MAY-03 04:15:26          99 % Hits/Pins
2004-MAY-03 04:16:24          98 % Hits/Pins
```

The *v$sysmetric_history* view is very handy to use for memory ratios and other performance statistics. It is a view that a DBA will likely become quite familiar with if working in Oracle10g or higher.

In Oracle10g, it is possible to let Oracle take over the management and distribution of SGA memory. By setting the *sga_target* parameter, Oracle takes 'x' amount of memory and allocates it among as many of the various memory regions as it desires. By setting this parameter to a non-zero number, it is no longer necessary to set the following parameters: *shared_pool_size*; *large_pool_size*; *db_cache_size*; and *java_pool_size*. Other memory parameters like the buffer recycle and keep caches still require manual tuning.

dba_hist_librarycache

The *dba_hist_librarycache* view contains statistical history for library cache activity. This view stores snapshots for the *v$librarycache* dynamic view. The library cache stores SQL cursors, Java classes, and PL/SQL programs in executable form. If library cache contention is significant, this view can be queried to get more details about particular library objects that may cause such a contention. These details will give users hints about ways to potentially reduce library cache contention.

In order to understand the importance of library cache tuning, the DBA must always be aware that a library and dictionary cache miss is more expensive in terms of resources than a data buffer miss because it involves a significant amount of CPU work.

```
SQL> desc DBA_HIST_LIBRARYCACHE

Name                  Null?     Type
-----------------     --------  ------------
SNAP_ID               NOT NULL  NUMBER
DBID                  NOT NULL  NUMBER
INSTANCE_NUMBER       NOT NULL  NUMBER
NAMESPACE             NOT NULL  VARCHAR2(15)
GETS                            NUMBER
GETHITS                        NUMBER
PINS                           NUMBER
PINHITS                        NUMBER
RELOADS                        NUMBER
INVALIDATIONS                  NUMBER
DLM_LOCK_REQUESTS              NUMBER
DLM_PIN_REQUESTS               NUMBER
DLM_PIN_RELEASES               NUMBER
DLM_INVALIDATION_              NUMBER
REQUESTS
DLM_INVALIDATIONS              NUMBER
```

The following *lib_cache_int_10g.sql* query can be used to retrieve a report for library cache statistics:

🖫 lib_cache_int_10g.sql

```
-- ***************************************************
-- Copyright © 2005 by Rampant TechPress
-- This script is free for non-commercial purposes
-- with no warranties.  Use at your own risk.
--
-- To license this script for a commercial purpose,
-- contact info@rampant.cc
-- ***************************************************

select b.namespace "Name Space"
    , e.gets - b.gets  "Get Requests"
    , to_number(decode(e.gets,b.gets,null,
      100 - (e.gethits - b.gethits) * 100/(e.gets - b.gets))) "Get Pct
Miss"
    , e.pins - b.pins "Pin Requests"
    , to_number(decode(e.pins,b.pins,null,
      100 - (e.pinhits - b.pinhits) * 100/(e.pins - b.pins))) "Pin Pct
Miss"
    , e.reloads - b.reloads                            "Reloads"
    , e.invalidations - b.invalidations
"Invalidations"
  from dba_hist_librarycache  b
    , dba_hist_librarycache  e
```

```
where b.snap_id            = &pBgnSnap
  and e.snap_id            = &pEndSnap
  and b.dbid               = &pDbId
  and e.dbid               = &pDbId
  and b.dbid               = e.dbid
  and b.instance_number    = &pInstNum
  and e.instance_number    = &pInstNum
  and b.instance_number    = e.instance_number
  and b.namespace          = e.namespace
```

The following is a possible result of this query:

```
SQL> @ Lib_cache_int_10g.sql

Name Space      Get Requests Get Pct Miss Pin Requests Pin Pct Miss  Reloads Invalids
--------------- ------------ ------------ ------------ ------------  -------- --------
BODY                 596338  .068417575        985463  .046272666        35        0
CLUSTER                2555  1.01761252          6534  .642791552        16        0
INDEX                  2183  85.6161246         10599  26.8232852         0        0
JAVA DATA               183           0             0                     0        0
JAVA RESOURCE             4         100             8          100        0        0
JAVA SOURCE               0                         0                     0        0
OBJECT                    0                         0                     0        0
PIPE                      0                         0                     0        0
SQL AREA            1593263  1.95730397      10746720  .758361621     18493     3083
TABLE/PROCEDURE      240318  3.66680815       2315873  1.72284922     12897        0
TRIGGER               19324  2.56158145         85401  .971885575       321        0
```

The report shows what particular types of library cache contents have the highest miss percentage. This means that these objects require additional work to reload them back into library cache thereby causing CPU overhead.

The WISE tool has a report named Library Cache, which generates charts against the *dba_hist_librarycache* view as shown in Figure 6.10:

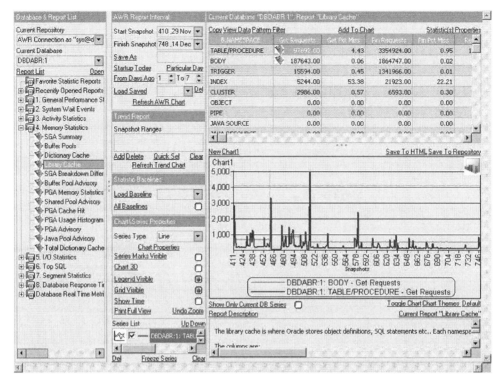

Figure 6.10: *AWR Library Cache chart in WISE.*

dba_hist_rowcache_summary

The *dba_hist_rowcache_summary* view stores history summary statistics for data dictionary cache activity. This view contains snapshots for the *v$rowcache* dynamic view. The data dictionary cache stores metadata information about schema objects that participate in SQL parsing or compilation of PL/SQL programs.

The following is a *describe* of the *dba_hist_rowcache_summary* view:

```
SQL> desc DBA_HIST_ROWCACHE_SUMMARY

Name                   Null?    Type
-----------------      -------- -----------
SNAP_ID                         NUMBER
DBID                            NUMBER
```

```
INSTANCE_NUMBER              NUMBER
PARAMETER                    VARCHAR2(32)
TOTAL_USAGE                  NUMBER
USAGE                        NUMBER
GETS                         NUMBER
GETMISSES                    NUMBER
SCANS                        NUMBER
SCANMISSES                   NUMBER
SCANCOMPLETES                NUMBER
MODIFICATIONS                NUMBER
FLUSHES                      NUMBER
DLM_REQUESTS                 NUMBER
DLM_CONFLICTS                NUMBER
DLM_RELEASES                 NUMBER
```

The following *rowcache_int_10g.sql* query can be used to retrieve historical statistical data for data dictionary cache:

🖫 rowcache_int_10g.sql

```
-- ***********************************************
-- Copyright © 2005 by Rampant TechPress
-- This script is free for non-commercial purposes
-- with no warranties.  Use at your own risk.
--
-- To license this script for a commercial purpose,
-- contact info@rampant.cc
-- ***********************************************

select
  param "Parameter",
  gets "Get Requests",
  getm "Pct Miss",
  scans "Scan Requests",
  scanm "Pct Miss",
  mods "Mod Req",
  usage "Final Usage"
From
(select lower(b.parameter)                              param
     , e.gets - b.gets                                  gets
     , to_number(decode(e.gets,b.gets,null,
       (e.getmisses - b.getmisses) * 100/(e.gets - b.gets)))  getm
     , e.scans - b.scans                                scans
     , to_number(decode(e.scans,b.scans,null,
       (e.scanmisses - b.scanmisses) * 100/(e.scans - b.scans))) scanm
     , e.modifications - b.modifications                mods
     , e.usage                                          usage
  from dba_hist_rowcache_summary  b
     , dba_hist_rowcache_summary  e
 where b.snap_id         = &pBgnSnap
   and e.snap_id         = &pEndSnap
   and b.dbid            = &pDbId
   and e.dbid            = &pDbId
   and b.dbid            = e.dbid
   and b.instance_number = &pInstNum
```

```
    and e.instance_number = &pInstNum
    and b.instance_number = e.instance_number
    and b.parameter       = e.parameter
    and e.gets - b.gets    > 0   )
order by param;
```

The following is sample output from the *rowcache_int_10g.sql* script that displays details about dictionary cache activity for a particular snapshot interval:

```
SQL> @rowcache_int_10g.sql
Parameter                Get Requests    Pct Miss Scan Reqs   Pct Miss   Mod Req Final Usage
----------------------   ------------    -------- ---------   --------   ------- -----------
dc_awr_control                  11858           0         0                  374           1
dc_constraints                   1324   50.8308157        0                 1311           1
dc_database_links                3309   .090661831        0                    3           1
dc_files                          650   1.84615385        0                    6          12
dc_global_oids                1176297   .074726026        0                    0          13
dc_histogram_data              151274   9.03724368        0                 7338         915
dc_histogram_defs              302695   29.5191529        0                14655        1645
dc_object_ids                 1674476   .609145787        0                  763         975
dc_objects                     258066   5.60244279        0                 2497         652
dc_profiles                     14968           0         0                    0           1
dc_rollback_segments           150163           0         0                    0          22
dc_segments                    270211   4.27517755        0                 3529         756
dc_sequences                     2398   2.91909925        0                 2398           3
dc_table_scns                    2144   8.11567164        0                    0           9
dc_tablespace_quotas              918   2.17864924        0                  573           0
dc_tablespaces                 414603   .000964778        0                    4          13
dc_usernames                    65367   .123915737        0                    2          19
dc_users                      4171619   .005057988        0                   20          71
global database name             1318   .227617602        0                    0           1
outstanding_alerts              16160   4.46163366        0                 1417          15
```

The WISE tool has a report named Dictionary Cache, which generates charts against *dba_hist_rowcache_summary* view as shown in Figure 6.11.

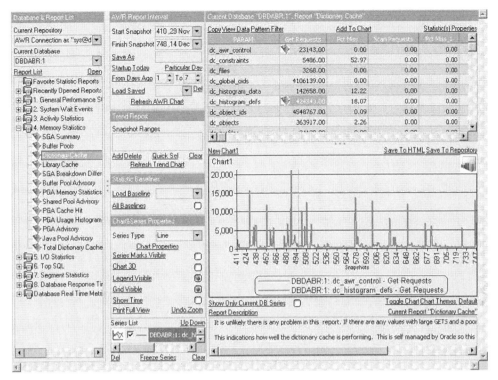

Figure 6.11: *AWR Dictionary Cache chart in WISE.*

dba_hist_buffer_pool_stat

The *dba_hist_buffer_pool_stat* view contains statistic history for all buffer pools configured for the instance. Additional non-default buffer caches can be used as *keep* and *recycle* caches in order to address atypical access patterns to data segments.

The following is a *describe* of the *dba_hist_buffer_pool_stat* view:

```
SQL> desc DBA_HIST_BUFFER_POOL_STAT

 Name                                      Null?    Type
 ----------------------------------------- -------- ------------
 SNAP_ID                                   NOT NULL NUMBER
 DBID                                      NOT NULL NUMBER
 INSTANCE_NUMBER                           NOT NULL NUMBER
 ID                                        NOT NULL NUMBER
 NAME                                               VARCHAR2(20)
 BLOCK_SIZE                                         NUMBER
 SET_MSIZE                                          NUMBER
 CNUM_REPL                                          NUMBER
 CNUM_WRITE                                         NUMBER
 CNUM_SET                                           NUMBER
 BUF_GOT                                            NUMBER
 SUM_WRITE                                          NUMBER
 SUM_SCAN                                           NUMBER
 FREE_BUFFER_WAIT                                   NUMBER
 WRITE_COMPLETE_WAIT                                NUMBER
 BUFFER_BUSY_WAIT                                   NUMBER
 FREE_BUFFER_INSPECTED                              NUMBER
 DIRTY_BUFFERS_INSPECTED                            NUMBER
 DB_BLOCK_CHANGE                                    NUMBER
 DB_BLOCK_GETS                                      NUMBER
 CONSISTENT_GETS                                    NUMBER
 PHYSICAL_READS                                     NUMBER
 PHYSICAL_WRITES                                    NUMBER
```

The following *Buf_pool_int_10g.sql* query can be used to review statistic history of buffer pools for a particular snapshot interval:

🖫 Buf_pool_int_10g.sql

```
-- ***************************************************
-- Copyright © 2005 by Rampant TechPress
-- This script is free for non-commercial purposes
-- with no warranties.  Use at your own risk.
--
-- To license this script for a commercial purpose,
-- contact info@rampant.cc
-- ***************************************************

select
     name
     , numbufs  "Number of Buffers"
     , buffs "Buffer Gets"
     , conget    "Consistent Gets"
     , phread   "Physical Reads"
     , phwrite  "Physical Writes"
     , fbwait   "Free Buffer Waits"
     , bbwait  "Buffer Busy Waits"
     , wcwait   "Write Complete Waits"
     , poolhr "Pool Hit %"
From
(select e.name
     , e.set_msize                                           numbufs
```

```
        , decode (    e.db_block_gets       - nvl(b.db_block_gets,0)
               +  e.consistent_gets    - nvl(b.consistent_gets,0)
               , 0, to_number(null)
               , (100* (1 - (   (e.physical_reads - nvl(b.physical_reads,0))
                           / (  e.db_block_gets      - nvl(b.db_block_gets,0)
                             + e.consistent_gets     -
nvl(b.consistent_gets,0))
                          )
                        )
                      )
                    )                                        poolhr
        ,     e.db_block_gets       - nvl(b.db_block_gets,0)
            +  e.consistent_gets    - nvl(b.consistent_gets,0)     buffs
        , e.consistent_gets      - nvl(b.consistent_gets,0)     conget
        , e.physical_reads       - nvl(b.physical_reads,0)       phread
        , e.physical_writes      - nvl(b.physical_writes,0)      phwrite
        , e.free_buffer_wait     - nvl(b.free_buffer_wait,0)     fbwait
        , e.write_complete_wait  - nvl(b.write_complete_wait,0)  wcwait
        , e.buffer_busy_wait     - nvl(b.buffer_busy_wait,0)     bbwait
   from dba_hist_buffer_pool_stat   b
        , dba_hist_buffer_pool_stat   e
 where b.snap_id(+)            = &pBgnSnap
   and e.snap_id              = &pEndSnap
   and b.dbid(+)              = &pDbId
   and e.dbid                 = &pDbId
   and b.dbid(+)              = e.dbid
   and b.instance_number(+)   = &pInst_Num
   and e.instance_number      = &pInst_Num
   and b.instance_number(+)   = e.instance_number
   and b.id(+)                = e.id)
 order by 1
```

The output of the query looks like:

```
SQL> @Buf_pool_int_10g.sql

NAME                    Number of Buffers Buffer Gets Consistent Gets
------------------- ----------------- ----------- ---------------
Physical Reads Physical Writes Free Buffer Waits Buffer Busy Waits
-------------- --------------- ----------------- -----------------
Write Complete Waits Pool Hit %
------------------- ----------
DEFAULT                             8016      5354123         4347376
       100070           41865                0              24
               0 98.1309731
```

The *buf_pool_int_10g.sql* script output provides users with valuable historical information about activity in configured data buffers. Analysis of this information will determine if pools are configured correctly and whether tables need to be re-assigned to a particular cache.

---

dba_hist_buffer_pool_stat

The WISE tool contains a report named Buffer Pools that shows history charts for buffer pools statistics as shown in Figure 6.12.

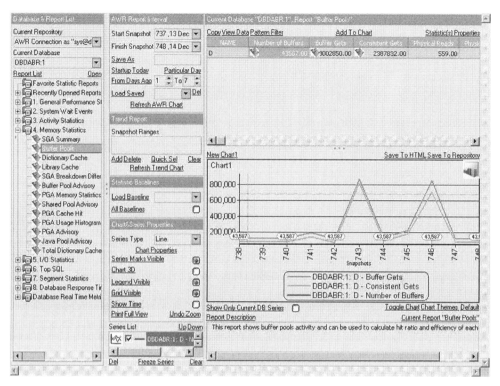

Figure 6.12: *AWR Buffer Pools chart in WISE.*

The chart in figure 6.12 displays two spikes in buffer gets and consistent gets. The next script, *rpt_10g_lib_missl.sql*, will display information on the *library cache*.

🖫 rpt_10g_lib_miss.sql

```
-- ************************************************
-- Copyright © 2005 by Rampant TechPress
-- This script is free for non-commercial purposes
-- with no warranties.  Use at your own risk.
--
-- To license this script for a commercial purpose,
-- contact info@rampant.cc
-- ************************************************

set lines 80;
```

```
set pages 999;

column mydate heading 'Yr.  Mo Dy  Hr.' format a16
column c1 heading "execs"     format 9,999,999
column c2 heading "Cache Misses|While Executing"     format 9,999,999
column c3 heading "Library Cache|Miss Ratio"     format 999.99999

break on mydate skip 2;

select
   to_char(sn.end_interval_time,'yyyy-mm-dd HH24')  mydate,
   sum(new.pins-old.pins)              c1,
   sum(new.reloads-old.reloads)        c2,
   sum(new.reloads-old.reloads)/
   sum(new.pins-old.pins)              library_cache_miss_ratio
from
   dba_hist_librarycache old,
   dba_hist_librarycache new,
   dba_hist_snapshot       sn
where
   new.snap_id = sn.snap_id
and
   old.snap_id = new.snap_id-1
and
   old.namespace = new.namespace
group by
   to_char(sn.end_interval_time,'yyyy-mm-dd HH24')
;
```

The following is a sample of the output. This report can easily be customized to alert the DBA when there are excessive executions or library cache misses:

```
                            Cache Misses  Library Cache
Yr.  Mo Dy  Hr.      execs While Executing   Miss Ratio
---------------- ---------- --------------- ---------------
2001-12-11 10        10,338               3          .00029
2001-12-12 10       182,477             134          .00073
2001-12-14 10       190,707             202          .00106
2001-12-16 10         2,803              11          .00392
```

Once this report identifies a time period where there may be a problem, STATSPACK provides the ability to run detailed reports to show the behavior of the objects within the *library cache*.

In the preceding example, it would appear that there is a RAM shortage in the shared pool between 10:00 a.m. and 11:00 a.m. each day. In this case, the shared pool could be dynamically reconfigured with additional RAM memory from the *db_cache_size* during this period. In the next

---

section the topic of what information the AWR provides about the buffer pool will be covered.

Plotting the Data Buffer Usage by Hour of the Day

The AWR can easily compute the average Data Buffer Hit Ratio (DBHR) by the hour of the day. The *rpt_bhr_awr_hr.sql* script below performs this function and references the *stats$buffer_pool_statistics* table. This table contains the values used for computing the DBHR. These values are time-specific and are only indicative of conditions at the time of the AWR snapshot. A technique that will yield an elapsed-time measure of the hit ratio is needed.

To convert the values into elapsed-time data, the *stats$buffer_pool_statistics* table can be joined against itself, and the original snapshot can be compared with each successive one. Since the desired collection interval is hourly, the script presented below will compute each hourly buffer hit ratio. The hourly DBHR for each day can be derived by selecting the *snap_time* column with a mask of HH24:

🖫 rpt_bhr_awr_hr.sql

```
-- ***************************************************
-- Copyright © 2005 by Rampant TechPress
-- This script is free for non-commercial purposes
-- with no warranties.  Use at your own risk.
--
-- To license this script for a commercial purpose,
-- contact info@rampant.cc
-- ***************************************************

set pages 999;

column bhr format 9.99
column mydate heading 'yr.  mo dy Hr.'

select
   to_char(snap_time,'HH24')        mydate,
   avg(
   (((new.consistent_gets-old.consistent_gets)+
   (new.db_block_gets-old.db_block_gets))-
   (new.physical_reads-old.physical_reads))
   /
   ((new.consistent_gets-old.consistent_gets)+
   (new.db_block_gets-old.db_block_gets))
   ) bhr
from
```

```
   dba_hist_buffer_pool_stat old,
   dba_hist_buffer_pool_stat new,
   dba_hist_sga                sn
where
   new.name in ('DEFAULT','FAKE VIEW')
and
   new.name = old.name
and
   new.snap_id = sn.snap_id
and
   old.snap_id = sn.snap_id-1
and
   new.consistent_gets > 0
and
   old.consistent_gets > 0
having
   avg(
   (((new.consistent_gets-old.consistent_gets)+
   (new.db_block_gets-old.db_block_gets))-
   (new.physical_reads-old.physical_reads))
   /
   ((new.consistent_gets-old.consistent_gets)+
   (new.db_block_gets-old.db_block_gets))
   ) < 1
group by
   to_char(snap_time,'HH24')
;
```

The output from the DBHR hourly average script has been plotted with WISE and is shown below. The output displays the average hit ratio for each day. The signature of the database becomes much more obvious when it is plotted with WISE.

Oracle professionals use the AWR to extract the signatures for all of the important metrics, and then to plot the metrics to reveal the trend-based patterns. The signatures are typically gathered by hour of the day and day of the week.

A plot of the data is shown in Figure 6.13. Signatures become more evident over longer periods of time. Nevertheless, the plot of this database already presents some interesting trends.

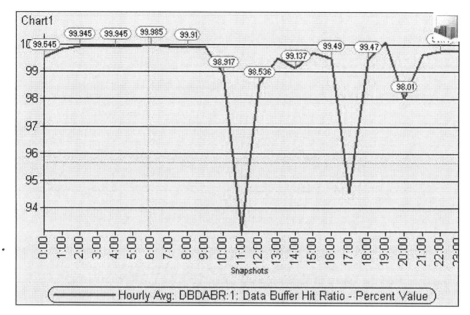

Figure 6.13: *A plot of buffer hit ratio averages by hour of day.*

Plotting the DBHR by Day of the Week

A similar analysis using *rpt_bhr_awr_dy.sql* will yield the average DBHR by day of the week. This is achieved by changing the script *snap_time* format mask from HH24 to "day":

🖫 **rpt_bhr_awr_dy.sql**

```
-- *************************************************
-- Copyright © 2005 by Rampant TechPress
-- This script is free for non-commercial purposes
-- with no warranties.  Use at your own risk.
--
-- To license this script for a commercial purpose,
-- contact info@rampant.cc
-- *************************************************

set pages 999;

column bhr format 9.99
column mydate heading 'yr.  mo dy Hr.'

select
   to_char(end_interval_time,'day')       mydate,
   avg(
   (((new.consistent_gets-old.consistent_gets)+
   (new.db_block_gets-old.db_block_gets))-
```

```
   (new.physical_reads-old.physical_reads))
   /
   ((new.consistent_gets-old.consistent_gets)+
   (new.db_block_gets-old.db_block_gets))
   ) bhr
from
   dba_hist_buffer_pool_stat old,
   dba_hist_buffer_pool_stat              new,
   dba_hist_snapshot sn
where
   new.name in ('DEFAULT','FAKE VIEW')
and
   new.name = old.name
and
   new.snap_id = sn.snap_id
and
   old.snap_id = sn.snap_id-1
and
   new.consistent_gets > 0
and
   old.consistent_gets > 0
having
   avg(
   (((new.consistent_gets-old.consistent_gets)+
   (new.db_block_gets-old.db_block_gets))-
   (new.physical_reads-old.physical_reads))
   /
   ((new.consistent_gets-old.consistent_gets)+
   (new.db_block_gets-old.db_block_gets))
   ) < 1
group by
   to_char(end_interval_time,'day')
;
```

The output from the script is shown below. The days must be manually re-sequenced because they are given in alphabetical order. This can be done after pasting the output into a spreadsheet for graphing:

```
Day        BHR
---------  -----
friday     .89
monday     .98
saturday   .92
sunday     .91
thursday   .96
tuesday    .93
wednesday  .91
```

The resulting graph is shown in Figure 6.14:

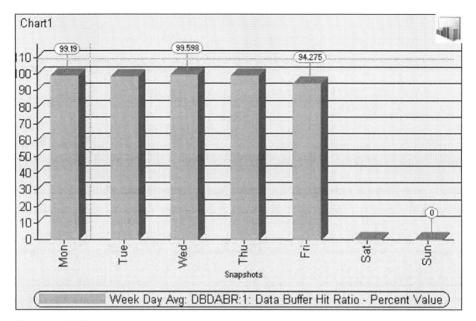

Figure 6.14: *Average data buffer hit ratio by day of the week.*

The chart in figure 6.14 shows a fairly consistent data buffer hit ratio, certainly nothing to be alarmed about. In the next section the *keep pool* in Oracle 10g will be examined.

Automating KEEP Pool Assignment

The Oracle documentation states:

"A good candidate for a segment to put into the KEEP pool is a segment that is smaller than ten percent of the size of the DEFAULT buffer pool and has incurred at least one percent of the total I/Os in the system."

It is easy to locate segments that are less than ten percent of the size of their data buffer, but Oracle does not have a mechanism to track I/O at the segment level. To get around this issue, some DBAs place each segment into an isolated tablespace so the AWR can show the total I/O.

This is not a practical solution for complex schemas with hundreds of segments.

Since the idea of the KEEP is to fully cache the object, the goal is to locate those objects that are small and experience a disproportional amount of I/O activity. Using this guideline, there are two approaches. Unlike the recommendation from the Oracle documentation, these approaches can be completely automated:

- Cache tables and indexes where the table is small, <50 blocks, and the table experiences frequent full-table scans.

- Cache any objects that consume more than ten percent of the size of their data buffer.

The first method that uses *v$sql_plan* to examine all execution plans searching for small-table, full-table scans, is found in *get_keep_pool_awr.sql*. This can automatically generate the KEEP syntax for any small table, with the DBA adjusting the table size threshold for tables that have many full-table scans.

get_keep_pool_awr.sql

```
-- ****************************************************
-- Copyright © 2005 by Rampant TechPress
-- This script is free for non-commercial purposes
-- with no warranties.  Use at your own risk.
--
-- To license this script for a commercial purpose,
-- contact info@rampant.cc
-- ****************************************************

select
   'alter table '||p.owner||'.'||p.name||' storage (buffer_pool keep);'
from
   dba_tables    t,
   dba_segments  s,
   dba_hist_sqlstat a,
   (select distinct
     pl.sql_id,
     pl.object_owner owner,
     pl.object_name name
   from
     dba_hist_sql_plan pl
   where
     pl.operation = 'TABLE ACCESS'
     and
     pl.options = 'FULL') p
where
```

```
   a.sql_id = p.sql_id
   and
   t.owner = s.owner
   and
   t.table_name = s.segment_name
   and
   t.table_name = p.name
   and
   t.owner = p.owner
   and
   t.owner not in ('SYS','SYSTEM')
   and
   t.buffer_pool <> 'KEEP'
having
   s.blocks < 50
group by
   p.owner, p.name, t.num_rows, s.blocks
UNION
-- ************************************************************

-- Next, get the index names

-- ************************************************************
select
   'alter index '||owner||'.'||index_name||' storage (buffer_pool keep);'
from
   dba_indexes
where
   owner||'.'||table_name in
(
select
   p.owner||'.'||p.name
from
   dba_tables       t,
   dba_segments     s,
   dba_hist_sqlstat a,
   (select distinct
     pl.sql_id,
     pl.object_owner owner,
     pl.object_name name
   from
     dba_hist_sql_plan pl
   where
     pl.operation = 'TABLE ACCESS'
     and
     pl.options = 'FULL') p
where
   a.sql_id = p.sql_id
   and
   t.owner = s.owner
   and
   t.table_name = s.segment_name
   and
   t.table_name = p.name
   and
   t.owner = p.owner
   and
   t.owner not in ('SYS','SYSTEM')
   and
```

```
   t.buffer_pool <> 'KEEP'
having
   s.blocks < 50
group by
   p.owner, p.name, t.num_rows, s.blocks
)
```

By running this script, the Oracle10g *v$* views can be used to generate suggestions for the KEEP syntax, based on the number of blocks in the object:

```
alter index DING.PK_BOOK storage (buffer_pool keep);
alter table DING.BOOK storage (buffer_pool keep);
alter table DING.BOOK_AUTHOR storage (buffer_pool keep);
alter table DING.PUBLISHER storage (buffer_pool keep);
alter table DING.SALES storage (buffer_pool keep);
```

Conclusion

Database memory usage monitoring is a complex topic involving the watching of latches, locks waits, and events. All of these are controlled through a series of settings controlled by the initialization parameters. The DBA must be aware of how to mine the Oracle DPTs, x$, and data dictionary views to obtain the required performance indicators for effective tuning to take place.

Other structures such as the shared pool and data block buffers control the flow of code and data in an Oracle system.

While the general idea that databases run better with more memory is valid, the DBA must be careful how RAM is distributed to the various memory regions in Oracle in order for it to be efficiently utilized. By following the points outlined in this chapter, it should be possible to:

- Determine how much RAM is currently devoted to the SGA in all databases.

- Quickly get a general snapshot of overall memory usage and efficiency using the *memsnap.sql* script.

- Drill down into the data cache and shared pool to determine how well each memory area is being utilized.

- Utilize the excellent memory features available in Oracle to make sure that data and code objects are stored appropriately.

- Get to the bottom of how each session is using memory on the database.

Knowing how to properly use memory in Oracle can help cut down on I/O time.

SQL

Sorting in Oracle9i and Above

Versions 9i and higher of the Oracle database have the option of running automatic Program Global Area (PGA) memory management.

Oracle9i introduced a parameter called *pga_aggregate_target*. When the *pga_aggregate_target* parameter is set while using dedicated Oracle connections, Oracle9i will ignore all of the PGA parameters in the Oracle file, including *sort_area_size*, *hash_area_size* and *sort_area_retained_size*. Oracle recommends that the value of *pga_aggregate_target* be set to the amount of remaining memory, less a 10% overhead for other UNIX tasks, on the UNIX server after the instance has been started.

Once the *pga_aggregate_target* has been set, Oracle will automatically manage PGA memory allocation based upon the individual needs of each Oracle connection. Oracle9i allows the *pga_aggregate_target* parameter to be modified at the instance level with the alter system command thereby allowing the DBA to dynamically adjust the total RAM region available to Oracle9i.

Oracle9i also introduced a parameter called *workarea_size_policy*. When this parameter is set to AUTOMATIC, all Oracle connections will benefit from the shared PGA memory. When this parameter is set to MANUAL, connections will allocate memory according to the values for the *sort_area_size* parameter. Under the automatic mode, Oracle tries to maximize the number of work areas that are using optimal memory and uses one-pass memory for the others.

In addition to increasing the amount of memory devoted to sorting, the DBA should consider hunting down inefficient SQL that cause needless sorts. For example, union all does not cause a sort; whereas, union does cause a sort in an SQL query in order to eliminate duplicate rows. The distinct keyword is often coded inappropriately, especially by users transferring from Microsoft Access, which used distinct for nearly every query.

Many DBAs prefer to avoid the continuous scanning of large tables because of the heavy logical and physical I/O cost.

The currently connected sessions causing such scans can be located in a couple of different ways. The *userscans.sql* query can be used on Oracle to pick out the worst large table scan offenders:

userscans.sql

```
-- **************************************************
-- Copyright © 2005 by Rampant TechPress
-- This script is free for non-commercial purposes
-- with no warranties.  Use at your own risk.
--
-- To license this script for a commercial purpose,
-- contact info@rampant.cc
-- **************************************************

select
      sid,
      username,
      total_user_scans,
      round(100 * total_user_scans/total_scans,2) pct_scans
from
(select
       b.sid sid,
       nvl(b.username,p.name) username,
       sum(value) total_user_scans
from
     sys.v_$statname c,
     sys.v_$sesstat a,
     sys.v_$session b,
     sys.v_$bgprocess p
where
     a.statistic#=c.statistic# and
     p.paddr (+) = b.paddr and
     b.sid=a.sid and
     c.name = 'table scans (long tables)'
group by
     b.sid,
     nvl(b.username,p.name)
order by
     3 desc),
(select
     sum(value) total_scans
from
     sys.v_$statname c,
     sys.v_$sesstat a
where
     a.statistic#=c.statistic# and

     c.name = 'table scans (long tables)');
```

A sample output from this query might look like this:

```
SID    USERNAME    TOTAL_USER_SCANS    PCT_SCANS
---------------------------------------------------
19     ORA_USER1            2286724        99.94
5          SMON               1397          .06
21      ERADMIN                 47            0
1          PMON                  0            0
```

With output like the one shown above, it would not be too difficult to identify which SID should be investigated. A DBA should normally focus on large table scans versus small table scans. Often, Oracle can actually digest a small table much easier if it scans it than if it uses an index.

Another way of getting a handle on sessions that are causing table scans is to look at wait events. The *db file scattered read* wait event is generally considered to be an indicator of table scan activity.

The *scatwait.sql* query will yield historical information regarding sessions that have caused *db file scattered read* wait events since the database has been up:

scatwait.sql

```
-- ***************************************************
-- Copyright © 2005 by Rampant TechPress
-- This script is free for non-commercial purposes
-- with no warranties.  Use at your own risk.
--
-- To license this script for a commercial purpose,
-- contact info@rampant.cc
-- ***************************************************
select
       b.sid,
       nvl(b.username,c.name) username,
       b.machine,
       a.total_waits,
       round((a.time_waited / 100),2)
       time_wait_sec,a.total_timeouts,
       round((average_wait / 100),2)
       average_wait_sec,
       round((a.max_wait / 100),2) max_wait_sec
  from
       sys.v_$session_event a,
       sys.v_$session b,
       sys.v_$bgprocess c
 where
       event = 'db file scattered read'
       and a.sid = b.sid
       and c.paddr (+) = b.paddr
order by
       3 desc,
       1 asc;
```

Again, it is not difficult to identify users who are the table scan gluttons are on this system. Figure 7.1 shows the detailed wait output for sessions with possible table scans:

	SID	USERNAME	MACHINE	TOTAL_WAITS	TIME_WAIT_SEC	TOTAL_TIMEOUTS	AVERAGE_WAIT_SEC	MAX_WAIT_SEC
1	13	USR1	EBT2K\EBT2K08	16	.04	0	0	.01
2	5	SMON	EBT2K04	93	0	0	0	0

Figure 7.1: *Detailed wait output for sessions with possible table scans*

The drawback of using the above query is that it cannot be accurately determined if the waits have been caused by small or large table scans.

While these queries will work well on Oracle8i and above, some new *v$* views can be utilized if Oracle9i or above is in use. The *v$* views provide more flexibility in the identification of problem table scan situations.

The *9ilarge_scanusers.sql* query can help ferret out the parsing users submitting SQL calls that have scanned tables over 1MB:

🖫 9ilarge_scanusers.sql

```
-- *************************************************
-- Copyright © 2005 by Rampant TechPress
-- This script is free for non-commercial purposes
-- with no warranties.  Use at your own risk.
--
-- To license this script for a commercial purpose,
-- contact info@rampant.cc
-- *************************************************

select
      c.username username,
      count(a.hash_value) scan_count
from
    sys.v_$sql_plan a,
    sys.dba_segments b,
    sys.dba_users c,
    sys.v_$sql d
where
    a.object_owner (+) = b.owner
    and   a.object_name (+) = b.segment_name
    and   b.segment_type in ('TABLE', 'TABLE PARTITIOn')
    and   a.operation like '%TABLE%'
    and   a.options = 'FULL'
    and   c.user_id = d.parsing_user_id
    and   d.hash_value = a.hash_value
```

```
    and    b.bytes / 1024 > 1024
group by
    c.username
order by
    2 desc;
```

The output from such a query might look like this:

```
USERNAME        SCAN_COUNT
----------    ----------------
SYSTEM                  15
SYS                     13
ORA_USR1                 2
```

The above query can be tweaked to locate scans on larger tables by changing the "and b.bytes / 1024 > 1024" clause. Large table scans identified in the *v$sesstat* view are generally thought to be scans that were performed on a table of five blocks or greater.

The above query allows the DBA the flexibility to define "large." Regardless of what query is used, if sessions are found that appear to be causing a lot of table scans, the next step is to capture the SQL calls those sessions are issuing and begin the SQL examination and tuning process.

Pinpointing Sessions with Problem SQL

The goal is to pinpoint the problem sessions that are currently issuing bad SQL calls rather than creating a historical analysis of the worst SQL issued on a system.

For example, to see the SQL currently running in a database session that has caused the most physical I/O, a query like the *curriosql.sql* script would do the trick for Oracle8i and above:

🖫 **curriosql.sql**

```
-- ************************************************
-- Copyright © 2005 by Rampant TechPress
-- This script is free for non-commercial purposes
-- with no warranties.  Use at your own risk.
--
-- To license this script for a commercial purpose,
```

```
-- contact info@rampant.cc
-- ************************************************

select
      sid,
      username,
      sql_text
from
    sys.v_$sqltext a,
    sys.v_$session b
where
    b.sql_address = a.address
    and b.sid =
(select
    sid
from
(select
      b.sid sid,
      nvl(b.username,p.name) username,
      sum(value) total_user_io
from
    sys.v_$statname c,
    sys.v_$sesstat a,
    sys.v_$session b,
    sys.v_$bgprocess p
where
      a.statistic#=c.statistic# and
      p.paddr (+) = b.paddr and
      b.sid=a.sid and
      c.name in ('physical reads','physical writes',
                 'physical reads direct',
                 'physical reads direct (lob)',
                 'physical writes direct',
                 'physical writes direct (lob)')
group by
      b.sid,
      nvl(b.username,p.name)
order by
      3 desc)
where
      rownum < 2)
order by
      a.piece;
```

The output from such a query might look like this:

```
SID  USERNAME      SQL_TEXT
------------------------------------------------------
19   ORA_MONITOR   SELECT COUNT(*) FROM ADMISSION
19   ORA_MONITOR   WHERE PATIENT_ID BETWEEN 1 AND 100;
```

Similar queries could be issued to uncover the SQL that the current memory or CPU is running as well. Of course, the above query will give only the currently running SQL for a session, which may or may not be the code that has contributed to the session's resource consumption.

With Oracle9i or above, a higher-level analysis can be done to answer the question of "What sessions have parsed Cartesian join statements?" by issuing the *cartsession.sql* script:

🖫 cartsession.sql

```
-- ***************************************************
-- Copyright © 2005 by Rampant TechPress
-- This script is free for non-commercial purposes
-- with no warranties.  Use at your own risk.
--
-- To license this script for a commercial purpose,
-- contact info@rampant.cc
-- ***************************************************

select
       username,
       count(distinct c.hash_value) nbr_stmts
from
     sys.v_$sql a,
     sys.dba_users b,
     sys.v_$sql_plan c
where
       a.parsing_user_id = b.user_id
       and    options = 'cartesian'
       and    operation like '%join%'
       and    a.hash_value = c.hash_value
group by
       username
order by
       2 desc;
```

Running this query on an Oracle9i server may yield results similar to this:

```
USERNAME        NBR_STMTS
---------       ---------
ORA_USR1                2
SYSMAN                  2
ERADMIN                 1
```

Once it has been determined that Cartesian joins have occurred on a system, a query like the *cartsql.sql* script can be used to find the actual SQL statements themselves. Again, this is valid only on Oracle9i or above.

cartsql.sql

```
-- ***********************************************
-- Copyright © 2005 by Rampant TechPress
-- This script is free for non-commercial purposes
-- with no warranties.  Use at your own risk.
--
-- To license this script for a commercial purpose,
-- contact info@rampant.cc
-- ***********************************************

select
     *
from
     sys.v_$sql
where
     hash_value in
(select
     hash_value
from
     sys.v_$sql_plan
where
     options = 'CARTESIAN'
     and operation LIKE '%JOIN%' )
order by
     hash_value;
```

The following output shows SQL statements that contain at least one Cartesian join:

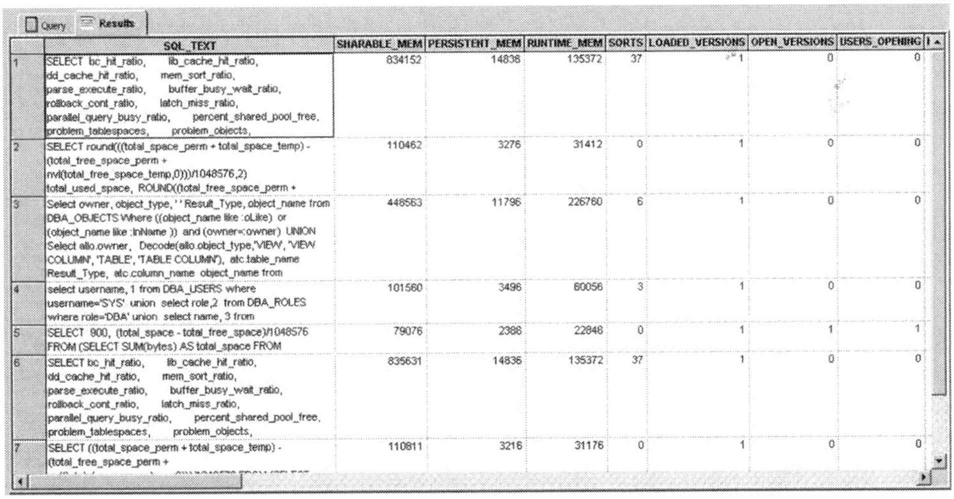

	SQL_TEXT	SHARABLE_MEM	PERSISTENT_MEM	RUNTIME_MEM	SORTS	LOADED_VERSIONS	OPEN_VERSIONS	USERS_OPENING
1	SELECT bc_hit_ratio, lib_cache_hit_ratio, dd_cache_hit_ratio, mem_sort_ratio, parse_execute_ratio, buffer_busy_wait_ratio, rollback_cont_ratio, latch_miss_ratio, parallel_query_busy_ratio, percent_shared_pool_free, problem_tablespaces, problem_objects,	834152	14836	135372	37	1	0	0
2	SELECT round(((total_space_perm + total_space_temp) - (total_free_space_perm + nvl(total_free_space_temp,0)))/1048576,2) total_used_space, ROUND((total_free_space_perm +	110462	3276	31412	0	1	0	0
3	Select owner, object_type, ' ' Result_Type, object_name from DBA_OBJECTS Where ((object_name like :oLike) or (object_name like :lnName)) and (owner=:owner) UNION Select allo.owner, Decode(allo.object_type,'VIEW', 'VIEW COLUMN', 'TABLE', 'TABLE COLUMN'), atc.table_name Result_Type, atc.column_name object_name from	448563	11796	226760	6	1	0	0
4	select username, 1 from DBA_USERS where username='SYS' union select role,2 from DBA_ROLES where role='DBA' union select name, 3 from	101560	3496	60056	3	1	0	0
5	SELECT 900, (total_space - total_free_space)/1048576 FROM (SELECT SUM(bytes) AS total_space FROM	79076	2388	22848	0	1	1	1
6	SELECT bc_hit_ratio, lib_cache_hit_ratio, dd_cache_hit_ratio, mem_sort_ratio, parse_execute_ratio, buffer_busy_wait_ratio, rollback_cont_ratio, latch_miss_ratio, parallel_query_busy_ratio, percent_shared_pool_free, problem_tablespaces, problem_objects,	835631	14836	135372	37	1	0	0
7	SELECT ((total_space_perm + total_space_temp) - (total_free_space_perm +	110811	3216	31176	0	1	0	0

Figure 7.2: *SQL statements that contain at least one Cartesian join*

The above script is quite valuable, as Cartesian joins can cause unnecessary system workload and be difficult to spot in SQL queries with many join predicates.

What is Bad SQL?

Before identifying problem SQL in the database, the following question must be asked: "What is bad SQL?" What criteria should be used when beginning the hunt for problem SQL in critical systems?

Even seasoned experts disagree on what constitutes efficient and inefficient SQL, so there is no way to sufficiently answer this question to every Oracle professional's satisfaction. The following information contains the general criteria that can be used when evaluating the output from various database monitors or personal diagnostic scripts:

- **Overall Response (Elapsed) Time** - This is how much time the query took to parse, execute, and fetch the data needed to satisfy the query. It should not include the network time needed to make the round trip from the requesting client workstation to the database server.

- **CPU Time** - This is how much CPU time the query took to parse, execute, and fetch the data needed to satisfy the query.

- **Physical I/O** - Often used as the major statistic in terms of identifying good SQL versus bad SQL, this is a measure of how many disk reads the query caused to satisfy the user's request. While one goal is to control disk I/O where possible, it's important to not focus solely on physical I/O as the single benchmark of inefficient SQL. Disk access is slower than memory access and consumes processing time making the physical to logical transition. However, it is necessary to look at the entire I/O picture of an SQL statement, which includes looking at a statement's logical I/O as well.

- **Logical I/O** - This is a measure of how many memory reads the query took to satisfy the user's request. The goal of tuning I/O for a query should be to examine both logical and physical I/O, and to use the appropriate mechanisms to keep both to a minimum.

- **Repetition** - This is a measure of how often the query has been executed. A problem in this area is not as easy to spot as the others unless the application is known well. A query that takes a fraction of a second to execute may still be causing a headache on the system if it is executed erroneously. One example would be a query that executes in a runaway PL/SQL loop over and over again.

There are other criteria that can be examined, such as sort activity or access plan statistics that show items such as Cartesian joins and the like. More often than not, these measures are reflected in the criteria listed above.

Fortunately, Oracle9i and higher record all the above measures, which makes tracking the SQL that has been submitted against an Oracle database much easier.

Pinpointing Bad SQL

When beginning the quest for inefficient SQL in a database, there are two primary questions to answer:

- What has been the worst SQL that has historically been run in the database?

- What is the worst SQL that is running right now in the database?

Historical SQL Analysis

The easiest way to perform historical SQL analysis is to use either a third-party software vendor tool, migrate to Oracle10g which offers built-in functionality for gathering SQL calls, or employ a homegrown solution to periodically collect SQL execution statistics into a database repository and then analyze the results.

While Oracle does record real-time SQL execution information in performance views, such data can be lost if a DBA flushes the shared pool or shuts down the database, so ad-hoc historical analysis using straight SQL scripts might produce misleading results. However, if the database is predictable in terms of SQL code being kept in the shared pool, it is possible to obtain good metrics to determine if inefficient SQL is being executed in the system.

A good Top SQL script to use for Oracle9i and above is the *top9isql.sql* query. It will pull the top 20 SQL statements as determined initially by disk reads per execution, but the sort order can be changed to sort on logical I/O, elapsed time, etc.:

🖫 top9isql.sql

```
-- ***************************************************
-- Copyright © 2005 by Rampant TechPress
-- This script is free for non-commercial purposes
-- with no warranties.  Use at your own risk.
--
-- To license this script for a commercial purpose,
-- contact info@rampant.cc
-- ***************************************************

select
        sql_text ,
        username ,
        disk_reads_per_exec,
        buffer_gets_per_exec,
        buffer_gets ,
        disk_reads,
        parse_calls ,
        sorts ,
        executions ,
        loads,
        rows_processed ,
        hit_ratio,
        first_load_time ,
        sharable_mem ,
        persistent_mem ,
        runtime_mem,
        cpu_time_secs,
        cpu_time_secs_per_execute,
        elapsed_time_secs,
        elapsed_time_secs_per_execute,
        address,
        hash_value
from
(select
        sql_text ,
        b.username ,
        round((a.disk_reads/
        decode(a.executions,0,1,a.executions)),2)
        disk_reads_per_exec,
        a.disk_reads ,
        a.buffer_gets ,
        round((a.buffer_gets/
```

```
        decode(a.executions,0,1,a.executions)),2)
        buffer_gets_per_exec,
        a.parse_calls ,
        a.sorts ,
        a.executions ,
        a.loads,
        a.rows_processed ,
        100 - round(100 *
        a.disk_reads/
        greatest(a.buffer_gets,1),2) hit_ratio,
        a.first_load_time ,
        sharable_mem ,
        persistent_mem ,
        runtime_mem,
        round(cpu_time / 1000000,3) cpu_time_secs,
        round((cpu_time / 1000000)/
        decode(a.executions,0,1,a.executions),3)
        cpu_time_secs_per_execute,
        round(elapsed_time / 1000000,3) elapsed_time_secs,
        round((elapsed_time /
        1000000)/decode(a.executions,0,1,a.executions),3)
        elapsed_time_secs_per_execute,
        address,
        hash_value
from
        sys.v_$sqlarea a,
        sys.all_users b
where
        a.parsing_user_id=b.user_id and
        b.username not in ('SYS','SYSTEM')
        order by 3 desc)
where
        rownum < 21;
```

The output from this query might resemble the following:

	SQL_TEXT	USERNAME	DISK_READS_PER_EXEC	BUFFER_GETS_PER_EXEC	BUFFER_GETS	DISK_READS	PARSE_CALLS	SORTS	EX
1	begin PERFCNTR_24x7_QUERIES.fetchcursor20_2(VAR1_	USR1	122.5	78886.5	157773	245	2	0	
2	SELECT 956, (INVALID_OBJECTS + UNUSABLE_INDEXES) AS TOTAL FROM (SELECT	USR1	94	45723.5	91447	188	1	0	
3	SELECT 'PERFCNTR_24x7_QUERIES', PERFCNTR_24x7_QUERIES.GetVersion from DUAL UNION	USR1	67	975	975	67	1	1	
4	SELECT 900, (total_space - total_free_space)/1048576 FROM (SELECT SUM(bytes) AS total_space FROM	USR1	18.5	238	476	37	1	0	
5	select 99 / 100, 1 - to_number(to_char(to_date('1997-11-0	USR1	11	86	86	11	1	0	
6	SELECT 955, COUNT(*) FROM SYS.DBA_TABLES WHER	USR1	5.5	30784	61568	11	1	0	
7	SELECT 998, COUNT(*) FROM (SELECT USERNAME FROM SYS.DBA_USERS WHERE	USR1	3.5	239.5	479	7	1	16	
8	select a.machine, b.count from (SELECT DISTINCT MACHINE FROM V$SESSION WHERE TYPE =	USR1	3	63	63	3	1	1	
9	SELECT 977, a.active active_jobs,b.due-a.active jobs_waiting,c.snp_processes - a.active idle_jobs,c.snp_processes total_jobs FROM (SELECT	USR1	2.5	70.5	141	5	1	2	
10	begin PERFCNTR_24x7_QUERIES.fetchcursor22_5(VAR1_	USR1	2.5	70.5	141	5	2	0	
11	begin PERFCNTR_24x7_QUERIES.fetchcursor18_3(VAR1_	USR1	1.67	114.5	687	10	6	0	
12	SELECT 948, ACTIVE_COUNT,ROUND(100 * (ACTIVE_COUNT / TOTAL_COUNT),2) AS ACTIVE_PCT	USR1	1.67	76.17	457	10	1	0	
13	begin PERFCNTR_24x7_QUERIES.fetchcursor1_2(VAR1_	USR1	1.33	156.17	937	8	6	0	
14	begin PERFCNTR_24x7_QUERIES.fetchcursor3_3(VAR1_	USR1	.83	107.83	647	5	6	0	

Figure 7.3: *Output from the top 20 SQL query*

If using a version of Oracle lower than 9i, the query can be modified and the references to *elapsed_time* and *cpu_time* removed. These are columns that were added to the *v$sqlarea* view in 9i. If using Oracle10g or above, add the following columns that convey wait time and other details:

- *application_wait_time*
- *concurrency_wait_time*
- *cl98uster_wait_time*
- *user_io_wait_time*
- *plsql_exec_time*
- *java_exec_time*
- *direct_writes*

It is important to examine the output of this query to see how it uses the criteria set forth at the beginning of this chapter to pinpoint problematic SQL.

A good first step would be to look at Figure 7.4 and focus on the circled columns.

	PERSISTENT_MEM	RUNTIME_MEM	CPU_TIME_SECS	CPU_TIME_SECS_PER_EXECUTE	ELAPSED_TIME_SECS	ELAPSED_TIME_SECS_PER_EXECUTE	ADDRESS	HASH_VALUE
1	549	276	1.642	.821	4.814	2.407	672621C0	3077230681
2	696	30300	.521	.26	1.204	.602	6746A26C	2965734772
3	1400	3664	.11	.11	.399	.399	674D57CC	2741343822
4	2388	22848	.06	.03	1.368	.684	6746A848	3829441909
5	700	876	.02	.02	.079	.079	674FA26C	1276527007
6	660	12748	.26	.13	.293	.147	6746A460	2911359602
7	692	100596	.05	.025	.07	.035	67469D84	3547812303
8	664	4036	.02	.02	.034	.034	674F4504	2966647892
9	852	4388	.02	.01	.054	.027	674688A0	482951707

Figure 7.4: *Output from the top 20 SQL query showing timing statistics.*

The output displays both CPU and elapsed times for each query. The times are shown both cumulatively, in seconds, and per execution, indicating that the first query in the result set has accumulated almost five seconds of total execution time and runs for about two and half seconds each time it is executed.

The query can be changed to sort by any of these timed statistics depending on the criteria needed to bubble the worst running SQL to the top of the result set. Unfortunately, these metrics are lost when running any database version under Oracle9i.

Referring back to Figure 7.1, the columns that will help examine the I/O characteristics of each SQL statement relate to the number of disk reads (physical I/O) and buffer gets (logical I/O), along with numbers that display the average I/O consumption of each SQL statement.

Queries that have only been executed once may have misleading statistics with respect to disk reads, since the data needed for the first run of the query was likely read in from disk to memory. Therefore, the number of disk reads per execution should drop for subsequent executions, and the hit ratio for the query should rise.

The executions column of the top SQL's result set will provide clues to the repetition metric for the query. When troubleshooting a slow system, the DBA should be on the lookout for any query that shows an execution count that is significantly larger than any other query on the system. It may be that the query is in an inefficient PL/SQL loop or other problematic programming construct. Only by bringing the query to the attention of the application developers can it be determined if the query is being mishandled from a programming standpoint.

Once the SQL statements are found through Oracle's diagnostic views, it is prudent to get the entire SQL text for the statements that appear inefficient.

Note the *hash_value*, or *sql_id* in Oracle10g and higher values for each SQL statement, and then issue the *fullsql.sql* script to obtain the full SQL statement:

Current SQL Analysis

If the phone begins to ring with complaints of a slow database, the DBA should quickly check to see what SQL is currently executing to understand if any resource intensive SQL is dragging down the database's overall performance levels.

This is very easy to do and only involves making one change to the *top9isql.sql* query. Add the following filter to the main query's where clause:

```
where
        a.parsing_user_id=b.user_id and
        b.username not in ('SYS','SYSTEM') and
        a.users_executing > 0
        order by 3 desc;
```

This query change will display the worst SQL that is currently running in the database. This way a DBA can quickly tell if any queries are to blame for a dip in database performance.

Once bad SQL in a database has been discovered by traditional means, new techniques for analyzing SQL execution presented in the next section will be very helpful.

New Techniques for Analyzing SQL Execution

The techniques and queries showcased above are the more traditional means of pinpointing problem SQL in a database. If Oracle9i or higher is in use, there are new methods that can be employed to get a handle on how well the SQL in the database is executing.

For example, an Oracle9i or 10g DBA may want to know how many total SQL statements are causing Cartesian joins on the system. The following *9icartcount.sql* query can answer that:

🖫 9icartcount.sql

```
-- *************************************************
-- Copyright © 2005 by Rampant TechPress
-- This script is free for non-commercial purposes
-- with no warranties.  Use at your own risk.
--
-- To license this script for a commercial purpose,
-- contact info@rampant.cc
-- *************************************************

select
       count(distinct hash_value) cartesian_statements,
       count(*) total_cartesian_joins
from
       sys.v_$sql_plan
where
       options = 'CARTESIAN' and
       operation like '%JOIN%';
```

It is possible for a single SQL statement to contain more than one Cartesian join. Output from this query might resemble the following:

```
CARTESIAN_STATEMENTS    TOTAL_CARTESIAN_JOINS
----------------------  ----------------------
                     4                       6
```

The DBA can then view the actual SQL statements containing the Cartesian joins, along with their performance metrics by using the *9icartsql.sql* query:

9icartsql.sql

```
-- **************************************************
-- Copyright © 2005 by Rampant TechPress
-- This script is free for non-commercial purposes
-- with no warranties.  Use at your own risk.
--
-- To license this script for a commercial purpose,
-- contact info@rampant.cc
-- **************************************************

select
    *
from
    sys.v_$sql
where
    hash_value in
(select
    hash_value
 from
    sys.v_$sql_plan
 where
    options = 'CARTESIAN'
 AND  operation LIKE '%JOIN%' )
order by hash_value;
```

Another big area of interest for DBAs concerned with tuning SQL is table scan activity. Most DBAs don't worry about small table scans since Oracle can often access small tables more efficiently through a full scan than through index access. In that situation, the small table is just cached and accessed. Large table scans, however, are another matter. Most DBAs prefer to avoid them, where possible, through smart index placement or intelligent partitioning.

Using the 9i/10g *v$sql_plan* view, a DBA can quickly identify any SQL statement that contains one or more large table scans and even define 'large' in their own terms.

The following *9itabscan.sql* query shows any SQL statement that contains a large table scan which is defined in this query as a table over 1MB. In addition, it also shows a count of how many large scans it causes for each execution, the total number of times the statement has been executed, and the sum total of all scans it has caused on the system:

🖫 9itabscan.sql

```
-- ****************************************************
-- Copyright © 2005 by Rampant TechPress
-- This script is free for non-commercial purposes
-- with no warranties.  Use at your own risk.
--
-- To license this script for a commercial purpose,
-- contact info@rampant.cc
-- ****************************************************

select
      sql_text,
      total_large_scans,
      executions,
      executions * total_large_scans sum_large_scans
from

(select
      sql_text,
      count(*) total_large_scans,
      executions

from
     sys.v_$sql_plan a,
     sys.dba_segments b,
     sys.v_$sql c

where
      a.object_owner (+) = b.owner
and   a.object_name (+) = b.segment_name
and   b.segment_type in ('TABLE', 'TABLE PARTITION')
and   a.operation like '%TABLE%'
and   a.options = 'FULL'
and   c.hash_value = a.hash_value
and   b.bytes / 1024 > 1024
group by
      sql_text, executions)
order by
      4 desc;
```

The following output shows 'large' table scan activity from an Oracle9i database:

	SQL_TEXT	TOTAL_LARGE_SCANS	EXECUTIONS	SUM_LARGE_SCANS
1	select o.owner#,o.obj#,decode(o.linkname,null, decode(u.name,null,'SYS',u.name),o.remoteowner),	1	19	19
2	SELECT 1 FROM SYS.DBA_OBJECTS WHERE ROWNUM = 1 MINUS SELECT 1 FROM SYS.DBA_EXTENTS WHERE ROWNUM = 1 MINUS	2	2	4
3	SELECT 1 FROM SYS.DBA_OBJECTS WHERE ROWNUM = 1 MINUS SELECT 1 FROM SYS.DBA_EXTENTS WHERE ROWNUM = 1 MINUS	2	1	2
4	SELECT OWNER,TABLE_NAME,NUM_ROWS,PCT_FREE,PCT_USED,TA	1	2	2
5	EXPLAIN PLAN SET STATEMENT_ID='10118429' INTO EMBARCADERO	1	1	1
6	SELECT OWNER,TABLE_NAME,NUM_ROWS,PCT_FREE,PCT_USED,TABLESPA	1	1	1
7	select count(*) from eradmin.emp	1	1	1
8	select distinct i.obj# from sys.idl_ub1$ i where i.obj#>=:1 and i.obj# not	1	1	1

Figure 7.5: *Output showing 'large' table scan activity from an Oracle9i database*

This query provides important output and poses a number of interesting questions. Should a DBA worry more about an SQL statement that causes only one large table scan, but has been executed 1,000 times or an SQL statement that has ten large scans in it, but has only been executed a handful of times?

Each DBA will likely have an opinion on this matter; however, it is evident that such a query can assist with identifying SQL statements that have the potential to cause system slowdowns.

Oracle 9.2 introduced another performance view, *v$sql_plan_statistics*, that can be used to get still more statistical data regarding the execution of inefficient SQL statements. This view can tell how many buffer gets, disk reads, etc., that each step in a SQL execution plan caused. It even goes so far as to list the cumulative and last executed counts of all held metrics.

DBAs can reference this view to get a great perspective of which step in a SQL execution plan is really responsible for most of the resource consumption. To enable the collection of data for this view, the Oracle configuration parameter *statistics_level* must be set to ALL.

An example that utilizes this 9i view, also available in 10g and above, is the following *9iplanstats.sql* script that shows the statistics for one problem SQL statement:

9iplanstats.sql

```
-- *****************************************************
-- Copyright © 2005 by Rampant TechPress
-- This script is free for non-commercial purposes
-- with no warranties.  Use at your own risk.
--
-- To license this script for a commercial purpose,
-- contact info@rampant.cc
-- *****************************************************

select
        operation,
        options,
        object_owner,
        object_name,
        executions,
        last_output_rows,
        last_cr_buffer_gets,
        last_cu_buffer_gets,
        last_disk_reads,
        last_disk_writes,
        last_elapsed_time
from
        sys.v_$sql_plan a,
        sys.v_$sql_plan_statistics b
where
        a.hash_value = b.hash_value and
        a.id = b.operation_id and
        a.hash_value = <enter hash value>
order by a.id;
```

The following output shows statistical metrics for each step in a 9i query execution plan:

	OPERATION	OPTIONS	OBJECT_OWNER	OBJECT_NAME	EXECUTIONS	LAST_OUTPUT_ROWS	LAST_CR_BUFFER_GETS	LAST_CU_BUFFER_GETS	LAST_DISK_READS	LAST
1	MERGE JOIN	CARTESIAN	[NULL]	[NULL]	1	31849	46	0	18	
2	TABLE ACCESS	FULL	ERADMIN	PATIENT	1	22	24	0	5	
3	BUFFER	SORT	[NULL]	[NULL]	1	31849	22	0	13	
4	PARTITION RANGE	ALL	[NULL]	[NULL]	1	1507	22	0	13	
5	TABLE ACCESS	FULL	ERADMIN	ADMISSION	1	1507	22	0	13	

Figure 7.6: *Example output showing statistical metrics for each step in a 9i query execution plan*

Interrogating SQL Execution Plans

The following script examines the execution plans of *plan9i.sql* and reports on the frequency of every type of table and index access, including full-table scans, index range scans, index unique scans, and index full scans. The script goes to the appropriate view, *v$sql_plan* in *plan9i.sql* and *dba_hist_sqlplan* in *plan10g.sql*, and parses the output, counting the frequency of execution for each type of access. The *plan10g.sql* script is included at the end of the Oracle 10g section of this chapter.

The *plan9i.sql* script will show the SQL that is currently inside the library cache:

plan9i.sql

```
-- *************************************************
-- Copyright © 2005 by Rampant TechPress
-- This script is free for non-commercial purposes
-- with no warranties.  Use at your own risk.
--
-- To license this script for a commercial purpose,
-- contact info@rampant.cc
-- *************************************************

set echo off;
set feedback on

set pages 999;
column nbr_FTS  format 999,999
column num_rows format 999,999,999
column blocks   format 999,999
column owner    format a14;
column name     format a24;
column ch       format a1;

column object_owner heading "Owner"            format a12;
column ct            heading "# of SQL selects" format 999,999;

select
   object_owner,
   count(*)   ct
from
   v$sql_plan
where
   object_owner is not null
group by
   object_owner
order by
   ct desc
;
--spool access.lst;

set heading off;
set feedback off;

set heading on;
```

```
set feedback on;
ttitle 'full table scans and counts|  |The "K" indicates that the table is
in the KEEP Pool (Oracle8).'
select
   p.owner,
   p.name,
   t.num_rows,
--    ltrim(t.cache) ch,
   decode(t.buffer_pool,'KEEP','Y','DEFAULT','N') K,
   s.blocks blocks,
   sum(a.executions) nbr_FTS
from
   dba_tables   t,
   dba_segments s,
   v$sqlarea    a,
   (select distinct
     address,
     object_owner owner,
     object_name name
   from
     v$sql_plan
   where
     operation = 'TABLE ACCESS'
     and
     options = 'FULL') p
where
   a.address = p.address
   and
   t.owner = s.owner
   and
   t.table_name = s.segment_name
   and
   t.table_name = p.name
   and
   t.owner = p.owner
   and
   t.owner not in ('SYS','SYSTEM')
having
   sum(a.executions) > 9
group by
   p.owner, p.name, t.num_rows, t.cache, t.buffer_pool, s.blocks
order by
   sum(a.executions) desc;

column nbr_RID  format 999,999,999
column num_rows format 999,999,999
column owner     format a15;
column name      format a25;

ttitle 'Table access by ROWID and counts'
select
   p.owner,
   p.name,
   t.num_rows,
   sum(s.executions) nbr_RID
from
   dba_tables t,
   v$sqlarea s,
   (select distinct
```

```
      address,
      object_owner owner,
      object_name name
   from
      v$sql_plan
   where
      operation = 'TABLE ACCESS'
      and
      options = 'BY ROWID') p
where
   s.address = p.address
   and
   t.table_name = p.name
   and
   t.owner = p.owner
having
   sum(s.executions) > 9
group by
   p.owner, p.name, t.num_rows
order by
   sum(s.executions) desc;

--***************************************************
--   Index Report Section
--***************************************************

column nbr_scans  format 999,999,999
column num_rows   format 999,999,999
column tbl_blocks format 999,999,999
column owner      format a9;
column table_name format a20;
column index_name format a20;

ttitle 'Index full scans and counts'
select
   p.owner,
   d.table_name,
   p.name index_name,
   seg.blocks tbl_blocks,
   sum(s.executions) nbr_scans
from
   dba_segments seg,
   v$sqlarea s,
   dba_indexes d,
   (select distinct
      address,
      object_owner owner,
      object_name name
   from
      v$sql_plan
   where
      operation = 'INDEX'
      and
      options = 'FULL SCAN') p
where
   d.index_name = p.name
   and
   s.address = p.address
   and
```

```
   d.table_name = seg.segment_name
   and
   seg.owner = p.owner
having
   sum(s.executions) > 9
group by
   p.owner, d.table_name, p.name, seg.blocks
order by
   sum(s.executions) desc;


ttitle 'Index range scans and counts'
select
   p.owner,
   d.table_name,
   p.name index_name,
   seg.blocks tbl_blocks,
   sum(s.executions) nbr_scans
from
   dba_segments seg,
   v$sqlarea s,
   dba_indexes d,
   (select distinct
      address,
      object_owner owner,
      object_name name
   from
      v$sql_plan

   where
      operation = 'INDEX'
      and
      options = 'RANGE SCAN') p
where
   d.index_name = p.name
   and
   s.address = p.address
   and
   d.table_name = seg.segment_name
   and
   seg.owner = p.owner
having
   sum(s.executions) > 9
group by
   p.owner, d.table_name, p.name, seg.blocks
order by
   sum(s.executions) desc;


ttitle 'Index unique scans and counts'
select
   p.owner,
   d.table_name,
   p.name index_name,
   sum(s.executions) nbr_scans
from
   v$sqlarea s,
   dba_indexes d,
   (select distinct
```

```
   address,
   object_owner owner,
   object_name name
from
   v$sql_plan
where
   operation = 'INDEX'
   and
   options = 'UNIQUE SCAN') p
where
   d.index_name = p.name
   and
   s.address = p.address
having
   sum(s.executions) > 9
group by
   p.owner, d.table_name, p.name
order by
   sum(s.executions) desc;
```

SQL Tuning Roadmap

There are large volumes of SQL tuning books on the market that provide minute detail on how to build and tune SQL code. A DBA could stay immersed in such manuals, and many of these manuals are very good, for a long time, but chances are they do not have the time.

If that is the case, the DBA can walk through the quick generic roadmap below, which can be used to remedy some of the problem SQL statements that have been identified using the techniques and scripts already outlined in this chapter.

With one or more problem queries in hand, the tuning process, which basically consists of these three broad steps, begins as follows:

- Understand the query and dependent objects.

- Look for SQL rewrite possibilities.

- Look for object-based solutions.

The following sections will address each of these steps in more detail.

Understand the Query and Dependent Objects

The DBA must first get a handle on what the query is trying to do, how the Oracle optimizer is satisfying the query's request, and what kind of objects the query is referencing.

In terms of understanding what the query is trying to accomplish and how Oracle will handle the query, the EXPLAIN plan is the main part of the process. Although the EXPLAIN plan has been around for as long as SQL itself, it might be surprising to learn that many seasoned database professionals are not proficient at reading EXPLAIN plan output.

Many DBAs can do the basics like recognize table scans, spot Cartesian joins, and zero in on unnecessary sort operations; however, when the EXPLAIN output wave starts rolling back and forth in large SQL EXPLAINs, some DBAs tend to get a little lost. The better SQL analysis tools are now sporting a new EXPLAIN format with better graphics and English-based explanations that makes it much easier to follow the access path trail.

For DBAs who are not good at reading traditional EXPLAIN output, getting to the root of a bad SQL statement becomes much simpler with the use of these SQL analysis tools.

If a third-party SQL analysis product with built-in EXPLAIN functionality is not being used, the standard EXPLAIN plan table and methods for performing a SQL statement EXPLAIN should be employed.

Users of Oracle9i, however, can get an EXPLAIN of any SQL statement that has already been executed in the database. A script like the 9iexpl.sql can be used:

9iexpl.sql

```
-- ****************************************************
-- Copyright © 2005 by Rampant TechPress
-- This script is free for non-commercial purposes
-- with no warranties.  Use at your own risk.
--
-- To license this script for a commercial purpose,
-- contact info@rampant.cc
-- ****************************************************

select
        lpad(' ',level-1)||operation||' '||options||' '||
        object_name "Plan",
        cost,
        cardinality,
        bytes,
        io_cost,
        cpu_cost
  from
        sys.v_$sql_plan
  connect by
        prior id = parent_id
        and prior hash_value = hash_value
  start with
        id = 0 and hash_value = <enter hash value>
  order by id;
```

The following example output shows an EXPLAIN plan generated for a SQL statement already in Oracle9i's shared pool:

	Plan	COST	CARDINALITY	BYTES	IO_COST	CPU_COST
1	SELECT STATEMENT	1502	[NULL]	[NULL]	[NULL]	[NULL]
2	MERGE JOIN CARTESIAN	1502	750000	52500000	1502	[NULL]
3	TABLE ACCESS FULL PATIENT	2	500	23500	2	[NULL]
4	BUFFER SORT	1500	1500	34500	1500	[NULL]
5	PARTITION RANGE ALL	[NULL]	[NULL]	[NULL]	[NULL]	[NULL]
6	TABLE ACCESS FULL ADMISSION	3	1500	34500	3	[NULL]

Figure 7.7: *Example output for an EXPLAIN plan generated for a SQL statement already in Oracle9i's shared pool*

Upon gaining understanding through an EXPLAIN, the DBA can begin to look into the objects the EXPLAIN plan is referencing. When writing efficient SQL, it is imperative to know the demographics and shape of the objects the code will bump up against. For most databases, all the information needed is found in the data dictionary. When querying the dictionary for object statistics, one must make sure to look at accurate information.

While some databases like SQL Server 2000 have automatic updating of object statistics into the dictionary, other RDBMS engines like Oracle require the DBA to manually and periodically refresh the database catalog with up-to-date object data. Fortunately, this is pretty easy to accomplish.

Oracle offers special packages to assist with the updating of objects in addition to the standard analyze command. The *dbms_utility* package contains several procedures to help database professionals update their schema objects. To update the dictionary for a single schema, the *dbms_utility.analyze_schema* procedure can be used, while the *dbms_utility.analyze_database* procedure has been introduced for larger updates. One must be careful when executing such a procedure against a monolithic database like often occur in Oracle's applications.

Whatever method is chosen to update the objects, DBAs must make a practice of keeping data in the dictionary current, especially for databases that are very dynamic in nature.

Scheduling object updates in a nightly maintenance plan would probably be a good plan for such a database, especially if the cost-based optimizer is used. Fresh statistics help the optimizer make more informed choices of what path to follow when routing queries to the requested data. If the database thinks there are only 100 rows in a table that actually contains a million, the map used by the optimizer might not be the right one and response times will show it.

When tuning SQL, what types of metrics should be looked for in objects to help make intelligent coding choices? Although this list is certainly not exhaustive for tables, taking a look at the following items is a good start:

- **Row Counts** - No heavy explanation is needed for why this statistic should be reviewed. Full scans on beefy tables with large row counts should be avoided. Proper index placement becomes quite important on such tables. Another reason for reviewing row counts is physical redesign decisions. Perhaps a table has grown larger than anticipated and is now eligible for partitioning? Scanning a single partition in a table is much less work than running through the entire table.

- **Chained Row Counts** - Row chaining and migration can be a thorn in the side of an otherwise well-written SQL statement. Chained rows are usually the result of invalid page or blocksize choices where rows for a wide table simply will not fit on a single page or block. Migration is caused when a row expands beyond the remaining size boundary of the original block it was placed into. The database is forced to move the row to another block and leaves a pointer behind to indicate its new location. While chaining and migration are different, they have one thing in common; extra I/O is needed to retrieve the row that is either chained or migrated. Knowing how many of these the table has can help determine if object reorganization is needed. Extreme cases may require a full database rebuild with a larger blocksize. Oracle9i users, however, can create new tablespaces with larger blocksizes and move/reorganize their objects into them.

- **Space Extents** - For some databases, objects that have moved into multiple extents can be slower to access than same-size objects that are contained within a single contiguous extent of space. Later versions of Oracle, however, don't suffer from this multi-extent problem anymore, especially when objects have been placed into new locally-managed tablespaces.

- **High-Water Marks** - Tables that experience a lot of insert and delete activity can pose special problems. Oracle will always scan up to a table's "high-water mark," which is the last block of space it thinks contains data. For example, a table that used to contain a million rows, but now only has a hundred, may be scanned like it still has a million! Checking the high-water marks of the tables to see if they are still set to abnormally high values can determine if a table needs to be reloaded. This is usually done by a reorg or truncate and load.

- **Miscellaneous Properties** - There are several other performance boosting properties that can be set for tables. For instance, large tables that are being scanned may benefit from having parallelism enabled so the table can hopefully be scanned much quicker. Small lookup tables may benefit from being permanently cached in memory to speed access times. In Oracle, placing them into the KEEP buffer pool may do this. The cache parameter may also be used, although it is not as permanent a fix as the KEEP buffer pool option.

Indexes have their own unique set of items that need occasional review. Some of these include:

- **Selectivity/Unique Keys** - Indexes by their nature normally work best when selectivity is high, in other words, the numbers of unique values are many. The exception to this rule is the bitmap index, which is designed to work on columns with very low cardinality such as a Yes/No column. The selectivity of indexes should be periodically examined to see if an index that used to contain many unique values is now one that is losing its uniqueness rank.

- **Depth** - The tree depth of an index will indicate if the index has undergone a lot of splits and other destructive activity. Typically, indexes with tree depths greater than three or four are good candidates for rebuilds. Hopefully, this activity will improve access speed.

- **Deleted Row Counts** - Indexes that suffer from high parent table maintenance may contain a lot of "dead air" in the form of deleted rows in the leaf pages. Again, a rebuild may be in order for indexes with high counts of deleted leaf rows.

There are, of course, other items can be reviewed on the table and index statistical front, as well as at the individual column level.

Understanding the current state and shape of the objects being used in the queries that are being tuned can unlock clues about how to restructure the SQL code. For example, it may be determined that critical foreign keys that are used over and over in various sets of join operations have not been indexed, or it may be determined that the million-row table is a perfect candidate for a bitmap index given the current *where* predicate.

Look for SQL Rewrite Possibilities

For complex and problematic systems, analyzing and attempting the rewrite of many SQL statements can consume much of a database professional's time. A book of this nature cannot possibly go into this vast subject as there are a plethora of techniques and SQL hints that can be used to turn a query that initially runs slowly into one that runs as fast as possible.

To save time, the DBA might consider using one of the third-party SQL tuning tools that can help with rewriting SQL statements. Some of these tools will even generate automatic rewrites that can be trialed and reviewed.

Some DBAs have found that using such tools can indeed cut down on the SQL tuning process if used properly, since they offer easy generation of hints and normally are a good benchmarking facility that allows easy execution and review of performance statistics.

Even without access to third-party SQL tuning products, it is possible to use SQL*Plus to perform comparison benchmarks. By using the SET AUTOTRACE ON feature of SQL*Plus, it is possible to get decent feedback from Oracle on how efficient a query is.

```
SQL> set autotrace on;
SQL> select count(*) from admission;

  COUNT(*)
----------
      1552

Execution Plan
----------------------------------------------------------
   0      SELECT STATEMENT Optimizer=CHOOSE (Cost=1 Card=1)
   1    0   SORT (AGGREGATE)
   2    1     INDEX (FAST FULL SCAN) OF 'ADMISSION_PK' (UNIQUE) (Cost=
          1 Card=1542)
```

```
Statistics
----------------------------------------------------------
          0  recursive calls
          4  db block gets
          5  consistent gets
          0  physical reads
          0  redo size
        368  bytes sent via SQL*Net to client
        425  bytes received via SQL*Net from client
          2  SQL*Net roundtrips to/from client
          0  sorts (memory)
          0  sorts (disk)
          1  rows processed
```

What are some things to look for in terms of rewriting SQL? While this is certainly a large topic, there are a few major items that stand out above the rest:

- The Cartesian Product

- The Table Scan

- The Unnecessary Sort

- The Nonselective Index Scan

What different coding approaches should be tried using hints? While there is no way to give a complete rundown of every option, there are a few mainstays that can be tried:

- **The Four Standbys** - These include RULE, FIRST ROWS, ALL ROWS, and COST. Believe it or not, many times a query has been dramatically improved just by going back to the rule base optimizer. Even with all the progress made by cost-based approaches, sometimes the old way is the best way.

- **Table Order Shuffle** - Try influencing the order in which the optimizer joins the tables used in the query. The ORDERED hint can force the database to use the right tables to drive the join operation, and hopefully reduce inefficient I/O.

- **Divide and Conquer** - When databases introduced parallel operations, they opened up a whole new avenue in potential speed gains. The PARALLEL hint can be a powerful ally in splitting large table scans into chunks that may be worked on separately in parallel, and then merged back into a single result set. One thing to ensure is that the database is set up properly with respect to having enough parallel worker bees or "slaves" to handle the degree of parallelism specified.

- **Index NOW** – The EXPLAIN plan may demonstrate where the optimizer is not using an available index. This may or may not be a good thing. The only way to really tell is to force an index access plan in place of a table scan with an index hint.

Look for Object-Based Solutions

Object-based solutions are another option for SQL tuning analysts. This route involves steps like intelligent index creation, partitioning, and more. To accomplish this, it is necessary to first find the objects that will benefit from such modification, which, in turn, will enhance the overall runtime performance. For users of Oracle9i and above, the new *v$* views can help with this type of analysis.

For example, to investigate better use of partitioning, the first step is to locate large tables that are the consistent targets of full table scans. The *9iltabscan.sql* query below will identify the actual objects that are the target of such scans. It displays the table owner, table name, the table type (standard or partitioned), the table size in KB, the number of SQL statements that cause a scan to be performed, the number of total scans for the table each time the statement is executed, the number of SQL executions to date, and the total number of scans that the table has experienced (total single scans * executions).

🖫 9iltabscan.sql

```
-- ***************************************************
-- Copyright © 2005 by Rampant TechPress
-- This script is free for non-commercial purposes
-- with no warranties.  Use at your own risk.
--
-- To license this script for a commercial purpose,
-- contact info@rampant.cc
-- ***************************************************

select
    table_owner,
    table_name,
    table_type,
```

```
      size_kb,
      statement_count,
      reference_count,
      executions,
      executions * reference_count total_scans
from
   (select
    a.object_owner table_owner,
    a.object_name table_name,
    b.segment_type table_type,
    b.bytes / 1024 size_kb,
    sum(c.executions ) executions,
    count( distinct a.hash_value ) statement_count,
    count( * ) reference_count
from
    sys.v_$sql_plan a,
    sys.dba_segments b,
    sys.v_$sql c
where
    a.object_owner (+) = b.owner
    and a.object_name (+) = b.segment_name
    and b.segment_type in ('TABLE', 'TABLE PARTITION')
    and a.operation like '%TABLE%'
    and a.options = 'FULL'
    and a.hash_value = c.hash_value
    and b.bytes / 1024 > 1024
group by
    a.object_owner, a.object_name, a.operation,
    b.bytes / 1024, b.segment_type
order by
    4 desc, 1, 2 );
```

The following output shows identifying tables or table partitions that have been scanned in Oracle9i:

	TABLE_OWNER	TABLE_NAME	TABLE_TYPE	SIZE_KB	STATEMENT_COUNT	REFERENCE_COUNT	EXECUTIONS	TOTAL_SCANS
1	ERADMIN	EMP	TABLE	19456	2	2	2	4
2	ERADMIN	PATIENT	TABLE	3496	1	1	1	1
3	ERADMIN	ADMISSION	TABLE	3136	4	7	31	217

Figure 7.8: *Identifying tables or table partitions that have been scanned in Oracle9i*

The above query will help determine which tables might benefit from better indexing or partitioning.

While only examination of the actual SQL statements can determine if the queries that are scanning the tables are using available indexes, the question of whether the tables have indexes can be answered by using the *9iunused_indx.sql* query:

💾 **9iunused_indx.sql**

```
-- ***************************************************
-- Copyright © 2005 by Rampant TechPress
-- This script is free for non-commercial purposes
-- with no warranties.  Use at your own risk.
--
-- To license this script for a commercial purpose,
-- contact info@rampant.cc
-- ***************************************************

select distinct
    a.object_owner table_owner,
    a.object_name table_name,
    b.segment_type table_type,
    b.bytes / 1024 size_kb,
    d.index_name
from
    sys.v_$sql_plan a,
    sys.dba_segments b,
    sys.dba_indexes d
where
    a.object_owner (+) = b.owner
    and a.object_name (+) = b.segment_name
    and b.segment_type in ('TABLE', 'TABLE PARTITION')
    and a.operation like '%TABLE%'
    and a.options = 'FULL'
    and b.bytes / 1024 > 1024
    and b.segment_name = d.table_name
    and b.owner = d.table_owner
order by
    1, 2;
```

The following output shows unused indexes for tables being scanned:

	TABLE_OWNER	TABLE_NAME	TABLE_TYPE	SIZE_KB	INDEX_NAME
1	ERADMIN	ADMISSION	TABLE	2048	I_ADMISSION1
2	ERADMIN	ADMISSION	TABLE	2048	I_ADMISSION2
3	ERADMIN	PATIENT	TABLE	3072	I_PATIENT1
4	ERADMIN	PATIENT	TABLE	3072	I_PATIENT2
5	ERADMIN	PATIENT	TABLE	3072	I_PATIENT3

Figure 7.9: *Output showing unused indexes for tables being scanned*

Such a query can create a mini Unused Indexes report that can be used to ensure that any large tables being scanned on the system have the proper indexing scheme.

The previous sections explored various methods of tuning SQL in Oracle 9i. Oracle 10g offers even more options to find poor performing SQL.

Oracle 10g

SQL Statistics

SQL statements are used to access data in an Oracle database. Thus, it is nearly impossible to overestimate the importance of SQL tuning work. Most performance problems in an Oracle database are caused by poor SQL statements; therefore, it is important to learn how AWR helps identify SQL statements that are candidates for tuning.

SQL tuning process usually consists of three steps:

- Find bad SQL statements that place a high workload on an Oracle database.

- Determine that the cost-based optimizer (CBO) provides a less than optimal execution plan for those statements.

- Implement actions which lead to alternative execution plans that provide better response times and lower workload for poor SQL statements.

The goals of SQL tuning can be identified as the minimization of SQL response time or reducing of the workload on an Oracle database while performing the same amount of work. In earlier Oracle releases, SQL tuning work was mostly a manual iterative process for finding an optimal execution plan.

Fortunately, Oracle10g introduces automated SQL tuning tools in the form of SQL Tuning Advisor and SQL Access Advisor. These intelligent tools give Oracle tuning experts recommendations and advice. Recommendations may take the form of ideas on the gathering of additional object statistics, creation or removal of indexes, restructuring of SQL statements, etc. Furthermore, all resulting recommendations contain an estimated benefit of its implementation.

Oracle DBAs have several options for the identification of poorly performing SQL statements:

- Use of the AWR.

- Use of the STATSPACK utility.

- Use of SQL related *v$* dynamic performance views as *v$sql*.

- Use of the SQL trace facility.

The AWR can be used to find resource intensive SQL statements. The AWR repository contains several SQL statistics related views:

- *dba_hist_sqlstat* view contains a history for SQL execution statistics and stores snapshots of *v$sql* view.

- *dba_hist_sqltext* view stores actual text for SQL statements captured from *v$sql* view.

- *dba_hist_sql_plan* view stores execution plans for SQL statements available in *dba_hist_sqlstat* view.

The *dba_hist_sqlstat* is the view that helps identify SQL candidates for tuning. A study of the structure of *dba_hist_sqlstat* view and the information available through it will further aid users in the identification of poor SQL statements.

dba_hist_sqlstat

This view contains more than 20 statistics related to SQL statements. The structure of *dba_hist_sqlstat* view is:

```
SQL> desc DBA_HIST_SQLSTAT

Name                                      Null?    Type
----------------------------------------- -------- --------------------
SNAP_ID                                            NUMBER
DBID                                               NUMBER
INSTANCE_NUMBER                                    NUMBER
SQL_ID                                             VARCHAR2(13)
PLAN_HASH_VALUE                                    NUMBER
OPTIMIZER_COST                                     NUMBER
OPTIMIZER_MODE                                     VARCHAR2(10)
OPTIMIZER_ENV_HASH_VALUE                           NUMBER
SHARABLE_MEM                                       NUMBER
LOADED_VERSIONS                                    NUMBER
VERSION_COUNT                                      NUMBER
MODULE                                             VARCHAR2(64)
ACTION                                             VARCHAR2(64)
SQL_PROFILE                                        VARCHAR2(64)
PARSING_SCHEMA_ID                                  NUMBER
FETCHES_TOTAL                                      NUMBER
FETCHES_DELTA                                      NUMBER
END_OF_FETCH_COUNT_TOTAL                           NUMBER
END_OF_FETCH_COUNT_DELTA                           NUMBER
SORTS_TOTAL                                        NUMBER
SORTS_DELTA                                        NUMBER
EXECUTIONS_TOTAL                                   NUMBER
EXECUTIONS_DELTA                                   NUMBER
LOADS_TOTAL                                        NUMBER
LOADS_DELTA                                        NUMBER
INVALIDATIONS_TOTAL                                NUMBER
INVALIDATIONS_DELTA                                NUMBER
PARSE_CALLS_TOTAL                                  NUMBER
PARSE_CALLS_DELTA                                  NUMBER
DISK_READS_TOTAL                                   NUMBER
DISK_READS_DELTA                                   NUMBER
BUFFER_GETS_TOTAL                                  NUMBER
BUFFER_GETS_DELTA                                  NUMBER
ROWS_PROCESSED_TOTAL                               NUMBER
ROWS_PROCESSED_DELTA                               NUMBER
CPU_TIME_TOTAL                                     NUMBER
CPU_TIME_DELTA                                     NUMBER
ELAPSED_TIME_TOTAL                                 NUMBER
ELAPSED_TIME_DELTA                                 NUMBER
IOWAIT_TOTAL                                       NUMBER
IOWAIT_DELTA                                       NUMBER
CLWAIT_TOTAL                                       NUMBER
CLWAIT_DELTA                                       NUMBER
APWAIT_TOTAL                                       NUMBER
APWAIT_DELTA                                       NUMBER
CCWAIT_TOTAL                                       NUMBER
CCWAIT_DELTA                                       NUMBER
DIRECT_WRITES_TOTAL                                NUMBER
DIRECT_WRITES_DELTA                                NUMBER
PLSEXEC_TIME_TOTAL                                 NUMBER
PLSEXEC_TIME_DELTA                                 NUMBER
JAVEXEC_TIME_TOTAL                                 NUMBER
JAVEXEC_TIME_DELTA                                 NUMBER
```

The statistics for every SQL statement are stored in two separate columns:

- <Statistic Name>_TOTAL column stores the total values of statistics since the last instance startup.

- <Statistic Name>_DELTA column reflects the change in a statistic's value between *end_interval_time* and *begin_interval_time* time interval, which is stored in the *dba_hist_snapshot* view.

Using this core *dba_hist_sqlstat* view, poor SQL statements can be identified using such criteria as:

- High number of buffer gets.

- High number of physical reads.

- Large execution count.

- High shared memory usage.

- High version count.

- High parse count.

- High elapsed time.

- High execution CPU time.

- High number of rows processed.

- High number of sorts, etc.

This view does not contain the actual text of SQL statements; however, it does contain a *sql_id* column. The SQL text can be retrieved by joining *dba_hist_sqlstat* with *dba_hist_sqltext* view. For example, the *high_sql_buf_gets.sql* script below retrieves high buffer gets SQL statements for a particular snapshot interval:

high_sql_buf_gets.sql

```
-- *****************************************************
-- Copyright © 2005 by Rampant TechPress
-- This script is free for non-commercial purposes
-- with no warranties.  Use at your own risk.
--
-- To license this script for a commercial purpose,
-- contact info@rampant.cc
```

```
-- **************************************************
select
                sql_id
              , buffer_gets_total "Buffer Gets"
              , executions_total "Executions"
              , buffer_gets_total/executions_total "Gets / Exec"
              , pct*100 "% Total"
              , cpu_time_total/1000000 "CPU Time (s)"
              , elapsed_time_total/1000000 "Elapsed Time (s)"
              , module "SQL Module"
              , stmt   "SQL Statement"
from
(select
                e.sql_id sql_id
              , e.buffer_gets_total - nvl(b.buffer_gets_total,0)
buffer_gets_total
              , e.executions_total - nvl(b.executions_total,0)
executions_total
              , (e.buffer_gets_total - nvl(b.buffer_gets_total,0))/
              (  select e1.value - nvl(b1.value,0)
                 from dba_hist_sysstat b1 , dba_hist_sysstat e1
                    where b1.snap_id(+)            = b.snap_id
                      and e1.snap_id               = e.snap_id
                      and b1.dbid(+)               = b.dbid
                      and e1.dbid                  = e.dbid
                      and b1.instance_number(+)    = b.instance_number
                      and e1.instance_number       = e.instance_number
                      and b1.stat_id               = e1.stat_id
                      and e1.stat_name             = 'session logical
reads'
) pct
              , e.elapsed_time_total - nvl(b.elapsed_time_total,0)
elapsed_time_total
              , e.cpu_time_total - nvl(b.cpu_time_total,0) cpu_time_total
              , e.module
              , t.sql_text   stmt
        from dba_hist_sqlstat   e
           , dba_hist_sqlstat   b
           , dba_hist_sqltext   t
       where b.snap_id(+)           = @pBgnSnap
         and b.dbid(+)              = e.dbid
         and b.instance_number(+)   = e.instance_number
         and b.sql_id(+)            = e.sql_id
         and e.snap_id              = &pEndSnap
         and e.dbid                 = &pDBId
         and e.instance_number      = &pInstNum
         and (e.executions_total - nvl(b.executions_total,0)) > 0
         and t.sql_id               = b.sql_id
)
       order by 2 desc
```

The WISE tool has several reports which allow the retrieval of top SQL statements from the AWR based on various criteria as shown in Figure 7.10.

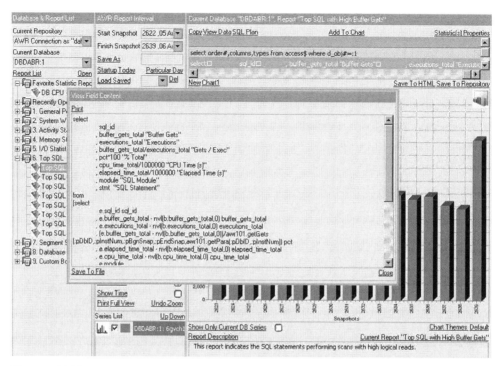

Figure 7.10: *AWR Top SQLs With High Buffer Gets Report in WISE.*

Furthermore, the WISE tool allows users to quickly drill down to execution plan details for every particular SQL statement. It also allows the easy creation and viewing of SQL Advisor recommendations in a GUI environment.

Thus, the *dba_hist_sqlstat* view provides valuable information about SQL statements that are querying the database. By regularly checking this view, the primary causes of most performance problems can easily be identified.

For a given session, an Oracle user may issue multiple SQL statements and it is the interaction between the SQL and the database that determines the wait conditions. The *v$active_session_history* table can be joined into the *v$sqlarea* and *dba_users* to quickly see the top SQL waits as well as the impacted user and session with which they are associated.

The *top_sql_waits.sql* script is an example of how these features can be combined effectively:

🖫 top_sql_waits.sql

```
-- ***************************************************
-- Copyright © 2005 by Rampant TechPress
-- This script is free for non-commercial purposes
-- with no warranties.  Use at your own risk.
--
-- To license this script for a commercial purpose,
-- contact info@rampant.cc
-- ***************************************************

select
   ash.user_id,
   u.username,
   sqla.sql_text,
   sum(ash.wait_time + ash.time_waited) wait_time
from
   v$active_session_history ash,
   v$sqlarea                sqla,
   dba_users                u
where
   ash.sample_time > sysdate-1
and
   ash.sql_id = sqla.sql_id
and
   ash.user_id = u.user_id
group by
   ash.user_id,
   sqla.sql_text,
   u.username
order by 4;
```

The following is a sample output from this script:

```
  USER_ID USERNAME
---------- ------------------------------
SQL_TEXT
--------------------------------------------------------------------------------
  WAIT_TIME
----------
       54 SYSMAN
DECLARE job BINARY_INTEGER := :job; next_date DATE := :mydate;  broken BOOLEAN :
= FALSE; BEGIN EMD_MAINTENANCE.EXECUTE_EM_DBMS_JOB_PROCS(); :mydate := next_date
; IF broken THEN :b := 1; ELSE :b := 0; END IF; END;
        0

       58 DABR
select tbsp      , reads "Reads"       , rps  "Reads / Second"       , atpr   "Avg
 Reads (ms)"      , bpr   "Avg Blks / Read"      , writes  "Writes"       , wps
"Avg Writes / Second"      , waits  "Buffer Waits"      , atpwt"Avg Buf Wait (m
s)" From ( select e.tsname tbsp      , sum (e.phyrds - nvl(b.phyrds,0))
        reads      , Round(sum (e.phyrds - nvl(b.phyrds,0))/awr101.getEla( :
pDbId,:pInstNum,:pBgnSnap,:pEndSnap,'NO' ),3)    rps       , Round(decode( sum(e.p
hyrds - nvl(b.phyrds,0))         , 0, 0        , (sum(e.readtim - nvl
(b.readtim,0)) /           sum(e.phyrds  - nvl(b.phyrds,0)))*10),3)
atpr       , Round(decode( sum(e.phyrds - nvl(b.phyrds,0))         , 0, to_n
umber(NULL)         , sum(e.phyblkrd - nvl(b.phyblkrd,0)) /
sum(e.phyrds  - nvl(b.phyrds,0)) ),3)     bpr      , sum (e.phywrts   - n
vl(b.phywrts,0))           writes      , Round(sum (e.phywrts   - nvl(b.ph
ywrts,0))/awr101.getEla( :pDbId,:pInstNu
     174

       58 DABR
select e.stat_name                  "E.STAT_NAME"      , (e.value - b.value
)/1000000       "Time (s)"      , decode( e.stat_name,'DB time'       ,
to_number(null)       , 100*(e.value - b.value)       )/awr101.get
DBTime(:pDbId,:pInstNum,:pBgnSnap,:pEndSnap) "Percent of Total DB Time"    from d
ba_hist_sys_time_model e      , dba_hist_sys_time_model b   where b.snap_id
       = :pBgnSnap    and e.snap_id         = :pEndSnap     and b.dbid
       = :pDbId    and e.dbid           = :pDbId     and b.ins
tance_number       = :pInstNum    and e.instance_number        = :pInstNum    a
nd b.stat_id            = e.stat_id    and e.value - b.value > 0  order by 2
 desc
```

Once the SQL details have been identified, the DBA can drill-down deeper by joining *v$active_session_history* with *dba_objects* and find important information about the interaction between the SQL and specific tables and indexes.   What follows is an ASH script, *obj_wait_ash.sql*, that can be used to show the specific objects that are causing the highest resource waits:

🖫 obj_wait_ash.sql

```
-- *************************************************
-- Copyright © 2005 by Rampant TechPress
-- This script is free for non-commercial purposes
-- with no warranties.  Use at your own risk.
--
-- To license this script for a commercial purpose,
-- contact info@rampant.cc
-- *************************************************

select
   obj.object_name,
   obj.object_type,
   ash.event,
   sum(ash.wait_time + ash.time_waited) wait_time
from
```

```
      v$active_session_history ash,
      dba_objects              obj
where
      ash.sample_time > sysdate -1
and
      ash.current_obj# = obj.object_id
group by
      obj.object_name,
      obj.object_type,
      ash.event
order by 4 desc;
```

The following is a sample output from this script:

```
OBJECT_NAME          OBJECT_TYPE    EVENT                         WAIT_TIME
-------------------  -----------    ----------------------------  ---------
SCHEDULER$_CLASS     TABLE          rdbms ipc message             199853456
USER$                TABLE          rdbms ipc message              33857135
USER$                TABLE          control file sequential read     288266
WRI$_ALERT_HISTORY   TABLE          db file sequential read           26002
OL_SCP_PK            INDEX          db file sequential read           19638
C_OBJ#               CLUSTER        db file sequential read           17966
STATS$SYS_TIME_MODEL TABLE          db file scattered read            16085
WRI$_ADV_DEFINITIONS INDEX          db file sequential read           15995
```

The results show that table *wri$_alert_history* experiences a high wait time on *db file sequential read* wait event. Based on this fact, the DBA can further investigate causes of such behavior in order to find the primary problem. It could be, for example, a non-optimal SQL query that performs large full table scans on this table.

Oracle10g SQL Tuning Scripts

The following *awr_high_scan_sql.sql* query could be submitted to determine what sessions have parsed SQL statements that caused large table scans on a system along with the total number of large scans by session. In this example, large is anything over 1 MB

🖫 awr_high_scan_sql.sql

```
-- ***************************************************
-- Copyright © 2005 by Rampant TechPress
-- This script is free for non-commercial purposes
-- with no warranties.  Use at your own risk.
--
-- To license this script for a commercial purpose,
-- contact info@rampant.cc
-- ***************************************************

select
      c.username username,
```

```
        count(a.hash_value) scan_count
from
    sys.v_$sql_plan a,
    sys.dba_segments b,
    sys.dba_users c,
    sys.v_$sql d
where
    a.object_owner (+) = b.owner
and
    a.object_name (+) = b.segment_name
and
    b.segment_type IN ('TABLE', 'TABLE PARTITION')
and
    a.operation like '%TABLE%'
and
    a.options = 'FULL'
and
    c.user_id = d.parsing_user_id
and
    d.hash_value = a.hash_value
and
    b.bytes / 1024 > 1024
group by
    c.username
order by
    2 desc
;
```

The output from the above query might look something like the following:

```
USERNAME    SCAN_COUNT
----------  ----------
SYSTEM              14
SYS                 11
ERADMIN              6
ORA_MONITOR          3
```

In like fashion, if a DBA wants to uncover what sessions have parsed SQL statements containing Cartesian joins along with the number of SQL statements that contain such joins, the following query could be used:

```
select
    username,
    count(distinct c.hash_value) nbr_stmts
from
    sys.v_$sql a,
    sys.dba_users b,
    sys.v_$sql_plan c
where
    a.parsing_user_id = b.user_id
and
```

```
    options = 'CARTESIAN'
and
    operation like '%JOIN%'
and
    a.hash_value = c.hash_value
group by
    username
order by
    2 desc
;
```

A result set from this query could look similar to the following:

```
USERNAME    NBR_STMTS
---------   ---------
SYS                 2
SYSMAN              2
ORA_MONITOR         1
```

The *v$sql_plan* view adds more meat to the process of identifying problem sessions in a database. When combined with the standard performance metrics query, DBAs can really begin to pinpoint the sessions that are wreaking havoc inside their critical systems.

Identify the Resource Intensive SQL

After identifying the top resource hogging sessions in a database, attention can be focused on the code they and others are executing that is likely causing system bottlenecks. As with Top Session monitors, many decent database monitors have a "Top SQL" feature that can help ferret out bad SQL code. If access to such a tool is not available, a script like the *awr_high_resource_sql.sql* shown below can be used:

🖫 awr_high_resource_sql.sql

```
-- ***************************************************
-- Copyright © 2005 by Rampant TechPress
-- This script is free for non-commercial purposes
-- with no warranties.  Use at your own risk.
--
-- To license this script for a commercial purpose,
-- contact info@rampant.cc
-- ***************************************************

select sql_text,
       username,
       disk_reads_per_exec,
       buffer_gets,
```

```
         disk_reads,
         parse_calls,
         sorts,
         executions,
         rows_processed,
         hit_ratio,
         first_load_time,
         sharable_mem,
         persistent_mem,
         runtime_mem,
         cpu_time,
         elapsed_time,
         address,
         hash_value
from
(select sql_text ,
         b.username ,
 round((a.disk_reads/decode(a.executions,0,1,
 a.executions)),2)
         disk_reads_per_exec,
         a.disk_reads ,
         a.buffer_gets ,
         a.parse_calls ,
         a.sorts ,
         a.executions ,
         a.rows_processed ,
         100 - round(100 *
         a.disk_reads/greatest(a.buffer_gets,1),2) hit_ratio,
         a.first_load_time ,
         sharable_mem ,
         persistent_mem ,
         runtime_mem,
         cpu_time,
         elapsed_time,
         address,
         hash_value
from
   sys.v_$sqlarea a,
   sys.all_users b
where
   a.parsing_user_id=b.user_id and
   b.username not in ('sys','system')
order by 3 desc)
where rownum < 21
```

The code in this script will pull the top twenty SQL statements as ranked by disk reads per execution. The ROWNUM filter can be changed at the end to show more or all SQL that has executed in a database. The DBA can also add WHERE predicates that only show the SQL for one or more of the top sessions previously identified. Note that in Oracle9i, Oracle has added the *cpu_time* and *elapsed_time* columns, which provide more data which can be used to determine the overall efficiency of an SQL statement.

The following is the sample output of this query:

	SQL_TEXT	USERI	DISK_REA	BUFFER_GETS	DISK_READS	PARS	SORTS	EXEC	ROWS	HIT_RAT
1	update lob$ set retention = :1 where retention >= 0	SYS	791	1005	791	1	0	1	511	
2	delete from sys.wri$_optstat_histgrm_history where s	SYS	759	846	759	1	0	1	0	
3	delete from WRH$_SYSMETRIC_SUMMARY tab w	SYS	691	7172	691	1	0	1	5831	
4	delete from WRH$_WAITCLASSMETRIC_HISTOR'	SYS	630	11132	630	1	0	1	9633	
5	delete from WRH$_SQL_PLAN tab where (:beg_sn	SYS	533	3743	533	1	0	1	993	
6	delete from wrh$_sqltext tab where (tab.dbid = :dbid	SYS	522	1196	522	1	0	1	99	
7	BEGIN prvt_advisor.delete_expired_tasks; END;	SYS	454	1424	454	1	0	1	1	
8	begin dbms_feature_usage_internal.exec_db_usage	SYS	453	433868	453	1	0	1	1	
9	delete from WRH$_ENQUEUE_STAT tab where (:t	SYS	427	10306	427	1	0	1	3137	
10	SELECT T.ID FROM WRI$_ADV_TASKS T, WRI$_	SYS	421	1133	421	1	0	1	0	
11	select s.synonym_name object_name, o.object_type	SYS	397.5	434481	1590	4	0	4	13536	
12	select o.owner#,o.obj#,decode(o.linkname,null, dec	SYS	362.5	6051	725	2	0	2	0	
13	select atc + ix, NULL, NULL from (select count(*) atc	SYS	296	293988	296	1	0	1	1	
14	delete from sys.wri$_optstat_histhead_history where	SYS	231	292	231	1	0	1	0	
15	delete from WRH$_BG_EVENT_SUMMARY tab wl	SYS	207	6895	207	1	0	1	2057	
16	delete from WRI$_ALERT_HISTORY where time_su	SYS	188	2071	188	1	0	1	582	
17	begin "SYS"."DBMS_REPCAT_UTL"."DROP_USE	SYS	163	4048	163	1	0	1	1	
18	BEGIN ECM_CT.POSTLOAD_CALLBACK(:1, :2); EI	SYSM	154	7904	308	2	0	2	2	
19	begin "CTXSYS"."CTX_ADM"."DROP_USER_OBJ	SYS	118	2395	118	1	0	1	1	
20	select table_objno, primary_instance, secondary_inst	SYS	111	688	111	1	0	1	0	

Figure 7.11: *The sample high_resource_sql.sql query output*

The Oracle9i *v$sql_plan* view can also help with identification of problem SQL. For example, a DBA may want to know how many total SQL statements are causing Cartesian joins on a system. The following *awr_cartesian_sum.sql* query can answer that question:

🖫 awr_cartesian_sum.sql

```
-- ************************************************
-- Copyright © 2005 by Rampant TechPress
-- This script is free for non-commercial purposes
-- with no warranties.  Use at your own risk.
--
-- To license this script for a commercial purpose,
-- contact info@rampant.cc
-- ************************************************

select
   count(distinct hash_value) carteisan_statements,
   count(*)                   total_cartesian_joins
from
   sys.v_$sql_plan
where
   options = 'CARTESIAN'
and
   operation like '%JOIN%'
```

Output from this query might resemble the following::

```
CARTESIAN_STATEMENTS     TOTAL_CARTESIAN_JOINS
---------------------- ----------------------
                    3                        3
```

It is possible for a single SQL statement to contain more than one Cartesian join. A DBA can then view the actual SQL statements containing the Cartesian joins, along with their performance metrics by using a query like *awr_sql_cartesian.sql* below:

🖫 awr_sql_cartesian.sql

```
-- ****************************************************
-- Copyright © 2005 by Rampant TechPress
-- This script is free for non-commercial purposes
-- with no warranties.  Use at your own risk.
--
-- To license this script for a commercial purpose,
-- contact info@rampant.cc
-- ****************************************************

select *
from
   sys.v_$sql
where
   hash_value in
      (select hash_value
       from
          sys.v_$sql_plan
       where
          options = 'CARTESIAN'
          and
          operation LIKE '%JOIN%' )
order by hash_value;
```

Another area of interest for DBAs is table scan activity. Most DBAs don't worry about small table scans because Oracle can many times access small tables more efficiency through a full scan than through index access. Large table scans, however, are another matter. Most DBAs prefer to avoid those where possible through smart index placement or intelligent partitioning.

Using the *v$sql_plan* view, a DBA can quickly identify any SQL statement that contains one or more large table scans. The following query, *awr_large_scan_count.sql*, shows any SQL statement containing a large table scan, along with a count of how many large scans it causes for each execution, the total number of times the statement has been executed, and then the sum total of all scans it has caused on the system:

💾 awr_large_scan_count.sql

```
-- ****************************************************
-- Copyright © 2005 by Rampant TechPress
-- This script is free for non-commercial purposes
-- with no warranties.  Use at your own risk.
--
-- To license this script for a commercial purpose,
-- contact info@rampant.cc
-- ****************************************************

select
    sql_text,
    total_large_scans,
      executions,
      executions * total_large_scans sum_large_scans
from
(select
      sql_text,
      count(*) total_large_scans,
      executions
 from
      sys.v_$sql_plan a,
      sys.dba_segments b,
      sys.v_$sql c
 where
      a.object_owner (+) = b.owner
   and
      a.object_name (+) = b.segment_name
   and
      b.segment_type IN ('TABLE', 'TABLE PARTITION')
   and
      a.operation LIKE '%TABLE%'
   and
      a.options = 'FULL'
   and
      c.hash_value = a.hash_value
   and
      b.bytes / 1024 > 1024
   group by
      sql_text, executions)
order by
  4 desc
;
```

This query produces the output shown below. Should the DBA worry more about an SQL statement that causes only one large table scan, but has been executed 1000 times; or care more about an SQL statement that has ten large scans in it, but has only been executed a handful of times? Note the following sample output from the above query:

	SQL_TEXT	TOTAL_U	EXECUTIONS	SUM_LARGE_SCANS
1	select name,type#,obj#,remoteowner,linkname,namespace, subname from obj$ v	1	71	71
2	select o.name,o.type#,o.obj#,o.remoteowner,o.linkname,o.namespace, o.subnan	1	16	16
3	select object_name, object_type from sys.user_objects o where o.object_type in	2	3	6
4	select s.synonym_name object_name, object_type from sys.all_synonyms s,	1	4	4
5	select name, type#, obj#, remoteowner, linkname, namespace, subname from ob	1	3	3
6	select object_name, object_type from sys.user_objects o where o.object_type in	2	1	2
7	SELECT NUM!["]IDX_OR_TABI!["]PTYPEI["]SUBPTYPEI["]PCNT!["]SUBPCNT	2	1	2
8	SELECT /*+ full(o) */ U.NAME, COUNT(DECODE(O.TYPE#, 7,1, 8,1, 9,1, 11,1,	1	1	1
9	delete from WRH$_SQL_PLAN tab where (:beg_snap <= tab.snap_id and	1	1	1
10	delete from WRH$_BG_EVENT_SUMMARY tab where (:beg_snap <= tab.snap	1	1	1
11	select name,type#,obj#,remoteowner,linkname,namespace, subname from obj$ v	1	1	1
12	select name, type#, obj#, remoteowner, linkname, namespace, subname from ob	1	1	1
13	select name, type#, obj#, remoteowner, linkname, namespace, subname from ot	1	1	1
14	delete from wrh$_sqltext tab where (tab.dbid = :dbid and :beg_snap <= tab.	1	1	1
15	select grantor#,ta.obj#,o.type# from objauth$ ta, obj$ o where grantee#=:1 and t	1	1	1
16	select name, type#, obj#, remoteowner, linkname, namespace, subname from ob	1	1	1
17	select name, type#, obj#, remoteowner, linkname, namespace, subname from ob	1	1	1
18	delete from WRH$_WAITCLASSMETRIC_HISTORY tab where (:beg_snap <= t	1	1	1
19	delete from WRH$_SYSMETRIC_SUMMARY tab where (:beg_snap <= tab.snaj	1	1	1
20	delete from WRH$_ENQUEUE_STAT tab where (:beg_snap <= tab.snap_id anc	1	1	1
21	delete from WRI$_ALERT_HISTORY where time_suggested < :1	1	1	1
22	select max(bytes) from dba_segments	1	1	1

Figure 7.12: *The sample large_scan_count.sql query output*

Each DBA will likely have an opinion on this, but regardless, use of this query can assist in identifying SQL statements that have the potential to cause system slowdowns.

dba_hist_sqlstat

This view is very similar to the *v$sql* view except that it contains important SQL metrics for each snapshot. These include important delta (change) information on disk reads and buffer gets, as well as time-series delta information on application, I/O and concurrency wait times and can be shown by applying the *awr_sqlstat_deltas.sql* code as follows:

🖫 awr_sqlstat_deltas.sql

```
-- ***************************************************
-- Copyright © 2005 by Rampant TechPress
-- This script is free for non-commercial purposes
-- with no warranties.  Use at your own risk.
--
-- To license this script for a commercial purpose,
-- contact info@rampant.cc
-- ***************************************************


col c1 heading 'Begin|Interval|time'    format a8
col c2 heading 'SQL|ID'                 format a13
col c3 heading 'Exec|Delta'             format 9,999
col c4 heading 'Buffer|Gets|Delta'      format 9,999
col c5 heading 'Disk|Reads|Delta'       format 9,999
```

```
col c6 heading 'IO Wait|Delta'          format 9,999
col c7 heading 'Application|Wait|Delta' format 9,999
col c8 heading 'Concurrency|Wait|Delta' format 9,999


break on c1

select
   to_char(s.begin_interval_time,'mm-dd hh24')  c1,
   sql.sql_id               c2,
   sql.executions_delta     c3,
   sql.buffer_gets_delta    c4,
   sql.disk_reads_delta     c5,
   sql.iowait_delta         c6,
   sql.apwait_delta         c7,
   sql.ccwait_delta         c8
from
   dba_hist_sqlstat         sql,
   dba_hist_snapshot          s
where
   s.snap_id = sql.snap_id
order by
   c1,
   c2
;
```

Here is a sample of the output. This is very important because the changes in SQL execution over time periods are shown. For each snapshot period, the change in the number of times that the SQL was executed as well as important performance information about the performance of the statement is revealed.

Begin Interval time	SQL ID	Exec Delta	Buffer Gets Delta	Disk Reads Delta	IO Wait Delta	Application Wait Delta	Concurrency Wait Delta
10-10 16	0sfgqjz5cs52w	24	72	12	0	3	0
	1784a4705pt01	1	685	6	0	17	0
	19rkm1wsf9axx	10	61	4	0	0	0
	1d5d88cnwxcw4	52	193	4	6	0	0
	1fvsn5j51ugz3	4	0	0	0	0	0
	1uym1vta995yb	1	102	0	0	0	0
	23yu0nncnp8m9	24	72	0	0	6	0
	298ppdduqr7wm	1	3	0	0	0	0
	2cpffmjm98pcm	4	12	0	0	0	0
	2prbzh4qfms7u	1	4,956	19	1	34	5
10-10 17	0sfgqjz5cs52w	30	90	1	0	0	0
	19rkm1wsf9axx	14	88	0	0	0	0
	1fvsn5j51ugz3	4	0	0	0	0	0
	1zcdwkknwdpgh	4	4	0	0	0	0
	23yu0nncnp8m9	30	91	0	0	0	5
	298ppdduqr7wm	1	3	0	0	0	0
	2cpffmjm98pcm	4	12	0	0	0	0
	2prbzh4qfms7u	1	4,940	20	0	0	0
	2ysccdanw72pv	30	60	0	0	0	0
	3505vtqmvvf40	2	321	5	1	0	0

This report is especially useful because the DBA can track the logical I/O (buffer gets) vs. physical I/O for each statement over time, thereby providing important information about the behavior of the SQL statement.

This output gives a quick overview of the top SQL during any AWR snapshot period and shows how the behavior has changed since the last snapshot period. Detecting changes in the behavior of commonly executed SQL statements is the key to time-series SQL tuning.

A WHERE clause can be easily added to the above script and plot the I/O changes over time as shown in the *awr_sqlstat_deltas_detail.sql* below:

🖫 awr_sqlstat_deltas_detail.sql

```
-- ***************************************************
-- Copyright © 2005 by Rampant TechPress
-- This script is free for non-commercial purposes
-- with no warranties.  Use at your own risk.
--
-- To license this script for a commercial purpose,
-- contact info@rampant.cc
-- ***************************************************

col c1 heading 'Begin|Interval|time'      format a8
col c2 heading 'Exec|Delta'               format 999,999
col c3 heading 'Buffer|Gets|Delta'        format 999,999
col c4 heading 'Disk|Reads|Delta'         format 9,999
col c5 heading 'IO Wait|Delta'            format 9,999
col c6 heading 'App|Wait|Delta'           format 9,999
col c7 heading 'Cncr|Wait|Delta'          format 9,999
col c8 heading 'CPU|Time|Delta'           format 999,999
col c9 heading 'Elpsd|Time|Delta'         format 999,999

accept sqlid prompt 'Enter SQL ID: '

ttitle 'time series execution for|&sqlid'

break on c1

select
  to_char(s.begin_interval_time,'mm-dd hh24')  c1,
  sql.executions_delta      c2,
  sql.buffer_gets_delta     c3,
  sql.disk_reads_delta      c4,
  sql.iowait_delta          c5,
  sql.apwait_delta          c6,
  sql.ccwait_delta          c7,
  sql.cpu_time_delta        c8,
```

```
    sql.elapsed_time_delta     c9
from
    dba_hist_sqlstat          sql,
    dba_hist_snapshot           s
where
    s.snap_id = sql.snap_id
and
    sql_id = '&sqlid'
order by
    c1
;
```

The following output shows the changes to the execution of a frequently used SQL statement and how its behavior changes over time:

Begin Interval time	Exec Delta	Buffer Gets Delta	Disk Reads Delta	IO Wait Delta	App Wait Delta	Cncr Wait Delta	CPU Time Delta	Elpsd Time Delta
10-14 10	709	2,127	0	0	0	0	398,899	423,014
10-14 11	696	2,088	0	0	0	0	374,502	437,614
10-14 12	710	2,130	0	0	0	0	384,579	385,388
10-14 13	693	2,079	0	0	0	0	363,648	378,252
10-14 14	708	2,124	0	0	0	0	373,902	373,902
10-14 15	697	2,091	0	0	0	0	388,047	410,605
10-14 16	707	2,121	0	0	0	0	386,542	491,830
10-14 17	698	2,094	0	0	0	0	378,087	587,544
10-14 18	708	2,124	0	0	0	0	376,491	385,816
10-14 19	695	2,085	0	0	0	0	361,850	361,850
10-14 20	708	2,124	0	0	0	0	368,889	368,889
10-14 21	696	2,088	0	0	0	0	363,111	412,521
10-14 22	709	2,127	0	0	0	0	369,015	369,015
10-14 23	695	2,085	0	0	0	0	362,480	362,480
10-15 00	709	2,127	0	0	0	0	368,554	368,554
10-15 01	697	2,091	0	0	0	0	362,987	362,987
10-15 02	696	2,088	0	0	0	2	361,445	380,944
10-15 03	708	2,124	0	0	0	0	367,292	367,292
10-15 04	697	2,091	0	0	0	0	362,279	362,279
10-15 05	708	2,124	0	0	0	0	367,697	367,697
10-15 06	696	2,088	0	0	0	0	361,423	361,423
10-15 07	709	2,127	0	0	0	0	374,766	577,559
10-15 08	697	2,091	0	0	0	0	364,879	410,328

In Figure 7.13, the WISE tool allows the DBA to plot time-series charts for particular *sql_id* of interest:

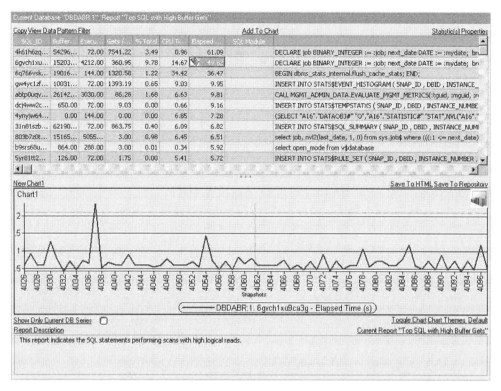

Figure 7.13: *The time-series plot for particular SQL statement.*

In the above example, the average elapsed time for the SQL statement over time is shown. Of course, the execution speed may change due to any number of factors:

- Different bind variables.

- Database resource shortage.

- High physical reads from data buffer shortage.

The good news is that the DBA can drill-down into those specific times when the SQL statement performed badly and see exactly why its execution time was slow.

For example, Figure 7.15 shows the average executions by day of the week.

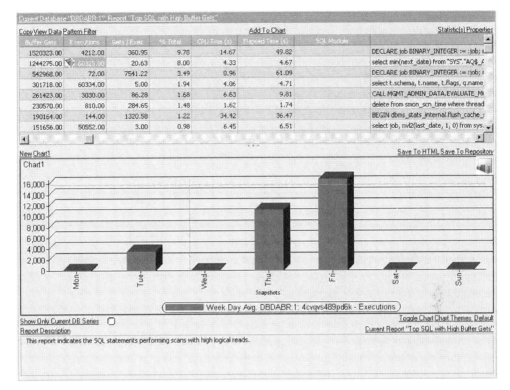

Figure 7.14: *Signature for a specific SQL statement in WISE tool.*

The *awr_sqlstat_deltas_detail.sql* script can also be changed slightly to examine logical I/O (consistent gets) versus physical I/O (disk reads) averages for any given SQL statement as shown in Figure 7.15.

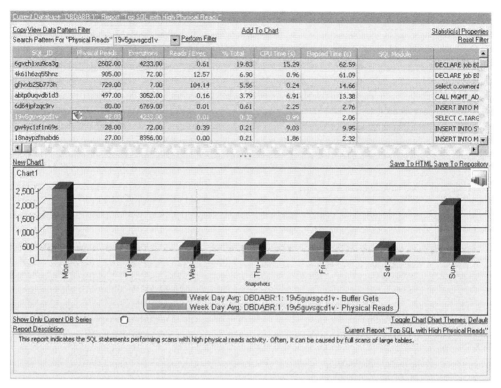

Figure 7.15: *Logical vs. physical I/O averages for a specific SQL statement in WISE tool.*

In this plot, the ratio of logical to physical reads changes depending on the day of the week. If execution speed for this SQL query is critical, examine those times when it has high physical disk reads and consider segregating the tables that participate in this query into our KEEP pool.

The *dba_hist_sql_plan* table that stores time-series execution details is covered in the next section.

dba_hist_sql_plan

The *dba_hist_sql_plan* table contains time-series data about each object, such as tables, indexes, and views, involved in the query. The important columns include the cost, cardinality, *cpu_cost*, *io_cost* and *temp_space* required for the object.

The *awr_high_cost_sql.sql* query below retrieves SQL statements which have high query execution cost identified by Oracle optimizer:

🖫 awr_high_cost_sql.sql

```
-- *************************************************
-- Copyright © 2005 by Rampant TechPress
-- This script is free for non-commercial purposes
-- with no warranties.  Use at your own risk.
--
-- To license this script for a commercial purpose,
-- contact info@rampant.cc
-- *************************************************

col c1 heading 'SQL|ID'           format a13
col c2 heading 'Cost'             format 9,999,999
col c3 heading 'SQL Text'         format a200


select
  p.sql_id            c1,
  p.cost              c2,
  to_char(s.sql_text) c3
from
  dba_hist_sql_plan    p,
  dba_hist_sqltext     s
where
      p.id = 0
  and
      p.sql_id = s.sql_id
  and
      p.cost is not null
order by
  p.cost desc
;
```

The output of the above query showing the high cost SQL statements over time might look like the following:

```
SQL
ID                  Cost SQL Text
------------- ---------- -----------------------------------------
847ahztscj4xw    358,456 select
                                s.begin_interval_time  c1,
                                pl.sql_id              c2,
                                pl.object_name         c3,
                                pl.search_columns      c4,
                                pl.cardinality         c5,
                                pl.access_predicates   c6,
                                pl.filter_predicates   c7
                         from
                                dba_hist_sql_plan pl,
                                dba_hist_snapshot s
                         order by
                                c1, c2

58du2p8phcznu      5,110 select
                                begin_interval_time  c1,
                                search_columns       c2,
                                count(*)             c3
                         from
                                dba_hist_sqltext
                         natural join
                                dba_hist_snapshot
                         natural join
                                dba_hist_sql_plan
                         where
                                lower(sql_text) like lower('%idx%')
                         group by
                                begin_interval_time,search_columns
```

Once a particular SQL statement is identified for which details are desired, its execution plan used by the optimizer to actually execute the statement can be viewed. The *awr_sql_details.sql* query below retrieves an execution plan for a particular SQL statement of interest:

awr_sql_details.sql

```
-- *************************************************
-- Copyright © 2005 by Rampant TechPress
-- This script is free for non-commercial purposes
-- with no warranties.  Use at your own risk.
--
-- To license this script for a commercial purpose,
-- contact info@rampant.cc
-- *************************************************

accept sqlid prompt 'Please enter SQL ID: '

col c1 heading 'Operation'              format a20
col c2 heading 'Options'                format a20
col c3 heading 'Object|Name'            format a25
col c4 heading 'Search Columns'         format 999,999
col c5 heading 'Cardinality'            format 999,999
```

```
select
   operation          c1,
   options            c2,
   object_name        c3,
   search_columns     c4,
   cardinality        c5
from
   dba_hist_sql_plan p
where
      p.sql_id = '&sqlid'
order by
   p.id;
```

This is one of the most important of all of the SQL tuning tools.

Here is a sample of the output from this script:

```
                                           Search
Operation         Options        Name      Cols Cardinality
----------------  -------------  ---------------------- --- -----------
SELECT STATEMENT                            0
VIEW                                        3          4
SORT              ORDER BY                  4          4
VIEW                                        2          4
UNION-ALL                                   0
FILTER                                      6
NESTED LOOPS      OUTER                     0          3
NESTED LOOPS      ANTI                      0          3
TABLE ACCESS      BY INDEX ROWID STATS$SYSTEM_EVENT     0         70
INDEX             RANGE SCAN     STATS$SYSTEM_EVENT_PK  3         70
INDEX             UNIQUE SCAN    STATS$IDLE_EVENT_PK    1         46
TABLE ACCESS      BY INDEX ROWID STATS$SYSTEM_EVENT     0          1
INDEX             UNIQUE SCAN    STATS$SYSTEM_EVENT_PK  4          1
FILTER                                      0
FAST DUAL                                   1          1
```

Interrogating Table Join Methods

The choice between a hash join and a nested loop join depends on several factors:

- The relative number of rows in each table.

- The presence of indexes on the key values.

- The settings for static parameters such as *index_caching* and *cpu_costing*.

- The current setting and available memory in *pga_aggregate_target*.

Hash joins do not use indexes and perform full-table scans, often using parallel query. As a result, hash joins with parallel full-table scans tend

---

to drive up CPU consumption. Additionally, PGA memory consumption becomes higher when hash joins are involved; however, if Automatic Memory Management (AMM) is enabled, that's usually not a problem.

The following *awr_hash_join_alert.sql* query produces a report alerting an Oracle DBA when hash join operations count exceeds some threshold:

🖫 awr_hash_join_alert.sql

```
-- ***************************************************
-- Copyright © 2005 by Rampant TechPress
-- This script is free for non-commercial purposes
-- with no warranties.  Use at your own risk.
--
-- To license this script for a commercial purpose,
-- contact info@rampant.cc
-- ***************************************************

col c1 heading 'Date'              format a20
col c2 heading 'Hash|Join|Count'   format 99,999,999
col c3 heading 'Rows|Processed'    format 99,999,999
col c4 heading 'Disk|Reads'        format 99,999,999
col c5 heading 'CPU|Time'          format 99,999,999


accept hash_thr char prompt 'Enter Hash Join Threshold: '

ttitle 'Hash Join Threshold|&hash_thr'

select
   to_char(sn.begin_interval_time,'yy-mm-dd hh24')  c1,
   count(*)                                          c2,
   sum(st.rows_processed_delta)                      c3,
   sum(st.disk_reads_delta)                          c4,
   sum(st.cpu_time_delta)                            c5
from
   dba_hist_snapshot sn,
   dba_hist_sql_plan  p,
   dba_hist_sqlstat   st
where
   st.sql_id = p.sql_id
and
   sn.snap_id = st.snap_id
and
   p.operation = 'HASH JOIN'
having
   count(*) > &hash_thr
group by
   begin_interval_time;
```

The sample output might look like the following, showing the number of hash joins during the snapshot period along with the relative I/O and CPU associated with the processing. The values for *rows_processed* are generally higher for hash joins, which do full table scans, as opposed to nested loop joins with generally involved a very small set of returned rows.

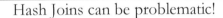

Hash Join Thresholds

Date	Hash Join Count	Rows Processed	Disk Reads	CPU Time
04-10-12 17	22	4,646	887	39,990,515
04-10-13 16	25	2,128	827	54,746,653
04-10-14 11	21	17,368	3,049	77,297,578
04-10-21 15	60	2,805	3,299	5,041,064
04-10-22 10	25	6,864	941	4,077,524
04-10-22 13	31	11,261	2,950	46,207,733
04-10-25 16	35	46,269	1,504	6,364,414

Hash Joins can be problematic!

In Oracle9i, the sorting default is that no single task may consume more than 5% of the *pga_aggregate_target* region before the sort pages-out to the TEMP tablespace for a disk sort. For parallel sorts, the limit is 30% of the PGA aggregate, regardless of the number of parallel processes.

In Oracle9i, if there are specialized hash joins that require more hash area, when *pga_aggregate_target* is set, no single hash join may consume more than five percent of the area.

To force hash joins in Oracle9i, there are two steps. It may not be enough to increase the *hash_area_size* if the CBO is stubborn and the DBA may need to force the hash join with a hint.

Step 1 - Increase the *hash_area_size* maximum

```
alter session set workarea_size_policy=manual;
alter session set hash_area_size=1048576000;
```

Step 2 - Add a *use_hash* hint to the SQL

```
select /*+ use_hash (a, b)*/
from . . .
```

The default sorting behavior can be overridden in one of two ways:

Option 1 - Manual override:

```
alter session set workarea_size_policy=manual;
alter session set sort_area_size=1048576000;
```

Option 2 - Bounce with special hidden parameter:

In this example, the DBA can increase the default amount of RAM available to sort operations from five percent to about 50%:

```
pga_aggregate_target=10g
_smm_max_size=4000000;
```

The number for *_smm_max_size* is expressed in k-bytes, so this value is about 4.5 Gigabytes. Hidden parameters are totally unsupported, so DBAs must understand that there is risk in using this technique.

The following script is the AWR version of the SQL execution plan script. Unlike the *plan9i.sql* script that only extracts current SQL from the library cache, the *plan10g.sql* script accesses the AWR *dba_hist_sqlplan* table and gives a time-series view of the ways that Oracle is accessing the tables and indexes:

🖫 **plan10g.sql**

```
-- ************************************************
-- Copyright © 2005 by Rampant TechPress
-- This script is free for non-commercial purposes
-- with no warranties.  Use at your own risk.
--
-- To license this script for a commercial purpose,
-- contact info@rampant.cc
-- ************************************************

spool plan.lst

set echo off
set feedback on

set pages 999;
column nbr_FTS  format 99,999
column num_rows format 999,999
```

```
column blocks    format 9,999
column owner     format a10;
column name      format a30;
column ch        format a1;
column time      heading "Snapshot Time"        format a15

column object_owner heading "Owner"             format a12;
column ct           heading "# of SQL selects" format 999,999;

break on time

select
   object_owner,
   count(*)    ct
from
   dba_hist_sql_plan
where
   object_owner is not null
group by
   object_owner
order by
   ct desc
;


--spool access.lst;

set heading on;
set feedback on;

ttitle 'full table scans and counts|  |The "K" indicates that the table is
in the KEEP Pool (Oracle8).'
select
   to_char(sn.end_interval_time,'mm/dd/rr hh24') time,
   p.owner,
   p.name,
   t.num_rows,
--   ltrim(t.cache) ch,
   decode(t.buffer_pool,'KEEP','Y','DEFAULT','N') K,
   s.blocks blocks,
   sum(a.executions_delta) nbr_FTS
from
   dba_tables    t,
   dba_segments s,
   dba_hist_sqlstat     a,
   dba_hist_snapshot sn,
   (select distinct
     pl.sql_id,
     object_owner owner,
     object_name name
   from
     dba_hist_sql_plan pl
   where
     operation = 'TABLE ACCESS'
     and
     options = 'FULL') p
where
   a.snap_id = sn.snap_id
   and
```

```
   a.sql_id = p.sql_id
   and
   t.owner = s.owner
   and
   t.table_name = s.segment_name
   and
   t.table_name = p.name
   and
   t.owner = p.owner
   and
   t.owner not in ('SYS','SYSTEM')
having
   sum(a.executions_delta) > 1
group by
   to_char(sn.end_interval_time,'mm/dd/rr hh24'),p.owner, p.name,
t.num_rows, t.cache, t.buffer_pool, s.blocks
order by
   1 asc;


column nbr_RID  format 999,999,999
column num_rows format 999,999,999
column owner    format a15;
column name     format a25;

ttitle 'Table access by ROWID and counts'
select
   to_char(sn.end_interval_time,'mm/dd/rr hh24') time,
   p.owner,
   p.name,
   t.num_rows,
   sum(a.executions_delta) nbr_RID
from
   dba_tables t,
   dba_hist_sqlstat    a,
   dba_hist_snapshot sn,
  (select distinct
     p1.sql_id,
     object_owner owner,
     object_name name
   from
     dba_hist_sql_plan p1
   where
     operation = 'TABLE ACCESS'
     and
     options = 'BY USER ROWID') p
where
   a.snap_id = sn.snap_id
   and
   a.sql_id = p.sql_id
   and
   t.table_name = p.name
   and
   t.owner = p.owner
having
   sum(a.executions_delta) > 9
group by
   to_char(sn.end_interval_time,'mm/dd/rr hh24'),p.owner, p.name, t.num_rows
order by
```

```
   1 asc;
-- ****************************************************
--   Index Report Section
-- ****************************************************

column nbr_scans   format 999,999,999
column num_rows    format 999,999,999
column tbl_blocks format 999,999,999
column owner       format a9;
column table_name format a20;
column index_name format a20;

ttitle 'Index full scans and counts'
select
   to_char(sn.end_interval_time,'mm/dd/rr hh24') time,
   p.owner,
   d.table_name,
   p.name index_name,
   seg.blocks tbl_blocks,
   sum(s.executions_delta) nbr_scans
from
   dba_segments seg,
   dba_indexes d,
   dba_hist_sqlstat      s,
   dba_hist_snapshot sn,
   (select distinct
      pl.sql_id,
      object_owner owner,
      object_name name
   from
      dba_hist_sql_plan pl
   where
      operation = 'INDEX'
      and
      options = 'FULL SCAN') p
where
   d.index_name = p.name
   and
   s.snap_id = sn.snap_id
   and
   s.sql_id = p.sql_id
   and
   d.table_name = seg.segment_name
   and
   seg.owner = p.owner
having
   sum(s.executions_delta) > 9
group by
   to_char(sn.end_interval_time,'mm/dd/rr hh24'),p.owner, d.table_name,
p.name, seg.blocks
order by
   1 asc;


ttitle 'Index range scans and counts'
select
   to_char(sn.end_interval_time,'mm/dd/rr hh24') time,
   p.owner,
```

```
   d.table_name,
   p.name index_name,
   seg.blocks tbl_blocks,
   sum(s.executions_delta) nbr_scans
from
   dba_segments seg,
   dba_hist_sqlstat    s,
   dba_hist_snapshot sn,
   dba_indexes d,
  (select distinct
     pl.sql_id,
     object_owner owner,
     object_name name
   from
     dba_hist_sql_plan pl
   where
     operation = 'INDEX'
     and
     options = 'RANGE SCAN') p
where
   d.index_name = p.name
   and
   s.snap_id = sn.snap_id
   and
   s.sql_id = p.sql_id
   and
   d.table_name = seg.segment_name
   and
   seg.owner = p.owner
having
   sum(s.executions_delta) > 9
group by
   to_char(sn.end_interval_time,'mm/dd/rr hh24'),p.owner, d.table_name,
p.name, seg.blocks
order by
   1 asc;

ttitle 'Index unique scans and counts'
select
   to_char(sn.end_interval_time,'mm/dd/rr hh24') time,
   p.owner,
   d.table_name,
   p.name index_name,
   sum(s.executions_delta) nbr_scans
from
   dba_hist_sqlstat    s,
   dba_hist_snapshot sn,
   dba_indexes d,
  (select distinct
     pl.sql_id,
     object_owner owner,
     object_name name
   from
     dba_hist_sql_plan pl
   where
     operation = 'INDEX'
     and
     options = 'UNIQUE SCAN') p
where
```

```
   d.index_name = p.name
   and
   s.snap_id = sn.snap_id
   and
   s.sql_id = p.sql_id
having
   sum(s.executions_delta) > 9
group by
   to_char(sn.end_interval_time,'mm/dd/rr hh24'),p.owner, d.table_name,
p.name
order by
   1 asc;

spool off
```

The following table represents the output. The DBA should start by viewing the counts of full-table scans for each AWR snapshot period. Then, the RECYCLE pool should be used for segregating large tables involved in frequent full-table scans. To locate these large-table full-table scans, return to the plan9i.sql full-table scan report.

```
                    full table scans and counts

Snapshot Time  OWNER      NAME                     NUM_ROWS C K  BLOCKS  NBR_FTS
-------------  ---------- ------------------------ -------- - -  ------- -------   12/08/04 14
APPLSYS    FND_CONC_RELEASE_DISJS       39 N K      2  98,864
           APPLSYS    FND_CONC_RELEASE_PERIODS     39 N K          2  98,864
           APPLSYS    FND_CONC_RELEASE_STATES       1 N K          2  98,864
           SYS        DUAL                            N K          2  63,466
           APPLSYS    FND_CONC_PP_ACTIONS       7,021 N      1,262  52,036
           APPLSYS    FND_CONC_REL_CONJ_MEMBER      0 N K         22  50,174

12/08/04 15    APPLSYS    FND_CONC_RELEASE_DISJS       39 N K          2  33,811
               APPLSYS    FND_CONC_RELEASE_PERIODS     39 N K          2   2,864
               APPLSYS    FND_CONC_RELEASE_STATES       1 N K          2  32,864
               SYS        DUAL                            N K          2  63,466
               APPLSYS    FND_CONC_PP_ACTIONS       7,021 N      1,262  12,033
               APPLSYS    FND_CONC_REL_CONJ_MEMBER      0 N K         22  50,174
```

One table in the listing is a clear candidate for inclusion in the RECYCLE pool. The FND_CONC_PP_ACTIONS table contains 1,262 blocks and has experienced many full-table scans.

These scripts also show counts for indexes that are accessed via *rowid*, indicative of non-range scan access.

```
Table access by ROWID and counts
Wed Dec 22


Snapshot Time  OWNER   NAME                             NUM_ROWS  NBR_RID
-------------  ------  -------------------------------  --------  --------
12/16/04 19    SYSMAN  MGMT_TARGET_ROLLUP_TIMES              110        10
12/17/04 06    SYSMAN  MGMT_TARGET_ROLLUP_TIMES              110        10
12/17/04 07    SYSMAN  MGMT_TARGET_ROLLUP_TIMES              110        10
12/17/04 08    SYSMAN  MGMT_TARGET_ROLLUP_TIMES              110        10
```

```
12/17/04 12   SYSMAN   MGMT_TARGET_ROLLUP_TIMES        110        10
12/17/04 13   SYSMAN   MGMT_TARGET_ROLLUP_TIMES        110        10
12/17/04 14   SYS      VIEW$                         2,583        84
              SYSMAN   MGMT_TARGET_ROLLUP_TIMES        110        10
12/17/04 17   SYS      VIEW$                         2,583        82
12/17/04 18   SYSMAN   MGMT_TARGET_ROLLUP_TIMES        110        10
12/17/04 20   SYSMAN   MGMT_TARGET_ROLLUP_TIMES        110        10
12/17/04 21   SYSMAN   MGMT_TARGET_ROLLUP_TIMES        110        10
12/17/04 22   SYSMAN   MGMT_TARGET_ROLLUP_TIMES        110        10
12/17/04 23   SYSMAN   MGMT_TARGET_ROLLUP_TIMES        110        10
12/18/04 00   SYSMAN   MGMT_TARGET_ROLLUP_TIMES        110        10
12/18/04 01   SYSMAN   MGMT_TARGET_ROLLUP_TIMES        110        20
12/18/04 02   SYSMAN   MGMT_TARGET_ROLLUP_TIMES        110        10
12/18/04 03   SYSMAN   MGMT_TARGET_ROLLUP_TIMES        110        10
12/18/04 04   SYSMAN   MGMT_TARGET_ROLLUP_TIMES        110        10
12/18/04 05   SYSMAN   MGMT_TARGET_ROLLUP_TIMES        110        10
12/18/04 09   SYSMAN   MGMT_TARGET_ROLLUP_TIMES        110        20
12/18/04 11   SYSMAN   MGMT_TARGET_ROLLUP_TIMES        110        20
```

Also obtained are counts of index full scans and index range scans, and this data is very useful for locating those indexes that might benefit from segregation onto a larger blocksize.

```
Index full scans and counts

Snapshot Time   OWNER    TABLE_NAME              INDEX_NAME            TBL_BLOCKS   NBR_SCANS
---------------  ------   --------------------   --------------------  ----------   ----------
12/08/04 14     SYSMAN   MGMT_FAILOVER_TABLE     PK_MGMT_FAILOVER              8          59
12/08/04 15     SYSMAN   MGMT_FAILOVER_TABLE     PK_MGMT_FAILOVER              8          58
12/08/04 16     SYS      WRH$_TEMPFILE           WRH$_TEMPFILE_PK             8          16
                SYSMAN   MGMT_FAILOVER_TABLE     PK_MGMT_FAILOVER              8          59
12/08/04 17     SYS      WRH$_STAT_NAME          WRH$_STAT_NAME_P             8         483
                SYSMAN   MGMT_FAILOVER_TABLE     PK_MGMT_FAILOVER              8          58
12/08/04 18     SYSMAN   MGMT_FAILOVER_TABLE     PK_MGMT_FAILOVER              8          59
12/08/04 19     SYSMAN   MGMT_FAILOVER_TABLE     PK_MGMT_FAILOVER              8          58
12/08/04 20     SYSMAN   MGMT_FAILOVER_TABLE     PK_MGMT_FAILOVER              8          59
12/08/04 21     SYSMAN   MGMT_FAILOVER_TABLE     PK_MGMT_FAILOVER              8          58
12/08/04 22     SYSMAN   MGMT_FAILOVER_TABLE     PK_MGMT_FAILOVER              8          58
12/08/04 23     SYSMAN   MGMT_FAILOVER_TABLE     PK_MGMT_FAILOVER              8          59
12/09/04 00     SYSMAN   MGMT_FAILOVER_TABLE     PK_MGMT_FAILOVER              8          58
12/09/04 01     SYSMAN   MGMT_FAILOVER_TABLE     PK_MGMT_FAILOVER              8          59
12/09/04 02     SYSMAN   MGMT_FAILOVER_TABLE     PK_MGMT_FAILOVER              8          59
12/09/04 03     SYSMAN   MGMT_FAILOVER_TABLE     PK_MGMT_FAILOVER              8          59
12/09/04 04     SYSMAN   MGMT_FAILOVER_TABLE     PK_MGMT_FAILOVER              8          58
12/09/04 05     SYSMAN   MGMT_FAILOVER_TABLE     PK_MGMT_FAILOVER              8          59
12/09/04 06     SYSMAN   MGMT_FAILOVER_TABLE     PK_MGMT_FAILOVER              8          58
12/09/04 07     SYSMAN   MGMT_FAILOVER_TABLE     PK_MGMT_FAILOVER              8          59
12/09/04 08     SYSMAN   MGMT_FAILOVER_TABLE     PK_MGMT_FAILOVER              8          58
12/09/04 09     SYSMAN   MGMT_FAILOVER_TABLE     PK_MGMT_FAILOVER              8          59


Index range scans and counts

Snapshot Time   OWNER    TABLE_NAME              INDEX_NAME                TBL_BLOCKS   NBR_SCANS
---------------  ------   --------------------   ------------------------  ----------   ----------
12/08/04 14     SYS      SYSAUTH$                I_SYSAUTH1                        8         345
                SYSMAN   MGMT_JOB_EXECUTION      MGMT_JOB_EXEC_IDX01              8        1373
                SYSMAN   MGMT_JOB_EXEC_SUMMARY   MGMT_JOB_EXEC_SUMM_IDX04         8          59
                SYSMAN   MGMT_METRICS            MGMT_METRICS_IDX_01             80          59
                SYSMAN   MGMT_PARAMETERS         MGMT_PARAMETERS_IDX_01           8         179
                SYSMAN   MGMT_TARGETS            MGMT_TARGETS_IDX_02              8          61
12/08/04 15     SYS      SYSAUTH$                I_SYSAUTH1                        8         273
                SYSMAN   MGMT_JOB_EXECUTION      MGMT_JOB_EXEC_IDX01              8        1423
                SYSMAN   MGMT_JOB_EXEC_SUMMARY   MGMT_JOB_EXEC_SUMM_IDX04         8          58
```

Conclusion

Tuning SQL is probably the most important tuning aspect of tuning an Oracle database. Nothing will trash a properly configured database more than poorly designed SQL. Most performance problems in an Oracle database are caused by poor SQL statements. In this chapter, many various methods and approaches to tuning SQL in both Oracle 9i and 10g have been demonstrated. This information arms the DBA with a wealth of scripts with which to tune SQL:

- Finding Problematic SQL

- Understanding the query and dependent objects.

- Looking for SQL rewrite possibilities.

- Looking for object-based solutions.

Storage and Space Management

Avoiding Database Downtime

From the DBA's perspective, it is anything but desirable to have something bring down the database or cause a hang that stops critical work from being done on a system. A storage problem has the potential to do both, so it is imperative to proactively put things in place that will prevent any downtime.

Free space, or the lack thereof, is at the heart of many storage related problems. The DBA should always ensure that both the server and the database have free space available so that when the need for more room arises, it can be accommodated. There are some very simple ways to accomplish this.

Automatic Growth

Way back in version 7, Oracle introduced the concept of auto-extendable datafiles. This simple addition to Oracle has silenced many a DBA's pager. It basically allows Oracle to automatically grow a datafile to meet the needs of incoming or changed data if not enough free space currently exists in the tablespace.

To enable this feature, the DBA can either create a tablespace with *autoextend* enabled or alter a tablespace after creation to turn the feature on. An example of creating a tablespace with *autoextend* initially enabled would be:

```
create tablespace
   users
datafile
   'd:\oracle\ora92\o92\users01.dbf' size 25600k
autoextend on next 1280k maxsize unlimited
extent management local autoallocate
logging
online;
```

Some DBAs have an aversion to using *autoextend*, and instead prefer to pre-allocate space to a tablespace. If proper capacity planning measures are used, this approach can work just fine. However, if the database is very dynamic and unpredictable, *autoextend* should be enabled for most tablespaces, especially temporary tablespaces that can be the object of large sort operations.

Some DBAs may not know whether *autoextend* is enabled for their tablespaces and datafiles. Furthermore, they may not know how much total space their storage structures are currently taking up.

If Oracle8i and above is being used, the *spacesum8i.sql* script will be necessary for making this determination:

⊟ spacesum8i.sql

```
-- ************************************************
-- Copyright © 2005 by Rampant TechPress
-- This script is free for non-commercial purposes
-- with no warranties.  Use at your own risk.
--
-- To license this script for a commercial purpose,
-- contact info@rampant.cc
-- ************************************************

select
      tablespace_name,
      autoextend,
      round ((total_space / 1024 / 1024), 2) as
      total_space,
      round ((total_free_space /
      1024 / 1024), 2) as total_free,
      round (((total_space - total_free_space) /
      1024 / 1024), 2) as used_space,
      to_char (
         nvl (
            round (
               (100 *
                  sum_free_blocks /
                  sum_alloc_blocks),2),0)) || '%'
            as pct_free
  from (select
            tablespace_name,
            max (autoextensible) autoextend,
            sum (blocks) sum_alloc_blocks,
            sum (bytes) as total_space
         from
            dba_data_files
         group by tablespace_name),
       (select
            b.tablespace_name fs_ts_name,
            nvl (sum (bytes), 0) as total_free_space,
            sum (blocks) as sum_free_blocks
         from
            dba_free_space a, dba_tablespaces b
         where
            a.tablespace_name (+) = b.tablespace_name
         group by b.tablespace_name,  status)
 where
      tablespace_name = fs_ts_name
union all
select
      d.tablespace_name, autoextend,
      round ((a.bytes / 1024 / 1024), 2),
      round ((a.bytes / 1024 / 1024) -
      (nvl (t.bytes, 0) / 1024 / 1024), 2),
      round (nvl (t.bytes, 0) / 1024 / 1024, 2),
      to_char (100 - (nvl (t.bytes /
      a.bytes * 100, 0)), '990.00')
  from
      sys.dba_tablespaces d,
      (select
            tablespace_name,
```

```
            max (autoextensible) autoextend,
            sum (bytes) bytes
      from
            dba_temp_files
      group by tablespace_name) a,
      (select
            tablespace_name, sum (bytes_cached) bytes
      from
            sys.v_$temp_extent_pool
      group by tablespace_name) t
where
      d.tablespace_name = a.tablespace_name (+)
  and d.tablespace_name = t.tablespace_name (+)
  and d.extent_management like 'LOCAL'
  and d.contents like 'TEMPORARY'
order by 1;
```

The following output displays summary space information and *autoextend* properties for tablespaces:

	TABLESPACE_NAME	AUTOEXTEND	TOTAL_SPACE	TOTAL_FREE	USED_SPACE	PCT_FREE
1	AUTOSEG	NO	5	4.94	.06	98.75%
2	DRSYS	YES	20	15.19	4.81	75.94%
3	INDX	YES	25	24.88	.13	99.5%
4	OEM_REPOSITORY	YES	35.01	3	32.01	8.57%
5	SYSTEM	YES	300	3.63	296.38	1.21%
6	TEMP	YES	556	1	555	0.18
7	TOOLS	YES	10	7.75	2.25	77.5%
8	UNDOTBS1	YES	210	208.69	1.31	99.38%
9	USERS	YES	25	15.13	9.88	60.5%
10	XDB	YES	38.13	.19	37.94	49%

Figure 8.1: *Output displaying summary space information and autoextend properties for tablespaces*

While the above queries will indicate whether a tablespace has *autoextend* enabled, it will not identify a specific datafile if the tablespace has multiple datafiles. For this determination, the datafileae.sql script will be needed and will work for all Oracle versions:

datafileae.sql

```
--  ****************************************************
--  Copyright © 2005 by Rampant TechPress
--  This script is free for non-commercial purposes
--  with no warranties.  Use at your own risk.
```

```
--
-- To license this script for a commercial purpose,
-- contact info@rampant.cc
-- ***************************************************

select
      b.file_name,
      b.tablespace_name,
      decode(c.inc,null,'no','yes') autoextend
  from
      sys.dba_data_files b,
      sys.filext$ c
 where
      c.file# (+)= b.file_id
 order by
      2, 1;
```

The following output shows information regarding which datafiles have *autoextend* enabled:

	FILE_NAME	TABLESPACE_NAME	AUTOEXTEND
1	D:\ORACLE\ORA92\O92\AUTOSEG.ORA	AUTOSEG	NO
2	D:\ORACLE\ORA92\O92\DRSYS01.DBF	DRSYS	YES
3	D:\ORACLE\ORA92\O92\INDX01.DBF	INDX	YES
4	D:\ORACLE\ORA92\O92\OEM_REPOSITORY.DBF	OEM_REPOSITORY	YES
5	D:\ORACLE\ORA92\O92\SYSTEM01.DBF	SYSTEM	YES
6	D:\ORACLE\ORA92\O92\TOOLS01.DBF	TOOLS	YES
7	D:\ORACLE\ORA92\O92\UNDOTBS01.DBF	UNDOTBS1	YES
8	D:\ORACLE\ORA92\O92\USERS01.DBF	USERS	YES
9	D:\ORACLE\ORA92\O92\XDB01.DBF	XDB	YES

Figure 8.2: *Information regarding what datafiles have autoextend enabled*

Unlimited Object Extents

When an object in Oracle (table, index, table partition, etc.) needs to expand, Oracle is kind enough to automatically allocate another extent of space to accommodate the incoming data.

Many DBAs, however, have horror stories about how a critical database suddenly froze in its tracks because a hub table or index had reached its maximum extent limit. The extent limit is the maximum number of extents that Oracle will allow an object to possess. If that limit was reached, a DBA could increase the maximum extent limit to a higher number, providing the object had not reached the ceiling of allowable extents for the Oracle version and operating system combination being used.

If the ceiling had indeed been reached, the DBA has no choice but to reorganize the object into fewer extents.

Such a situation can be quite time consuming, but it can be completely avoided if objects are created or altered to have unlimited extents, which is allowed in Oracle versions at least back to Oracle 7.3. For example, to alter an object to have unlimited extents a DDL command like the following can be issued:

```
alter table
   schemaname.tablename
   storage(maxextents unlimited);
```

Unlimited extents are the rule in locally-managed tablespaces, so if the decision is made to use these storage structures in the database, there will be no worry about an object reaching a maximum extent limit. Still, some DBAs have expressed concerns over whether an object having hundreds or thousands of extents will experience performance problems when full table scans or similar operations are performed against them. The next section explores how to find and analyze fragmentation.

Detecting Tablespace Fragmentation

How can a DBA tell if tablespaces are suffering from fragmentation problems and identify the type of fragmentation? The detection and diagnosis is not difficult to make at all. To determine if tablespaces are having a problem with fragmentation, the *tsfrag.sql* script can be used:

🖫 tsfrag.sql

```
-- ***************************************************
-- Copyright © 2005 by Rampant TechPress
-- This script is free for non-commercial purposes
-- with no warranties.  Use at your own risk.
--
-- To license this script for a commercial purpose,
```

```
-- contact info@rampant.cc
-- ************************************************

select
      tablespace_name,
      count(*) free_chunks,
      decode(round((max(bytes) / 1024000),2),null,0,
      round((max(bytes) / 1024000),2)) largest_chunk,
      nvl(round(sqrt(max(blocks)/sum(blocks)) *
   (100/sqrt(sqrt(count(blocks)) )),2),0)
      fragmentation_index
from
      sys.dba_free_space
group by
      tablespace_name
order by
      2 desc, 1;
```

The following output shows tablespace fragmentation:

	TABLESPACE_NAME	FREE_CHUNKS	LARGEST_CHUNK	FRAGMENTATION_INDEX
1	TEMP	2208	.44	.81
2	USER_DATA	73	63.23	31.33
3	RBS	36	18.94	15.77
4	USER_DATA2	8	4.66	57.06
5	ER_DATA	5	2.47	47.33
6	BROKER_DATA	3	8.26	72.94
7	BROKER_INDEXES	1	10.18	100
8	OEM_REPOSITORY	1	2.82	100
9	USER_DATA3	1	12.28	100
10	SYSTEM	1	.24	100
11	TEST	1	1.02	100
12	TEST_TS	1	14.27	100
13	TOOLS	1	5.08	100
14	USER_INDEXES	1	.38	100

Figure 8.3: *Checking for tablespace fragmentation*

When examining the script's output, the fragmentation index column is one column of interest. This column shows an overall ranking for the tablespace with respect to how badly it is actually fragmented. A 100% score indicates no fragmentation at all. Lesser scores verify the presence of fragmentation.

Another column of interest is the free chunks count column that will show how many segments of free space are scattered throughout the tablespace. One thing to keep in mind is that tablespaces with multiple datafiles will always show a free chunk count greater than one because each datafile will likely have at least one pocket of free space.

To drill down a little further and discover how badly fragmented each datafile in the database is use the *dffrag.sql* script:

💾 dffrag.sql

```
-- ************************************************
-- Copyright © 2005 by Rampant TechPress
-- This script is free for non-commercial purposes
-- with no warranties.  Use at your own risk.
--
-- To license this script for a commercial purpose,
-- contact info@rampant.cc
-- ************************************************

select
     b.file_name, b.tablespace_name,
     nvl(round(sqrt(max(a.blocks)/
     sum(a.blocks))*(100/sqrt(sqrt(count(a.blocks)) )),2),0)
     fragmentation_index,
     decode(c.inc,null,'no','yes') autoextend,
     count (*) free_chunks,
     decode (
         round ((max (a.bytes) / 1024000), 2),
         null, 0,
         round ((max (a.bytes) / 1024000), 2)) largest_chunk
  from
     sys.dba_free_space a,
     sys.dba_data_files b,
     sys.filext$ c
  where
     b.tablespace_name = a.tablespace_name (+) and
     c.file# (+)= a.file_id and
     b.file_id = a.file_id (+)
  group
     by b.file_name,
     decode(c.inc,null,'no','yes'),
     b.tablespace_name
  order
     by 5 desc, 1;
```

The following output shows datafile fragmentation:

Query Results

	FILE_NAME	TABLESPACE_NAME	FRAGMENTATION_INDEX	AUTOEXTEND	FREE_CHUNKS	LARGEST_CHUNK
1	D:\ORACLE\ORADATA\O817\TEMP01.DBF	TEMP	.81	YES	2208	.44
2	D:\ORACLE\ORADATA\O817\USERS01.DBF	USER_DATA	32.08	YES	68	63.23
3	D:\ORACLE\ORADATA\O817\RBS01.DBF	RBS	15.77	YES	36	18.94
4	D:\ORACLE\ORADATA\O817\USER_DATA2.DBF	USER_DATA2	57.06	NO	8	4.66
5	D:\ORACLE\ORADATA\O817\ER_DATA.DBF	ER_DATA	47.33	NO	5	2.47
6	D:\ORACLE\ORADATA\O817\USERS02.DBF	USER_DATA	43.98	YES	5	.38
7	D:\ORACLE\ORADATA\O817\BROKER_DATA.DBF	BROKER_DATA	72.94	YES	3	8.26
8	D:\ORACLE\ORADATA\O817\BIGADMIN.DBF	BIG_ADMISSION	0	NO	1	0
9	D:\ORACLE\ORADATA\O817\BROKER_INDEXES.DBF	BROKER_INDEXES	100	YES	1	10.18
10	D:\ORACLE\ORADATA\O817\INDX01.DBF	USER_INDEXES	100	YES	1	.38
11	D:\ORACLE\ORADATA\O817\OEM_REPOSITORY.ORA	OEM_REPOSITORY	100	YES	1	2.82
12	D:\ORACLE\ORADATA\O817\USER_DATA3.DBF	USER_DATA3	100	NO	1	12.28
13	D:\ORACLE\ORADATA\O817\SYSTEM01.DBF	SYSTEM	100	YES	1	.24
14	D:\ORACLE\ORADATA\O817\TEST01.DBF	TEST	100	YES	1	1.02
15	D:\ORACLE\ORADATA\O817\TEST_TS.ORA	TEST_TS	100	YES	1	14.27
16	D:\ORACLE\ORADATA\O817\TOOLS01.DBF	TOOLS	100	YES	1	5.08

Figure 8.4: *Checking for datafile fragmentation*

Another important fact about detecting tablespace fragmentation is that even if there are numerous free chunk counts in locally-managed tablespaces, it really is not an issue.

Since every object placed in the tablespace will have the same extent size, sooner or later the pockets of free space will be reused, whether new objects are placed into the tablespace or existing objects extended.

If fragmentation is found in the tablespaces, the DBA should identify whether it is of the honeycomb or bubble variety.

To answer this question, the DBA will need to produce a tablespace map that plots the entire tablespace in datafile/block id order. Doing so will show a number of interesting things, including where the actual objects in the tablespace reside, along with where the pockets of free space are located.

A clean tablespace will normally show one large segment of free space at the end. A badly fragmented tablespace will show bubbles of free space interspersed throughout. Two free space segments that reside next to one another can identify honeycombs.

If version 8 or higher of Oracle is being used, the *tsmap8.sql* script should be used:

tsmap8.sql

```
-- ********************************************************
-- Copyright © 2005 by Rampant TechPress
-- This script is free for non-commercial purposes
-- with no warranties.  Use at your own risk.
--
-- To license this script for a commercial purpose,
-- contact info@rampant.cc
-- ********************************************************

select
       'free space' object_owner,
       '    ' object_type,
       '    ' object_name,
       file_id,
       block_id,
       bytes / 1024 size_kb,
       blocks
from
       sys.dba_free_space
where
       tablespace_name = <:tablespace name>
union all
select
       owner,
       segment_type,
       decode (partition_name,null,segment_name,segment_name ||
       '.' || partition_name),
       file_id,
       block_id,
       bytes / 1024,
       blocks
from
       sys.dba_extents
where
       tablespace_name = <:tablespace name>
order by
       4,5;
```

The following output shows a mapping of the contents of a tablespace:

	OBJECT_OWNER	OBJECT_TYPE	OBJECT_NAME	FILE_ID	BLOCK_ID	SIZE_KB	BLOCKS
1	USER21	TABLE	TAB1	3	2	128	16
2	ERADMIN	INDEX	PK22	3	18	128	16
3	free space			3	34	128	16
4	USER21	TABLE	INDEX1	3	50	128	16
5	EMBT_CP	INDEX	REF61	3	66	128	16
6	EMBT_CP	INDEX	REF63	3	82	128	16
7	EMBT_CP	INDEX	REF62	3	98	128	16
8	free space			3	114	128	16
9	ERADMIN	LOBSEGMENT	SYS_LOB0000034196C00001$$	3	130	128	16
10	free space			3	146	128	16
11	EMBT_CP	TABLE	CP_TABLE	3	162	128	16
12	EMBT_CP	INDEX	REF67	3	178	128	16
13	ERADMIN	TABLE	TEST_RAW	3	194	128	16
14	BILLY	TABLE	PLAN_TABLE	3	210	128	16
15	ERADMIN	TABLE	EMP_BKP	3	226	128	16
16	ERADMIN	TABLE	CREATE$JAVA$LOB$TABLE	3	242	128	16
17	BAD_GUY	TABLE	ROB	3	258	128	16
18	ERADMIN	TABLE	DOCTOR_PROCEDURE	3	274	128	16
19	ERADMIN	INDEX	PK10	3	290	128	16
20	ERADMIN	TABLE	EMPLOYEE	3	306	128	16
21	ERADMIN	TABLE	MEDICATION	3	322	128	16
22	ERADMIN	INDEX	PK11	3	338	128	16
23	ERADMIN	TABLE	MEDICATION_DISP	3	354	128	16
24	ERADMIN	INDEX	PK12	3	370	128	16
25	ERADMIN	TABLE	MEDICATION_DISPM	3	386	128	16
26	ERADMIN	INDEX	PK13	3	402	128	16
27	ERADMIN	TABLE	NURSE	3	418	128	16
28	ERADMIN	LOBINDEX	SYS_IL0000034196C00002$$	3	434	128	16

Figure 8.5: *Mapping the contents of a tablespace*

These results display the contents of a particular tablespace in blockid order. Of particular interest are the fragmented pieces of freespace for file id #3. The next section will explain how to eliminate this fragmentation.

Eliminating Tablespace Fragmentation

Once tablespace fragmentation is identified, what should be done about it? Honeycomb fragmentation is easy to fix. All that needs to be done is the combination of adjacent free segments into one by issuing a coalesce statement similar to this one:

```
alter tablespace USERS coalesce;
```

Bubble fragmentation is more difficult to handle. The best course of action is to prevent it in the first place. The best weapon for prevention is the use of locally -managed tablespaces. It may sound too simple, but in reality, implementing these storage structures in the database can just about remove the need to perform full tablespace reorganizations.

What should be done if a situation exists in which there are many databases that were set up with dictionary-managed tablespaces? If running at least Oracle 8i, new locally-managed tablespaces in the database should be created, and a final full-tablespace reorganization performed of all the database objects into the new tablespaces.

Needless to say, this can be a difficult task if there are large databases and no third-party reorganization tool is available. However, it will be worth the effort as it is likely the tablespaces will never have to be reorganized again, and the objects should never again encounter a maximum extent limit.

Another option if using Oracle 8.1.6 or higher, is to convert any current dictionary-managed tablespaces to locally-managed tablespaces. Buried in the Oracle documentation is a procedure for converting a tablespace's extent management from dictionary to local or vice-versa.

The additions to the *sys.dbms_space_admin* package make it quite simple to convert a dictionary-managed tablespace to a locally-managed tablespace or vice versa, if desired. For example, to convert a dictionary-managed tablespace called USERS to a locally-managed tablespace in Oracle, this single command should be issued:

```
sys.dbms_space_admin.tablespace_migrate_to_local('USERS')
```

DBAs should not be afraid of how long this procedure might take on large tablespaces. It actually runs very fast. To take a tablespace that is locally-managed back to dictionary management, the following command can be issued:

```
sys.dbms_space_admin.tablespace_migrate_from_local('USERS')
```

There are a few restrictions on these conversion procedures. For example, 9i UNDO tablespaces currently cannot be converted, so check the Oracle documentation for the specifics of using these new procedures. Converting a dictionary-managed tablespace that has existing objects to locally-managed will not magically rebuild all the existing object extents to conform to the sizing guidelines used by locally-managed tablespaces.

If the situation precludes the use of locally-managed tablespaces, what choices remain to control tablespace fragmentation? One solution is to manually mimic the mechanisms of locally-managed tablespaces. This is done by:

Creating a tablespace that has same-sized extents for every object's INITIAL and NEXT extent values.

Setting the tablespace's PCTINCREASE property to zero.

Creating new objects in the tablespace without storage properties so they will inherit the tablespace's default storage properties.

Setting each object's maximum extent limit to unlimited.

This wraps up a brief examination of what to do for tablespace fragmentation. The next section goes deeper and explores object fragmentation

Detecting Object Fragmentation

Object fragmentation can damage performance in one of two ways:

- If there are objects in dictionary-managed tablespaces that have a maximum extent limit set to something other than unlimited, the objects could run out of space.

- As a result of repeated insert and delete activity, tables can become internally fragmented and contain a lot of wasted space. In the same way, indexes can become fragmented so that their depth reaches unacceptable levels. This predicament will be covered in the next section.

How can a DBA tell if the objects are getting close to hitting their maximum extent limit? This is quite easy to do. If using version 8 or higher of Oracle, the *maxext8.sql* script can be used:

🗔 maxext8.sql

```
-- ****************************************************
-- Copyright © 2005 by Rampant TechPress
-- This script is free for non-commercial purposes
-- with no warranties.  Use at your own risk.
--
-- To license this script for a commercial purpose,
-- contact info@rampant.cc
-- ****************************************************

select
      owner,
      decode(partition_name,NULL,segment_name,segment_name ||
      '.' || partition_name) segment_name,
      segment_type,
      extents,
      max_extents,
      initial_extent,
      next_extent,
      tablespace_name
from
      sys.dba_segments
where
      max_extents - extents <= 5 and
      segment_type <> 'CACHE'
order by
      1,2,3;
```

The following output shows objects nearing their maximum extent limit:

	OWNER	SEGMENT_NAME	SEGMENT_TYPE	EXTENTS	MAX_EXTENTS	INITIAL_EXTENT	NEXT_EXTENT	TABLESPACE_NAME
1	ERADMIN	CANT_EXTEND	TABLE	3	4	131072	131072	USER_DATA
2	USER21	TABLE1	TABLE	1	1	16384	6144000	USER_DATA
3	USER21	TABLE2	TABLE	1	1	106496	8192	USER_DATA
4	USER21	TABLE3	TABLE	1	1	106496	8192	USER_DATA

Figure 8.6: *Output showing objects nearing their maximum extent limit*

Another extent problem arises when an object in a dictionary-managed tablespace cannot extend because of a lack of contiguous free space. To uncover this type of problem, the *objdef.sql* script can be used:

objdef.sql

```
-- ***************************************************
-- Copyright © 2005 by Rampant TechPress
-- This script is free for non-commercial purposes
-- with no warranties.  Use at your own risk.
--
-- To license this script for a commercial purpose,
-- contact info@rampant.cc
-- ***************************************************

select
    a.owner,
    a.segment_name,
    a.segment_type,
    a.tablespace_name,
    a.next_extent,
    max(c.bytes) max_contig_space
from
    sys.dba_segments a,
    sys.dba_free_space c
where
    a.tablespace_name = c.tablespace_name and
    a.next_extent >
       (select
            max(bytes)
       from
            sys.dba_free_space b
       where
            a.tablespace_name = b.tablespace_name and
            b.tablespace_name = c.tablespace_name)
group by
        a.owner,
        a.segment_name,
        a.tablespace_name,
        a.segment_type,
        a.next_extent
```

The following output shows objects that have a space deficit in their parent tablespace:

	OWNER	SEGMENT_NAME	SEGMENT_TYPE	TABLESPACE_NAME	NEXT_EXTENT	MAX_CONTIG_SPACE
1	BAD_GUY	ADMISSION	TABLE PARTITION	USER_DATA	104857600	64749568
2	ERADMIN	ADMISSION	TABLE PARTITION	USER_DATA	104857600	64749568
3	ERADMIN	REF440	INDEX	USER_DATA	102400000	64749568
4	USER21	TABLE1	TABLE	USER_DATA	6144000	4767744
5	SYS	C_FILE#_BLOCK#	CLUSTER	SYSTEM	335872	245760
6	SYS	EMBARCADERO_EXPLAIN_PLAN	TABLE	SYSTEM	507904	245760
7	SYS	I_IDL_SB41	INDEX	SYSTEM	335872	245760
8	SYS	I_IDL_UB11	INDEX	SYSTEM	1146880	245760
9	SYS	I_IDL_UB21	INDEX	SYSTEM	335872	245760
10	SYS	JAVASNM$	TABLE	SYSTEM	507904	245760

Figure 8.7: *Output showing objects that have a space deficit in their parent tablespace*

Correcting Object Fragmentation

The prescription for correcting object fragmentation is generally total object reorganization. Such a procedure used to be fraught with errors and fear even when third party software products were used. Fortunately, this is not the case any longer as Oracle has provided more built-in reorganization capabilities with each new release. Oracle has even gone so far as to grant online reorganization abilities for certain object types.

The next section will cover the reorganization techniques and methods that can be used to fix objects when they need to be reorganized. Object space fragmentation is covered in detail in Chapter 5, *Objects*.

Correcting Space-Related Object Performance Problems

While the use of locally-managed tablespaces can just about make full tablespace reorganizations a thing of the past, object reorganizations are still necessary for the removal of headaches like wasted table space, chained/migrated table rows, deep index levels, and etc.

Oracle used to leave reorganization capabilities to third party software vendors, but newer versions of the RDBMS engine provide a number of built-in features that allow the reorganization of objects with simple DDL commands or packages.

Table 8.1 below summarizes the methods that can be used to reorganize objects when the need arises.

ORACLE VERSION	OBJECT TYPE	DDL COMMAND/METHOD	OFFLINE	ONLINE
7.x	Table	Drop/recreate table	Yes	No
	Index	Drop/recreate index	Yes	No
		ALTER INDEX REBUILD	Yes	No
8.0	Table	Drop/recreate table	Yes	No
	Table Partition	Drop/recreate table	Yes	No

ORACLE VERSION	OBJECT TYPE	DDL COMMAND/METHOD	OFFLINE	ONLINE
	Index	Drop/recreate index	Yes	No
		ALTER INDEX REBUILD	Yes	No
	Index Partition	ALTER INDEX REBUILD PARTITION	Yes	No
8.1	Heap Table	Drop/recreate table	Yes	No
		ALTER TABLE MOVE	Yes	No
	Table Partition	ALTER TABLE MOVE PARTITION	Yes	No
	Index-Organized table	ALTER TABLE MOVE	Yes	Yes
	Index	Drop/recreate index	Yes	No
		ALTER INDEX REBUILD*	Yes	Yes
	Index Partition	ALTER INDEX REBUILD PARTITION*	Yes	Yes
9.x	Heap Table	Drop/recreate table	Yes	No
		ALTER TABLE MOVE	Yes	No
		Online Table Redefinition	NA	Yes
	Table Partition	ALTER TABLE MOVE PARTITION	Yes	No
	Index-Organized table	ALTER TABLE MOVE	Yes	Yes
	Index	Drop/recreate index	Yes	No
		ALTER INDEX REBUILD*	Yes	Yes
	Index Partition	ALTER INDEX REBUILD PARTITION*	Yes	Yes
10.0	Heap Table	ALTER TABLE COMPACT SPACE	NA	Yes

Table 8.1: *Reorganization methods summary*

Restrictions apply as to what indexes can and can't be rebuilt online. Consult the Oracle documentation for specifics.

Reorganizations are just one task that DBAs need to perform periodically, and most include them as part of an overall database maintenance plan.

Database Maintenance Plans

"You can pay me now or pay me later" is a familiar phrase spoken by auto mechanics. Because of time and money, many folks put off taking their car in for preventative maintenance work.

The thing is that a little work performed over defined intervals in a car's life can really go a long way in ensuring peak performance, as well as stopping those unexpected breakdowns that can really cost a person time and money.

The same thing is true of a database. Although a database may seem well tuned and ready to go the first day a production application goes in, it can break down, sometimes rather quickly, over time, unless a DBA periodically performs preventative maintenance to keep it running well.

For storage diagnostic scripts to accurately perform their calculations, a maintenance plan should be designed to include periodic updates of dynamic objects' statistics by using *analyze* or *dbms_stats*. It is also advisable to schedule periodic reorganizations of objects that continually falter because of sub-optimal storage structures. In Oracle10g and above, the database can automatically gather statistics whenever desired.

Only by observing the database over time can the actual timing of such planned runs be determined. By instituting scheduled maintenance operations, it is possible to proactively nip any critical problems in the bud before they cause any real pain.

The next section will explain the new features of Oracle 10g for optimizing a database's storage.

Oracle 10g

Oracle10g Storage Diagnostics

With Oracle10g, a new segment advisor has been made available to help troubleshoot object storage problems. Part of the *dbms_advisor* package series, the new advisor is graphically available through the new Oracle Enterprise Manager. It can be issued in an ad-hoc fashion to find problem objects, or it can be set up to run on a scheduled basis. If the advisor in OEM finds problems with one or more objects, it provides the ability to reorganize them.

Oracle 10g ASSM

An Oracle10g database can reclaim space within data segments online without affecting the end users access to their data. The only thing the DBA must ensure before using the on-line segment reorganization capability is that the tablespaces have the Automatic Segment Space Management (ASSM) feature enabled. Oracle10g introduces the ability to reclaim space from a segment by shrinking the segment. Shrinking a segment will make unused space available to other segments in the tablespace and may improve the performance of queries and DML operations.

With the introduction of the powerful ASSM tool, the DBA can effectively and easily manage database space. However, it must be known which data segments experience high space wastage in order to reclaim free space to the database and shrink segments. The *awr_list_seg_block_space.sql* sample function reports percentages of free space for data segments:

🖫 awr_list_seg_block_space.sql

```
-- ******************************************************
-- Copyright © 2005 by Rampant TechPress
-- This script is free for non-commercial purposes
-- with no warranties.  Use at your own risk.
--
-- To license this script for a commercial purpose,
```

```
-- contact info@rampant.cc
-- **************************************************

drop type BlckFreeSpaceSet;
drop type BlckFreeSpace;

create type BlckFreeSpace as object
(
 seg_owner varchar2(30),
 seg_type varchar2(30),
 seg_name varchar2(100),
 fs1 number,
 fs2 number,
 fs3 number,
 fs4 number,
 fb  number
 );

create type BlckFreeSpaceSet as table of  BlckFreeSpace;

create or replace function BlckFreeSpaceFunc (seg_owner IN varchar2,
seg_type in varchar2 default null) return BlckFreeSpaceSet
pipelined
is
   outRec BlckFreeSpace :=
BlckFreeSpace(null,null,null,null,null,null,null,null);
   fs1_b number;
   fs2_b number;
   fs3_b number;
   fs4_b number;
   fs1_bl number;
   fs2_bl number;
   fs3_bl number;
   fs4_bl number;
   fulb number;
   fulbl number;
   u_b number;
   u_bl number;
begin
  for rec in (select s.owner,s.segment_name,s.segment_type from dba_segments
s where owner = seg_owner and segment_type = nvl(seg_type,segment_type) )
  loop
    dbms_space.space_usage (
      segment_owner       => rec.owner,
      segment_name        => rec.segment_name,
      segment_type        => rec.segment_type,
      fs1_bytes           => fs1_b,
      fs1_blocks          => fs1_bl,
      fs2_bytes           => fs2_b,
      fs2_blocks          => fs2_bl,
      fs3_bytes           => fs3_b,
      fs3_blocks          => fs3_bl,
      fs4_bytes           => fs4_b,
      fs4_blocks          => fs4_bl,
      full_bytes          => fulb,
      full_blocks         => fulbl,
      unformatted_blocks  => u_bl,
      unformatted_bytes   => u_b
    );
```

```
  outRec.seg_owner := rec.owner;
  outRec.seg_type := rec.segment_type;
  outRec.seg_name := rec.segment_name;

  outRec.fs1 := fs1_bl;
  outRec.fs2 := fs2_bl;
  outRec.fs3 := fs3_bl;
  outRec.fs4 := fs4_bl;
  outRec.fb  := fulbl;

  Pipe Row (outRec);

  end loop;
  return;
end;
/
```

Now, the *awr_report_seg_block_space.sql* can be used to generate a report showing which data segments are good candidates for segment shrinking, and thus can reuse wasted space to the database:

🖫 awr_report_seg_block_space.sql

```
-- ************************************************
-- Copyright © 2005 by Rampant TechPress
-- This script is free for non-commercial purposes
-- with no warranties.  Use at your own risk.
--
-- To license this script for a commercial purpose,
-- contact info@rampant.cc
-- ************************************************

col seg_owner heading 'Segment|Owner'  format a10
col seg_type heading 'Segment|Type'    format a10
col seg_name heading 'Segment|Name'    format a30

col fs1 heading '0-25%|Free Space'     format 9,999
col fs2 heading '25-50%|Free Space'    format 9,999
col fs3 heading '50-75%|Free Space'    format 9,999
col fs4 heading '75-100%|Free Space'   format 9,999
col fb  heading 'Full|Blocks'          format 9,999

accept user_name prompt 'Enter Segment Owner: '

break on seg_owner

select
  *
from
  Table ( BlckFreeSpaceFunc ('&user_name', 'TABLE' ) )
order by
  fs4 desc
;
```

The following is the sample output of the above script for PERFSTAT
schema that owns STATSPACK utility:

Segment Owner	Segment Type	Segment Name	0-25% Free Space	25-50% Free Space	50-75% Free Space	75-100% Free Space	Full Blocks
PERFSTAT	TABLE	STATS$EVENT_HISTOGRAM	0	0	2	47	321
	TABLE	STATS$LATCH	0	0	1	35	522
	TABLE	STATS$SQL_SUMMARY	0	1	0	28	1,285
	TABLE	STATS$SYSSTAT	1	0	1	13	355
	TABLE	STATS$LIBRARYCACHE	0	0	0	7	13
	TABLE	STATS$SQL_WORKAREA_HISTOGRAM	0	0	1	7	5
	TABLE	STATS$ROWCACHE_SUMMARY	0	0	1	6	43
	TABLE	STATS$ENQUEUE_STATISTICS	0	0	1	6	66
	TABLE	STATS$RESOURCE_LIMIT	1	0	1	6	5
	TABLE	STATS$TIME_MODEL_STATNAME	0	0	0	5	0
	TABLE	STATS$DATABASE_INSTANCE	0	0	0	5	0
	TABLE	STATS$LEVEL_DESCRIPTION	0	0	0	5	0
	TABLE	STATS$IDLE_EVENT	0	0	0	5	0
	TABLE	STATS$WAITSTAT	1	0	1	5	13
	TABLE	STATS$STATSPACK_PARAMETER	0	0	0	5	0
	TABLE	STATS$TEMP_HISTOGRAM	0	1	0	4	0
	TABLE	STATS$INSTANCE_RECOVERY	0	1	0	4	0
	TABLE	STATS$SQL_STATISTICS	0	0	1	4	0
	TABLE	STATS$SGASTAT	0	0	2	4	44
	TABLE	STATS$THREAD	0	0	1	4	0
	TABLE	STATS$ROLLSTAT	0	1	1	4	14
	TABLE	STATS$PARAMETER	1	0	0	4	301

From the above output, one might notice that tables *stats$event_histogram*,
stats$latch, *stats$sql_summary*, and *stats$sysstat* are good candidates for
segment shrinking. The following SQL statements can be issued to
shrink the segments mentioned:

```
SQL> alter table stats$event_histogram enable row movement;

Table altered.

SQL> alter table stats$event_histogram shrink space compact;

Table altered.

SQL>
SQL> alter table stats$latch enable row movement;

Table altered.

SQL> alter table stats$latch shrink space compact;

Table altered.

SQL>
SQL> alter table stats$sql_summary enable row movement;

Table altered.

SQL> alter table stats$sql_summary shrink space compact;

Table altered.

SQL>
SQL> alter table stats$sysstat  enable row movement;
```

```
Table altered.

SQL> alter table stats$sysstat  shrink space compact;

Table altered.
```

Now, again the *awr_report_seg_block_space.sql* script can be issued to verify Oracle reclaimed space:

```
SQL> @ awr_report_seg_block_space.sql

Segment   Segment Segment                       0-25%       25-50%      50-75%      75-100%   Full
Owner     Type    Name                       Free Space  Free Space  Free Space  Free Space  Blocks
--------- ------- ---------------------------- ---------- ----------- ----------- ----------- -------
PERFSTAT  TABLE   STATS$LIBRARYCACHE                 0           0           0           7       13
          TABLE   STATS$SQL_WORKAREA_HISTOGRAM       0           0           1           7        5
          TABLE   STATS$ROWCACHE_SUMMARY             0           0           1           6       43
          TABLE   STATS$RESOURCE_LIMIT               1           0           1           6        5
          TABLE   STATS$ENQUEUE_STATISTICS           0           0           1           6       66
.......
          TABLE   STATS$SHARED_POOL_ADVICE           1           0           0           2       17
          TABLE   STATS$BUFFER_POOL_STATISTICS       0           0           2           2        1
          TABLE   STATS$EVENT_HISTOGRAM              0           1           0           1      320
          TABLE   STATS$SYSSTAT                      0           0           1           1      356
          TABLE   STATS$SGA                          0           1           1           1        2
          TABLE   STATS$BUFFERED_QUEUES              0           1           2           1        1
          TABLE   STATS$PGASTAT                      1           1           1           1        9
          TABLE   STATS$SYS_TIME_MODEL               0           1           1           1       10
.....
          TABLE   STATS$PGA_TARGET_ADVICE            1           0           1           0       11
          TABLE   STATS$LATCH_PARENT                 0           0           0           0        0
          TABLE   STATS$LATCH_CHILDREN               0           0           0           0        0
          TABLE   STATS$LATCH                        0           1           1           0      521
          TABLE   STATS$DB_CACHE_ADVICE              0           1           0           0       27
          TABLE   STATS$SQL_SUMMARY                  1           0           0           0    1,284
          TABLE   STATS$SEG_STAT_OBJ                 0           0           0           0        0
          TABLE   STATS$SQL_PLAN                     0           0           0           0        0
          TABLE   STATS$SESS_TIME_MODEL              0           0           0           0        0
          TABLE   STATS$DLM_MISC                     0           0           0           0        0
          TABLE   STATS$CR_BLOCK_SERVER              0           0           0           0        0
          TABLE   STATS$CURRENT_BLOCK_SERVER         0           0           0           0        0
          TABLE   STATS$CLASS_CACHE_TRANSFER         0           0           0           0        0
```

From the listing above, one might notice that the tables on which the shrink operation was performed subsequently consume much less space. The DBA is now able to reset HWM for tables using SQL statement like ALTER TABLE SHRINK SPACE. The shrink operation is performed completely online without affecting end users. If the SHRINK clause option is added to CASCADE, Oracle will compact indexes created on the target table.

How Can I Shrink Segments?

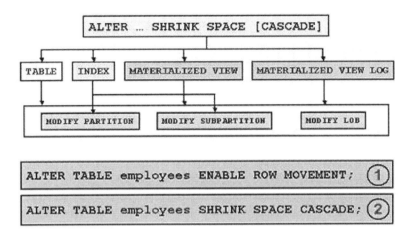

Figure 8.8: *Database objects that support SHRINK SPACE operation.*

In Figure 8.8, the database objects that support the SHRINK SPACE operation are shown. Oracle10g provides the ability to perform an in-place reorganization of data for optimal space utilization by shrinking it. This feature also provides the ability to both compact the space used in a segment and then de-allocate it from the segment.

The de-allocated space is returned to the tablespace and is available to other objects in the tablespace. Sparsely populated tables may cause a performance problem for full table scans. By performing shrink, data in the table is compacted and the HWM of the segment is pushed down. This makes full table scans read less blocks. As a result, they run faster. Also, during compaction, row chaining is eliminated whenever possible.

The ASSM tool allows DBAs to estimate the sizes of indexes they intend to create on a table. The procedure, *create_index_cost*, from the *dbms_space* package allows the DBA to get an estimate for space usage of the future

---

index. This can be accomplished by using the *awr_estimate_index_cost.sql* query that follows:

🖫 awr_estimate_index_cost.sql

```
-- ***************************************************
-- Copyright © 2005 by Rampant TechPress
-- This script is free for non-commercial purposes
-- with no warranties.  Use at your own risk.
--
-- To license this script for a commercial purpose,
-- contact info@rampant.cc
-- ***************************************************

declare
   u_bytes number;
   a_bytes number;
begin
   dbms_space.create_index_cost (
      ddl => 'create index stats$sysstat_idx on stats$sysstat '||
         '(value) tablespace sysaux',
      used_bytes => u_bytes,
      alloc_bytes => a_bytes
   );
   dbms_output.put_line ('Used Bytes      = '|| u_bytes);
   dbms_output.put_line ('Allocated Bytes = '|| a_bytes);
end;
/
```

The result of this PL/SQL block looks like the following:

```
SQL>
  1  declare
  2     u_bytes number;
  3     a_bytes number;
  4  begin
  5     dbms_space.create_index_cost (
  6        ddl => 'create index stats$sysstat_idx on stats$sysstat '||
  7           '(value) tablespace sysaux',
  8        used_bytes => u_bytes,
  9        alloc_bytes => a_bytes
 10     );
 11     dbms_output.put_line ('Used Bytes      = '|| u_bytes);
 12     dbms_output.put_line ('Allocated Bytes = '|| a_bytes);
 13* end;
SQL> /
Used Bytes      = 392886
Allocated Bytes = 851968

PL/SQL procedure successfully completed.
```

This approach is very useful because it allows the adjustment of some storage parameters before an index is actually created. The *create_table_cost* procedure for table space size estimates is also available within the *dbms_space* package.

Planning for segment space growth will be presented in the next section.

Segment Space Growth Prediction

Most production databases grow over the course of time. Planning for growth is a primary task of every professional Oracle DBA. If resources are planned well in advance, such problems as "out of space" are likely to be avoided. Of course, alerts will still be issued when the space utilization crosses the established alert thresholds. However, it is very good to proactively resolve such space related issues.

The most important feature of ASSM is the ability to predict the growth of the segments. The ASSM prediction mechanism is based on data collected and stored by the AWR. The growth trend reporting is also built in into the Oracle database kernel and is available by default.

The active space monitoring of individual segments in the database makes available to the database, the up to the minute status of individual segments in the system. This information is periodically written to the AWR. It provides sufficient information over time to perform growth trending of individual objects in the database as well as the database as a whole.

The query below allows the DBA to estimate the segment growth trend for *stats$sysstat* table:

```
SQL> select
*
from
table(dbms_space.OBJECT_GROWTH_TREND
('PERFSTAT','STATS$SYSSTAT','TABLE'));
```

The output of this query might look the following:

```
TIMEPOINT                      SPACE_USAGE SPACE_ALLOC QUALITY
------------------------------ ----------- ----------- -----------
```

```
02.10.04 15:58:04,218000        592359    1048576  INTERPOLATED
03.10.04 15:58:04,218000        592359    1048576  INTERPOLATED
04.10.04 15:58:04,218000        592359    1048576  INTERPOLATED
05.10.04 15:58:04,218000        592359    1048576  INTERPOLATED
06.10.04 15:58:04,218000        592359    1048576  INTERPOLATED
07.10.04 15:58:04,218000        592359    1048576  INTERPOLATED
08.10.04 15:58:04,218000        592359    1048576  INTERPOLATED
09.10.04 15:58:04,218000        592359    1048576  INTERPOLATED
10.10.04 15:58:04,218000        592359    1048576  INTERPOLATED
11.10.04 15:58:04,218000        592359    1048576  INTERPOLATED
12.10.04 15:58:04,218000        592359    1048576  INTERPOLATED
13.10.04 15:58:04,218000        592359    1048576  INTERPOLATED
14.10.04 15:58:04,218000        592359    1048576  INTERPOLATED
15.10.04 15:58:04,218000        592359    1048576  INTERPOLATED
16.10.04 15:58:04,218000        592359    1048576  INTERPOLATED
17.10.04 15:58:04,218000        592359    1048576  INTERPOLATED
18.10.04 15:58:04,218000        592359    1048576  INTERPOLATED
19.10.04 15:58:04,218000        592359    1048576  INTERPOLATED
20.10.04 15:58:04,218000        592359    1048576  INTERPOLATED
21.10.04 15:58:04,218000        592359    1048576  GOOD
22.10.04 15:58:04,218000        786887    1048576  INTERPOLATED
23.10.04 15:58:04,218000        826610    1048576  INTERPOLATED
24.10.04 15:58:04,218000        839843    1048576  INTERPOLATED
25.10.04 15:58:04,218000        846459    1048576  INTERPOLATED
26.10.04 15:58:04,218000       3072829    3145728  INTERPOLATED
27.10.04 15:58:04,218000       3072829    3145728  INTERPOLATED
28.10.04 15:58:04,218000       3072829    3145728  INTERPOLATED
29.10.04 15:58:04,218000       3072829    3145728  INTERPOLATED
30.10.04 15:58:04,218000       3072829    3145728  INTERPOLATED
31.10.04 15:58:04,218000       3072829    3145728  INTERPOLATED
01.11.04 15:58:04,218000       3072829    3145728  INTERPOLATED
02.11.04 15:58:04,218000       3678280    3678280  PROJECTED
03.11.04 15:58:04,218000       3764774    3764774  PROJECTED
04.11.04 15:58:04,218000       3851267    3851267  PROJECTED
05.11.04 15:58:04,218000       3937760    3937760  PROJECTED
06.11.04 15:58:04,218000       4024253    4024253  PROJECTED
```

The *space_usage* column reveals how many bytes the table *stats$sysstat* actually consumes, and the *space_alloc* column reports the size in bytes of space used by the table.

Conclusion

In this chapter, scripts have been shown providing methodologies for detecting space management issues. Additionally, many of the features for Oracle 10g ASSM for managing database storage were reviewed.

Miscellaneous Scripts

Workspaces in Oracle9*i*

The concept of a database workspace was introduced with Oracle9i. A workspace is an environment for a long-term transaction that allows multiple versions of objects and can be shared among many users. The workspace environment is managed through a series of short transactions and multiple data versions that lead to a complete long-term transaction event. This process maintains atomicity, as well as concurrency.

The Workspace Manager (WKS) is installed by default in all seed and DBCA databases. If it is needed in a manually created database, it must be installed following the guide in the Oracle9i Application Developers

---

Guide--Workspace Manager, Release 1 9.0.1, PART# A88806-01, Oracle Corporation, June 2001.

💾 workspace_status.sql

```
-- ************************************************
-- Copyright © 2005 by Rampant TechPress
-- This script is free for non-commercial purposes
-- with no warranties.  Use at your own risk.
--
-- To license this script for a commercial purpose,
-- contact info@rampant.cc
-- ************************************************

COLUMN WORKSPACE FORMAT a10 HEADING 'Workspace'
COLUMN owner FORMAT a10 HEADING 'Owner'
COLUMN freeze_status FORMAT a8 HEADING 'Freeze|Status'
COLUMN resolve_status FORMAT a8 HEADING 'Resolve|Status'
COLUMN parent_workspace FORMAT a10 HEADING 'Parent|Workspace'
COLUMN freeze_mode FORMAT a8 HEADING 'Freeze|Mode'

ttitle 'Workspace Status'
spool workspace_status

select
  workspace,
  NVL(parent_workspace,'NONE') parent_workspace,
  owner,
  freeze_status,
  NVL(freeze_mode,'NONE') freeze_mode,
  resolve_status
from
  dba_workspaces
;
spool off
ttitle off
```

The following is a sample listing from the above query:

Workspace	Parent Workspace	Owner	Freeze Status	Freeze Mode	Resolve Status
LIVE	NONE	SYS	UNFROZEN	NONE	INACTIVE

Other items, such as workspace privileges and save points, can also be monitored using the *dba_* series of views. The next section will examine the *pga_aggregate_target*

---

pga_aggregate_target in Oracle9*i*

In Oracle9i, the sort and hash area parameters such as *sort_area_size*, *hash_area_size* and their associated multi-block read parameters can be turned over to Oracle for management by using the *pga_aggregate_target* and *workarea_size_policy* parameters.

The *pga_aggregate_target* parameter is set to the size of memory for the projected aggregate PGA, including sort area and context areas, for all users, and the *workarea_size_policy* parameter is set to AUTO to turn on automated tuning.

However, how does the DBA know if these are set correctly? Oracle provides the *v$pga_target_advice* DPT to offer guidance as to the appropriateness of the settings. By using a simple select, such as the one in the script below, it can easily be seen if the *pga_aggregate_target* value is set correctly.

🖫 pga_advice.sql

```
-- ***************************************************
-- Copyright © 2005 by Rampant TechPress
-- This script is free for non-commercial purposes
-- with no warranties.  Use at your own risk.
--
-- To license this script for a commercial purpose,
-- contact info@rampant.cc
-- ***************************************************

ttitle 'PGA Target Advice Report'
set lines 80 pages 47
spool pga_advice
SELECT round(PGA_TARGET_FOR_ESTIMATE/1024/1024) target_mb,
       ESTD_PGA_CACHE_HIT_PERCENTAGE cache_hit_perc,
       ESTD_OVERALLOC_COUNT FROM    v$pga_target_advice
/
spool off
ttitle off
```

The output from the above SQL select will resemble the following:

```
TARGET_MB CACHE_HIT_PERC ESTD_OVERALLOC_COUNT
---------- --------------- --------------------
        13              31                 2046
        25              31                 1999
        38              32                  926
        50              34                  591
        60              36                  461
        70              37                  353
        80              38                  251
        90              38                  168
       100              39                  100
       150              45                    8
       200              47                    0
       300              58                    0
       400              59                    0

13 rows selected.
```

The above report reveals that the over-allocation values indicate that the setting is too small and should be increased to at least 150 megabytes. The next section will explore how to find security holes in databases.

Uncovering Security Holes

One of a DBA's highest security priorities should be to ensure that no user account can access any storage or database object that should not be accessed by that user. While identifying such accounts can get tricky, depending on the complexity of the database, there are a few general sweeps that should be made from time to time to uncover potential security holes in a system.

First, check to see that no general users are granted powerful roles, such as DBA. A query like the *dbagranted.sql* script can determine if such is the case:

🖫 dbagranted.sql

```
-- **************************************************
-- Copyright © 2005 by Rampant TechPress
-- This script is free for non-commercial purposes
-- with no warranties.  Use at your own risk.
--
-- To license this script for a commercial purpose,
-- contact info@rampant.cc
-- **************************************************

select
   grantee
from
   sys.dba_role_privs
where
   granted_role = 'DBA'
and
   grantee not in ('SYS','SYSTEM');
```

The results of this script might look like this example.

```
GRANTEE
------------------------------
HACKER
```

Likewise, check to see if any user accounts have been granted sensitive privileges or roles that provide them with the potential to cause serious damage to the database. For example, a user with the *unlimited tablespace* privilege can place data in the SYSTEM tablespace, which should only be reserved for data dictionary objects. The *sensprivs.sql* script can help quickly locate such accounts:

🖫 sensprivs.sql

```
-- **************************************************
-- Copyright © 2005 by Rampant TechPress
-- This script is free for non-commercial purposes
-- with no warranties.  Use at your own risk.
--
-- To license this script for a commercial purpose,
-- contact info@rampant.cc
-- **************************************************

select
   grantee,
   privilege,
   admin_option
from
   sys.dba_sys_privs
where
 (privilege like '%ANY%'
```

```
   or
   privilege like '%DROP%'
   or
   privilege in
      ('ALTER SYSTEM',
       'ALTER TABLESPACE',
        'BECOME USER',
        'UNLIMITED TABLESPACE'))
   and
   grantee not in ('SYS','SYSTEM')
   and
   grantee not in
(select role from sys.dba_roles)
union all
select
   grantee,
   privilege,
   admin_option
from
   sys.dba_sys_privs
where
   (privilege like '%ANY%'
   or
    privilege like '%DROP%'
   or
    privilege in
    ('ALTER SYSTEM',
     'ALTER TABLESPACE',
     'BECOME USER',
     'UNLIMITED TABLESPACE'))
   and
      grantee not in ('SYS','SYSTEM')
   and
   grantee in
    (select role
     from sys.dba_roles
     where role not in
     ('DBA',
      'AQ_ADMINISTRATOR_ROLE',
      'IMP_FULL_DATABASE',
      'SNMPAGENT',
      'OEM_MONITOR',
      'EXP_FULL_DATABASE'));
```

If any users do indeed have sensitive privileges or roles, the output from the query above might look like this:

```
GRANTEE     PRIVILEGE                       ADMIN_OPTION
-------------------------------------------------------
BAD_GUY     ALTER ANY PROCEDURE                NO
BAD_GUY     ALTER ANY TRIGGER                  NO
BAD_GUY     CREATE ANY INDEX                   NO
BAD_GUY     CREATE ANY PROCEDURE               NO
BAD_GUY     CREATE ANY TABLE                   NO
BAD_GUY     CREATE ANY TRIGGER                 NO
BAD_GUY     DROP ANY PROCEDURE                 NO
```

```
BAD_GUY    DROP ANY TRIGGER           NO
BAD_GUY    EXECUTE ANY PROCEDURE      NO
BAD_GUY    UNLIMITED TABLESPACE       NO
```

Users found with these two queries should be examined to see if they really need the special privileges that they have been granted. In addition to users having sensitive privileges or roles, the DBA should determine if any user account has undesired abilities with respect to storage.

User accounts with unchecked storage powers can cause major headaches for a DBA by incorrectly using up storage. The *badstorage.sql* script can be used to find such accounts:

🖫 **badstorage.sql**

```
-- *************************************************
-- Copyright © 2005 by Rampant TechPress
-- This script is free for non-commercial purposes
-- with no warranties.  Use at your own risk.
--
-- To license this script for a commercial purpose,
-- contact info@rampant.cc
-- *************************************************

select
     a.name username,'system as default' privilege
from
     sys.user$ a,
     sys.ts$ dts,
     sys.ts$ tts
where
     (a.datats# = dts.ts# and a.tempts# = tts.ts#) and
     (dts.name = 'SYSTEM' or tts.name = 'SYSTEM') and
     a.name not in ('SYS', 'SYSTEM')
union
select
     username,'system quotas'
from
     sys.dba_ts_quotas
where
     tablespace_name = 'system' and
     username not in ('SYS', 'SYSTEM')
union
select
     grantee,'unlimited tablespace'
from
     dba_sys_privs
where
     privilege = 'unlimited tablespace' and
     grantee not in ('SYS', 'SYSTEM')
order by
```

```
        1;
```

If there are user accounts with unchecked storage capabilities, the output from this query might look like this:

```
USERNAME                     PRIVILEGE
------------------------------------------------
AQ_ADMINISTRATOR_ROLE        SYSTEM AS DEFAULT
BAD_GUY                      UNLIMITED TABLESPACE
BAD_ROLE                     SYSTEM AS DEFAULT
BILLY                        UNLIMITED TABLESPACE
BRKADMIN                     UNLIMITED TABLESPACE
CODER                        UNLIMITED TABLESPACE
```

Any user account that is identified in the *badstorage.sql* query should be altered so that their storage settings do not have the potential to negatively impact the database.

Finally, although it is surprising that DBAs in today's very security-conscious environment would allow this to occur, the appropriately cautious DBA must make sure that no critical database exists with default passwords for the SYS and SYSTEM accounts.

Once any database security holes have been plugged, the DBA should examine each session's storage capabilities.

Finding Storage Hogs

One thing that a DBA should monitor closely in the database is the amount of storage space that each user account is consuming. It is not uncommon for developers to create object backups of their object backups when working on a critical project. If those objects are left indefinitely in the database, there will be a considerable amount of unusable space that may be needed at a later time.

The *totuserspace.sql* script is a good query to run to see how much space each user account has consumed:

🖫 totuserspace.sql

```
-- **************************************************
-- Copyright © 2005 by Rampant TechPress
-- This script is free for non-commercial purposes
-- with no warranties.  Use at your own risk.
--
-- To license this script for a commercial purpose,
-- contact info@rampant.cc
-- **************************************************

select
        owner,
        round((byte_count / 1024 / 1024),2) space_used_mb,
        round(100 * (byte_count / tot_bytes),2) pct_of_database
from
(select
        owner ,
        sum(bytes) as byte_count
from
        sys.dba_segments
where
        segment_type not in ('TEMPORARY','CACHE')
group by
        owner
order by
        2 desc),
(select
        sum(bytes) as tot_bytes
from
        sys.dba_segments);
```

The partial output from the above query might look something like this:

```
OWNER       SPACE_USED_MB  PCT_OF_DATABASE
-------------------------------------------
ERADMIN            807.10            58.48
SYS                322.36            23.36
USER1               45.47             3.29
REPO                27.19             1.97
SYSTEM              22.88             1.66
```

The above script should be run and the output examined periodically to see if any user accounts are hogging the majority of space in a database. Some databases only have one schema account that contains application objects. In that case, there should not be anything to worry about.

If, however, a number of accounts with large amounts of data are found, each user should be checked to ensure that bogus objects have not been left that both clutter up user database files and add to the size of the Oracle data dictionary.

Finding Storage Hogs

Another storage issue that should be examined from time to time is the amount of temporary space used by connected sessions. Many DBAs have experienced the sad fact that large disk sorts can cause out of space conditions to manifest quickly at both the database and operating system level.

To get an idea of historical temporary tablespace (sort) usage, the *sortusage.sql* query can be executed:

🖫 sortusage.sql

```
-- ***************************************************
-- Copyright © 2005 by Rampant TechPress
-- This script is free for non-commercial purposes
-- with no warranties.  Use at your own risk.
--
-- To license this script for a commercial purpose,
-- contact info@rampant.cc
-- ***************************************************

select
      tablespace_name,
      current_users,
      total_extents,
      used_extents,
      free_extents,
      max_used_size,
      max_sort_size
from
      sys.v_$sort_segment
order by 1;
```

The following is the output from the *sortusage.sql* query:

TABLESPACE_NAME	CURRENT_USERS	TOTAL_EXTENTS	USED_EXTENTS	FREE_EXTENTS	MAX_USED_SIZE	MAX_SORT_SIZE
1	TEMP	0	3	0	3	3	2

Figure 9.1: *Output from the sortusage.sql query*

The output will display how many users are currently using space in each temporary tablespace along with the current used extent and free extent numbers. The last two columns will display the largest number of total extents ever used for all sorts and the size of the single largest sort, in extents, since the database has been up.

Such knowledge can help the DBA plan the size of the temporary tablespace(s). Many DBAs will size very large temporary tablespaces in anticipation of heavy sort activity only to find that such sorts do not occur. If there is not heavy temporary tablespace usage, it may be possible to resize the temporary tablespace datafiles and reclaim space on the server.

If the *sortusage.sql* query shows that users are currently using space in a temporary tablespace, the DBA should dig deeper to see exactly what they are doing. The *sortdet.sql* query can provide this exact detail:

🖫 sortdet.sql

```
-- *************************************************
-- Copyright © 2005 by Rampant TechPress
-- This script is free for non-commercial purposes
-- with no warranties.  Use at your own risk.
--
-- To license this script for a commercial purpose,
-- contact info@rampant.cc
-- *************************************************

select
        sql_text,
        sid,
        c.username,
        machine,
        tablespace,
        extents,
        blocks
from
        sys.v_$sort_usage a,
        sys.v_$sqlarea b,
        sys.v_$session c
where
        a.sqladdr = b.address and
        a.sqlhash = b.hash_value and
        a.session_addr = c.saddr
order by
        sid;
```

The output from the above query might look like the following:

```
SQL_TEXT        SID   USERNAME  MACHINE TABLESPACE EXTENTS   BLOCKS
-------------------------------------------------------------------
```

```
SELECT * FROM  10    ERADMIN  ROBS    TEMP     10      80
```

Using this query, the SQL call, current session information, and details on how much temporary space the SQL call is using can be obtained. Red flags should begin to run up the flagpole if continuous large disk sorts are occurring on the system.

Sort activity that occurs on disk is much slower than sort activity that occurs in memory. The DBA should begin an analysis of sort activity by examining memory settings as well as the SQL statements that are revealed from this query to see if unnecessary sorts are occurring or if the *init.ora*/spfile parameters relating to sorting are set too low.

The following section reviews some various scripts and views for Oracle 10g

Oracle10g

Metric *dba_hist* Views

Metric *dba_hist* data dictionary views are organized into several groups such as system, session, service, file, tablespace, and event metrics. All available metric groups can be found by using the *v$metricgroup* dynamic view as follows:

```
SQL> select * from V$METRICGROUP;

  GROUP_ID NAME                                  INTERVAL_SIZE MAX_INTERVAL
  -------- ------------------------------------- ------------- ------------
         0 Event Metrics                                  6000            1
         1 Event Class Metrics                            6000           60
         2 System Metrics Long Duration                   6000           60
         3 System Metrics Short Duration                  1500           12
         4 Session Metrics Long Duration                  6000           60
         5 Session Metrics Short Duration                 1500            1
         6 Service Metrics                                6000           60
         7 File Metrics Long Duration                    60000            6
         9 Tablespace Metrics Long Duration               6000            0
```

All available metrics for which the Automatic Workload Repository (AWR) keeps history are in the *dba_hist_metric_name* view that stores snapshots for *v$metric_name* view. There are approximately 184 different metrics available.

Metrics are actively used by sophisticated automation features of Oracle10g such as Automatic Memory Management (AMM), Sequential data Access via Metadata (SAM) and advisory engines such as the Automatic Database Diagnostic Monitor (ADDM), SQL Advisor, etc. For example, ADDM uses a goal-based algorithm designed to minimize DB time. This metric is computed as a cumulative time spent.

```
SQL> select METRIC_NAME  from DBA_HIST_METRIC_NAME;
```

The following is a list of several metrics computed by the AWR snapshot engine; however, the list is not exhaustive:

```
METRIC_NAME
-------------------------------------
Average File Read Time (Files-Long)
Average File Write Time (Files-Long)
Average Users Waiting Counts
Background Checkpoints Per Sec
Blocked User Session Count
Branch Node Splits Per Sec
Branch Node Splits Per Txn
Buffer Cache Hit Ratio
CPU Time (Session)
CPU Time Per User Call
CPU Usage Per Sec
```

The following sections provide a general overview of selected metric *dba_hist* views that are available and a short description of information they provide.

dba_hist_sysmetric_history

The *dba_hist_sysmetric_history* view collects history for all system-wide metrics belonging to such metric groups as System Metrics Long Duration and System Metrics Short Duration. This view stores snapshots of the *v$sysmetric_history* dynamic view as shown below:

```
SQL> desc DBA_HIST_SYSMETRIC_HISTORY

Name                                     Null?     Type
--------------------------------------   --------  ------------
SNAP_ID                                  NOT NULL  NUMBER
DBID                                     NOT NULL  NUMBER
INSTANCE_NUMBER                          NOT NULL  NUMBER
BEGIN_TIME                               NOT NULL  DATE
END_TIME                                 NOT NULL  DATE
INTSIZE                                  NOT NULL  NUMBER
GROUP_ID                                 NOT NULL  NUMBER
METRIC_ID                                NOT NULL  NUMBER
METRIC_NAME                              NOT NULL  VARCHAR2(64)
VALUE                                    NOT NULL  NUMBER
METRIC_UNIT                              NOT NULL  VARCHAR2(64)
```

This view also contains important metrics for database time-series tuning approach such as:

- Buffer Cache Hit Ratio

- Database CPU Time Ratio

- Database Time Per Sec

- Database Wait Time Ratio

- Physical Reads Per Sec

- Response Time Per Txn

- SQL Service Response Time.

Note that this view also contains a *metric_unit* column that helps identify measure units for every metric.

dba_hist_sysmetric_summary

The *dba_hist_sysmetric_summary* view shows a history for system-wide metrics that belong to the System Metrics Long Duration metric group. This view stores snapshots for the *v$sysmetric_summary* dynamic view as shown below:

```
SQL> desc DBA_HIST_SYSMETRIC_SUMMARY

 Name                            Null?       Type
 ------------------------------- ----------- ---------------
 SNAP_ID                         NOT NULL    NUMBER
 DBID                            NOT NULL    NUMBER
 INSTANCE_NUMBER                 NOT NULL    NUMBER
 BEGIN_TIME                      NOT NULL    DATE
 END_TIME                        NOT NULL    DATE
 INTSIZE                         NOT NULL    NUMBER
 GROUP_ID                        NOT NULL    NUMBER
 METRIC_ID                       NOT NULL    NUMBER
 METRIC_NAME                     NOT NULL    VARCHAR2(64)
 METRIC_UNIT                     NOT NULL    VARCHAR2(64)
 NUM_INTERVAL                    NOT NULL    NUMBER
 MINVAL                          NOT NULL    NUMBER
 MAXVAL                          NOT NULL    NUMBER
 AVERAGE                         NOT NULL    NUMBER
 STANDARD_DEVIATION              NOT NULL    NUMBER
```

The following simple query, *metric_summary.sql*, can be used to retrieve metrics for a particular snapshot:

🖫 metric_summary.sql

```
-- *************************************************
-- Copyright © 2005 by Rampant TechPress
-- This script is free for non-commercial purposes
-- with no warranties.  Use at your own risk.
--
-- To license this script for a commercial purpose,
-- contact info@rampant.cc
-- *************************************************

select
  metric_name "Metric Name",
  metric_unit "Metric Unit",
  minval "Minimum Value",
  maxval "Maximum Value",
  average "Average Value"
from
  DBA_HIST_SYSMETRIC_SUMMARY
where
      snap_id            = &pEndSnap
  and dbid               = &pDbId
  and instance_number    = &pInstNum
```

This view contains pre-computed metric values as they appeared in *v$sysmetric_summary* dynamic view. The sample output of the *metric_summary.sql* script looks like the following:

```
SQL> @ metric_summary.sql

Metric Name                 Metric Unit             Minimum Value Maximum Value Average Value
--------------------------  ----------------------  ------------- ------------- -------------
Host CPU Utilization (%)    %Busy/(Idle+Busy)                   1            55            16
Database Time Per Sec       CentiSeconds Per Second             0             9             0
Txns Per Logon              Txns Per Logon                      1            17             4
Executions Per Sec          Executes Per Second                 0            17             1
Executions Per Txn          Executes Per Txn                   10           357            28
Session Limit %             % Sessions/Limit                   10            12            10
Process Limit %             % Processes/Limit                   9            12            10
PGA Cache Hit %             % Bytes/TotalBytes                 97            97            97
Shared Pool Free %          % Free/Total                       10            11            10
Library Cache Miss Ratio    % Misses/Gets                       0             6             0
Library Cache Hit Ratio     % Hits/Pins                        93           100            99
Row Cache Miss Ratio        % Misses/Gets                       0            24             1
```

The *metric_summary.sql* query output shows that database workload statistics can be easily retrieved directly from the AWR for any time interval, without any additional computing overhead.

The WISE tool has a report called System Metric Summary History that allows the production of time-series charts for all of the metrics available as shown in Figure 9.2.

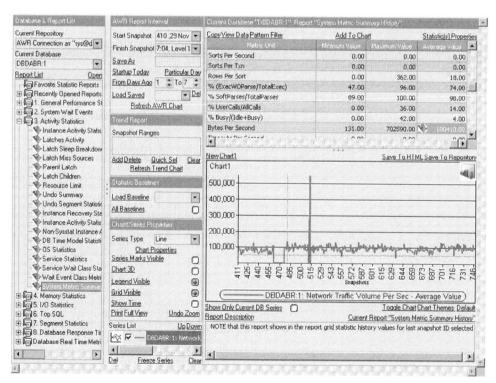

Figure 9.2: *AWR System Metric Summary History chart in WISE.*

This display is given as only one example of the charting capabilities of WISE respective to AWR System Metrics.

System Statistics

The AWR stores history for a large number of instance cumulative statistics. These statistics are generally available through the *v$sysstat* dynamic view. The AWR stores snapshots for this view in the *dba_hist_sysstat* view.

dba_hist_sysstat

The *dba_hist_sysstat* view contains a history for system statistics from the *v$sysstat* view. With more than 300 statistics available, statistic names can be retrieved from the *dba_hist_statname* view.

```
SQL> desc  DBA_HIST_SYSSTAT

Name                  Null?     Type
----------------- --------  ------------
SNAP_ID                         NUMBER
DBID                            NUMBER
INSTANCE_NUMBER                 NUMBER
STAT_ID                         NUMBER
STAT_NAME                       VARCHAR2(64)
VALUE                           NUMBER
```

System statistics for a particular snapshot interval can be viewed using the *sys_stat_int_10g.sql* query as follows:

🖫 sys_stat_int_10g.sql
```
-- *****************************************************
-- Copyright © 2005 by Rampant TechPress
-- This script is free for non-commercial purposes
-- with no warranties.  Use at your own risk.
--
-- To license this script for a commercial purpose,
-- contact info@rampant.cc
-- *****************************************************

select e.stat_name        "Statistic Name"
    , e.value - b.value   "Total"
    , round((e.value - b.value)/
    ( select
```

```
            avg( extract( day from (e1.end_interval_time-b1.end_interval_time)
)*24*60*60+
            extract( hour from (e1.end_interval_time-b1.end_interval_time)
)*60*60+
            extract( minute from (e1.end_interval_time-b1.end_interval_time)
)*60+
            extract( second from (e1.end_interval_time-b1.end_interval_time))
)
      from dba_hist_snapshot   b1
          ,dba_hist_snapshot   e1
     where b1.snap_id            = b.snap_id
       and e1.snap_id            = e.snap_id
       and b1.dbid               = b.dbid
       and e1.dbid               = e.dbid
       and b1.instance_number    = b.instance_number
       and e1.instance_number    = e.instance_number
       and b1.startup_time       = e1.startup_time
       and b1.end_interval_time < e1.end_interval_time ),2) "Per Second"
  from  dba_hist_sysstat   b
     ,  dba_hist_sysstat   e
 where b.snap_id            = &pBgnSnap
   and e.snap_id            = &pEndSnap
   and b.dbid               = &pDbId
   and e.dbid               = &pDbId
   and b.instance_number = &pInstNum
   and e.instance_number = &pInstNum
   and b.stat_id            = e.stat_id
   and e.stat_name not in (  'logons current'
                          , 'opened cursors current'
                          , 'workarea memory allocated'
                          )
   and e.value              >= b.value
   and e.value              >  0
 order by 1 asc
```

The query output looks like the following:

```
SQL> @Sys_stat_int_10g.sql

Statistic Name                              Total Per Second
------------------------------------- ---------- ----------
CPU used by this session                     4307          1
CPU used when call started                   4307          1
CR blocks created                             200          0
DB time                                    959909        115
DBWR checkpoint buffers written              3228          0
DBWR checkpoints                                9          0
DBWR object drop buffers written               75          0
DBWR tablespace checkpoint buffers written     71          0
DBWR transaction table writes                  92          0
DBWR undo block writes                        822          0
IMU CR rollbacks                               20          0
IMU Flushes                                   103          0
IMU Redo allocation size                   761060         92
IMU commits                                   383          0
IMU contention                                  0          0
IMU ktichg flush                                4          0
```

```
IMU pool not allocated                   1702        0
IMU undo allocation size               1772624      213
```

The *sys_stat_int_10g.sql* script allows users to easily identify all instance activity statistics for a particular snapshot interval in two representations: cumulative, and per second. The next section will review the available operating statistics.

Operating System Statistics

Operating system (OS) statistics such as CPU, disk input/output (I/O), virtual memory, and network statistics help identify possible bottlenecks where system hardware is stressed.

The AWR has a view called *dba_hist_osstat* that stores snapshots of the *v$osstat* dynamic view. OS statistics indicate how the hardware and OS are working thus reflecting workload placed on the database. These statistics can give an indication of where to first search the database for possible hot spots.

The structure of the *dba_hist_osstat* view is:

```
SQL> desc DBA_HIST_OSSTAT

Name                                     Null?    Type
---------------------------------------- -------- ------------
SNAP_ID                                           NUMBER
DBID                                              NUMBER
INSTANCE_NUMBER                                   NUMBER
STAT_ID                                           NUMBER
STAT_NAME                                         VARCHAR2(64)
VALUE                                             NUMBER
```

To view history statistics for a particular snapshot interval, the *os_stat_int_10g.sql* query below should be used:

🖫 os_stat_int_10g.sql

```
-- ****************************************************
-- Copyright © 2005 by Rampant TechPress
-- This script is free for non-commercial purposes
-- with no warranties.  Use at your own risk.
--
-- To license this script for a commercial purpose,
```

```
-- contact info@rampant.cc
-- ***************************************************

select e.stat_name "Statistic Name"
     , decode(e.stat_name, 'NUM_CPUS', e.value, e.value - b.value) "Total"
     , decode( instrb(e.stat_name, 'BYTES'), 0, to_number(null)
            , round((e.value - b.value)/( select
       avg( extract( day from (e1.end_interval_time-b1.end_interval_time)
)*24*60*60+
         extract( hour from (e1.end_interval_time-b1.end_interval_time)
)*60*60+
         extract( minute from (e1.end_interval_time-b1.end_interval_time)
)*60+
         extract( second from (e1.end_interval_time-b1.end_interval_time))
)
     from dba_hist_snapshot  b1
         ,dba_hist_snapshot  e1
     where b1.snap_id          = b.snap_id
       and e1.snap_id          = e.snap_id
       and b1.dbid             = b.dbid
       and e1.dbid             = e.dbid
       and b1.instance_number  = b.instance_number
       and e1.instance_number  = e.instance_number
       and b1.startup_time     = e1.startup_time
       and b1.end_interval_time < e1.end_interval_time ),2)) "Per Second"
 from   dba_hist_osstat  b
     ,  dba_hist_osstat  e
 where b.snap_id           = &pBgnSnap
   and e.snap_id           = &pEndSnap
   and b.dbid              = &pDbId
   and e.dbid              = &pDbId
   and b.instance_number   = &pInstNum
   and e.instance_number   = &pInstNum
   and b.stat_id           = e.stat_id
   and e.value            >= b.value
   and e.value            >  0
 order by 1 asc
```

The query output looks like the following:

```
SQL> @os_stat_int_10g.sql

Statistic Name                       Total    Per Second
------------------------------ ----------    ----------
AVG_BUSY_TICKS                    1,974,925
AVG_IDLE_TICKS                    7,382,241
AVG_IN_BYTES                  2,236,256,256    23881,91
AVG_OUT_BYTES                   566,304,768     6047,8
AVG_SYS_TICKS                       727,533
AVG_USER_TICKS                    1,247,392
BUSY_TICKS                        1,974,925
IDLE_TICKS                        7,382,241
IN_BYTES                      2,236,256,256    23881,91
NUM_CPUS                                  1
OUT_BYTES                       566,304,768     6047,8
SYS_TICKS                           727,533
USER_TICKS                         1247,392
```

The *os_stat_int_10g.sql* script allows a view of OS statistics in two forms: cumulative, and per second. Thus, users are able to identify hot areas in the OS and hardware.

The WISE tool has a corresponding report called OS Statistics that is used to produce history charts as shown in Figure 9.3.

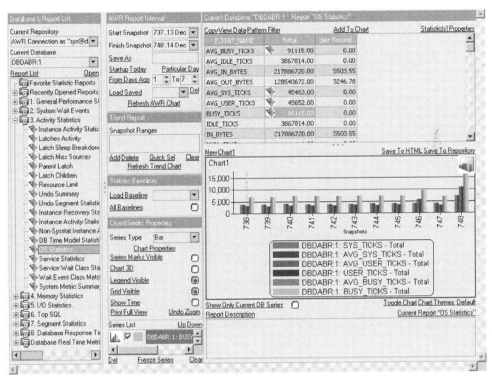

Figure 9.3: *AWR OS Statistics chart in WISE.*

This display is given as only one example of the charting capabilities of WISE respective to Operating System Statistics.

Conclusion

This chapter has given some additional scripts and areas of insight into an Oracle database. The scripts were included in this chapter as they may not have fit exactly into the topics of the previous chapters. Also provided where the new metrics and statistics now available in 10g.

Inside AWR Scripts

Oracle AWR

Because AWR branched off from STATSPACK in Oracle 10g, they remain remarkably similar and undergo many of the same enhancements. Table 10.1 below shows the comparison of Oracle STATSPACK tables to their AWR equivalents. Note that the *wrh$* fixed views are the building blocks for AWR, built into the Oracle software. Fortunately, many of the names of the *wrh$* tables are identical to their *stats$* equivalents making it easy to migrate STATSPACK scripts to AWR.

DBA HIST TABLE	WRH$ VIEW	STATSPACK TABLE
dba_hist_event_summary	wrh$_bg_event_summary	stats$bg_event_summary
dba_hist_buffer_pool_statistics	wrh$_buffer_pool_statistics	stats$buffer_pool_statistics
dba_hist_filestatxs	wrh$_filestatxs	stats$filestatxs
dba_hist_latch	wrh$_latch	stats$latch
dba_hist_latch_children	wrh$_latch_children	stats$latch_children
dba_hist_librarycache	wrh$_librarycache	stats$librarycache
dba_hist_rowcache_summary	wrh$_rowcache_summary	stats$rowcache_summary
dba_hist_sgastat	wrh$_sgastat	stats$sgastat
dba_hist_sql_summary	wrh$_sql_summary	stats$sql_summary
dba_hist_sysstat	wrh$_sysstat	stats$sysstat
dba_hist_system_event	wrh$_system_event	stats$system_event
dba_hist_waitstat	wrh$_waitstat	stats$waitstat

Table 10.1: *STATSPACK, DBA HIST and wrh$ Equivalencies*

Fortunately, Oracle has kept the column definitions almost identical between STATSPACK and AWR, making it easy to downgrade to STATSPACK if you don't want to pay the thousands of dollars to license AWR. Conversely, if you have just purchased an AWR license, it's easy to port your STATSPACK scripts to AWR.

To begin, let's revisit this simple example of an AWR query. The script below gathers physical disk read counts, the phyrds column of *dba_hist_filestatxs*. It then joins this data into the *dba_hist_snapshot* view to get the *begin_interval_time* column.

🖫 awr_disk_reads.sql

```
break on begin_interval_time skip 2

column phyrds  format 999,999,999
column begin_interval_time format a25

select
   begin_interval_time,
   filename,
   phyrds
from
   dba_hist_filestatxs
  natural join
   dba_hist_snapshot;
```

Executing this script shows a running total of physical reads, organized by datafile. In this case, the AWR snapshots are collected every half-hour, but it is possible to adjust the snapshot collection interval depending on data needs.

```
SQL> @reads


BEGIN_INTERVAL_TIME        FILENAME                                       PHYRDS
-------------------------  -------------------------------------------  ----------
24-FEB-04 11.00.32.000 PM  E:\ORACLE\ORA92\FSDEV10G\SYSTEM01.DBF          164,700
                           E:\ORACLE\ORA92\FSDEV10G\UNDOTBS01.DBF          26,082
                           E:\ORACLE\ORA92\FSDEV10G\SYSAUX01.DBF          472,008
                           E:\ORACLE\ORA92\FSDEV10G\USERS01.DBF             1,794
                           E:\ORACLE\ORA92\FSDEV10G\T_FS_LSQ.ORA            2,123


24-FEB-04 11.30.18.296 PM  E:\ORACLE\ORA92\FSDEV10G\SYSTEM01.DBF          167,809
                           E:\ORACLE\ORA92\FSDEV10G\UNDOTBS01.DBF          26,248
                           E:\ORACLE\ORA92\FSDEV10G\SYSAUX01.DBF          476,616
                           E:\ORACLE\ORA92\FSDEV10G\USERS01.DBF             1,795
                           E:\ORACLE\ORA92\FSDEV10G\T_FS_LSQ.ORA            2,244
```

```
25-FEB-04 12.01.06.562 AM E:\ORACLE\ORA92\FSDEV10G\SYSTEM01.DBF      169,940
                         E:\ORACLE\ORA92\FSDEV10G\UNDOTBS01.DBF       26,946
                         E:\ORACLE\ORA92\FSDEV10G\SYSAUX01.DBF       483,550
                         E:\ORACLE\ORA92\FSDEV10G\USERS01.DBF          1,799
                         E:\ORACLE\ORA92\FSDEV10G\T_FS_LSQ.ORA         2,248
```

This small, simple script is quite powerful. This script can be enhanced by adding to the *where* clause to create a unique time-series exception report on any specific data file or any specific time periods.

Let's look at how these tables are assembled. The following shows how the *dba_hist_sysstat* view is built from *wrm$_snapshot*, *wrh$_sysstat* and *dba_hist_stat_name tables:*.

```
create table
   dba_hist_sysstat
as
select
   s.snap_id,
   s.dbid,
   s.instance_number,
   s.statistic#,
   s.statistic_hash,
   nm.statistic_name, value
from
   wrm$_snapshot       sn,
   wrh$_sysstat        s,
   dba_hist_stat_name nm
where
   s.statistic_hash = nm.statistic_hash
and s.statistic# = nm.statistic#
and s.dbid = nm.dbid
and s.snap_id = sn.snap_id
and s.dbid = sn.dbid
and s.instance_number = sn.instance_number
and sn.status = 0
and sn.bl_moved = 0
union all
select
   s.snap_id,
   s.dbid,
   s.instance_number,
   s.statistic#,
   s.statistic_hash,
   nm.statistic_name, value
from
   WRM$_SNAPSHOT sn,
   WRH$_SYSSTAT_BL s,
   DBA_HIST_STAT_NAME nm
where
   s.statistic_hash = nm.statistic_hash
```

```
and s.statistic# = nm.statistic#
and s.dbid = nm.dbid
and s.snap_id = sn.snap_id
and s.dbid = sn.dbid
and s.instance_number = sn.instance_number
and sn.status = 0
and sn.bl_moved = 1;
```

Generating reports with SQL and Scripts using AWR

There are many techniques for running STATSPACK and AWR queries and you can even use Oracle analytic functions to display changes over time. This script compares the changes between snapshot periods, in this case the time period between snapshots 313 and 320:

```
select
   s1.ucomment,
   w1.event,
   s1.snap_id,
   w1.total_waits,
   lag(w1.total_waits)
   over (order by s1.snap_id) prev_val,
   w1.total_waits -
   lag(w1.total_waits)
   over (order by s1.snap_id) delta_val
from
   stats$snapshot      s1,
   stats$system_event w1
where
   s1.snap_id between 313 and 320
and
   s1.snap_id = w1.snap_id
and
   w1.event = 'db file sequential read'
order by
   w1.event, s1.snap_id;
```

You can also use Oracle analytic functions for comparing two periods in STATSPACK. In this example, out SQL specifies a list of valid snapshots.

```
select
   sy.snap_id,
   sy.statistic# statistic#,
   sy.name statname,
   sy.value - (LAG(sy.value)
   over (partition by sy.name
   order by sy.snap_id)) statdelta
```

```
from
   stats$sysstat sy
where
   sy.snap_id in (12208,12599,13480,13843)
and
   sy.name IN
   ('consistent gets','consistent changes',
   'db block gets', 'db block changes')
order by
   sy.name, sy.snap_id;
```

It's also easy to put a STATSPACK or AWR alert into a UNIX/Linux shell script that will e-mail the DBA whenever an exceptional condition is detected.   Below is a script that will look for significant wait events in STATSPACK and e-mail the alert to the DBA.

🖫 wait_alert_email.ksh

```
#!/bin/ksh

# First, we must set the environment . . . .
ORACLE_SID=proderp
export ORACLE_SID
ORACLE_HOME=`cat /var/opt/oracle/oratab|grep \^$ORACLE_SID:|cut -f2 -d':'`
export ORACLE_HOME
PATH=$ORACLE_HOME/bin:$PATH
export PATH

SERVER_NAME=`uname -a|awk '{print $2}'`
typeset -u SERVER_NAME
export SERVER_NAME

# sample every 10 seconds
SAMPLE_TIME=10

while true
do

   #****************************************************************
   # Test to see if Oracle is accepting connections
   #****************************************************************
   $ORACLE_HOME/bin/sqlplus -s /<<! > /tmp/check_$ORACLE_SID.ora
   select * from v\$database;
   exit
!

   #****************************************************************
   # If not, exit immediately . . .
   #****************************************************************
   check_stat=`cat /tmp/check_$ORACLE_SID.ora|grep -i error|wc -l`;
   oracle_num=`expr $check_stat`
   if [ $oracle_num -gt 0 ]
     then
```

```
    exit 0
  fi

  rm -f /export/home/oracle/statspack/busy.lst

  $ORACLE_HOME/bin/sqlplus -s perfstat/perfstat<<!> /tmp/busy.lst

  set feedback off;
  select
     sysdate,
     event,
     substr(tablespace_name,1,14),
     p2
  from
     v\$session_wait a,
     dba_data_files  b
  where
     a.p1 = b.file_id
  ;
!

var=`cat /tmp/busy.lst|wc -l`

echo $var
if [[ $var -gt 1 ]];
 then
  echo
********************************************************************"
  echo "There are waits"
  cat /tmp/busy.lst|mailx -s "Prod block wait found"\
  info@remote-dba.net \
  Larry_Ellison@oracle.com
  echo
********************************************************************"
 exit
fi

sleep $SAMPLE_TIME
done
```

This query shows a technique that computes wait times for sequential and scattered reads:

💾 event_read_waits.sql

```
select to_char(snap_time,'mm/dd/yyyy hh24:mi:ss') snaptime
, max(decode(event,'db file scattered read', nvl(wait_ms,0), null))
wait_ms_dbfscatrd
, max(decode(event,'db file sequential read',nvl(wait_ms,0), null))
wait_ms_dbfseqrd
, max(decode(event,'db file scattered read', nvl(waits,0), null))
waits_dbfscatrd
, max(decode(event,'db file sequential read',nvl(waits,0), null))
waits_dbfseqrd
```

```
from
(
select ps.snap_time
, event
, case
when (total_waits - lag_total_waits > 0)
then round(( (time_waited_micro - lag_time_waited_micro) / (total_waits -
lag_total_waits)) / 1000)
else -1
end wait_ms
, (total_waits - lag_total_waits) waits
, (time_waited_micro - lag_time_waited_micro) time_waited
from (
select se.snap_id
, event
, se.total_waits
, se.total_timeouts
, se.time_waited_micro
, lag(se.event) over (order by snap_id, event) lag_event
, lag(se.snap_id) over (order by snap_id, event) lag_snap_id
, lag(se.total_waits) over (order by snap_id, event) lag_total_waits
, lag(se.total_timeouts) over (order by snap_id, event) lag_total_timeouts
, lag(se.time_waited_micro) over (order by snap_id, event)
lag_time_waited_micro
from perfstat.stats$system_event se
where event = 'db file sequential read'
and snap_id in (select snap_id from stats$snapshot
where snap_time > trunc(sysdate) - 1
)
union all
select se.snap_id
, event
, se.total_waits
, se.total_timeouts
, se.time_waited_micro
, lag(se.event) over (order by snap_id, event) lag_event
, lag(se.snap_id) over (order by snap_id, event) lag_snap_id
, lag(se.total_waits) over (order by snap_id, event) lag_total_waits
, lag(se.total_timeouts) over (order by snap_id, event) lag_total_timeouts
, lag(se.time_waited_micro) over (order by snap_id, event)
lag_time_waited_micro
from perfstat.stats$system_event se
where event = 'db file scattered read'
and snap_id in (select snap_id from stats$snapshot
where snap_time > trunc(sysdate) -1
)
order by event, snap_id
) a
, perfstat.stats$snapshot ss
, perfstat.stats$snapshot ps
where a.lag_snap_id = ps.snap_id
and a.snap_id = ss.snap_id
and a.lag_total_waits != a.total_waits
and a.event = a.lag_event
order by a.snap_id, event
)
group by snap_time
;
```

```
SNAPTIME              RD WAIT_MS WAITS_DBFSCATRD WAITS_DBFSEQRD
------------------- -- ------- --------------- --------------
06/06/2009 03:00:00     5                               52911
06/06/2009 05:00:02     5                               39646
06/06/2009 06:00:04  1  2            3966              1191959
06/06/2009 07:00:00     2                              130977
06/06/2009 09:00:03     3                              367850
06/06/2009 20:00:03  4  3               1              562774
```

This type of STATSPACK data can also be summarized by day of the week to show overall trends on a daily basis. Now, that we get the general idea about using STATSPACK, let's move on and look at the AWR tables.

Inside the AWR Tables

Originally, the AWR was added in Oracle 10g to provide data for Oracle's extra-cost diagnostic and performance packs, but it has much of the same information as the free STATSPACK utility. We also discussed that the *dba_hist* views that comprise AWR are built from their underlying *wrh$* equivalents. These views serve to provide the data source for a wealth of customizable reports for identification of trends and time-series performance optimization.

All custom queries that are written against the *dba_hist* views require a join into the *dba_hist_snapshot* view, which is the main anchor for the AWR history views. Figure 10.1 shows the anchor *dba_hist_snapshot* view and samples of summary and detail *dba_hist* views.

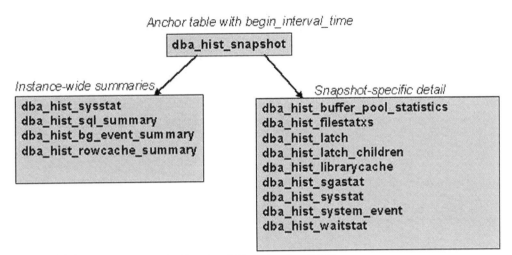

Anchor table with begin_interval_time

dba_hist_snapshot

Instance-wide summaries

```
dba_hist_sysstat
dba_hist_sql_summary
dba_hist_bg_event_summary
dba_hist_rowcache_summary
```

Snapshot-specific detail

```
dba_hist_buffer_pool_statistics
dba_hist_filestatxs
dba_hist_latch
dba_hist_latch_children
dba_hist_librarycache
dba_hist_sgastat
dba_hist_sysstat
dba_hist_system_event
dba_hist_waitstat
```

Figure 10.1: *A Sample of the dba_hist Views for the AWR*

Within these *dba_hist* views, there are thousands of possible statistics to examine, a virtual gold mine of performance data. The trick to success with AWR reports is to start simple and add successive detail. From the simple reports, more sophisticated reports can be created for exception reporting, trend identification, correlation analysis, and hypothesis testing.

Database Wait Events in AWR

Database wait event statistics are critical to tuning because they show us how much time a process had to wait for a particular resource. These wait events are grouped by Oracle into several categories including Administrative, Application, Cluster, Commit, Concurrency, Configuration, Idle, Network, Other, Scheduler, System I/O, and User I/O events.

Wait event data is most effective when they are ordered by wait time. This way, the most significant wait events are displayed first as the lead candidates for further investigation. Even though there is a standard AWR report which contains a wait events section that displays top wait events, I like to use the following query to retrieve the top wait events for a particular AWR snapshot interval:

wt_events_int.sql

```
select event
     , waits "Waits"
     , time "Wait Time (s)"
     , pct*100 "Percent of Tot"
     , waitclass "Wait Class"
from (select e.event_name event
                    , e.total_waits - nvl(b.total_waits,0)  waits
                    , (e.time_waited_micro -
nvl(b.time_waited_micro,0))/1000000  time
                    , (e.time_waited_micro - nvl(b.time_waited_micro,0))/
                      (select sum(e1.time_waited_micro -
nvl(b1.time_waited_micro,0)) from dba_hist_system_event b1 ,
dba_hist_system_event e1
                    where b1.snap_id(+)            = b.snap_id
                      and e1.snap_id               = e.snap_id
                      and b1.dbid(+)               = b.dbid
                      and e1.dbid                  = e.dbid
                      and b1.instance_number(+)    = b.instance_number
                      and e1.instance_number       = e.instance_number
                      and b1.event_id(+)           = e1.event_id
                      and e1.total_waits           > nvl(b1.total_waits,0)
                      and e1.wait_class            <> 'Idle'
     )  pct
                    , e.wait_class waitclass
                from
                  dba_hist_system_event b ,
                  dba_hist_system_event e
                where b.snap_id(+)            = &pBgnSnap
                  and e.snap_id               = &pEndSnap
                  and b.dbid(+)               = &pDbId
                  and e.dbid                  = &pDbId
                  and b.instance_number(+)    = &pInstNum
                  and e.instance_number       = &pInstNum
                  and b.event_id(+)           = e.event_id
                  and e.total_waits           > nvl(b.total_waits,0)
                  and e.wait_class            <> 'Idle'
        order by time desc, waits desc
     );
```

The sample output of this query looks like:

```
SQL> @ wt_events_int.sql

EVENT                       Waits Wait Time(s) Percent of Tot Wait Class
--------------------------- ----- ------------ -------------- ----------
control file parallel write 11719       119.13   34,1611762 System I/O
class slave wait               20       102.46   29,3801623 Other
Queue Monitor Task Wait        74        66.74   19,1371008 Other
log file sync                 733        20.60    5,90795938 Commit
db file sequential read      1403        16.27    4,09060416 User I/O
log buffer space              178        10.17    2,91745801 Configuration
process startup               114         7.65    2,19243344 Other
db file scattered read        311         2.14     ,612767501 User I/O
control file sequential read 7906         1.33     ,380047642 System I/O
latch free                    254         1.13     ,324271668 Other
log file switch completion     20         1.11     ,319292495 Configuration
```

The output of the script displays the wait events ordered by wait times in seconds.

The dba_hist_system_event table

The *dba_hist_system_event* table displays information about the count of total waits and time waited in microseconds, gathering the data from the *v$system_event* view. The following query can be used to retrieve wait events data for a particular snapshot interval:

🖫 awr_system_events.sql

```
select
    event "Event Name",
    waits "Waits",
    timeouts "Timeouts",
    time "Wait Time (s)",
    avgwait "Avg Wait (ms)",
    waitclass "Wait Class"
from
    (select e.event_name event
        , e.total_waits - nvl(b.total_waits,0)  waits
        , e.total_timeouts - nvl(b.total_timeouts,0) timeouts
        , (e.time_waited_micro - nvl(b.time_waited_micro,0))/1000000  time
        , decode ((e.total_waits - nvl(b.total_waits, 0)), 0,
to_number(NULL),
            ((e.time_waited_micro - nvl(b.time_waited_micro,0))/1000) /
(e.total_waits - nvl(b.total_waits,0)) ) avgwait
        , e.wait_class waitclass
    from
        dba_hist_system_event b ,
        dba_hist_system_event e
    where
                b.snap_id(+)            = &pBgnSnap
            and e.snap_id               = &pEndSnap
            and b.dbid(+)               = &pDbId
            and e.dbid                  = &pDbId
            and b.instance_number(+)    = &pInstNum
            and e.instance_number       = &pInstNum
            and b.event_id(+)           = e.event_id
            and e.total_waits           > nvl(b.total_waits,0)
            and e.wait_class            <> 'Idle' )
order by time desc, waits desc;
```

In the above and some subsequent queries, the following parameters need to have appropriate values substituted for them:

- *BgnSnap*: the start snapshot number for the AWR snapshot interval of interest

- *EndSnap*: the finish snapshot number for the AWR snapshot interval of interest

- *DbId*: the database identified of the target database

- *InstNum*: the instance number of the target database

The sample output for this query looks like the following:

```
SQL> @ Sys_event_int.sql

Event Name                 Waits Timeouts Wait Time (s) Avg Wait (ms) Wait Class
-------------------------- ----- -------- ------------- ------------- ----------
control file parallel write 11719        0        119.13         10.17 System I/O
class slave wait               20       20        102.46      5,122.91 Other
Queue Monitor Task Wait        74        0         66.74        901.86 Other
log file sync                 733        6         20.60         28.11 Commit
db file sequential read      1403        0         16.27         10.17 User I/O
log buffer space              178        0         10.17         57.16 Configurat
process startup               114        0          7.65         67.07 Other
db file scattered read        311        0          2.14          6.87 User I/O
control file sequential read 7906        0          1.33           .17 System I/O
latch free                    254        0          1.13          6.45 Other
log file switch completion     20        0          1.11         55.67 Configurat
```

The dba_hist_bg_event_summary table

The *dba_hist_bg_event_summary* data dictionary table is very similar to the *dba_hist_system_event* table. The difference is that the *dba_hist_bg_event_summary* table displays historical information about wait events caused by Oracle background process activities.

These OS background processes form the "kernel software" of an Oracle instance, and they interface with the SGA memory region and perform many types of important jobs.

In a concurrent access environment, these Oracle background processes can see contention for shared system resources in much the same way as the foreground user processes might experience contention. Hence, we may need to know what part of database waits are caused by background Oracle processes.

The following query can be used to retrieve background wait event data for a particular snapshot interval:

💾 show_background_waits.sql

```
select
    event       "Event Name",
    waits       "Waits",
    timeouts    "Timeouts",
    time        "Wait Time (s)",
    avgwait     "Avg Wait (ms)",
    waitclass   "Wait Class"
from
    (select e.event_name event
        , e.total_waits - nvl(b.total_waits,0)  waits
        , e.total_timeouts - nvl(b.total_timeouts,0) timeouts
        , (e.time_waited_micro - nvl(b.time_waited_micro,0))/1000000  time
        ,  decode ((e.total_waits - nvl(b.total_waits, 0)), 0,
to_number(NULL),
            ((e.time_waited_micro - nvl(b.time_waited_micro,0))/1000) /
(e.total_waits - nvl(b.total_waits,0)) ) avgwait
        , e.wait_class waitclass
    from
        dba_hist_bg_event_summary b ,
        dba_hist_bg_event_summary e
    where
                    b.snap_id(+)           = &pBgnSnap
            and e.snap_id                  = &pEndSnap
            and b.dbid(+)                  = &pDbId
            and e.dbid                     = &pDbId
            and b.instance_number(+)       = &pInstNum
            and e.instance_number          = &pInstNum
            and b.event_id(+)              = e.event_id
            and e.total_waits              > nvl(b.total_waits,0)
            and e.wait_class               <> 'Idle' )
order by time desc, waits desc;
```

The output of this script looks similar to the output of the script shown in the previous *dba_hist_system_event* section with the exception that wait events are displayed for background processes.

The dba_hist_waitstat table

The *dba_hist_waitstat* table displays historical statistical information about block contention, and the AWR gets this information from the *v$waitstat* view. This table is useful if we see buffer busy waits with a large wait time because we can query *dba_hist_waitstat* to see what block has DML contention.

The *dba_hist_active_sess_history* table can be queried to identify particular sessions and objects that caused the high contention. In AWR, the datafile and object's IDs can be found in the *v$session_wait* dynamic view. The following query can be used to retrieve historical block contention statistics:

🖫 wait_stat_int.sql

```
select e.class                             "E.CLASS"
     , e.wait_count   - nvl(b.wait_count,0) "Waits"
     , e.time         - nvl(b.time,0)       "Total Wait Time (cs)"
     , (e.time        - nvl(b.time,0)) /
       (e.wait_count  - nvl(b.wait_count,0)) "Avg Time (cs)"
  from dba_hist_waitstat b
     , dba_hist_waitstat e
 where b.snap_id         = &pBgnSnap
   and e.snap_id         = &pEndSnap
   and b.dbid            = &pDbId
   and e.dbid            = &pDbId
   and b.dbid            = e.dbid
   and b.instance_number = &pInstNum
   and e.instance_number = &pInstNum
   and b.instance_number = e.instance_number
   and b.class           = e.class
   and b.wait_count      < e.wait_count
 order by 3 desc, 2 desc;
```

The sample query output looks like this and total waits over time are seen:

```
SQL> @wait_stat_int.sql
```

E.CLASS	Waits	Total Wait Time (cs)	Avg Time (cs)
undo header	97	121	1,24742268
file header block	2	114	57

The output of the script shows which particular buffer wait events play a significant role.

The dba_hist_enqueue_stat table

The *dba_hist_enqueue_stat* table displays statistical information about requests for various types of enqueues or locks. At snapshot time, *dba_hist_enqueue_stat* gets its data from the *v$enqueue_statistics* view.

Oracle enqueues provide a lock mechanism for the coordination of concurrent access to numerous database resources. The name of the enqueue is included as part of the wait event name and takes the form *enq: enqueue_type-related_details*. There are several types of enqueues available:

- **ST enqueues:** The ST enqueues control dynamic space allocation.

- **HW enqueues:** HW enqueues are used to serialize the allocation of space beyond the high water mark (HWM).

- **Waits for TM locks:** These are usually caused by missing indexes on foreign key constraints.

- **TX locks:** The TX locks are placed in various modes on data blocks when a transaction modifies data within this block. There are several types of TX locks: *enq: TX - allocate ITL entry; enq: TX – contention; enq: TX - index contention; enq: TX - row lock contention.*

If you see any wait events appear with "enqueue" in their name, the *dba_hist_enqueue_stat* table can be used to drill down to details about what particular enqueue has a long wait time. Here is a script to see these important enqueue statistics:

🖫   enq_stat_int.sql

```
select
  ety "Enqueue",
  reqs "Requests",
  sreq "Successful Gets",
  freq "Failed Gets",
  waits "Waits",
  wttm "Wait Time (s)",
  awttm "Avg Wait Time(ms)"
from (
select /*+ ordered */
        e.eq_type || '-' || to_char(nvl(l.name,' '))
     || decode( upper(e.req_reason)
             , 'CONTENTION', null
             , '-',             null
```

```
                 , ' ('||e.req_reason||')')                    ety
      , e.total_req#      - nvl(b.total_req#,0)                 reqs
      , e.succ_req#       - nvl(b.succ_req#,0)                  sreq
      , e.failed_req#     - nvl(b.failed_req#,0)                freq
      , e.total_wait#     - nvl(b.total_wait#,0)               waits
      , (e.cum_wait_time - nvl(b.cum_wait_time,0))/1000         wttm
      , decode(  (e.total_wait#   - nvl(b.total_wait#,0))
               , 0, to_number(NULL)
               , (  (e.cum_wait_time - nvl(b.cum_wait_time,0))
                 / (e.total_wait#   - nvl(b.total_wait#,0))
                 )
             )                                                  awttm
   from dba_hist_enqueue_stat e
      , dba_hist_enqueue_stat b
      , v$lock_type            l
  where b.snap_id(+)           = &pBgnSnap
    and e.snap_id              = &pEndSnap
    and b.dbid(+)              = &pDbId
    and e.dbid                 = &pDbId
    and b.dbid(+)              = e.dbid
    and b.instance_number(+)   = &pInstNum
    and e.instance_number      = &pInstNum
    and b.instance_number(+)   = e.instance_number
    and b.eq_type(+)           = e.eq_type
    and b.req_reason(+)        = e.req_reason
    and e.total_wait# - nvl(b.total_wait#,0) > 0
    and l.type(+)              = e.eq_type
  order by wttm desc, waits desc);
```

The output will look like the following:

```
SQL> @Enq_stat_int.sql

Enqueue              Requests Successful Gets Failed Gets Waits Wait Time (s) Avg Wait Time(ms)
---------------------  --------  ---------------- ----------- ----- -------------- --------
RO-Multiple Object     1806        1806           0    153     4,554         29,7647059

TC-Tablespace            81          81           0     27     4,016         148,740741
Checkpoint

TQ-Queue table        19878       19878           0     16     3,596         224,75
enqueue

CF-Controlfile       308733      308732           1      2      ,692         346
Transaction
```

This script output shows activity statistics for particular types of enqueues which allows users to find the enqueues that cause most waits and wait times. Now, let's take a look at the AWR metric tables.

The AWR Metric Tables

The metric *dba_hist* data dictionary tables are organized into several groups: system, session, service, file, tablespace, and event metrics. All available metric groups can be found in the *v$metricgroup* dynamic view:

```
SQL> select * from V$METRICGROUP;

GROUP_ID NAME                              INTERVAL_SIZE MAX_INTERVAL
-------- --------------------------------- ------------- ------------
       0 Event Metrics                              6000            1
       1 Event Class Metrics                        6000           60
       2 System Metrics Long Duration               6000           60
       3 System Metrics Short Duration              1500           12
       4 Session Metrics Long Duration              6000           60
       5 Session Metrics Short Duration             1500            1
       6 Service Metrics                            6000           60
       7 File Metrics Long Duration                60000            6
       9 Tablespace Metrics Long Duration           6000            0
```

All of the metrics in AWR and kept in the *dba_hist_metric_name* table that stores snapshots for the *v$metric_name* view. There are over 180 different metrics in Oracle 11g, a whole lot of information!

These metrics are actively used by Oracle's automation features, providing the data that drives AMM as well as advisory engines such as ADDM and the SQLTuning and SQLAccess Advisors. For example, the ADDM uses a goal-based algorithm designed to minimize db time. This metric is computed as a cumulative time spent.

```
select
   metric_name
from
   dba_hist_metric_name;
```

The following is a list of several metrics that are computed by the AWR snapshot engine; however, the list is not exhaustive.

```
METRIC_NAME
------------------------------------
Average File Read Time (Files-Long)
Average File Write Time (Files-Long)
Average Users Waiting Counts
Background Checkpoints Per Sec
```

```
Blocked User Session Count
Branch Node Splits Per Sec
Branch Node Splits Per Txn
Buffer Cache Hit Ratio
CPU Time (Session)
CPU Time Per User Call
CPU Usage Per Sec
```

The usage of metric statistics in time-series tuning approach will be presented later in this book. This next section provides a general overview of metric *dba_hist* tables that are available and a short description of information they provide.

The dba_hist_filemetric_history table

The *dba_hist_filemetric_history* table collects metrics history for datafile I/O related activity such as average file read/write times, number of physical read/write operations, and blocks. Along with this *dba_hist_filemetric_history* table, there is a corresponding AWR data dictionary table called *dba_hist_sysmetric_summary* that contains several useful datafile I/O related metrics.

```
select
   metric_name
from
   dba_hist_metric_name
where
   group_name like 'File Metrics%';
```

```
METRIC_NAME
-----------------------------------
Physical Block Writes (Files-Long)
Physical Block Reads (Files-Long)
Physical Writes (Files-Long)
Physical Reads (Files-Long)
Average File Write Time (Files-Long)
Average File Read Time (Files-Long)
```

The above query output shows all of the metrics available for datafile I/O activity.

The *dba_hist_sessmetric_history* table

The *dba_hist_sessmetric_history* table collects history information for important session related metrics such as:

```
select
   metric_name
from
   dba_hist_metric_name
where
   group_name like 'Session Metrics%';
```

```
METRIC_NAME
-------------------------------------
Blocked User Session Count
Logical Reads Ratio (Sess/Sys) %
Physical Reads Ratio (Sess/Sys) %
Total Parse Count (Session)
Hard Parse Count (Session)
PGA Memory (Session)
Physical Reads (Session)
CPU Time (Session)
User Transaction Count (Session)
```

The *dba_hist_sessmetric_history* table can be queried to find additional metric details about particular sessions of interest. This table contains a *metric_unit* column that helps identify the units of measure for every metric.

The *dba_hist_sysmetric_history* table

The *dba_hist_sysmetric_history* table collects history for all system-wide metrics which belong to such metric groups as System Metrics Long Duration and System Metrics Short Duration, gathering its data from the *v$sysmetric_history* view.

This *dba_hist_sysmetric_history* table contains important metrics for database time-series tuning approach such as:

- Buffer cache hit ratio

- Database CPU time ratio

- Database time per sec

- Database wait time ratio
- Physical reads per sec
- Response time per TXN
- SQL service response time

This table also contains a *metric_unit* column that helps identify measure units for every metric.

The dba_hist_sysmetric_summary table

The *dba_hist_sysmetric_summary* table shows a history for system-wide metrics that belong to the System Metrics Long Duration metric group. This table stores snapshots for the *v$sysmetric_summary* dynamic view.

The following simple query can be used to retrieve metrics for a particular snapshot.

⊟ metric_summary.sql

```
select
  metric_name "Metric Name",
  metric_unit "Metric Unit",
  minval "Minimum Value",
  maxval "Maximum Value",
  average "Average Value"
from
  dba_hist_sysmetric_summary
where
  snap_id        = &pEndSnap
and
  dbid           = &pDbId
and
  instance_number = &pInstNum;
```

This table contains pre-computed metric values as they appeared in *v$sysmetric_summary* dynamic view. The sample output of this script shows the minimum and maximum values for the chosen metric:

```
SQL> @ metric_summary.sql

Metric Name              Metric Unit            Minimum Value Maximum Value Average Value
------------------------ ---------------------- ------------- ------------- -------------
Host CPU Utilization (%) % Busy/(Idle+Busy)                 1            55            16
Database Time Per Sec    CentiSeconds Per Second            0             9             0
```

Txns Per Logon	Txns Per Logon	1	17	4
Executions Per Sec	Executes Per Second	0	17	1
Executions Per Txn	Executes Per Txn	10	357	28
Session Limit %	% Sessions/Limit	10	12	10
Process Limit %	% Processes/Limit	9	12	10
PGA Cache Hit %	% Bytes/TotalBytes	97	97	97
Shared Pool Free %	% Free/Total	10	11	10
Library Cache Miss Ratio	% Misses/Gets	0	6	0
Library Cache Hit Ratio	% Hits/Pins	93	100	99
Row Cache Miss Ratio	% Misses/Gets	0	24	1

The output from *dba_hist_sysmetric_summary* can be easily retrieved directly from the AWR for any time interval, without any additional computing overhead.

The *dba_hist_sys_time_model* table

The *dba_hist_sys_time_model* table displays snapshots for the *v$sys_time_model* dynamic view and stores history for system time model statistics.

The statistic names are also available in the *dba_hist_stat_name* table that displays all the statistic names gathered by the AWR and stores snapshots for the *v$statname* view. The *dba_hist_stat_name* table is also used with the *dba_hist_sysstat* table as shown below where information from *dba_hist_sys_time_model* table for a particular AWR snapshot interval is retrieved.

sys_time_model_int.sql

```
column "Statistic Name" format A40
column "Time (s)" format 999,999
column "Percent of Total DB Time" format 999,999

select e.stat_name "Statistic Name"
    , (e.value - b.value)/1000000        "Time (s)"
    , decode( e.stat_name,'DB time'
            , to_number(null)
            , 100*(e.value - b.value)
            )/
    ( select nvl((e1.value - b1.value),-1)
    from dba_hist_sys_time_model  e1
       , dba_hist_sys_time_model  b1
    where b1.snap_id              = b.snap_id
    and e1.snap_id                = e.snap_id
    and b1.dbid                   = b.dbid
    and e1.dbid                   = e.dbid
    and b1.instance_number        = b.instance_number
    and e1.instance_number        = e.instance_number
    and b1.stat_name              = 'DB time'
    and b1.stat_id                = e1.stat_id
```

```
)
    "Percent of Total DB Time"
  from dba_hist_sys_time_model e
     , dba_hist_sys_time_model b
 where b.snap_id              = &pBgnSnap
   and e.snap_id              = &pEndSnap
   and b.dbid                 = &pDbId
   and e.dbid                 = &pDbId
   and b.instance_number      = &pInst_Num
   and e.instance_number      = &pInst_Num
   and b.stat_id              = e.stat_id
   and e.value - b.value > 0
 order by 2 desc;
```

The output of this query looks like:

```
SQL> @sys_time_model_int.sql

Statistic Name                       Time (s) Percent of Total DB Time
-------------------------------      -------- ------------------------
DB time                                   169
sql execute elapsed time                  156                       93
DB CPU                                    153                       90
PL/SQL execution elapsed time              77                       46
background cpu time                        53                       31
parse time elapsed                          6                        4
hard parse elapsed time                     4                        3
connection management call elapsed time     0                        0
Java execution elapsed time                 0                        0
PL/SQL compilation elapsed time             0                        0
sequence load elapsed time                  0                        0
hard parse (sharing criteria) elapsed ti    0                        0
hard parse (bind mismatch) elapsed time     0                        0
```

This simple script provides valuable information about the percentage of total database processing time and actual the time (in seconds) for each metric. With this query, we can quickly identify the areas in which Oracle consumes processing time (not wait time) and, thereby, isolate the most resource intensive tasks.

The next section will provide an overview of performance information that the AWR stores about instance-wide system activity.

AWR System Statistics

The AWR stores history for a large number of instance cumulative statistics. These statistics are generally available through the *v$sysstat* dynamic view. The AWR stores snapshots for this table in the *dba_hist_sysstat* table. The following sections provide more details on these system statistics AWR tables.

The *dba_hist_sysstat* table

The *dba_hist_sysstat* table contains a history for system statistics from the *v$sysstat view*. Statistic names can be retrieved from the *dba_hist_statname* table where more than 300 statistics are available.

System statistics for a particular snapshot interval can be viewed using the following query.

🖫   sys_stat_int.sql

```
select e.stat_name         "Statistic Name"
     , e.value - b.value  "Total"
     , round((e.value - b.value)/
     ( select
       avg( extract( day from (e1.end_interval_time-b1.end_interval_time)
)*24*60*60+
            extract( hour from (e1.end_interval_time-b1.end_interval_time)
)*60*60+
            extract( minute from (e1.end_interval_time-b1.end_interval_time)
)*60+
            extract( second from (e1.end_interval_time-b1.end_interval_time)) )
       from dba_hist_snapshot  b1
           ,dba_hist_snapshot  e1
      where b1.snap_id         = b.snap_id
        and e1.snap_id         = e.snap_id
        and b1.dbid            = b.dbid
        and e1.dbid            = e.dbid
        and b1.instance_number = b.instance_number
        and e1.instance_number = e.instance_number
        and b1.startup_time    = e1.startup_time
        and b1.end_interval_time < e1.end_interval_time ),2) "Per Second"
 from  dba_hist_sysstat  b
     , dba_hist_sysstat  e
 where b.snap_id          = &pBgnSnap
   and e.snap_id          = &pEndSnap
   and b.dbid             = &pDbId
   and e.dbid             = &pDbId
   and b.instance_number  = &pInstNum
   and e.instance_number  = &pInstNum
```

```
   and b.stat_id        = e.stat_id
   and e.stat_name not in (  'logons current'
                    , 'opened cursors current'
                    , 'workarea memory allocated'
                    )
   and e.value       >= b.value
   and e.value       >  0
 order by 1 asc;
```

The query output will look like this:

```
SQL> @sys_stat_int.sql

Statistic Name                                  Total Per Second
----------------------------------- ---------- ----------
CPU used by this session                        4,307          1
CPU used when call started                      4,307          1
CR blocks created                                 200          0
DB time                                       959,909        115
DBWR checkpoint buffers written                 3,228          0
DBWR checkpoints                                    9          0
DBWR object drop buffers written                   75          0
DBWR tablespace checkpoint buffers written         71          0
DBWR transaction table writes                      92          0
DBWR undo block writes                            822          0
IMU CR rollbacks                                   20          0
IMU Flushes                                      103          0
IMU Redo allocation size                      761,060         92
IMU commits                                       383          0
IMU contention                                      0          0
IMU ktichg flush                                    4          0
IMU pool not allocated                          1,702          0
IMU undo allocation size                    1,772,624        213
```

This script allows users to easily identify all instance activity statistics for a particular snapshot interval in two representations: cumulative and per second.

The *dba_hist_latch* table

The *dba_hist_latch* table contains historical latch statistics, gathered at snapshot time from *v$latch*. The statistics in the *dba_hist_latch* table are grouped by latch names and allows us to tune applications whenever wait events show a significant amount of latch contention. For example, latch resource usage can be greatly reduced if the application is properly tuned and shared pool is configured optimally.

The following query can be used to retrieve historical data about latches from AWR.

💾 **latch_int.sql**

```
select e.latch_name "Latch Name"
    , e.gets    - b.gets  "Get Requests"
    , to_number(decode(e.gets, b.gets, null,
      (e.misses - b.misses) * 100/(e.gets - b.gets)))    "Percent Get Misses"
    , to_number(decode(e.misses, b.misses, null,
      (e.sleeps - b.sleeps)/(e.misses - b.misses)))    "Avg Sleeps / Miss"
    , (e.wait_time - b.wait_time)/1000000 "Wait Time (s)"
    , e.immediate_gets - b.immediate_gets "No Wait Requests"
    , to_number(decode(e.immediate_gets,
                b.immediate_gets, null,
                (e.immediate_misses - b.immediate_misses) * 100 /
                (e.immediate_gets  - b.immediate_gets)))    "Percent
No Wait Miss"
 from  dba_hist_latch  b
     , dba_hist_latch  e
 where b.snap_id         = &pBgnSnap
   and e.snap_id         = &pEndSnap
   and b.dbid            = &pDbId
   and e.dbid            = &pDbId
   and b.dbid            = e.dbid
   and b.instance_number = &pInstNum
   and e.instance_number = &pInstNum
   and b.instance_number = e.instance_number
   and b.latch_hash      = e.latch_hash
   and e.gets - b.gets   > 0
 order by 1, 4;
```

The results of the query show latch activity statistics and identify the particular type of latch that produces miss events that cause processes to wait.

```
SQL> @latch_int.sql

Latch Name              Get Requests
----------------------- ------------
Percent Get Misses Avg Sleeps / Miss Wait Time (s) No Wait Requests
------------------ ----------------- ------------- ----------------
Percent No Wait Miss
-------------------
Consistent RBA           5,670           0           0              0

FOB s.o list latch         203           0           0              0

In memory undo latch    22,929           0           0          5,163

JOX SGA heap latch       1,173           0           0              0
```

The *dba_hist_latch_misses_summary* table

The *dba_hist_latch_misses_summary* table displays historical summary statistics about missed attempts to get latches.

The following query can be used to get statistics on latch misses for a particular snapshot interval.

🖫 latch_miss_int.sql

```
select    latchname "Latch Name",
          nwmisses "No Wait Misses",
          sleeps "Sleeps",
                waiter_sleeps "Waiter Sleeps"
From (
select e.parent_name||' '||e.where_in_code  latchname
    , e.nwfail_count - nvl(b.nwfail_count,0) nwmisses
    , e.sleep_count - nvl(b.sleep_count,0)  sleeps
    , e.wtr_slp_count - nvl(b.wtr_slp_count,0)   waiter_sleeps
  from dba_hist_latch_misses_summary  b
    , dba_hist_latch_misses_summary  e
 where b.snap_id(+)          = &pBgnSnap
   and e.snap_id             = &pEndSnap
   and b.dbid(+)             = &pDbId
   and e.dbid                = &pDbId
   and b.dbid(+)             = e.dbid
   and b.instance_number(+)  = &pInstNum
   and e.instance_number     = &pInstNum
   and b.instance_number(+)  = e.instance_number
   and b.parent_name(+)      = e.parent_name
   and b.where_in_code(+)    = e.where_in_code
   and e.sleep_count         > nvl(b.sleep_count,0)
)
 order by 1, 3 desc;
```

The output of the query provides additional details about sleeps that occur while the database attempts to acquire a particular latch.

```
SQL> @latch_miss_int.sql

Latch Name                                   No Wait Misses  Sleeps Waiter Sleeps
-------------------------------------------- -------------- ------- -------------
KWQMN job cache list latch kwqmnuji: update job it    0          8        0
cache buffers chains kcbgcur: kslbegin                0          2        0
cache buffers chains kcbgtcr: fast path               0          2        0
cache buffers lru chain kcbzgws_1                      0          1        1
latch wait list No latch                              0      1,163    1,163
library cache kgldti: 2child                          0          3        0
library cache kglhdgc: child:                         0          1        0
library cache kglic                                   0          3        0
library cache kglobld                                 0          1        2
library cache kglobpn: child:                         0         11       15
library cache kglpin                                  0          4        0
```

```
library cache kglpnc: child                          0        51  1,606
library cache kglpndl: child: after processing       0         7      0
library cache kglpndl: child: before processing      0     1,016     40
```

There is other data inside the library cache, and AWR has a view for this information.

The *dba_hist_librarycache* table

The *dba_hist_librarycache* table contains the statistical history of library cache activity, and it gets its data from the *v$librarycache view*. As we know from DBA 101 class, the library cache stores SQL, Java classes, and PL/SQL programs in an executable form. If our library cache contention is significant, *dba_hist_librarycache* can be queried to get more details about particular library objects that may cause such a contention. These details will give us clues on how to reduce library cache contention.

In order to understand the importance of library cache tuning, we must remember that a library and dictionary cache miss is more expensive, in terms of resources, than a data buffer miss. This is because it involves a significant amount of CPU.

The following query can be used to get a report for library cache statistics.

💾   **lib_cache_int.sql**

```
select b.namespace "Name Space"
    , e.gets - b.gets  "Get Requests"
    , to_number(decode(e.gets,b.gets,null,
       100 - (e.gethits - b.gethits) * 100/(e.gets - b.gets))) "Get Pct Miss"
    , e.pins - b.pins "Pin Requests"
    , to_number(decode(e.pins,b.pins,null,
       100 - (e.pinhits - b.pinhits) * 100/(e.pins - b.pins))) "Pin Pct Miss"
    , e.reloads - b.reloads                            "Reloads"
    , e.invalidations - b.invalidations                "Invalidations"
  from dba_hist_librarycache  b
    , dba_hist_librarycache  e
 where b.snap_id          = &pBgnSnap
   and e.snap_id          = &pEndSnap
   and b.dbid             = &pDbId
   and e.dbid             = &pDbId
   and b.dbid             = e.dbid
   and b.instance_number  = &pInstNum
   and e.instance_number  = &pInstNum
   and b.instance_number  = e.instance_number
   and b.namespace        = e.namespace;
```

The following is a result of this query.

```
SQL> @lib_cache_int.sql

Name Space       Get Req Get Pct Miss Pin Requests Pin Pct Miss   Reloads Invalidat
--------------- ------- ------------ ------------ ------------- ---------- ------
BODY               1840   5,76086957         3117    4,39525184        24       0
CLUSTER             216   2,31481481          532    1,12781955         1       0
INDEX                37   97,2972973           41     87,804878         0       0
JAVA DATA             3   33,3333333            5            40         0       0
JAVA RESOURCE         0                         0                       0       0
JAVA SOURCE           0                         0                       0       0
OBJECT                0                         0                       0       0
PIPE                  0                         0                       0       0
SQL AREA          31706     7,459156       120148    2,84482472       495      60
TABLE/PROCEDURE   13926   17,6576188        83460     5,5415768       425       0
TRIGGER             119   14,2857143          488    3,89344262         2       0
```

The report shows what particular types of library cache contents have the highest miss percentage.

The *dba_hist_rowcache_summary* table

The *dba_hist_rowcache_summary* table stores history summary statistics for data dictionary cache activity, gathered at snapshot time from *v$rowcache*. This data dictionary cache stores information about schema objects that participate in SQL parsing or compilation of PL/SQL programs.

The following query can be used to retrieve historical statistical data for the data dictionary cache:

rowcache_int.sql

```
select
  param    "Parameter",
  gets     "Get Requests",
  getm     "Pct Miss"
From
(select lower(b.parameter)                                      param
     , e.gets - b.gets                                          gets
     , to_number(decode(e.gets,b.gets,null,
       (e.getmisses - b.getmisses) * 100/(e.gets - b.gets)))    getm
     , e.scans - b.scans                                        scans
     , to_number(decode(e.scans,b.scans,null,
       (e.scanmisses - b.scanmisses) * 100/(e.scans - b.scans))) scanm
     , e.modifications - b.modifications                        mods
     , e.usage                                                  usage
  from dba_hist_rowcache_summary  b
     , dba_hist_rowcache_summary  e
```

```
where b.snap_id         = &pBgnSnap
  and e.snap_id         = &pEndSnap
  and b.dbid            = &pDbId
  and e.dbid            = &pDbId
  and b.dbid            = e.dbid
  and b.instance_number = &pInstNum
  and e.instance_number = &pInstNum
  and b.instance_number = e.instance_number
  and b.parameter       = e.parameter
  and e.gets - b.gets   > 0   )
order by param;
```

The following is a sample output from this script that displays details about dictionary cache activity for a particular snapshot interval.

```
SQL> @rowcache_int.sql


Parameter                       Get Requests    Pct Miss
-------------------------------  ------------   -----------
dc_awr_control                        23,167          .00
dc_constraints                           558        33.51
dc_files                               2,748          .00
dc_global_oids                     3,018,842          .00
dc_histogram_data                     55,080        15.47
dc_histogram_defs                    225,507        16.29
dc_object_ids                      3,269,890          .05
dc_objects                           265,208         1.34
dc_profiles                           29,205          .00
dc_rollback_segments                 155,231          .00
dc_segments                          348,808          .31
dc_sequences                             763         1.31
dc_table_scns                             38       100.00
dc_tablespace_quotas                       6          .00
dc_tablespaces                       582,952          .00
dc_usernames                          65,451          .02
dc_users                           3,753,587          .00
outstanding_alerts                    13,822         3.43
```

The *dba_hist_buffer_pool_stat* table

The *dba_hist_buffer_pool_stat* table contains statistical history for all buffer pools configured for the instance. Additional non-default buffer caches can be used as keep and recycle caches in order to address atypical access patterns to data segments. This query can be used to review the statistical history of buffer pools for a particular snapshot interval:

```
select
    name
    , numbufs     "Number of Buffers"
    , buffs       "Buffer Gets"
    , conget      "Consistent Gets"
    , phread      "Physical Reads"
    , phwrite     "Physical Writes"
    , fbwait      "Free Buffer Waits"
    , bbwait      "Buffer Busy Waits"
    , wcwait  "Write Complete Waits"
    , poolhr  "Pool Hit %"
From
(select e.name
    , e.set_msize                                           numbufs
    , decode(   e.db_block_gets       - nvl(b.db_block_gets,0)
            +  e.consistent_gets      - nvl(b.consistent_gets,0)
          , 0, to_number(null)
          , (100* (1 - (   (e.physical_reads - nvl(b.physical_reads,0))
                    / (  e.db_block_gets      - nvl(b.db_block_gets,0)
                       + e.consistent_gets    - nvl(b.consistent_gets,0))
                     )
                  )
              )
           )
          )                                                 poolhr
    ,    e.db_block_gets      - nvl(b.db_block_gets,0)
      +  e.consistent_gets    - nvl(b.consistent_gets,0)    buffs
    , e.consistent_gets       - nvl(b.consistent_gets,0)    conget
    , e.physical_reads        - nvl(b.physical_reads,0)        phread
    , e.physical_writes       - nvl(b.physical_writes,0)    phwrite
    , e.free_buffer_wait      - nvl(b.free_buffer_wait,0)   fbwait
    , e.write_complete_wait   - nvl(b.write_complete_wait,0) wcwait
    , e.buffer_busy_wait      - nvl(b.buffer_busy_wait,0)   bbwait
  from dba_hist_buffer_pool_stat  b
    , dba_hist_buffer_pool_stat  e
where b.snap_id(+)          = &pBgnSnap
  and e.snap_id             = &pEndSnap
  and b.dbid(+)             = &pDbId
  and e.dbid                = &pDbId
  and b.dbid(+)             = e.dbid
  and b.instance_number(+)  = &pInst_Num
  and e.instance_number     = &pInst_Num
  and b.instance_number(+)  = e.instance_number
  and b.id(+)               = e.id)
order by 1;
```

The output of the query looks like:

```
SQL> @buf_pool_int.sql

NAME                  Number of Buffers Buffer Gets Consistent Gets
-------------------- ----------------- ----------- ----------
Physical Reads Physical Writes Free Buffer Waits Buffer Busy Waits
------------- --------------- ----------------- -----------
Write Complete Waits Pool Hit %
-------------------- ----------

DEFAULT                            8016    5,354,123       4,347,376
       100,070            41,865                 0              24
                   0 98.1309731
```

The script output provides users with valuable history information about activity in their data buffers. Analysis of buffer cache usage can determine if the pools are configured correctly and whether or not tables need to be reassigned to a particular cache.

The next section provides more details about a *dba_hist* table that exposes operating system performance statistics gathered by database server.

Operating System Statistics in AWR

Oracle does not run in a vacuum, and it's critical to search outside the box and see what is happening with your CPU, RAM, network and disk I/O subsystems. Operating system (OS) statistics such as CPU, disk input/output (I/O), virtual memory, and network statistics help identify possible bottlenecks where system hardware is stressed.

The AWR has a table called *dba_hist_osstat* that stores snapshots of the *v$osstat* dynamic view. OS statistics indicate how the hardware and OS are working, and thus, they reflect the workload placed on the database. To view history statistics for a particular snapshot interval, the following query can be used:

💾 **os_stat_int.sql**

```
select e.stat_name "Statistic Name"
     , decode(e.stat_name, 'NUM_CPUS', e.value, e.value - b.value) "Total"
     , decode( instrb(e.stat_name, 'BYTES'), 0, to_number(null)
```

```
           , round((e.value - b.value)/( select
      avg( extract( day from (e1.end_interval_time-b1.end_interval_time)
)*24*60*60+
           extract( hour from (e1.end_interval_time-b1.end_interval_time)
)*60*60+
           extract( minute from (e1.end_interval_time-b1.end_interval_time)
)*60+
           extract( second from (e1.end_interval_time-b1.end_interval_time)) )
     from dba_hist_snapshot  b1
         ,dba_hist_snapshot  e1
    where b1.snap_id         = b.snap_id
      and e1.snap_id         = e.snap_id
      and b1.dbid            = b.dbid
      and e1.dbid            = e.dbid
      and b1.instance_number = b.instance_number
      and e1.instance_number = e.instance_number
      and b1.startup_time    = e1.startup_time
      and b1.end_interval_time < e1.end_interval_time ),2)) "Per Second"
 from  dba_hist_osstat  b
     , dba_hist_osstat  e
 where b.snap_id          = &pBgnSnap
   and e.snap_id          = &pEndSnap
   and b.dbid             = &pDbId
   and e.dbid             = &pDbId
   and b.instance_number  = &pInstNum
   and e.instance_number  = &pInstNum
   and b.stat_id          = e.stat_id
   and e.value            >= b.value
   and e.value            >  0
 order by 1 asc;
```

The query output looks like the following, a valuable peek outward into the operating system:

```
SQL> @os_stat_int.sql

Statistic Name                      Total      Per Second
----------------------------  ----------    ----------
AVG_BUSY_TICKS                    1,974,925
AVG_IDLE_TICKS                    7,382,241
AVG_IN_BYTES                  2,236,256,256   23,881.91
AVG_OUT_BYTES                   566,304,768    6047.8
AVG_SYS_TICKS                       727,533
AVG_USER_TICKS                    1,247,392
BUSY_TICKS                        1,974,925
IDLE_TICKS                        7,382,241
IN_BYTES                      2,236,256,256   23,881.91
NUM_CPUS                                  1
OUT_BYTES                       566,304,768    6,047.8
SYS_TICKS                           727,533
USER_TICKS                        1247,392
```

This script allows a OS statistics in two forms, both cumulative and per second. With the per-second rates, we can identify hot areas in the OS and hardware, possible external bottlenecks.

The next section describes the very important *dba_hist* tables that contain performance history information for SQL statements executed in the Oracle database.

SQL Statistics in AWR

At the highest level, Oracle is just a SQL statement processor, so SQL optimization is a critical area of Oracle tuning. Almost all performance problems are related to sub-optimal SQL statements and it is important to learn how the AWR helps identify SQL statements that are candidates for tuning. The SQL tuning process usually consists of three steps:

1. Find "bad" SQL statements that place a high workload on an Oracle database

2. Determine that the cost-based optimizer (CBO) created a sub-optimal execution plan for those statements

3. Implement actions which lead to alternative execution plans that provide better response times and lower workload for poor SQL statements

The goals of SQL tuning can be identified as the minimization of SQL response time or reduction of the workload on an Oracle database while performing the same amount of work. In previous Oracle releases, SQL tuning work was mostly a manual process, tuning the workload as a whole by adjusting init.ora parameters and CBO statistics, followed by individual SQL tuning where we found a sub-optimal execution plan, fixed it, and moved on to the next SQL statement.

The *dba_hist_sqlstat* Table

This table contains more than 20 statistics related to SQL statement execution. The statistics for every SQL statement are stored in two separate columns:

- *<Statistic Name>_total* column stores the total values of statistics since the last instance startup

- *<Statistic Name>_delta* column reflects the change in a statistic's value between *end_interval_time* and *begin_interval_time* that is stored in the *dba_hist_snapshot* table.

Using this core *dba_hist_sqlstat* table, poor SQL statements can be identified using such criteria as:

- High buffer gets

- High physical reads

- Large execution count

- High shared memory usage

- High version count

- High parse count

- High elapsed time

- High execution CPU time

- High number of rows processed

- High number of sorts

This table does not contain the actual text of SQL statements; however, it does contain a *sql_id* column. The SQL text can be retrieved by joining *dba_hist_sqlstat* with the *dba_hist_sqltext* table. For example, the *high_sql_buf_gets.sql* script below retrieves high buffer gets SQL statements for a particular snapshot interval.

🖫 high_sql_buf_gets.sql

```
select
        sql_id
      , buffer_gets_total                      "Buffer Gets"
      , executions_total                       "Executions"
      , buffer_gets_total/executions_total "Gets / Exec"
      , pct*100                                "% Total"
      , cpu_time_total/1000000                 "CPU Time (s)"
      , elapsed_time_total/1000000             "Elapsed Time (s)"
      , module                                 "SQL Module"
      , stmt                                   "SQL Statement"
```

```
from
(select
            e.sql_id sql_id
          , e.buffer_gets_total - nvl(b.buffer_gets_total,0)
buffer_gets_total
          , e.executions_total - nvl(b.executions_total,0) executions_total
          , (e.buffer_gets_total - nvl(b.buffer_gets_total,0))/
            (  select e1.value - nvl(b1.value,0)
               from dba_hist_sysstat b1 , dba_hist_sysstat e1
                    where b1.snap_id(+)              = b.snap_id
                      and e1.snap_id                 = e.snap_id
                      and b1.dbid(+)                 = b.dbid
                      and e1.dbid                    = e.dbid
                      and b1.instance_number(+)      = b.instance_number
                      and e1.instance_number         = e.instance_number
                      and b1.stat_id                 = e1.stat_id
                      and e1.stat_name               = 'session logical reads'

) pct
          , e.elapsed_time_total - nvl(b.elapsed_time_total,0)
elapsed_time_total
          , e.cpu_time_total - nvl(b.cpu_time_total,0) cpu_time_total
          , e.module
          , t.sql_text   stmt
       from dba_hist_sqlstat  e
          , dba_hist_sqlstat  b
          , dba_hist_sqltext  t
      where b.snap_id(+)              = @pBgnSnap
        and b.dbid(+)                 = e.dbid
        and b.instance_number(+)      = e.instance_number
        and b.sql_id(+)               = e.sql_id
        and e.snap_id                 = &pEndSnap
        and e.dbid                    = &pDBId
        and e.instance_number         = &pInstNum
        and (e.executions_total - nvl(b.executions_total,0)) > 0
        and t.sql_id                  = b.sql_id
)
    order by 2 desc;
```

Aas we see, the *dba_hist_sqlstat* view provides valuable information about SQL statements that are querying the database. By regularly checking this table, the primary causes of most performance problems can easily be identified. The next section of this chapter introduces the segment-related AWR tables.

Segment Statistics in AWR

The AWR repository stores table-level statistics such as logical reads, physical reads and writes, buffer busy waits and row lock waits in

---

dba_hist_seg_stat, gathering this data at snapshot time from data inside *v$segstat*.

Oracle also has a more view called *v$segment_statistics* which shows the basic table and index statistics along with additional owner and segment names and tablespace name. These segment-level statistics can be selected from the *v$segstat_name* view:

```
SQL> select name from V$SEGSTAT_NAME;

NAME
-------------------------------------
logical reads
buffer busy waits
gc buffer busy
db block changes
physical reads
physical writes
physical reads direct
physical writes direct
gc cr blocks received
gc current blocks received
ITL waits
row lock waits
space used
space allocated
segment scans
```

Reviewing the segment-level statistics history helps us to identify hot segments, revealing those tables and indexes that are experiencing performance problems. For example, if the database has a high value of TX enqueue waits, the *dba_hist_seg_stat* table can be queried to find actual segments that are experiencing high row lock activity.

We can query the *dba_hist_seg_stat* table using various criteria to identify hot segments. For example, the *seg_top_logreads.sql* script retrieves top segments that have high logical reads activity:

seg_top_logreads.sql

```
select
    object_name "Object Name"
  , tablespace_name "Tablespace Name"
  , object_type "Object Type"
  , logical_reads_total "Logical Reads"
  , ratio "%Total"
```

```
from(
select
n.owner||'.'||n.object_name||decode(n.subobject_name,null,null,'.'||n.subobject
_name) object_name
    , n.tablespace_name
    , case when length(n.subobject_name) < 11 then
            n.subobject_name
        else
            substr(n.subobject_name,length(n.subobject_name)-9)
    end subobject_name
    , n.object_type
    , r.logical_reads_total
    , round(r.ratio * 100, 2) ratio
 from dba_hist_seg_stat_obj  n
    , (select *
        from (select e.dataobj#
                    , e.obj#
                    , e.dbid
                    , e.logical_reads_total - nvl(b.logical_reads_total, 0)
logical_reads_total
                    , ratio_to_report(e.logical_reads_total -
nvl(b.logical_reads_total, 0)) over () ratio
                from dba_hist_seg_stat  e
                    , dba_hist_seg_stat  b
                where b.snap_id   = 2694
                    and e.snap_id   = 2707
                    and b.dbid      = 37933856
                    and e.dbid      = 37933856
                    and b.instance_number  = 1
                    and e.instance_number  = 1
                    and e.obj#          = b.obj#
                    and e.dataobj#      = b.dataobj#
                    and e.logical_reads_total - nvl(b.logical_reads_total, 0)  >
0
                order by logical_reads_total desc) d
        where rownum <= 100) r
 where n.dataobj# = r.dataobj#
    and n.obj#       = r.obj#
    and n.dbid       = r.dbid
)
order by logical_reads_total desc;
```

This script allows the identification of hot segments which experience high logical reads activity. This information may help with the selection of tuning actions such as the optimization of corresponding queries that access these segments, redistribute segments across different disks, and more.

```
SQL> @seg_top_logreads.sql

Object Name                    Tablespace Object Type Logical Reads %Total
------------------------------ ---------- ----------- ------------- ------
SYSMAN.MGMT_METRICS_RAW_PK     SYSAUX     INDEX              46,272   8.68
SYS.SMON_SCN_TIME              SYSTEM     TABLE              43,840   8.23
```

```
SYS.JOB$                          SYSTEM    TABLE         30,640   5.75
SYS.I_SYSAUTH1                    SYSTEM    INDEX         27,120   5.09
PERFSTAT.STATS$EVENT_HISTOGRAM SYSAUX    INDEX         26,912   5.05
```

The Ion tool also has several reports for the retrieval of hot segments using the following criteria:

- Top logical reads

- Top physical reads

- Top physical writes

- Top buffer busy waits

- Top row lock waits

- Top block changes

The *dba_hist_seg_stat* table has two columns for each statistic: the accumulated total and the delta values. The *total* column shows the cumulative value of the statistic and the *delta* column shows change in the statistic value between *begin_interval_time* and *end_interval_time*.

The next chapter section introduces the *dba_hist* tables that are related to the I/O activity of the database.

Datafile I/O Statistics in AWR

The AWR has several tables that can be used to isolate datafile I/O statistics as well as tablespace space usage statistics. The *dba_hist_filestatxs* and *dba_hist_tempstatxs* tables display information about I/O activity over time.

The *dba_hist_tempstatxs* table has the identical structure to *dba_hist_filestatxs*. Both tables can be queried to monitor overall database I/O activity for a particular snapshot interval grouped by tablespaces using the *db_tbsp_io.sql* query.

🖫   **db_tbsp_io.sql**

```
select tbsp "Tablespace"
     , ios "I/O Activity"
```

```
From (
select e.tsname tbsp
     , sum (e.phyrds  - nvl(b.phyrds,0))  +
       sum (e.phywrts - nvl(b.phywrts,0)) ios
  from dba_hist_filestatxs  e
     , dba_hist_filestatxs  b
 where b.snap_id(+)           = &pBgnSnap
   and e.snap_id              = &pEndSnap
   and b.dbid(+)              = &pDbId
   and e.dbid                 = &pDbId
   and b.dbid(+)              = e.dbid
   and b.instance_number(+)   = &pInstNum
   and e.instance_number      = &pInstNum
   and b.instance_number(+)   = e.instance_number
   and b.file#                = e.file#
   and ( (e.phyrds  - nvl(b.phyrds,0) ) +
         (e.phywrts - nvl(b.phywrts,0)) ) > 0
 group by e.tsname
union
select e.tsname tbsp
     , sum (e.phyrds  - nvl(b.phyrds,0))  +
       sum (e.phywrts - nvl(b.phywrts,0)) ios
  from dba_hist_tempstatxs  e
     , dba_hist_tempstatxs  b
 where b.snap_id(+)           = &pBgnSnap
   and e.snap_id              = &pEndSnap
   and b.dbid(+)              = &pDbId
   and e.dbid                 = &pDbId
   and b.dbid(+)              = e.dbid
   and b.instance_number(+)   = &pInstNum
   and e.instance_number      = &pInstNum
   and b.instance_number(+)   = e.instance_number
   and b.file#                = e.file#
   and ( (e.phyrds  - nvl(b.phyrds,0) ) +
         (e.phywrts - nvl(b.phywrts,0) ) ) > 0
 group by e.tsname
);
```

This script allows users to look at the I/O activity on a per tablespace basis. It assists in finding hot tablespaces that experienced a large workload and may be candidates for further tuning consideration.

```
SQL> @db_tbsp_io.sql

Tablespace                      I/O Activity
-----------------------------   ------------
SYSAUX                               9,630
SYSTEM                               3,658
UNDOTBS1                             1,104
USERS                                   14
```

Conclusion

This chapter is a quick overview of the evolution of time-series tuning scripts from STATSPACK to AWR. We should now understand how the AWR table data creates the foundation from the *wrh$* tables for input to the intelligent ADDM and the SQLTuning Advisor.

The main points of this chapter include:

- AWR was built into Oracle 10g and beyond as an extra-cost feature requiring the purchase of the Oracle Performance Pack and Oracle Diagnostic Pack

- The AWR *dba_hist* views are similar to well-known STATSPACK tables, making it easy to migrate existing performance reports between these utilities.

- STATSPACK and AWR provides the foundation for sophisticated performance analysis including exception reporting, trend analysis, correlation analysis, hypothesis testing and data mining

- The AWR data is used as input to "intelligent advisor" tools such as ADDM, the SQLTuning Advisor, the SQLAccess Advisor and the SQL Performance Analyzer. As of 2010, none of these tools can replicate the ability of a human tuning expert, but these tools are an excellent way for a beginner to get started.

- STATSPACK remains an excellent low-cost alternative to the expensive AWR

- AWR and STATSPACK provide a set of history tables, and the AWR tables are actually views built upon the *wrh$* tables, all prefixed with *dba_hist*

- The AWR and STATSPACK repository stores time-series history for all major performance database statistics

- The AWR information can be easily accessed using simple SQL queries

Index

About Harry Conway

Harry Conway is an experienced Oracle DBA and Database manager with more than 25 years of full-time Information Technology experience. Expert in both Oracle and IDMS, Harry is a seasoned DBA and Database manager with that rare combination of exceptional technical and management skills.

As a veteran US Marine and a former Director of Database Development, Harry has outstanding leaderships and management skills with over a decade of experience managing multi-million dollar database projects.

About Mike Ault

Mike Ault is one of the leading names in Oracle technology. The author of more than 20 Oracle books and hundreds of articles in national publications, Mike Ault has five Oracle Masters Certificates and was the first popular Oracle author with his landmark book *Oracle7 Administration and Management*. Mike also wrote several of the *Exam Cram* books, and enjoys a reputation as a leading author and Oracle consultant.

Mike started working with computers in 1979 right out of a stint in the Nuclear Navy. He began working with Oracle in 1990 and has since become a World Renowned Oracle expert. Mike is currently a Senior Technical Management Consultant and has two wonderful daughters. Mike is kept out of trouble by his wife of 29 years, Susan.

About Don Burleson

Don Burleson is one of the world's top Oracle Database experts with more than 20 years of full-time DBA experience. He specializes in creating database architectures for very large online databases and he has worked with some of the world's most powerful and complex systems.

A former Adjunct Professor, Don Burleson has written 32 books, published more than 100 articles in National Magazines, and serves as Editor-in-Chief of Oracle Internals and Senior Consulting Editor for DBAZine and Series Editor for Rampant TechPress. Don is a popular lecturer and teacher and is a frequent speaker at OracleWorld and other international database conferences.

As a leading corporate database consultant, Don has worked with numerous Fortune 500 corporations creating robust database architectures for mission-critical systems. Don is also a noted expert on eCommerce systems, and has been instrumental in the development of numerous Web-based systems that support thousands of concurrent users.

In addition to his services as a consultant, Don also is active in charitable programs to aid visually impaired individuals. Don pioneered a technique for delivering tiny pigmy horses as guide animals for the blind and manages a non-profit corporation called the Guide Horse Foundation dedicated to providing Guide horses to blind people free-of-charge. The Web Site for The Guide Horse Foundation is www.guidehorse.org.

About Mike Reed

When he first started drawing, Mike Reed drew just to amuse himself. It wasn't long, though, before he knew he wanted to be an artist. Today he does illustrations for children's books, magazines, catalogs, and ads.

He also teaches illustration at the College of Visual Art in St. Paul, Minnesota. Mike Reed says, "Making pictures is like acting — you can paint yourself into the action." He often paints on the computer, but he also draws in pen and ink and paints in acrylics. He feels that learning to draw well is the key to being a successful artist.

Mike is regarded as one of the nation's premier illustrators and is the creator of the popular "Flame Warriors" illustrations at www.flamewarriors.com, a website devoted to Internet insults. "To enter his Flame Warriors site is sort of like entering a hellish Sesame Street populated by Oscar the Grouch and 83 of his relatives." – Los Angeles Times. (http://redwing.hutman.net/%7Emreed/warriorshtm/lat.htm)

Mike Reed has always enjoyed reading. As a young child, he liked the Dr. Seuss books. Later, he started reading biographies and war stories. One reason why he feels lucky to be an illustrator is because he can listen to books on tape while he works. Mike is available to provide custom illustrations for all manner of publications at reasonable prices. Mike can be reached at www.mikereedillustration.com.

Made in the USA
Middletown, DE
17 January 2022

58979769R00274